K. Dyck
Christ Church '86

THE CONCEPT OF GRACE
IN THE RADICAL REFORMATION

BIBLIOTHECA

HUMANISTICA & REFORMATORICA

VOLUME XVII

THE CONCEPT OF GRACE IN THE RADICAL REFORMATION

by

ALVIN J. BEACHY

NIEUWKOOP
B. DE GRAAF
1977

TO VERA

WHO WALKS IN GRACE

© ALVIN J. BEACHY, HARRISONBURG, U.S.A. 1976
ISBN 90 6004 338 3

Pages 1-351 form part of a doctoral thesis presented to Harvard Divinity School, 1960.

CONTENTS

PREFACE	IX
FOREWORD by Dr. George H. Williams	XIII
ABBREVIATIONS	XV
INTRODUCTION	1

Chapter

I   ACCUSATIONS AND REPLIES   6

A.	The Charge			6
	1.	The Pauline-Augustinian Concept of Grace		10
		(a)	The Accusation of Legalism	13
		(b)	The Accusation of Pelagianism	15
		(c)	The Accusation of Universalism	16
		(d)	The Legitimate Basis for These Accusations	17
			(1) The Absence of Legalism among the South German Anabaptists	20
B.	The Refutation of the Charge			25
	1.	The Johannine Concept of Salvation as the Divinization of Man		28
	2.	The Counter-Accusations to Which This Led		29
		(a)	The Theologians and Ministers are Antinomian	29
		(b)	The Theologians and Ministers are Hucksters of "Cheap Grace"	32
C.	Freedom of the Will as Opposed to the Bondage of the Will			33

II   ANABAPTIST OR RADICAL ANTHROPOLOGY   35

A.	The Creation and Fall of Man		35
	1.	The Extent of the Fall	36
B.	Original Sin and Its Consequences		37
C.	Actual Sin		42
D.	The Freedom versus the Bondage of the Will		46
E.	Man in the Eschatological Framework		56
	1.	The "Age of the Spirit"	56
	2.	The Brevity of the "Time of Grace"	58

III   THE GRACE OF GOD IN CHRIST   62

A.	The "Time of Grace" in Contrast to the "Time of Law"	62
B.	The Appropriation of Grace through Conversion	67
C.	The Appropriation of Grace through Regeneration	70
D.	The Significance of the Celestial Flesh Christology	79

Chapter

IV		THE GRACE OF CHRIST AND THE CHURCH OF CHRIST	87
	A.	The Church as the Community of the New Covenant of Grace	87
	B.	The Church and the Sacraments	99
		1. The Definition and Function of Sacrament	100
		2. The Repudiation of the Practice of Infant Baptism	100
		3. The Significance of Believer's Baptism and the Lord's Supper	103
	C.	The Place of the Ban	117
	D.	Vocation outside the Community of Grace	122
	E.	Suffering as a Mark of the True Church	124
V		THE HERMENEUTICS OF GRACE	129
	A.	The Rupture of an Ancient Synthesis	129
		1. The Three Main Hermeneutical Groups	130
		2. The Influence of the Mystics	131
		3. The Inner and Outer Word as the Distinction between Letter and Spirit	140
	B.	The Importance of the Epistle to the Hebrews	142
		1. Dirk Philips: The "Time of Law" and the "Time of Grace"	142
		2. Menno Simons and the hermeneutics of the Old and New Covenants	146
		3. Pilgram Marbeck: the "Covenant of Yesterday" and the "Covenant of Today"	149
VI		ANABAPTIST OR RADICAL ETHICS AND THE WORKS OF GRACE	153
	A.	The Role of the Holy Spirit in the Development of a Rigorous Ethic	153
	B.	The Ethics of Grace in Relation to the State	155
		1. The Legitimate Place and Function of the State	155
		2. The Limits of the State's Sphere of Activity Defined by the Ethic of Grace	162
	C.	The Ethics of Grace and the Refusal to Take the Oath	165
	D.	The Irreconcilable Conflict between the Duties of the Soldier and the Conduct of the Disciple	167
VII		SUMMARY AND EVALUATION	173
	A.	A Synoptic View of the Concept of Grace in the Radical Reformation	173

VI

B.		The Strenghts of the Radical or Anabaptist Concept of Grace	174
	1.	The Ontological Base for the Christian Life and the Constant Source of Renewal for the Church	174
	2.	The Principle of Voluntarism as Rooted in the Radical Concept of Grace	176
	3.	The Abiding Values of the Hermeneutics of Grace	177
C.		Weakness Inherent in the Radical Concept of Grace	178
	1.	The Tendency to Classify Sins into Major and Minor Categories	178
	2.	The Concept of Grace as Related to the Celestial Flesh Christology and Its Consequent Effect upon the Created Order and the Doctrine of the Atonement	178
	3.	The Limits Placed upon the Acceptance of Social Responsibility by the Ethics of Grace	179

BIBLIOGRAPHY

APPENDIX

Section

I. ANABAPTISM: THE RADICALIZATION OF PROTESTANTISM OR THE SURVIVAL OF MEDIEVAL MYSTICISM? ... 187

    A. Introduction ... 187
    B. An Analysis of the Mystical Anthropology of Johannes Tauler ... 189
    C. An Analysis of the Mystical Anthropology of Jean Gerson ... 191
    D. An Analysis of Luther's Rejection of the Mystical Anthropology ... 193
    E. Luther's Initial Approval and Eventual Rejection of the *Theologia Deutsch* ... 195
    F. The Continued Use of the Mystical Tradition by Anabaptists and Other Dissenters ... 197
    G. Hans Denck and Taulerian Mysticism ... 199
    H. Gersonian Mysticism in the Tripartite Anthropology of Balthasar Hubmaier and Modifications thereof within Anabaptism ... 200
    I. The Anabaptists as Heirs of Late Medieval Mysticism ... 202

II. ANABAPTIST MODIFICATIONS OF THE MYSTICAL HERITAGE ... 208

    A. The Sources of the Anabaptist Concept of Christ as the Second Adam and the Impact of this Concept upon Their Theology ... 208
    B. The Difference between Mystical and Anabaptist Anthropology: A Question of the Difference between *Before* and *After* ... 214

III. THE CHURCH ON EARTH AS THE PARTIAL REALIZATION OF PARADISE REGAINED ... 218

IV. ANABAPTIST PACIFISM: STRATEGY FOR SURVIVAL OR PRINCIPLE OF CHRISTIAN EXISTENCE? ... 219

V. CONCLUSION ... 227

BIBLIOGRAPHY ... 231

INDEX ... 233

PREFACE

The genesis of this book can be traced to a conversation between the author and George Huntston Williams, distinguished Hollis Professor of Divinity at Harvard University. Our personal friendship is by no means the least of the treasures that remain from the time spent at Harvard Divinity School, 1956–60. The occasion for this conversation was prompted by a letter which my mentor and friend had just received from William Klassen, then a doctoral candidate at Princeton University. Klassen, who is now head of the Department of Religion at the University of Manitoba, had written that he was well under way with a doctoral thesis devoted to an exploration of the hermeneutics of Pilgram Marbeck.[1] At that precise moment this new information seemed nothing short of calamitous. Klassen's forthcoming thesis was not only in the same area of what was then my particular interest; it was also devoted to the same man whose life and writings I had intended to study in the development of my own thesis!

What then appeared to be a calamity has since proved to be a blessing in disguise. George Williams was too polite to state forthrightly that he was not eager to have Harvard sponsor a second thesis in the same area and on the same person as the one already underway at Princeton. This reluctance could be clearly sensed, though it remained unspoken. At this point I shared with Williams a slowly forming conviction that an exploration of the Anabaptist concept of grace might be a fruitful field of research. During the course of my reading in the original sources of both sides of the sixteenth-century Reformation movement I had become aware of a literal chorus of accusations and counter-accusations. Anabaptists saw the Magisterial position on forensic justification as a new system of indulgences. The Magisterial Reformers saw the Anabaptists as a new form of monasticism. Reflection upon this controversy brought about a slowly forming conviction, which was initially no more than a nebulous surmise, that the two sides of the Reformation were working with two entirely different concepts of grace. In the caricatures that always result from theological polemics neither side was aware that what was at issue in the debate between them involved differing concepts of grace and how it is appropriated in the Christian experience of salvation.

When the possibility of writing a doctoral thesis on the concept of grace within Anabaptism was first mentioned to George Williams, his response was, "I don't think you can do that. The word *Gnade* does not even appear in their writings." However, encouragement was given to use the summer months to develop a prospectus for a thesis on this subject in order to test the durability of this then nebulous surmise. Fortunately that surmise survived not only the development of the prospectus but also the thesis, which later emerged from it under the title, *The Concept of Grace in the Radical Reformation.* Professor Williams, who had earlier expressed doubt about the feasibility of the project, was one of the first persons to extend his warm congratulations upon its successful completion.

Not only has this once nebulous surmise survived the writing of both the

---

1 This thesis has since been published under the title, *Covenant and Community, The Life and Writings of Pilgram Marpeck*, by William B. Eerdmans Pub. Co., Grand Rapids, MI, 1968.

prospectus and the thesis, but as William Keeney, Director of Experiential Learning, Bethel College, North Newton, Kansas, has stated, "The thesis itself has not been superseded by anything that has appeared in print since it was first successfully defended in the summer of 1960." Those several books and various scholarly articles published since that time which further help to clarify as well as modify the original conclusions are duly noted in the Appendix. I gratefully acknowledge the various ways in which I am indebted to William Keeney in the publication of this book – for his encouragement to pursue the task of publication, for his assistance in preparation of the index, and for the valuable suggestions he made for the improvement of the Appendix after reading the first draft. While I regret that I have neither time, energy, nor means to rewrite the entire volume in a more popular style, I am grateful to B. de Graaf of Nieuwkoop, Holland, for his willingness and ability to publish the book in its present form. Though it will continue to bear the unmistakable marks of a thesis, it will, nevertheless, be available to a much wider segment of the scholarly world than through the several manuscript and microfilm copies now available, largely in the libraries of the various Mennonite colleges and seminaries within the continental United States.

The basic writings of the seven men considered in this study were used as the primary sources. If these were available in critical editions, they were used for the purposes of translation with the exception of *The Complete Writings of Menno Simons*. Here the English translation of Leonard Verduin has been used almost exclusively. If critical editions of the works of the other six men were not available, these were, nevertheless, read in the original Dutch or German. The English translations in each case except the writings of Menno are my own. The English translations of the works of Hans Denck, Melchior Hoffmann, and Balthasar Hubmaier, which were made by George H. Williams and now appear in Volume XXV of *The Library of Christian Classics*, published by Westminster Press, were also used but not without comparison with the originals.

The careful reader will be aware of variant spellings in the names of Melchior Hoffmann and Pilgram Marbeck. This is due to the fact that F. O. zur Linden, who first introduced Hoffmann to the scholarly world, used the double "f" and double "n". I have chosen to follow his spelling except when quoting other authors. The same is true with the spelling of Marbeck. I have chosen to follow the example of most European scholars and use "b" rather than "p" except when quoting authors who use the "p".

The original study did not include the Swiss Brethren. The felt need to reply to James M. Stayer's *Anabaptists and the Sword* made it necessary to include a brief section on them in the Appendix. Stayer's interpretation, I believe, would reduce Anabaptist pacifism to a strategy for survival. I maintain that for the Anabaptists it was a principle of Christian existence.

In the course of writing this book my indebtedness to many people has grown beyond measure. It includes, first of all, the members of my original thesis committee, Professors James Luther Adams, Paul Louis Lehmann, and George Huntston Williams, each of whom rendered invaluable assistance in his way. Professor Adams with his interest in the principle of voluntarism gave provocative suggestions for the main thrust of the book in the area of church-state relationships. Professor Lehmann, who was my advisor during the initial research stage, assisted in the technical matters related to research. Professor Williams' vast knowledge of original Anabaptist sources was a tremendous asset. To each of these men I am most grateful.

Another group of people to whom I owe thanks are the librarians of the various institutions where I have either studied or taught while this book was in the process of formation. Without their always gracious assistance this task could neither have been begun nor completed. To James Tanis, librarian at Andover-Harvard Theological Library, while the thesis was being written; to Robert Kreider, Director of Mennonite Historical Library and Archives, and to Miss Marianne Harms, librarian and assistant archivist, Bethel College, North Newton, Kansas; to Miss Martha Stucky, Bethel College librarian; and to Miss Grace Showalter, librarian of the Mennonite Historical Library, Eastern Mennonite College, Harrisonburg, Virginia, I express my deep gratitude and thanks.

Last but by no means least, I owe a special debt of gratitude to my wife, Vera. Her editorial suggestions were invaluable, and her skillful typing of the original manuscript and the appendix has made the publication of this book possible.

The following publishers have given permission for extensive quotations from works to which they hold the copyright: G. Bertelsmann Verlag; E. J. Brill; Conrad Press; Coronado Press; B. de Graaf; Harper & Row, Publishers, Inc.; Herald Press; Chr. Kaiser Verlag; Mennonite Historical Society; *Review and Expositor*; Westminster Press; and Yale University Press.

Alvin J. Beachy
Bethel College
North Newton, Kansas

FOREWORD

Anabaptist research in North America, especially in the United States, concerned itself largely with the origins and spread of Anabaptism. The mainspring of the intensive concentration on the historical parameters was to lift from the shoulders of contemporary Mennonites (and Hutterites) the onus of the bellicose Anabaptist theocracy of Münster, 1534–35. Outside Mennonite circles from that episode, down into the late nineteenth century and some times much later, scholars have tried to legitimate their charge that Anabaptism was latently seditious and fanatic. It was inevitable, therefore, that with the full maturation of North American Mennonite scholarship, extensive efforts would be made on an imposing archival and monographic scale to document the wide range of regional types of Anabaptism and to isolate the Münsterite theocracy as a wholly aberrant anomaly. Given the regnant concern to explain but also to explain away the Münsterite whirlwind that even touched down at Amsterdam, it is understandable that much of what was most distinctive in the Anabaptist vision should become blurred even with the pens of the most conscientious modern Mennonite scholars of the Anabaptist past. Sixteenth-century Anabaptist leaders and other spokesmen whose conduct and theology were not substantially in harmony with the consensus of the latter-day Mennonite community tended to be read out of the authentic Anabaptist camp. This is true, for example, of the Italian Anabaptists as virtually a group, who, though they had one root in common with the Germanic type, largely succumbed to an alien force and by 1550 had become largely Unitarian, even though they remained consistently pacifist and opposed the oath and participation in magistracy because of its capital responsibilities. The desire to present Anabaptism with its emphasis on discipleship as primarily a radicalization of the Protestant principle of justification by grace through faith served to obscure further what was distinctively Anabaptist and, therefore, neither Catholic nor Protestant in the sixteenth-century development.

In any case, Mennonite scholarship and often that by others sympathetic with the problematic of ascertaining normative sixteenth-century Anabaptism tended to work on archival, historical, biographical, sociological, and religio-political matters – with enormous industry and productivity – to the relative neglect of the full range of Anabaptist theology, from Revelation to Last Things; and here, too, there was some inhibition in that Menno Simons had adopted and defended the unusual Christology of Melchior Hofmann, who surely participated in the movement that eventuated in the Münsterite theocracy, even though he himself died pathetically in Strassburg. Mennonite theologians thus on more than one count were indisposed to draw afresh upon Anabaptist materials excavated by the historians in huge heaps until the genetic lines had been first clearly laid down.

Of these theological matters the doctrine of grace was, among others, largely overlooked; and, here again, because justification and sanctification had been so radically severed theologically and soteriologically by Martin Luther, it took special courage for a Mennonite theologian to tackle the problem within the programmatic strictures of "Mennonitism as the consequential radicalization of Protestantism."

The author of the present book had precisely the courage to deal with the problem of grace before all the other problems had been solved; and in his doctoral dissertation on a fundamental and uniquely Anabaptist perception of God's grace, man's will, and scriptural authority he broke out of the mold set by the first three decades of Mennonite and philo-Mennonite Anabaptist research in the United States. Professor Beachy of Bethel College, North Newton, Kansas, a major center of American Anabaptist and Mennonite research, in his Harvard doctorate in theology shows how the experience and conceptualization of grace affected the Anabaptist *viator* of the sixteenth century differently from the conceptualization thereof of his imposing theological contemporaries, who, alas, all too easily derided him or her for lack of formal education rather than marvelling at the theological and scriptural cunning and the courage to expound Scripture in fair debate before great Reformers, inquisitors, and magistrates.

Because grace within the Anabaptist perspective means the ontological change within the believer, that is, a clear motion toward personal and group sanctification and discipline, rather than the state of one declared righteous forensically by virtue of the Work of Christ, discipleship, in which the life of Jesus Christ serves as the model for the life of every earnest Christian, becomes not only a possibility but also a requirement — much as in the pre-Constantinian Church. This demand led Anabaptists on their particular quest for a Christocentric hermeneutic, pivotal for almost all groupings, and with it the renunciation of coercion in matters of faith. Inevitably this emphasis upon religious voluntarism, both personal and ecclesiological, shaped the Anabaptist modalities for relating their churches with other churches and the structures of society at large, notably the magistracy.

All these uniquely Anabaptist concepts are dealt with in the book before us. Whether the reader in all cases agrees with the author, one may trust that the sources upon which the conclusions are based have been carefully and comprehensively documented. The author himself, recognizing that the definitive word on the Anabaptist experience and concept of grace may not be spoken until the full corpus of surviving *Anabaptistica*, Dutch, German, Swiss, and other has been published, would, however, maintain that the study represents a breakthrough in Anabaptist research. From the largely historical and often defensive stance of the first three decades of modern Mennonite research in North America, the book moves forthrightly in a theological direction and, without hesitancy, into the high sense of confessional apologetic in an irenic ecumenical context.

The reaffirmation of the abiding necessity of a tension between the Church of Christ and the world has significance not only for a better understanding of the deep motivation of the martyred thousands who in the sixteenth century regarded themselves as Christ's most faithful spiritual and ethical militia but also for all of us today facing comparable tensions in our own society and the world at large.

The book, without substantial change in its original format, has the advantage of an extensive Appendix in which the author and teacher, having long mused over the implications of his work on grace in the Anabaptists, has come to grips with much of the literature relating to this theme; and these mature reflections greatly enhance the present volume.

George H. Williams
Hollis Professor of Divinity
Harvard University

ABBREVIATIONS

BRN   *Bibliotheca Reformatoria Neerlandica*

CR   *Corpus Reformatorum*

CS   *Corpus Schwenckfeldianorum*

CWMS   *The Complete Writings of Menno Simons*

ME   *Mennonite Encyclopedia*

Opera *Opera Omnia Theologia*

QRF   *Quellen und Forschungen zur Reformationsgeschichte*

SAW   *Spiritualist and Anabaptist Writers*

WA   *Weimar Ausgabe, Luther's Works*

INTRODUCTION

A. Definition and Use of Terms

Historians when writing about the continental Reformation have generally used the four terms, Roman Catholic, Lutheran, Reformed, and Anabaptist, to designate the four distinct groups involved within the crisis of the Reformation. While the first three terms are in themselves reasonably adequate designations which require little definition, the term, Anabaptist, by itself has proved woefully inadequate for the fourth group. The reason for its inadequacy lies, as Harold S. Bender has said, in the fact that "it is commonly used in English to describe a motley collection of groups of no common faith."[1]

Currently an attempt is being made to find a nomenclature that is more adequately descriptive for the whole Anabaptist movement. John McNeill and Roland Bainton have popularized the term, "the left wing of the Reformation," to cover more adequately what Bender calls this "motley collection" within the Anabaptist camp.[2] Franklin Littell, following a modified application of the church-sect typology suggested by Ernst Troeltsch,[3] has attempted to give a more precise definition of the "left wing" by paying particular attention to the Anabaptist concept of the Church. Littell suggests at least a threefold division of the Anabaptists into three major types: the revolutionary groups with a chiliastic eschatology; the biblical Anabaptists with a quietistic eschatology and a concern for the Church as a gathered and disciplined community; and the Spirituals, who had little concern for an organized church.[4]

While Littell's typology is an improvement over the term, "left wing," it is not completely satisfactory, as he is himself aware. The most recent, and thus far the most satisfactory, attempt to develop an adequate system of classification is that of George H. Williams in the introduction to Volume XXV of the *Library of Christian Classics*.[5] Williams uses the term, *Magisterial* Reformation, to designate both Calvinistic and Lutheran branches of the continental Reformation, because both groups, as well as the later *papal* counter-Reformation, linked Church and State together. For the overall Anabaptist movement Williams uses the term, Radical Reformation, rather than the earlier "left wing," because this term best describes their common rejection of the union of Church and State.

Within the Radical Reformation Williams finds three main divisions: the Anabaptists proper; the Spiritualists; and the Evangelical Rationalists. The Anabaptists are again subdivided into the Revolutionaries, the Evangelicals, and the Contem-

---

1 Harold S. Bender, *Conrad Grebel, c. 1498–1526, the Founder of the Swiss Brethren* (Goshen, Ind.: The Mennonite Historical Society, 1950), p. 11 of preface.
2 *Spiritual and Anabaptist Writers*, ed. George H. Williams, Library of Christian Classics (Philadelphia: The Westminster Press, 1957), XXV, 20, esp. n. 2.
3 Ernst Troeltsch, *The Social Teachings of the Christian Churches*, trans. Olive Wyon (London: George Allen & Unwin Ltd.; New York: The Macmillan Co., 1931), II, 691–705.
4 Franklin H. Littell, *The Anabaptist View of the Church* (American Society of Church History, 1952), pp. 19–47.
5 Williams, pp. 19–36.

platives; while the Spiritualists are subdivided into the categories of the Revolutionaries, the Evangelicals, and the Rationalists.

The typology suggested by Williams is derived from the programatic characteristics of each specific group, as well as from theological differentiations within each group. Because it is the most satisfactory nomenclature so far suggested, it will be employed in this study. Of the seven representatives of the Radical Reformation considered in the study Balthasar Hubmaier, Melchior Hoffmann, Pilgram Marbeck, Dirk Philips, and Menno Simons are classified as Evangelical Anabaptists. Hans Denck is classified as a Contemplative Anabaptist, and Caspar Schwenckfeld, as an Evangelical Spiritualist. Where the term, Revolutionary Anabaptist, appears in the study, it refers to the Münsterite movement of 1534.[6]

B. Geographic Scope and Time Span of Study

Geographically this study is limited in scope to the Netherlands and South Germany. The area which today comprises Holland is considered as the territory in which Dutch Anabaptism arose and developed under the leadership of Melchior Hoffmann, Dirk Philips, and Menno Simons. The South German Anabaptists, who flourished for a time in Augsburg but who were later expelled from the city, owe their origin, in my opinion, to the early work of Hans Denck.[7] Pilgram Marbeck became the recognized leader of the South German brethren soon after his banishment from Strasbourg in 1531 and remained so until the time of his death in Ulm, some distance from Augsburg in 1556.[8]

For the sake of convenience in the handling of the material Hubmaier is, in this study, considered as a South German Anabaptist. The device is a purely arbitrary one and can only be defended on the basis that Hubmaier wrote in German and that chronologically he is closer to Denck and to Marbeck than to Dirk and Menno. It was in Zurich that Hubmaier first made contact with Anabaptism through the Swiss Brethren and in Nicolsburg in Austrian Moravia that his most extensive Anabaptist labors were conducted. If, therefore, the device of considering him along with the South German Anabaptists is too arbitrary, I alone must bear the responsibility for it.

Caspar Schwenckfeld's work was not restricted to one specific geographical area. He is included in this study because of his controversy with Marbeck and because he shares in common with Hoffmann, Menno, and Dirk the Celestial Flesh Christology with its consequent effects upon soteriology and the Lord's Supper. His writings are considered at those points where the controversy with Marbeck is at its sharpest and where the similarity of his thought to that of Hoffmann, Menno, and Dirk appears most clearly.

Since Hans Denck is considered as one of the founders of South German Ana-

---

6 See C. A. Cornelius, *Geschichte des Münsterischen Aufruhrs* (2 vols.; Leipzig: T. O. Weigel, 1855–1860).
7 Jan J. Kiwiet, "The Life of Hans Denck," *Mennonite Quarterly Review*, XXXI, No. 4 (October, 1957), 245.
8 John C. Wenger, *"The Life and Work of Pilgram Marpeck."* MQR, XII, No. 2 (July, 1938), 165.

baptism, January, 1525, the date of his "Confession" to the city council at Nürnberg, marks the beginning of the study. The Frankenthal Disputation of 1571, because it was the last serious attempt at dialogue between representatives of the Magisterial and Radical Reformation groups, is regarded as the terminal date during the formative period of the Reformation.

C. Method of Handling the Material

In the handling of the material it has seemed best to resort at times to a logical rather than a chronological scheme. In this way it has been possible not only to present the thought of the various men considered, but also to contrast and compare the Dutch Anabaptists with their South German brethren. Where the logical rather than the chronological method has been used, it is so indicated in an appropriate footnote.

D. Source Limitations

Original sources for the study of the Radical Reformation are on the increase in this country. The most abundant depository of materials on the Evangelical Anabaptists is in the Mennonite Historical Library at Goshen College, Indiana. Bethel College in North Newton, Kansas, has the best collection of Dutch Anabaptist materials. Yet, under the inspiration and leadership of George H. Williams, Andover Library of the Harvard Divinity School has accumulated a collection of Anabaptist materials which rivals that of Goshen. Between the resources available at Andover and Widener Libraries there has been a serious lack of original source materials only on Melchior Hoffmann. Of the various works by Hoffmann only the *Ordinance of God* and the *Explanation of the Bound and Freewill of Man* were available in full. Excerpts from his *Commentary on Romans* are also printed in Volume V of the *Bibliotheca Reformatoria Neerlandica.*

This lack has been supplemented somewhat by making use of all the excerpts from Hoffmann's other works, which are printed in the works on Hoffmann by Leendertz and zur Linden. Extensive use has also been made of the article on Hoffmann in Volume II of the *Mennonite Encyclopedia* and Peter Kawerau's *Melchior Hoffman als Religiöser Denker.* The gaps in original sources by Hoffmann in this country remain serious, and at this point could be overcome only by study abroad.

The difficulty with the other six representatives of the Radical Reformation lay not in the fact that not all the original sources were available but in the fact that critical editions are lacking, except for the works of Hans Denck, Dirk Philips. and Caspar Schwenckfeld. Since no critical edition of Menno Simons' writings is yet available, I have used the English translation of Menno's works by Leonhard Verduin rather than the Dutch edition in *Opera Omnia*, except for those places where the Dutch becomes critical for an understanding of Menno's Christology on the one hand and his soteriology on the other. The sixteenth century Dutch and German, in which the leaders of the Radical Reformation wrote, contained many archaic forms and grammatical corruptions. Therefore, all the sources used in the thesis have been translated into English. An effort has been made to render these translations accurately though not literally. Again I alone must bear the responsibility for such misrepresentations as may have occurred in the course of translation.

E. The Need for Such a Study

The need for such a study arises from two sides. From the side of the Magisterial Reformation the charge against the Radical Reformers has always been that they were "work's righteousness people," who knew not the meaning of grace. The truth of the charge has always been denied by the Radicals, yet they have been slow in giving a definition of their concept of grace on the basis of which this charge can be justly repudiated. How tardy the present-day descendants of the Radical Reformers have been in doing this is revealed by the fact that neither the *Mennonitisches Lexikon* nor the *Mennonite Encyclopedia* contain articles on grace.

F. A Digest of the Central Argument of This Thesis

The concept of grace which prevailed within the Magisterial Reformation was inseparably linked with predestination and the bondage of the will. Within this framework grace from God's side is the eternal decrees of divine election. From man's side it is God's act of forensic justification wherein the righteousness of the Christian becomes the imputed righteousness of Christ. Where grace is understood in this manner, spiritual health or wholeness is not something that becomes possible within this world. The Christian is throughout life both justified and sinner. He stumbles through this life as one who is half ill and as one who has the promise that eventually he will be well; but the promise of health is not health itself.[9]

Luther and Calvin were in essential agreement on this forensic view of grace as expressed in the formula, *simul justus et peccator*. The Magisterial Reformers arrived at this concept of grace by reading Paul through the eyes of Augustine. So understood, justification by grace through faith means a change of status before God, who for Christ's sake regards the sinner as righteous. It does not mean that within this life there is an ontological or metaphysical change in the believer himself.

The Radical Reformers reached back beyond Paul to the Gospels, and among the Gospels they had a preference for the Gospel of John. Five of the seven representatives of the Radical Reformation considered is this study specifically state that their concept of salvation is that of the divinization of man, which is also true of the fourth Gospel and of the Johannine epistles. Among the early fathers of the Church Irenaeus and Athanasius are the continuation of this aspect of Johannine thought. Their concept of grace was consequently colored by their concept of salvation. Thus, grace is for the Radical Reformers not so much a

---

9 Martin Luther, *Vorlesung über den Römerbrief, 1515–1516* (München: Chr. Kaiser Verlag, 1957), II, 151–52.

forensic change in status before God as it is an ontological change within the individual believer. Grace is God's act whereby He renews the divine image in man through the Holy Spirit and makes the believer a participant in the divine nature. The Radicals did not think that this grace could be earned through any meritorious work. It came as a sheer gift from God. Yet once received, the gift of grace so understood did enable one to rise higher in the scale of Christian perfection than was generally thought possible where the forensic concept of grace prevailed. Even for Balthasar Hubmaier and Pilgram Marbeck, who do not make the Johannine concept of salvation their own, grace is thought of as an act of God, which brings about an ontological change within the believer himself rather than a forensic change in status before God. There was present also throughout the Radical Reformation a rudimentary doctrine of natural law which was sometimes referred to as a first grace. The break between nature and grace was not as abrupt for them as it was for either Luther or Calvin.

The emphasis upon good works as the fruit of grace in the Radical Reformation led to the accusation of "work's righteousness" by the Magisterial side. On the other hand, the emphasis upon forensic justification by the Magisterial Reformers often led the Radicals to denounce them as peddlers of "cheap grace." That the two sides of the Reformation were in effect working with two different concepts of grace was not, I think, clear to the participants in the struggle of the sixteenth century. Nor, for that matter, is it always clear to the descendants of the two groups today. It is my hope that this study will help to clarify the issues involved in both sides of a continuing debate.

CHAPTER I

ACCUSATIONS AND REPLIES

A. *The Charge*

In nearly all of the major contacts between representative leaders of the Radical Reformation and those of the Magisterial Reformation, during the sixteenth century Reformation period, the most frequent charge which the latter bring against the former is that they have no adequate concept of grace. This is true even when the leaders of the Magisterial Reformation are kindly disposed toward the leaders of the Radical wing, as was Wolfgang Capito toward Michael Sattler when the two men met in Strasbourg during 1526. After Sattler's martyrdom at Rottenburg[1] Capito wrote to the council of Horb that Sattler had been known to the Strasbourg Reformers and that they had admired him because of his zeal for the honor of God and the Church of Christ, but that they had rejected his method and articles of faith, because "he wanted to make pious Christians through a fixed creed and outward compulsion which we considered the beginning of a new monasticism."[2] Regardless, too, of whether the Magisterial Reformers stand within the Lutheran or the Reformed tradition, their accusations against the Radicals when these take on a more hostile tone contain with almost monotonous regularity the affirmation that the Radicals are "heaven stormers," "merit men," or "work's righteousness people," whose assurance of justification and salvation does not ultimately rest upon God's grace given in Christ upon the cross, but rather upon their own good works. So Martin Bucer in his *Getrewe Warnung* of 1527 complained that Hans Denck, during his brief sojourn in Strasbourg (November, 1526, to Christmas Day, December, 1526),[3] "did not ascribe righteousness to Jesus Christ alone but also to our good works and free will."[4] Bucer had interpreted Denck as holding a position which made the objective effectiveness of Christ's atonement dependent upon its subjective appropriation by the believer, which appropriation had then to be made manifest in a Christlike life. To this interpretation of Denck's position on the atonement Bucer replied as follows:

---

1 *The Mennonite Encyclopedia* (4 vols.; Scottdale, Pa.: Mennonite Publishing House, 1956–1959), IV, 427–34.
2 Johann Wilhelm Baum, *Capito und Butzer, Strassburgs Reformatoren* (Elberfeld: R. L. Friderichs, 1860), p. 411.
3 *ME*, II, 34. See also Walter Fellmann (ed.), *Hans Denck Schriften*, 2. Teil, Religiose Schriften, *Quellen und Forschungen zur Reformationsgeschichte*, Band XXIV (Gütersloh: C. Bertelsmann Verlag, 1956), p. 14. Pp. 18–19 of the latter work contain a brief but excellent review of Denck's life. This review shows that Bucer was mainly responsible for securing Denck's banishment from the city.
4 Martin Bucer, *Getrewe Warnung der Prediger des Evangelii zu Strassburg über die Artickel, so Jakob Kautz, Prediger zu Wormbs, kürtzlich hat lassen ausgohn, die frucht der schrifft und Gottes worts, den kinder Tauff, und erlösung unsers herren Jesu Christi, sambt anderm, darin sich Hans Dencken, und anderer widertäuffer schwere yrrtumb erregen, betreffend. Beweren die geyster, ob sie aus Got sind, dann es sind vil falscher propheten inn die welt ausgangen. I. Johan. IV.* (Strasbourg, 1527). From a photostat copy now in the Mennonite Historical Library, Goshen, Ind. No pagination appears in the original.

> Therefore, it is a worse error than has ever occurred or even can occur. It wishes to make the redemption of Christ powerless, except as we walk in the way which he has traveled, as though the whole thing depended on us. No! When we were enemies, dead in our sins, says Paul, we were reconciled to God through the blood of Christ, and herein, in an act of God, created for good works in Jesus Christ. Ephesians 2. See, the beginning, middle, and end is the grace of God through the death of Christ. How then can one say [how does it sound to say] that Christ should have suffered for us or made satisfaction in no other way, except as we stand in his footsteps?[5]

Martin Luther had little or no direct contact with the Anabaptists,[6] but in 1530 he wrote an approving preface to the book of Justus Menius against the Anabaptists, which was titled *Der Widder Taüfer und Geheminus*, in which he said that the Anabaptists "say of me that I teach that good works are not worth a farthing. I contend that it is not good works which save a man, but rather faith alone. But that does not mean that one should not live a good life."[7]

In Luther's *Commentary on Galatians*, based upon lectures by Luther at the University of Wittenberg in 1531, and first published in 1535, the Anabaptists are always referred to as being among those who do not understand the righteousness of grace.

> The fantastical sects [writes Luther] teach nothing, neither can teach anything aright concerning this righteousness of grace. The words, indeed, they have taken out of our mouths and writings, and these only do they speak and write. But the thing itself they are not able to deliver and straitly urge, because they neither do nor can understand it, since they cling only to the righteousness of the Law.[8]

Luther does not identify any of the Anabaptists who used his works in support of their own program without grasping his central theological position. The statements which are lifted from the *Commentary on Galatians* are not intended in any sense to be an exhaustive definition of his attitude toward the Anabaptists, but simply to be illustrative of the fact that Luther, like Capito and Bucer, thought that the Anabaptists or Radicals had no adequate concept of grace. One other statement from the *Commentary* is, therefore, sufficient for our purpose at this point. Luther writes near the close, when the foundation for his doctrine of justification by grace through faith alone has been well laid, as follows:

---

5 *Ibid.* This quotation appears on what would be p. 13, if any pagination were added.
6 John Oyer, "The Writings of Luther Against the Anabaptists," *MQR*, XXVII, No. 2 (April, 1953), 100–10. Oyer points out that Luther did not bother to search for the origins of the Anabaptists and that he seems to have been indifferent toward them except when his opinion was sought, on which occasions he generally linked them with Carlstadt and the Zwickau prophets. Luther did, of course, have direct contact with Melchior Hoffmann before he became an Anabaptist and even gave his warm approval to Hoffmann's preaching in 1525, though he later recalled it. See *ME*, II, 779, col. I.
7 Oyer, p. 102.
8 Luther, *A Commentary on St. Paul's Epistle to the Galatians*, based on lectures delivered at the University of Wittenberg in 1531, and first published in 1535 (revised and completed translation based on the Middleton edition of the English version of 1575; London: James Clark & Co., 1956), p. 26.

> For when Christ, the chief cornerstone, is removed, the seekers of salvation cannot otherwise judge than that they which do such great and splendid works are acceptable to God. So at this day the Anabaptists dream that they which are poor, suffer hunger and cold, and wear mean apparel, etc., are saints, but these are not saints which have possessions.[9]

Heinrich Bullinger in his *Tegen de Wederdoopers* of 1531 complained that the Anabaptists reproached the Evangelical preachers, because they taught that Christ had made satisfaction for our sins, and also because they taught men became righteous before God through faith rather than through good works; while the Anabaptists held that one must emphasize much more good works and the doing of them in this present evil world.[10] As the Synod of Strasbourg met from the third to the fifteenth of June in 1533, it was again Martin Bucer, who this time found Melchior Hoffmann guilty of expounding doctrines that minimized the grace of God. In the opinion of the Synod, Hoffmann "began to cry to the world against the grace of God's elect, to minimize the redemption of Christ, and to erect human possibility."[11] This, said Bucer, speaking for the Synod, "amounts to a denial that God is God, and that all utilization of divine grace and whatever man can think of as good are purely the presents and gifts and works of God."[12]

Although the Anabaptists continued to insist that they did not seek their salvation by their own good works, the suspicion that the Radicals were not orthodox on the doctrine of grace continued to linger among the theologians and ministers of the Magisterial Reformation until the very end of the formative period in the Reformation era. John Calvin accused the Anabaptists of "work's righteousness" in a French work written from Geneva in 1544. For the purpose of clarity in presentation the exact nature of Calvin's accusation, the occasion for it, and the theological standpoint from which it was made will be discussed at a later point in this chapter.[13] The charge of "work's righteousness" was in essence the charge of Gellius Faber against Menno Simons and the Dutch Anabaptists in 1552, when he wrote that "they have a proud faith, one-half of which is founded on the merits of Christ, and the other upon their own good works."[14] In the Frankenthal Disputa-

---

9 *Ibid.*, p. 493.
10 Syste Hoekstra, *Beginselen en Leer der Oude Doopsgezinden...* (Amsterdam: P. N. van Kampen, 1863), p. 272, quoting Heinrich Bullinger, *Von dem unverschampten fräfel, ergerlichem Verwyrren, und unwarhafften leern, der selbsgesanden Widertouffern* (Zurich: Christoffel Froschauer, 1531), I, cols. 13 and 14).
11 *Bibliotheca Reformatoria Neerlandica*, eds. Samuel Cramer and Fredrik Pijper (10 vols.; The Hague: Martinus Nijhoff, 1903–14), V, 269.
12 *Ibid.*, p. 278.
13 The work referred to above appeared under the title, *Brieve Instruction Pour Armer tous bons fidels contre les Erreurs de la secte des Anabaptistes*, and was written as a refutation of the *Schleitheim Confession* of 1527, the earliest of several Anabaptist confessions of faith. The *Brieve Instruction* is found in its entirety in the *Corpus Reformatorum*, ed. Carolus Gottlieb Bretschneider (Halis Saxonum: C. A. Schwetschke et Filium, 1868), XXXV.
14 *The Complete Writings of Menno Simons*, trans. Leonard Verduin; ed. John C. Wenger; biography by Harold S. Bender (Scottdale: Mennonite Publishing House, 1956), p. 760. *Reply to Gellius Faber*, 1554, was Menno's longest, but not his most important writing. Gellius Faber, also known as Jelle Smit, had been a Catholic priest at Jelsum near Leeuwarden, Fries-

tion of 1571, the suspicion that the Radicals are not orthodox on the doctrine of grace again manifested itself in the manner in which the sixth item discussed at the Disputation was worded:

> Whether the perfect obedience of Jesus Christ, grasped and received through true faith is the only and sufficient payment for our sins and the reason for our salvation, or whether we are saved partly through faith in Christ and partly through bearing the cross and good works.[15]

After the proposition was put before the convocation, the Anabaptists requested a clarification. Peter Dathenus, a minister in the Reformed Church and chaplain during the Disputation, made the clarification. He emphasized that because of man's enslavement in sin no good work which took place before or after his conversion could be regarded as the ground for his justification. This could be found alone in the perfect obedience of Jesus Christ, so that man is saved by the grace of God and by the merits of Jesus Christ rather than by his own works.[16]

To this clarification Rauf Bitsch, spokesman for the Anabaptists, replied, "We do not believe that good works, the cross [of discipleship], or anything whatever saves us, but we confess that we wish to call good works the duty of obedience and the fruit of faith."[17] Dathenus had to admit that the answer which the Anabaptists gave to the question as stated in the sixth proposition was on this occasion orthodox. Yet he felt that there were weaknesses in their understanding of grace as related to the doctrine of justification which had been elsewhere expressed in Anabaptist literature. At the close of the discussion on this point Dathenus said:

> We ask these men in a contemplative manner that they should also speak of this article according to the will of the Lord. For in the *Ausbund* or *Spiritual Songs* there are many peculiar expressions through which the simple can easily be led astray to an opinion of

---

land, but left his home community nearly the same time that Menno did and joined the Reformed Church, where he became a minister, serving churches both at Norden and Emden. In 1552 Faber published a 78-page booklet against the Dutch Anabaptists under the title, *Eine Antwert Gellij Fabri dener des hilligen wordes binnen Emden op einen bitter honischen breeff der Wedderdoper...* (Magdenburg). See ME, II, 285. A copy of the Faber book is on deposit at the Universitätsbibliothek in Munich, Germany, and a microfilm copy is available at the Bluffton College Mennonite Historical Library. In his attack Faber names Obbe Philips as one who teaches a "proud faith" and as one who "plainly asserts that the justification of man results not from faith alone, but from faith and love and good works". *CWMS*, p. 760. Menno replies that Obbe has left the Anabaptist movement, and that his "proud faith", as Faber calls it, is not representative of the true Anabaptist position on grace and justification. Obbe's *Confession*, in which he explains why he left the Anabaptists, appears in *SAW*, pp. 206–25.

15 *Protocol dat is de Gansche Handelinge des Gespreche to Franckenthal inder Tuerhorstelicher, met dien welche men Wederdoopers noemt, den 28 May begonnen, ende den 19 June deses Jares 1571 Voleyndicht* (Dortrecht, 1571).
16 *Ibid.*, p. 458.
17 *Ibid.*, p. 461.

justification by works, of which one should read several and point them out. But we do not wish to detain our audience any longer at this time in order that we may progress.[18]

From the time of Hans Denck's expulsion from Strasbourg at the instigation of Martin Bucer on Christmas Day of 1526 to the end of the Frankenthal Disputation[19] on June 19, 1571, is a period of approximately fifty years. And at the end of the period, as in the beginning, the leaders of the Magisterial Reformation who contact the Radicals are convinced that the latter are "work's righteousness people," who do not know the meaning of grace. What was the theological center of the Magisterial Reformation which always caused its theologians and ministers to see the Anabaptists in this light?

1. The Pauline-Augustinian Concept of Grace

Zwingli, Capito, Bucer, and Bullinger may well be thought of as the Calvinists before Calvin. The position of all four on the truth of the Reformed faith as measured by the Scriptures, and of the mistaken position of the Radicals in regard to grace, are summed up rather well in Bullinger's *Handbuch oder Summa der Christlicher Religion* of 1556. Bullinger begins this work with an attack upon the doctrine of the freedom of the will as opposed to the bondage of the will, which, as will later be seen in Chapter II, was one of the basic differences between all the leaders of the Radical Reformation considered in this study and the leaders of the Magisterial Reformation with whom they had contact, whether these were in the Lutheran or the Reformed tradition.

Although the Anabaptists are not identified by name in Bullinger's *Handbuch*, a veiled polemic against them runs through the whole of it. This polemic becomes particularly clear in Bullinger's answer to the seventh question in the *Handbuch*, where he asks "whether man becomes righteous before God alone through faith in Jesus Christ or also through good works."[20] In answer to this seventh question Bullinger lists seven reasons why the Reformed faith is true according to the Scriptures and why the Radicals, by implication, have either an inadequate or a false concept of grace. First, he says that to be made righteous before God means

---

18 *Ibid.*, p. 464. The *Ausbund* is an early collection of Anabaptist hymns, which in its final form numbered more than 800, but the nucleus of the book, now Part II, beginning with hymn No. 81, consists of fifty-one hymns written by a number of Anabaptists, while they were imprisoned in the dungeons of the castle of Passau on the Danube between 1535–1540. Though it originated among the Swiss Brethren, it was apparently used by all German-speaking Anabaptists, and it is still in use among the Amish of America today. See *ME*, I, 191. It is regrettable that Dathenus did not take time to point out the passages which he considered heretical on the issue of justification by faith alone.
19 The Frankenthal Disputation was the most important of a number of disputations held between representatives of the Magisterial Reformation and the South German Anabaptists during the sixteenth century. It was a method by which princes tried to persuade the Anabaptists to join the church of a particular prince through the arguments of trained theologians, when the most severe persecutions failed in the accomplishment of that purpose. See *ME*, II, pp. 373–75.
20 Carl Pestalozzi (ed.), *Heinrich Bullinger, Leben und Ausgewahelte Schriften* (Elberfeld, 1858), p. 544.

to be pardoned before the judgment seat of God, where all men are guilty sinners and worthy of being given over to eternal damnation. In the second place, says Bullinger, one must now see why it is that God takes away our sins and delivers us from damnation, and the only ground for this is the mercy and the grace of God, who for Christ's sake considers us righteous. In the third place, according to Bullinger, all the benefits of Christ, his righteousness, redemption, and eternal life, are imputed to us through the gift of the Spirit of God, in whom all graces and gifts are shared with us. And this is necessary in the fourth place, because if it were otherwise man would boast in himself and trust in his works rather than in grace alone.[21]

The doctrine of grace as these men, as well as Luther, understood it was inseparably linked with the doctrine of divine election, predestination, and the bondage of the will as a consequence of the fall and original sin. Since all men are sinners before God, helpless in their sin and worthy of eternal damnation, it is wholly by an act of grace on God's part that any should be elected for salvation.

J. I. Packer and O. R. Johnston in the introduction to a new translation of Martin Luther's Bondage of the Will observe that Luther, Calvin, Bucer, and all the leading Protestant theologians stood on precisely the same ground, "namely, the helplessness of man in sin and the sovereignty of God in grace."[22] The translators of De Servo Arbitrio content further in their introduction that the heart of the Reformer's theology was found not in the doctrine of free justification by faith only, but at a deeper level where the question they asked

> was not simply whether God justified believers without works of law, but the broader question, whether sinners are wholly helpless in their sin and whether God is to be thought of as saving them by free unconditional invincible grace, not only justifying them for Christ's sake when they come to faith, but also raising them from the death of sin by his quickening Spirit in order to bring them to faith.[23]

Reduced to its simplest terms and pushed to its deepest theological implications the question asked is:

> *What is the source and status of faith? Is it the Godgiven means whereby the God-given justification is received, or is it a condition of justification which is left to man to fulfil? Is it a part of God's gift of salvation, or is it man's own contribution to salvation? Is our salvation wholly of God or does it ultimately depend on something that we do for ourselves?*[24] (Italic mine)

---

21 Ibid., pp. 544–45.
22 Martin Luther, The Bondage of the Will, a New Translation of De Servo Arbitrio (1525) by J. I. Packer and O. R. Johnston (London: James Clark & Co., 1957), p. 58.
23 Ibid., pp. 58–59.
24 Ibid., p. 59. Martin Bucer in Getrewe Warnung says:
"It is true that all children of God have been predestined to be conformed to the image of Christ, because all such conformity must be fulfilled in the elect. For those whom He predestines He also calls and makes them holy through the Spirit of God. For we can do nothing good of ourselves, except at the time and to the degree which it pleases God. That is what the Scriptures teach; that is what we preach, Dr. Luther, and all who curse the Denckian spirit which accuses us of making an idol out of Christ."

Luther, Bucer, and Bullinger all answered that since man is helpness in sin, the "beginning, middle, and end" of his salvation rests wholly in the invincible grace of God. For all of them the principle of *sola fide* was "anchored in the broader principle of *sola gratia.*"²⁵

Walther Koehler further clarifies Luther's theological standpoint with reference to grace as follows. Luther, he says, insisted that the confession of one's sinfulness as the will of God is the beginning of the way of salvation. Behind this confession of sinfulness is not man's search but God's act; not man searching after God, but man found by God. Luther's favorite example here was the Canaanite woman (Matt. 15:21ff.),²⁶ whose humility before Christ was for Luther an illustration of the truth that the confession of oneself as sinner may be at the same moment the source of deepest joy. Since man himself cannot become righteous, inasmuch as he cannot overcome sin, there is only one place where he may be declared so, and that is *coram Dei*, before God, where the sentence of guilty is at the same time the word of pardon. The righteousness of the Christian becomes here the imputed righteousness of Christ through the atoning death on the cross and remains so throughout this life as expressed in the formula, *simul iustus et peccator*. As the believer looks at himself, he is and remains sinner. As he looks at Christ on the cross, he is and remains righteous, since God for Christ's sake does not reckon his sin as sin.²⁷

---

25 *Ibid.*, p. 59.
26 Martin Luther, *Auff den andern Sontag hynn der fasten Evangelion*, in *D. Martin Luther's Werke*, kritische Gesamtausgabe (Weimar: Herman Böhlaus Nochfolger, 1907), XVII, 200–04.
27 Walther Koehler, *Doemengeschichte als Geschichte des Christlichen Selbstbewusstseins des Zeitalter der Reformation* (Zurich: Max Niehans Verlag A.C., 1951), a translation, paraphrase, and summary of pp. 336–47. The correctness of Koehler's interpretation of Luther's position on this point is, I think, substantiated by the following excerpt from Luther's *Commentary on Romans*:

"Es ist gleich wie mit einem Kranken, der dem Artz, der ihm aufs gewisseste die Gesundheit verspricht, Glauben schenkt und in der Hoffnung auf die versprochene Genesung seinem Gebote gehorcht und sich inzwischen dessen enthält, was ihm verboten ist, dass er nicht die verheissene Gesundung gefährde und die Krankheit steigere, bis der Arzt erfüllt, was er versprochen hat. Ist dieser Kranke nun etwa gesund? Nein, er ist zugleich krank und gesund. Krank in Wircklichkeit, gesund aber kraft der gewissen Zusage des Arztes, dem er glaubt, der ihn schon gleichsam für gesund rechnet, weil er dessen gewiss ist, dass er ihn heilen wird; denn er hat schon begonnen, ihn zu heilen, und er rechnet ihm darum die Krankheit nicht zum Tode an. In gleicher Weise hat auch unser Samariter Christus den halbtoten Menschen, seinen Kranken, zur Pflege in die Herberge aufgenommen und begonnen, ihn zu heilen, nachdem er ihm völlige Gesundheit zum ewigen Leben zugesagt hat. Er rechnet ihm die Sünde, d.h. die Begierden, nicht zum Tode an, sondern verwehrt ihm nur inzwischen in der Hoffnung auf die verheissene Gesundung das zu tun und zu lassen, wodurch jene Genesung aufgehalten und die Sünde, d.h. die böse Begierde gesteigert werden könnte. Ist er damit vollkommen gerecht? Nein, sondern er ist zugleich ein Sünder und ein Gerechter; Sünder in Wirklichkeit, aber gerecht kraft der Ansehung und der gewissen Zusage Gottes, dass er ihn von der Sünde erlösen wolle, bis er ihn völlig heilt, und so ist er vollkommen heil in Hoffnung, in Wirklichkeit aber ein Sünder; doch besitzt er die Erstlingsgabe der Gerechtigkeit, auf dass er immer weiter suche, immer in dem Bewusstsein ungerecht zu sein. [Wenn nun aber dieser Kranke aus Liebe zu seiner Schwachheit gar nicht alles heilen lassen will, wird er dann nicht sterben? So ist's mit denen, die ihren bösen Lüsten in der Welt nachgeben. Oder wenn ein Kranker sich einbildet,

This forensic view of grace, linked with the Pauline anthropology of Romans 6 and 7, and read through Augustinian eyes, must be kept in mind as the theological standpoint from which the theologians of the Magisterial Reformation accuse the Radicals as having not only an inadequate concept of grace, but also an inadequate concept of sin.

(a) The Accusation of Legalism

Legalism is here used as an expression of the distinction between *nomos* and *agape*. The difference between *nomos* and *agape* has been sharply drawn by Nygren as follows. *Nomos* as the righteousness of Law is based upon the worth of its subject, while *agape* as the love of God is sovereign and shows its sovereignty most clearly in the fact that it is directed toward the sinner.[28] In the *Commentary on Galatians* Luther takes the Anabaptists to task because they say that baptism is not a work of God unless the person receiving it is a believer. This, says Luther, makes the work of God depend upon the worth of the person. He asks:

> Who cannot see here in the Anabaptists, not men possessed by demons, but demons themselves possessed by worse demons? So also the papists still to this day insist on works and worthiness of the person, contrary to grace, thus giving strong support (in words at least) to their brethren, the Anabaptists. For these foxes are tied together by their tails, even though their heads look in opposite directions. While they outwardly profess to be

---

er sei nicht krank, sondern gesund, und darob den Arzt verschmäht, so bedeutet das so viel, wie durch seine eigenen Werke gerechtfertigt und gesund sein wollen.]
"Verhält es sich aber so, dann habe entweder ich's niemals verstanden oder es haben die scholastischen Theologen nicht zutreffend genug über Sünde und Gnade geredet, die davon träumen, dass die ganze Erbsünde so gut wie die Tatsünde hinweggenommen werde, wie wenn sie gewisse Dinge wären, die man im Augenblick wegräumen Könnte, so wie Finsternis durch das Licht vertrieben wird, während doch die alten heiligen Väter Augustinus und Ambrosius ganz anders darüber geredet haben nach der Weise der Schrift, jene aber nach der Weise des Aristoteles in seiner Ethik, der die Sünde und die Gerechtigkeit auf die Werke gründete und demgemäss darauf, ob sie vorhanden sind oder fehlen." (From *Vorlesung über den Römerbrief, 1515–1516*, II, 151–52.)

The influence of Augustine upon Luther is well known. It is evident, not only in *The Bondage of the Will*, but also in the *Commentary on Romans*, written during 1515–1516, nearly ten years before the latter work and a full year before the *Ninety-Five Theses*. In the recently published *Saint Augustin Dans L'oeuvre de Jean Calvin* (Assen: Van Gorcum & Comp. N.V. – G. A. Hak & H. J. Prakke, 1957) by Luchesius Smits has shown that with every succeeding edition of the *Institutes* Calvin shows a greater familiarity with and a greater dependence upon Augustine. This manifests itself specifically in those areas where Calvin found himself in conflict with the Anabaptists. See Vol. I, 45, 46, and 71.

28 Anders Nygren, *Eros und Agape*, Gestaltwandlungen der christlichen Liebe (Gutersloh: T. Bertelsmann, 1930), I, 54. Nygren maintains that Luther's break with Rome came about as the direct result of his rediscovery of the pristine meaning of *agape* in the Pauline theology of the cross; and that this meaning had become blurred in synthesis of *eros* and *agape* in the Augustinian doctrine of *caritas*. Luther, says Nygren, saw both *nomos*, where the love of God is dependent upon the worth of its object, and *caritas*, where the sinner is no longer loved because he is a sinner, but because of what he can become through infused grace, as a threat to the sovereignty of God in grace. (A summary of the central argument from Vol. II of the work cited above.)

great enemies, inwardly they think, teach, and defend one and the same against our only Saviour Christ, who alone is our righteousness.[29]

There are other comments on the Anabaptists in the *Commentary*, and they are nearly always made in this same vein. Papists, Zwinglians, and Anabaptists are alike ignorant of the righteousness of Christ and hence "must make of Christ Moses and of the Law Christ,"[30] while the fantastical sects who hold that faith is not true faith unless the cross, passion, and the shedding of blood are present "do darken and deface the benefits of Christ again at this day: They take away from him the glory of a justifier and make him a minister of sin."[31]

It was on this same basis that the grace of God is not dependent upon the merit or worthiness of the person receiving it that John Calvin criticized the Anabaptists on their position that a Christian should not or could not be a magistrate. This criticism is found in the *Brieve Instruction* of 1544, previously referred to in footnote 1, page 15. The *Brieve Instruction* was written as a refutation of the *Schleitheim Confession* and deals with the seven articles of that confession, as well as with two additional items, the Celestial Flesh of Christ and the Sleep of the Soul.[32] In his criticism of the *Schleitheim Confession* with regard to the office and power of the prince, Calvin refers to the Pauline admonition, that every man

---

29 Luther, *Commentary on Galatians*, p. 19.
30 *Ibid.*, pp. 146–47.
31 *Ibid.*, p. 148.
32 The doctrine of the Celestial Flesh of Christ was never accepted by the South German Anabaptists, but it was taught by both Menno Simons and Dirk Philips, who had received it from Melchior Hoffmann. Caspar Schwenckfeld also taught the doctrine in a slightly modified form. See Chapter III of thesis for details.

The *ME*, IV, 543, states that there is *no convincing evidence* (italics mine) that the doctrine of the Sleep of the Soul was ever held among the Anabaptists or Mennonites anywhere. The writer found, however, that some of the South German Anabaptists both held and taught this doctrine. Leonhard Schiemer, who, as Robert Friedmann says, belonged to the line of South German Anabaptists, represented by such names as Hans Denck, Hans Hut, Hans Schlaffer, and others, states this doctrine explicitly as follows:

"Yes, if I know God rightly, I will rejoice so greatly in my spirit and soul, that this joy will overflow into the body, and the body, in an indefinable way [*gantz unemfindlich*], will be glorified as unsuffering and immortal. Therefore, when man is cleansed of all love of the creaturely, God imparts this through sleep, for the holy ones all sleep until the resurrection of the dead."

See Leonhard Schiemer, "Von Drierlei Gnad," in *Glaubenszeugnisse oberdeutscher Taufgesinnter*, ed. Lydia Müller, *Quellen und Forschungen zur Reformationsgeschichte*, Band XX (Leipzig: M. Heinsius Nachfolger, 1938), 67.

Socinus and Servetus also held this doctrine. In their view only the righteous dead were raised up, while the wicked were simply annihilated. (See *The Radical Reformation*, by George H. Williams.) Calvin's tract, *Psychopannychia*, written during the 1530's, was aimed against this doctrine. He may have had in mind the South German Anabaptists as well as Servetus and Socinus.

It is interesting to note that this doctrine, which Calvin considered heretical in the sixteenth century, is closer to the modern understanding of the biblical view of man than Calvin himself was. Modern biblical scholarship stresses the fact that the Bible views man as psychosomatic unity. Consequently, its stress is on eternal life as the resurrection of the whole man, rather than upon the immortality of the soul as some element within man that is in itself immortal.

should remain in the vocation or state in which he was called (I Cor. 7:20), and he maintains that princes, because they must maintain the duties of the princely office, are not thereby excluded from God's grace.

The grace of God is given, argues Calvin, not because of the worth or fitness of the person who receives it, but solely on the basis of the merit and worth of Christ himself. Calvin builds his argument on the example of the Ethiopian eunuch (Acts 8:26–40), whose conversion took place, not on condition that he should first leave the service of Queen Candace, but alone on the basis of faith in Jesus Christ. Calvin's position, as outlined in the *Brieve Instruction*, was simply *that any condition laid down which one had to meet prior to faith, automatically shifted the ground of confidence for salvation from the "sola Gratia" to one's own ability to meet* that previously imposed condition.[33]

(b) The Accusation of Pelagianism

Standing as they did within the context of the Pauline-Augustinian anthropology with its emphasis upon the bondage of the will and man's utter helplessness in sin, it is not difficult to see why the Magisterial Reformers often felt that the Radicals were guilty of the Pelagian heresy. These accusations, which involve an atomistic view of sin, the reduction of Christ from the status of Redeemer to that of example, and in effect, a denial of original sin, are both veiled and direct. One of the complaints of Martin Bucer against Hans Denck in the *Getrewe Warnung* of 1527 was that Denck had "denied original sin by setting a free will within our nature which is entirely corrupted,"[34] and that he had taught that sin was as nothing and a vain delusion. Bucer felt that Denck had reduced the status of Christ as Redeemer to the point where he became only an example, and men became righteous as the result of their own efforts to follow that example.

In Calvin's *Institutes* Calvin speaks of the claim of Pelagius that Adam in his sin ruined only himself and that such injury as is received from Adam by his descendants is received by imitation rather than by propagation. Calvin asks in reply if the sin of Adam is propagated by imitation. "Do we then receive no other advantage from the righteousness of Christ than the proposal of an example for our imitation?"[35] In Book IV of the *Institutes*, II, where Calvin develops his doctrine of the Church, there are numerous thrusts at claims to Christian perfection which appear to be aimed at the Anabaptists. A favorite Anabaptist text with reference to the nature of the Church as *the holy community*, for example, was Eph. 5:26–27, where the Church is referred to as "a glorious church, not having

---

33 *CR*, XXXV, 83–85. Apparently Calvin also had some contact with or knowledge of Radical groups who renounced the ownership of personal property. He mentioned this, along with the prohibition to Christians to become magistrates or to wield the sword as a condition with which Anabaptists diminish the grace of Christ. See *Brieve Instruction*, p. 90, for the latter point.
34 Bucer. A rather full account of Bucer's accusations against Denck in the *Getrewe Warnung* appears in the article on Bucer in *ME*, I, 456–57.
35 John Calvin, *Institutes of the Christian Religion*, trans. John Allen (2 vols.; 7th American ed.; Philadelphia: Presbyterian Board of Christian Education, n.d.), I, 272.

spot or wrinkle." Calvin maintains that this passage indicates "what Christ is daily performing in his church . . . rather than anything he has already accomplished,"[36] and that any view of the Church which imagines her to be already perfect must be linked with the Pelagians, who "with the Cathari and Donatists must allow no infirmity in the church."[37] William Keeney in an unpublished paper on Calvin and the Anabaptists has shown that this stricture against the Anabaptists was already present in germinal form in the 1536 edition of the *Institutes,* and that in the second edition of 1539 strictures of this nature are both more numerous and more fully developed.[38]

(c) The Accusation of Universalism

George H. Williams has written that "predestination and the bondage of the will in the realm of saving faith constituted the theological center of Lutheranism."[39] The same statement can be made with equal accuracy of the theologians of the Reformed tradition. From the theological standpoint which they occupied, any denial of predestination seemed immediately to be a statement in favor of universal salvation. On the grounds that he had denied predestination and had taught the universal salvation of all men, Hans Denck was expelled from the city of Nürnberg in January of 1525 through the influence of the Lutheran clergyman, Andreas Osiander,[40] and when he arrived nearly a year later in Strasbourg, it was the Reformed leader, Martin Bucer, who was active in securing his banishment from that city for the same reason. There were, of course, other reasons why Bucer sought Denck's expulsion from the city, but Bucer considered his tendency toward Universalism as Denck's greatest heresy. After listing Denck's Christology, his attitude toward Scripture, and the civil government as being suspect, Bucer writes in the *Getrewe Warnung*:

> And after this, though they also cast many holy and elect members of Christ out of the kingdom of Christ, they maintain that if they would only cry to heaven once, devils and the damned would finally be saved.[41]

Written on the margin of the page on which this sentence appears are the words, "Summa Denckisher Leer."[42]

---

36 *Ibid.,* II, 428.
37 *Ibid.,* p. 428.
38 William Keeney, "An Analysis of Calvin's Treatment of the Anabaptists in the *Institutes*," (unpublished paper written for Ford Lewis Battles, Hartford Theological Seminary, 1958), p. 2. A chart on p. 2 shows Calvin's treatment of the Anabaptists in the editions of 1536, 1539, 1543, and 1559. According to the chart the greatest number of references to Anabaptist perfectionism as growing out of a Pelagian view of sin are in Book IV of the 1539 edition.
39 *SAW,* p. 86.
40 There were other charges as well which led to Denck's expulsion from Nürnberg, but the charge that he denied predestination and taught universal salvation was one of them.
41 Bucer.
42 *Ibid.*

The Synod of Strasbourg in 1533 condemned Melchior Hoffmann for teaching among other heresies the heresy of universal salvation. The following propositions provide the theological frame of reference from which the Synod made its condemnation:

(1) God has made all people out of nothing, but has only ordained some to eternal life through Jesus Christ, whose death is payment and satisfaction for our sins.

(2) Those whom God has predestined for salvation He grants the necessary measure of faith in Jesus Christ.

(3) Those who are are not redeemed are children of the world who have neither confessed Christ nor received him, because they are vessels of wrath whom God has prepared for damnation.

(4) The vessels of wrath are also granted knowledge of the truth by God, but in a less compelling way than the elect. Still that knowledge of truth is sufficient so that those who are appointed vessels of wrath will be accused by the testimonies of their own consciences, and God alone will be found righteous.

(5) Since God has made us all, He is indebted to no one, and He may use us as He will. Man cannot ascribe anything good to himself or accomplish anything good.[43]

After Bucer and the other Strasbourg Reformers had defined their theological position with the above propositions, they wrote:

> Melchior Hoffman began to go against this and to cry to the world against the grace of the elect ones, and he falsified the redemption of Christ and erected human ability, saying that all men are elected to eternal life and that all are redeemed through Christ. And [in order] that the people should be prepared to believe this, he brought forth several scriptures with which he thought to show that redemption through our Lord Jesus Christ had become common for the whole world.[44]

(d) The Legitimate Basis for These Accusations

To what extent are these charges of legalism, Pelagianism, and Universalism, as made by the theologians of the Magisterial Reformation against the Radicals, supported by what the Radicals themselves say about sin and grace and salvation? Chapter II will show that the charges of Pelagianism and Universalism have no solid foundation, and, therefore, these need not be discussed here. The charge of legalism in the sense of a *nomos*, as over against an *agape* stance, can be supported to some extent among the Radicals in Holland, who there came into the Anabaptist movement directly from Roman Catholicism. There is much less evidence of legalism among the South German Radicals, who there came into the Anabaptist movement by passing first through a Lutheran stage after their break with Catholicism.[45]

---

43 *Handelinge van der disputacie in Synodo te Straesburch teghen Melchior Hoffman door die predicanten derseluer stadt*, BRN, V, 263–69, summary and paraphrase.
44 *Ibid.*, p. 269.
45 This is not true in the case of Balthasar Hubmaier, who came into the Swiss Brethren

One can see the more legalistic attitude of the Dutch Anabaptists in the function which they ascribe to the Law in bringing men into the relationship of faith. The Word is divided into Law and Gospel, as it is for Luther, but the function of Law is not, as it is for Luther, to crush the sinner and drive him to despair, but to drive out sin and make him worthy of forgiveness. A good example of this is found in Dirk Philips' *Vande Gemeynte Godts.* Dirk places the beginning of the Church of God with the angels in heaven and its first reconstitution with Adam and Eve in the Garden of Eden. Dirk's concern is to show that the Church of God has always been made up of those who are holy and righteous, since God has never tolerated anything unholy or impure in His church. Therefore, those who would enter into the Church must first of all repent of their sins. To prepare men for, or to lead them to, repentance God has given His Word, which is twofold, in that it consists of both Law and Gospel. The function of the Law is threefold. It teaches first the knowledge of sin, and from this knowledge comes the fear of God, which is the beginning of wisdom, and from this fear comes the broken and contrite heart, which is acceptable to God.[46] For Dirk, as well as for Menno, the beginning of the way of salvation is not as it was for Luther and Calvin, the confession of oneself as sinner, but rather repentance. Dirk writes that the Law serves, or is conducive in part, to the new birth,

> *in view of the fact that no one can be born again or spiritually quickened, and no one can believe the Gospel except he first sincerely repent, as the Lord Jesus Christ himself testifies [Matt. 3:2], for he taught the people repentance first of all and then faith, and so he also commanded his apostles to do.*[47] (Italics mine)

This is the position which is taken consistently by Menno and Dirk in all of their writings. *Repentance*, not faith as the joyful trust in God because of His sovereignty in grace, is for them the beginning of the Christian life. This is true even of children who, when they come to the knowledge of good and evil, or through their own disobedience and transgression sin against God, should first be

> heartily admonished to repentance with the Law... in order that they might improve themselves, bewail their sins before God, confess them and bear remorse because of them. Afterwards they must again be comforted by the Gospel.[48]

For Menno, as well as for Dirk, the Word of God consists of both the threatening Law and the comforting Gospel. Here faith is not joyful trust in God and the sovereignty of His grace, but rather belief that both the dreadful threats of the Law and the comforting promises of the Gospel are dependable and true.[49] Throughout his writings and throughout his life Menno stresses the "threatening

---

wing of the Anabaptist movement via the influence of Zwingli and who is grouped with the South Germans in this study simply as a matter of convenience in the handling of material.
46 *BRN*, X, 379–414.
47 *SAW*, p. 236. Also *BRN*, X, 389.
48 Dirk Philips, *Vander Doope, BRN*, X, 75.
49 Menno Simons, *Meditation on the Twenty-Fifth Psalm, CWMS*, p. 80.

Law" and the "comforting Gospel" as the two sides of the Word of God. The Law must always precede the Gospel, because "it produces first of all the fear of God."[50] Through the fear of God, produced by the Law, the heart

> becomes affrighted, fears, and is amazed before God, and, therefore, does not do, counsel, or agree to anything which it acknowledges through the Word, in the Spirit that God, the righteous Judge, hates in His soul and has forbidden in His holy Word.[51]

To Menno the fear of the Lord was "an excellent pleasing fruit,"[52] inasmuch as this fear "is the power which expels, buries, slays, crushes, and destroys the sins of believers and is the first part of true repentance."[53] It is this fear, produced by the Law, which drives out sin, and, therefore, it is impossible to become righteous without the fear of God.[54] Those who reverse the apostolic order and preach first faith and then repentance, or the Gospel without the Law, have a false faith, and are the children of the world who like to walk upon the broad way.[55] Dirk Philips said that even as a good husbandman rids a plot of ground of weeds before sowing good seeds in it, so the true minister of the Gospel will preach first the Law in order to cleanse the heart and drive men to repentance and remorse for their sins.[56]

Obviously, this is very different from the *agape* standpoint as rediscovered by Luther and defined by Nygren. Calvin in Book III, Chapter III, of the *Institutes* writes of repentance and is at pains to show that the correct order for the beginning of the Christian life is "from faith to repentance."[57]

> Those who imagine [says Calvin] that repentance rather precedes faith, than is produced by it, as fruit by a tree, have never been acquainted with its power, and are induced to adopt that sentiment by a very insufficient argument.[58]

At a further point in the discussion Calvin writes:

> But there is not the least appearance of reason in the notion of those, who in order to begin with repentance, prescribe to their young certain days, during which they must exercise themselves in repentance; after which they then admit them to the communion of evangelical grace. I speak of many of the Anabaptists, especially of those who wonderfully delight in being accounted spiritual; and their companions, the Jesuits, and other such worthless men.[59]

---

50 Menno Simons, *The True Christian Faith*, first written in 1541 and revised in 1556, *CWMS*, p. 329.
51 *Ibid.*, pp. 328–29.
52 *Ibid.*, p. 337.
53 *Ibid.*, p. 337.
54 *Ibid.*, p. 337.
55 Menno Simons, *Reply to Gellius Faber*, 1554, *CWMS*, p. 659.
56 Dirk Philips, *Van der Sendinge der Predicanten oft Leeraers*, BRN, X, 217.
57 John Calvin, *Institutes*, I, 649.
58 *Ibid.*, pp. 649–50.
59 *Ibid.*, p. 651.

Syste Hoekstra was aware of this legalistic tendency on the part of the Dutch Anabaptists in his *Beginselen en Leer der Oude Doopsgezinden* of 1863. The book is primarily an analysis of the writings of Dirk Philips and Menno Simons, together with occasional comparisons at salient points between the *Augsburg* and *Heidelberg Confessions* and the confession of Hans de Reis. Hoekstra notes that the Dutch Anabaptists made repentance the condition for the reception of grace, and that for them *obedience* to that which God has commanded in the Scriptures came very near to being what faith was among the Evangelicals, the organ whereby grace is received.[60] Hoekstra says of the Dutch Anabaptists:

> They also preached salvation by grace, it is true, but they regarded grace ultimately much more as a gracious or judicial rule, than as the gracious activity of God directly in the soul of the sinner.[61]

The Dutch Anabaptists, in my opinion, can be absolved of the charge of legalism in the sense of a *nomos* as over against an *agape* point of view, only insofar as their doctrine of the freedom of the will (see Chapter II of thesis) is based upon the universal effects of Christ's atonement. And even here the Dutch Anabaptists cannot entirely escape this condemnation, for the South German Anabaptists, too, held a doctrine of the freedom of the will as opposed to the bondage of the will without, however, falling so deeply into the pit of legalism.

(1) The Absence of Legalism among the South German Anabaptists

The representatives who will speak for the South German Anabaptists on this point are Balthasar Hubmaier, Hans Denck, and Pilgram Marbeck. All three men are closer to Luther in the function which they attribute to the Law in bringing the individual into the relationship of saving faith than were either Menno or Dirk. With these men the function of the Law is not to cleanse the heart from sin and rid it of evil thoughts and deeds, even as men rid a plot of ground of weeds before sowing it with good seeds. The function of the Law is rather that of a schoolmaster to bring us to Christ. Through the Law the individual comes to know himself as a sinner who stands in need of God's redeeming grace. Hans Denck in his confession before the council at Nürnberg said:

> Unbelief alone is sin which the righteousness of God breaks through the Law. As soon as the Law has fulfilled its office, the Gospel comes to the fore, and through the hearing of the Gospel comes faith. Faith has no sin. Where there is no sin, there dwells the righteousness of God.[62]

The mystical strand in Denck's thought also influenced his thought in regard to the proper function of the Law. The purpose of the Law, as one side of that Word which was from the beginning, is to mortify those who are unbelieving, in order

---

60 Hoekstra, pp. 221–22.
61 *Ibid.*, p. 162.
62 Hans Denck, *Bekenntnis fur den Rat zu Nürnberg*, 1525, QFR, Band XXIV, 2 Teil, 22.

that through Christ they may be made alive and live no longer an earthly but a heavenly life.[63] The language here is reminiscent of the manner in which the mystics described the purgative stage on the way to the mystical union with God.

After his confession at Nürnberg in 1525 Denck wrote during the following year two of his major works, *Was geredt sei, dass die Schrift sagt* and *Vom Gesetz Gottes*. Walter Fellmann, who edited the critical edition of Denck's works, notes that the latter is the first of Denck's writings to come from the Anabaptist epoch in his life. Fellmann says that Denck's *Vom Gesetz Gottes* is a criticism of the Lutheran doctrine of the Law and thereby of the Lutheran doctrine of justification.[64]

Fellmann's analysis of the above work is essentially correct, and yet, even as Denck criticizes Luther's view of the function of the Law, he remains closer to Luther's view than to that of Menno and Dirk. Many of Denck's works are written in the form of a dialogue, in which the reader is engaged in an imaginary conversation with the author. This is the case with *Vom Gesetz Gottes*. After the reader has been taken through a series of questions and answers concerning the function of the Law, so that he appears to have given his consent to the proposition that the Law itself is nearly adequate to meet man's needs, Denck engages him in dialogue as follows:

> You may say: If then the Law is almost sufficient [*wann dann dem gsatz so gar gnug geschehen soll*], then is Christ vain. Here merit is established and grace is cast down.
>
> Answer: No one can satisfy the demands of the Law [*mag dem gsatz gnug thun*] who does not know and love Christ in truth. He who fulfils the Law, indeed, has merit, but no room to boast before God, for all glory belongs to God, through whose grace a way is given which was impossible for the whole world. Therefore, merit belongs not to man but to Christ, through whom everything that he has was given him by God. But he who seeks glory in his merit, as though he had it from himself, he, indeed, nullifies the grace through Christ.[65]

Denck did not object to the Lutheran doctrine that the Law was given so that through it man might be revealed to himself as sinner. What he did object to was the inference that obeying the commandments of the Law was *equally impossible* for Christian and non-Christian alike. Yet Denck never saw the Law as the instrument which God used alone to arouse men to repentance, so that He might lead them through repentance to faith, as was the case with Menno and Dirk.

In the thought of Denck the initiative in the way of salvation always resides in God's grace, who in His own time draws all men to Himself.

> No one [writes Denck] comes to Christ himself except the Father draw him, which He also truly does in His goodness. But whoever in his own mind wishes to come of himself without being drawn, he undertakes to give God something which he did not receive from

---

63 *Ibid.*, p. 23.
64 Hans Denck, *Vom Gesetz Gottes*, 1526, *QFR*, Band XXIV, 2 Teil, 48.
65 *Ibid.*, pp. 57–58.

God. He wishes to merit God [umb Gott verdienen] in order that he need not thank Him for His grace.[66]

Here can be seen the influence of Denck's Lutheran associations, even though much of what he says is written in criticism of Luther and even though those associations were all too brief in duration.

Balthasar Hubmaier also saw the Law as the instrument which is used of God to drive men to despair of themselves as miserable sinners. The Law, in Hubmaier's thought, is analogous to the baptism of John. This baptism, wrote Hubmaier,

> is nothing other than an open testimony which man receives and gives, because he considers and acknowledges himself a miserable sinner, who can neither counsel nor help himself, nor accomplish anything good, but whose righteousnesses are all foul and full of imperfections on account of which he must despair of himself. He must also, if a strange righteousness does not come to his aid, be eternally damned. This his conscience shows him out of the Law through which is taught the knowledge of sin. Now John is here and shows him to Christ, in whom he is released from his sin, finds rest and certainty, so that he does not linger in doubt and become eternally lost. In summary, God leads through John down into hell, and through Christ up again.[67]

Hubmaier's position in regard to the proper function of the Law was, however, not identical with that of Luther. Carl Sachsse has pointed out that when Hubmaier made the inner enlightenment of the Spirit a precondition for the perception of the truth of the preached Word, he fearfully withdrew from conclusions which the other Reformers drew without hesitation;

> namely, that in the last analysis the God-granted appeal of the heart of man depends upon that to which God had predestinated man. Luther expresses it completely otherwise and much more consequently, "In every man God comes first and works with grace before we call for it or cooperate with it."[68]

Pilgram Marbeck's conflict with the Strasbourg Reformers in 1531 revolved in part around the proper place for the preaching of the Law, and at first glance it appears that Marbeck held to a view of the function of the Law, which was similar to that of Menno and Dirk.[69] But excerpts from Marbeck's confession of faith, written for the Strasbourg Council before his banishment from the city in 1531,

---

66 Hans Denck, *Was geredt sei, dass die Schrift sagt*, 1526, *QFR*, Band XXIV, 2 Teil, 44. This work appears in an English translation in *SAW* under the title, *Whether God Is the Cause of Evil.*
67 Balthasar Hubmaier, *Vom christlichen Tauf der Gläubigen*, ca. 1525 (microfilm of Hubmaier's complete works, Andover-Harvard Library, Harvard Divinity School, Cambridge, Mass.) This translation was made from the modern translation of Hubmaier's work by Johannes Fundhenk, which was made available to the writer through the courtesy of Rollin Armour.
68 Carl Sachsse, *D. Balthasar Hubmaier als Theologe, Neue Studien zur Geschichte der Theologie und der Kirche*, ed. N. Bonwetsch und R. Seeberg (Berlin: Trowitzch & Sohn, 1914) XX, 172. The reference to Luther is found in *Werke, WA* I, 710.
69 John C. Wenger, "The Life and Work of Pilgram Marpeck," *MQR*, XII, No. 2 (July, 1938), 150.

and from his *Verantwortung* to Schwenckfeld of 1544, where he specifically answers the charge of legalism, indicate that Marbeck thought of the function of the Law in much the same terms as did Luther. Christ, says Marbeck, does not come for the sake of those who are well, and there is no need of a physician except where sin takes the upper hand. Marbeck refers to the passage in Rom. 5:20 and says that

> Paul does not mean here for sin to take the upper hand in the sense in which it is proper for God's wrath to assert itself, as it did in the destruction of Sodom and Gomorrah, but rather the sense of despair which comes with a knowledge of sin which is imparted by the Law. Without the knowledge of sin which is brought by the Law, the sinner is not driven to Christ, the true physician, who alone can heal him with his grace.[70]

Therefore, Marbeck can speak of the law as a "first grace," which is also given to us through Christ. Thus, the function of the Law, as Marbeck sees it, is to drive man either in idolatry to himself or in desperation to God.[71]

It is sometimes difficult to know whether Marbeck speaks of the Law with reference to the Decalogue or whether he has an incipient doctrine of natural law, or whether he equates the two. Marbeck did maintain, on the basis of Rom. 1 and Wisd. 13, that man had a natural knowledge of good and of God, which he had received from God at his creation as a result of the inbreathed breath (*ein blasen athem*) of God.[72] This natural knowledge of good and of God shines in man as a good light which is given him of God and enables man to be aware of what is good and of what is sinful, and so brings him through this Law to penitence and improvement.[73] This natural knowledge is not to be equated with the Christian supernatural knowledge which comes through the new birth and by which Christians gain a knowledge of spiritual things. But, says Marbeck, no mature man can deny that he has within himself, as a gift from God, the knowledge of both good and evil.[74] To be sure, men allow this light to shine in different degrees.

> One allows it to burn only partly or halfway; the other lets it shine at full strength; while a third extinguishes it entirely within himself, as all the godless do in whom then the darkness itself is very great.[75]

Nevertheless, "this light of nature," if man allows it to shine, is sufficient to show man to Christ, and God gave this light to man in order that through the Law he might come to the knowledge of sin, know that he is stricken, wounded and ill, and has need of a physician.[76] Marbeck speaks of this natural knowledge of good and evil as the "first grace," and he sometimes refers to the Old Testament in the

---

70 Pilgram Marbeck, "Confession of Faith," ed. John C. Wenger, *MQR*, XII, No. 3 (July, 1938), 178.
71 *Ibid.*, pp. 178–79.
72 Pilgram Marbeck, *Verantwortung* (Vienna and Leipzig: Johann Loserth, 1929), p. 231.
73 *Ibid.*, p. 233.
74 *Ibid.*
75 *Ibid.*, pp. 233–34.
76 *Ibid.*, p. 234.

same terms. The thought of Marbeck here is strikingly similar to that of Leonhard Schiemer in an epistle written to the Church of God at Rottenberg in 1527.[77]

Schiemer maintains that the Old and New Testaments speak of three levels or kinds of grace. The word, grace, he says, is much talked about and tossed to and fro in the mouths of the learned (*schrift geleerten*), but when they are pressed for a definition of grace, they cannot tell what they mean by it. They (the criticism is aimed at the Lutheran clergy) take refuge in Latin expressions whose meaning, they maintain, cannot be translated into German.[78]

Schiemer's purpose is to do away with this sophistry and to give a definition of what grace is according to the Scriptures, which speak of three kinds of grace. The "first grace" is the light of conscience, which is given by the preincarnate *Logos* to every man. This is the light which enlightens every man who comes into the world. Luther is wrong in applying John 1:8–9 to the Incarnate Word, for it refers to the Word within us, rather than to the Word among us. This light within is the Law or the "first grace," and Moses is but an external witness to this inward and "first grace."[79] This light shines in all men, for God shows no partiality and has given to every man this light, which shows man what is good or bad. Lutherans who say, "I would gladly do what is right, but I have not the grace," blaspheme God, who gives this grace to all men.[80]

The light of the eternal Word shines in the darkness of our flesh and blood, and directs us to all that is good, while the flesh (our fallen human nature) directs us toward all that is evil. The soul of man is between the flesh and the light of this "first grace," and since we have all, with the exception of Christ, turned toward the flesh with our soul, we have died in our soul. Therefore, Christ is the physician who makes us alive through his Word, so that through the power of his Word we have again a desire (for the good) but not the possibility of achieving it.[81]

Yet, while the light of this "first grace" shines within all men, one can distinguish among men three different levels of response to this light. The first group resist the light of conscience so strongly that they succeed in extinguishing it completely. Unlike Saint Peter, who went out and wept bitterly at the first crowing of the cock, they muzzle the cock's beak, so that he cannot crow at all, and at least they no longer hear him. Then they stumble blindly on, and no one can frighten them away from sin. From this first group, who respond to the light by resisting it with all their powers, come the best soldiers, for they do not fear to murder or kill, as is required of soldiers.[82]

The response of the second group to the "light within" is like that of the five foolish virgins, half-hearted. They do not entirely muzzle the beak of Saint Peter's cock, but they do not allow it to remain entirely open either. They do everything half-heartedly, fear God half-heartedly, pray half-heartedly, etc. One cannot tell the difference between these and real Christians at first glance, for in outward

---

77 Schiemer, "Von Drierlei Gnad," *QFR*, XX, 58–71.
78 *Ibid.*, pp. 58–59.
79 *Ibid.*, p. 61.
80 *Ibid.*, p. 62.
81 *Ibid.*, p. 63.
82 *Ibid.*, pp. 63–64.

appearance they are the same. But when the cross comes, they flee from it, and then their real character is revealed.[83]

The third group, as soon as they become aware of the "light within," turn to the Word of God with all their hearts. They pray, they listen much to preaching, and they inquire much with a true heart. Because they have not despised the "first grace," through which comes the knowledge of sin, God gives them the "second grace," which is given alone to those who do not despise the "first."[84] For a further contrast between Marbeck and Schiemer see Chapter III, Sections B and C.

The South German Anabaptists were thus a considerable distance removed from the *nomos* standpoint of their Dutch brethren, Menno Simons and Dirk Philips, and removed in the direction of Luther's *agape*, though insofar as they posited either natural law or free will, their position was not identical with that of Luther.

B. The Refutation of the Charge

Although a significant difference has been found to exist between the Dutch and South German Anabaptists on the function of the Law and, hence, obversely of grace in man's experience of justification, the replies which both groups make to the accusation of the Magisterial Reformers that they are "work's righteousness people" are strikingly similar. Both meant by "works of merit" primarily the whole cultic sacramental system of worship within late medieval Roman Catholicism. They saw works of love to the neighbor, not as the cause of faith but as evidence that faith was alive and not dead. From the time of Balthasar Hubmaier's proposed debate with John Eck in 1525 over all that concerns a true Christian life[85] to Menno Simon's *Confession of Distressed Christians* in 1552, the Radicals insisted that they "do not believe nor teach that we are to be saved by our merits and works as the envious assert without truth."[86] Much of what the Radicals say, as they reply to the accusation that they teach that men are saved by works and merit rather than by grace, is based upon their total rejection of all "works of merit" as practiced within the Roman Catholicism of the sixteenth century. Hubmaier, for example, maintained in the proposed debate with Eck that before God one is justified by faith alone, and that here all works of merit such as penance, the eating of fish on certain days, unleavened bread, the carrying of palms in religious processions, have been cast out as whey water.[87] The only good works, according to Hubmaier, are the deeds of brotherly love which God has commanded, but these are acts of gratitude in response to God's mercy.

Menno Simons in *The New Birth*, written in 1537, rejected the whole system of matins, masses, pilgrimages, and prayers for the dead as "works of merit," which tend to diminish the significance of Christ, who is the only sign or means of

---

83 *Ibid.*, p. 63.
84 *Ibid.*, p. 65.
85 Hubmaier, *Schluszreden die Balthazar Fridberger dem J. Eckio die meysterlich zu examinieren fürbotten hat*, n.d.
86 Menno Simons, *Confession of Distressed Christians, CWMS*, p. 506.
87 The German word is *weywasser* and evidently refers to the refuse that results from the making of cheese.

grace. The entire system is, therefore, "accursed heathenish idolatry,"[88] in which infant baptism and the daily sacrifice of the mass (see Chapter IV) are the most serious threat to the grace of God in Christ.

Pilgram Marbeck in his confession of 1531 stated his conviction that the Reformers had done well in rooting out masses and images from the worship of the Christ, but he regretted the fact that they had not seen fit to abandon the practice of infant baptism, which he saw as the root of all the other idolatrous ceremonies of the whole cultic system. Marbeck saw the sacramental system of Roman Catholicism as a continuation of the figurative ceremonies of the Old Testament, which before Christ had their place as "tokens of God's assurance to the faithful that He would redeem them eventually."[89] Now that Christ has come, however, "men are justified without merit through the redemption which has occurred in Jesus Christ, whom God has put forward as a throne of grace."[90]

Marbeck's position was simply that the continued use of ceremonies, masses, pilgrimages, prayers for the dead, etc., tended to lead men away from trust in the grace of God in Christ, and that which God has done for man's salvation in Him, to trust in that which men do for themselves in and through the ceremonies.[91]

Dirk Philips, about 1544, makes equally strong assertions that the Dutch Anabaptists trust only in the grace of Christ and not in their own works or merits nor in any external sign. Dirk was aware of the charge of "work's righteousness" made by the ministers of the Reformed Church in Holland against the Dutch Anabaptists, and in the preface of the *Enchiridion* he denies the truth of the charge, saying that men are saved alone through the grace of Christ and that they have forgiveness of sins through his blood.[92] Says Dirk, Christ makes us righteous out of grace without merit, through the redemption in which he is set before us by God as a throne of grace and to whom we have free access in the Holy Spirit. Heb. 4:14–16.[93]

Hence, for Dirk Philips, as for Menno Simons and Pilgram Marbeck, nothing is permissible in the Church of Christ which tends to diminish the grace of Christ. Dirk looked upon infant baptism, as practiced in both Roman Catholic and Magisterial churches, and upon all the ceremonies of the medieval Church of Rome as a new Pharisaism, which had been instituted according to man's own imagination of what was good without specific command from God. Dirk felt that the practice of anything not commanded of God in the Scriptures made men trust

---

88 Menno Simons, *The New Birth*, ca. 1537, *CWMS*, p. 89.
89 Marbeck, *Verantwortung*, p. 187.
90 *Ibid.*
91 Marbeck had in mind particularly the practice of infant baptism. See Chapter IV for the theological basis on which he rejected the practice.
92 *BRN*, X, 58. William Keeney in "The Writings of Dirk Philips," *MQR*, XXXII, No. 4 (October, 1958), p. 298, estimates that Dirk began publishing on a modest scale about 1544, reprinted some of his works about 1562, and that they reached their final and most expanded form about 1564. Says Keeney, "Several of Dirk's writings are completely undated. It is difficult to establish even the general period in which they were written. Through most of his life he was hunted by the authorities and wandered about as a fugitive."
93 Dirk Philips, *Bekentenisse vander scheppinge, verlossinge, ende salichmakinghe*, *BRN*, X, 65.

in their own works and humanly devised ordinances, and that any ceremony or ordinance that had no foundation in Scripture was, therefore, a diminution (*vercleyninghe*)[94] of the grace of Christ.

> For this is a word not to be doubted, and the ground of unchangeable truth, that we are not saved through any commands or ceremonies of men, but through the grace of Christ and faith in his name.[95]

Dirk states that the reason he and his followers feel compelled to separate themselves from both Roman Catholic and Magisterial churches is that both are involved in and promote these idolatrous practices, which tend to diminish Christ and his grace. To be sure, both Lutheran and Reformed groups had made a good beginning toward removing some of these practices by eliminating the daily sacrifice of the mass, prayers for the dead and to the saints, etc., but like Jeroboam in the Old Testament times the Magisterial Reformers had allowed the high places dedicated to the worship of Baal stand.[96]

Hans Denck makes his refutation of the charge of "work's righteousness," not so much from the angle of the total rejection of the system of meritorious works within Roman Catholicism and those vestiges of the system which the other Radicals saw as remaining within the Magisterial churches, but rather from the angle of one who rejects the doctrine of predestination as it is developed in Luther's *Bondage of the Will*. Yet, while Denck rejected this doctrine, he did not feel that the possibility of faith lay entirely within man's volition. In his confession before the Nürnberg Council in 1525 Denck stated that he had to await the grace of God through the work of the Holy Spirit before he could claim to have faith. To do otherwise, he said, would be to undertake for oneself the work which belongs to the Holy Spirit.[97] The significance of this statement is that Denck does not see anything within man by means of which he can create saving faith. Nor is there any good work by means of which man can compel God to grant this faith to him. Man can only wait for the stroke of God's grace and the work of the Holy Spirit in a state of *"gelassenheit"*[98]

In *Was geredt sei, dass die Schrift sagt* of 1526 there is a somewhat similar passage where Denck says that Christ alone has brought perfection to fruition which no one else has ever done. Insofar as others have partaken of perfection they have received it from Christ. This, says Denck, "is righteousness out of grace. But he [Christ] has received it from no one and this is grace out of righteousness."[99]

Denck thought of every degree of human perfection as derived from Christ, and

---

94 Dirk Philips, *Een Apologia, ofte verantwoordinghe*, BRN, X, 187.
95 *Ibid.*, p. 187.
96 *Ibid.*, p. 192.
97 Hans Denck, *Bekenntnis für den Rat zu Nürnberg*, 1525, QFR, Band XXIV, 2 Teil, 21–22.
98 The best English translation for 'gelassenheit' is, in my opinion, self-emptying or self-surrender.
99 Hans Denck, *Was geredt sei, dass die Schrift sagt*, 1526, QFR, Band XXIV, 2 Teil, 37.

every further step in the direction of a greater degree of perfection was for him the result of the activity of the grace of Christ within the individual. Denck says further that men seek the perfection which Christ never lost.[100]

Christ is necessary, because God desires no one in His service by means of compulsion, and yet that does not alter His will that all men should be saved. Therefore, God has given His Word, which is Christ, so that men might be redeemed through the same Word by which they were created.

> In this Word the mercy and righteousness of God are both hidden, so that what was impossible through the omnipotence of God now becomes possible. For as man may not receive grace without grace, so God may not share His righteousness with unrighteousness without the mediator.[101]

In *Vom Gesetz Gottes*, 1526, Denck asserted that whatever possibility one had of keeping the Law came through the grace of Christ, and he who keeps it has, therefore, no room to boast before God, because God through Christ has given him everything that he has.[102] Denck's so-called *Widerruf* (Retraction) of 1528, which was his last work before his death from the plague, contains an article on "good works," in which he says that

> good works are well pleasing to God, and He does reward them, not that they originate from us, but that we may not receive the grace which He has offered us in vain and nullify [*ausschlahen*] it completely.[103]

Clearly, neither Hans Denck nor any of the other representative leaders of the Radical Reformation considered in this study thought that they were without an adequate concept of grace, as the Magisterial Reformers repeatedly maintained. Yet as one analyzes what the Radicals say about grace, it becomes evident that they understood by grace neither the eternal decrees of God's election nor primarily the righteousness by imputation of forensic justification as expressed in the formula, *simul iustus et peccator*.

1. The Johannine Concept of Salvation as the Divinization of Man

A study of the statements made by the Radicals, as they set forth their own concept of grace, either independently of the accusations made by the Magisterial Reformers that they had no concept of grace, or in reply to those accusations, reveals the fact that among the Radicals the concept of grace was always related to the Johannine concept of salvation as the divinization of man. Whereas the central text for the forensic concept of grace, which prevailed within the Magisterial Reformation, was II Cor. 5:21, "For our sake He made him to be sin who

---

100 *Ibid.*, p. 37.
101 *Ibid.*, p. 38.
102 Hans Denck, *Vom Gesatz Gottes*, 1526, *QFR*, Band XXIV, 2 Teil, pp. 57–58.
103 Hans Denck, *Widerruf*, 1528, *QFR*, Band XXIV, 2 Teil, 107–08.

knew no sin, so that in him we might become the righteousness of God,"[104] the central text for the concept of grace, which was dominant within the Radical Reformation, was either John 1:12–13, "But to all who received him, who believed in his name, he gave power to become children of God; who were born, not of blood nor of the flesh nor of the will of man, but of God,"[105] or John 3:3, "Jesus answered him, 'Truly, truly, I say to you, unless one is born anew, he cannot see the kingdom of God.'"[106]

Hans Denck, Melchior Hoffmann, Dirk Philips, Menno Simons, and Caspar Schwenckfeld all state explicitly that their concept of salvation is that of the divinization of man. This is not the case with Balthasar Hubmaier and Pilgram Marbeck, and yet their ideas of an ontological change that is wrought by grace within man's nature are influenced by these Johannine presuppositions.

The impact of this concept of salvation upon the concept of grace within the Radical Reformation was far-reaching. It meant that for them the possibility of an *actual* righteousness in this life, as opposed to an *imputed* righteousness, lay nearer at hand. Syste Hoekstra saw this difference between the Dutch Anabaptists and the other Protestants as early as 1863, when he wrote that he found among them no trace of *Christ's imputed active righteousness*, although they taught his *imputed passive righteousness* just as did the other Protestants.[107] Hoekstra did not see the connection between this fact and the concept of salvation among the Dutch Anabaptists. The importance of the concept of salvation in its influence upon the concept of grace within the Radical Reformation is fully explored in Chapter III, Section B.

2. *The Counter-Accusations to Which This Led*

(a) *The Theologians and Ministers are Antinomian*

Standing as they did upon this position where the concept of grace was related to a concept of salvation, which involved both the renewal of the divine image in the believer and participation on his part in the divine nature itself, it becomes easy to see why the Radical Reformers regarded the forensic concept of grace which prevailed within the Magisterial Reformation as a perversion of grace. Walther Koehler has observed that both Anabaptists and Spiritualists reached back beyond Paul to the gospel of Jesus in their formulation of the doctrine of justification.[108] Koehler's analysis is, I think, correct, but one could justifiably maintain that among the Gospels the Radicals had a preference for the Gospel of John.[109]

---

104 The Holy Bible (Revised Standard Version; New York: Thomas Nelson & Sons, 1952).
105 *Ibid.*
106 *Ibid.*
107 Hoekstra, pp. 266–69.
108 Koehler, p. 358.
109 If one pushes further than this and asks what accounts for the fact that the Radicals had a preference for the Gospel of John and its concept of salvation, the answers lies, I think, in the influence of late medieval mysticism upon them. Among the South German Anabaptists this was mediated through the influence of the Friends of God and the

In any case, from the least to the greatest among them the Radicals infer that they look upon the theologians and ministers of the Magisterial Reformation as being antinomian. Hans Denck in *Vom Gesetz Gottes*, 1526, and in *Was geredt sei, dass die Schrift sagt* of the same year protests against an interpretation of grace which allows the Christian to continue in his old sinful life, when the possibility of a life that is in a larger measure triumphant over sin has been opened up through the grace that has now appeared in Christ. In the latter work Denck says, "Is it not a shame that we wish to learn to know Christ and nevertheless retain our old godless nature [*wesen*]."[110] Denck felt that the interpretation which his contemporaries within the Magisterial Reformation gave to the Pauline admonition that every man should remain in that state in which he was called (I Cor. 7:20) was wrongly applied, so that it gave people license to continue in the old godless life, while Paul spoke only of those who were married or single.[111] He who says that the Law was given merely in order that through it man might learn to know himself as sinner and that he need not or cannot keep it "does not confess that Jesus Christ has come in the flesh. He says in his heart, 'Christ is ten thousand miles away from me.'"[112] To confess Christ in such a way that the confession is without improvement in the moral life is to confess him as those who desire Christ, the son of the living God, as their king, but who do not wish this king to rule over them.[113] For Denck the experience of grace meant at least in part the God-given ability to pattern one's own life after the example of Christ's life. Man is man under the Gospel as well as under Law, even as was Saint Paul, but a new man, who, through the grace that has appeared in Christ, continues to struggle against sin with some hope of success.[114]

Balthasar Hubmaier in 1527 complained in much the same vein of the lack of the desired moral fruits of the Magisterial Reformation in the preface to his work on *The Freedom of the Will*. Hubmaier writes, "As soon as one says to them, 'Cease from evil and do good,' they answer, 'We can do nothing good. All things occur under the direction [*shickung*] of God.' And they understand by this that they are allowed to sin."[115] Hubmaier went on to say that those who were reminded that God punishes those who commit evil with eternal fire would instantly cover up their blasphemy with the excuse (*wadel*), "Faith alone saves us and not our works."[116] Hubmaier declares that he has heard many people say that they have neither prayed nor fasted nor given alms for a long time, because their priests tell them that their works are worthless before God. Hubmaier looks upon these statements, "Faith alone saves us and not our works," and "Our works are worthless before God," as half truths with which men adorned all the freedom of

---

Theologia Germanica. In Holland it came, so far as can be ascertained, through the influence of Wessel Gansfort and the Brethren of the Common Life.
110 Hans Denck, *Was geredt sei, dass die Schrift sagt*, 1526, QFR, Band XXIV, 2 Teil, 43.
111 *Ibid.*
112 Hans Denck, *Vom Gesetz Gottes*, 1526, QFR, Band XXIV, 2 Teil, 57–58.
113 Hans Denck, *Ordnung Gottes*, 1527, QFR, Band XXIV, 2 Teil, 99.
114 Hans Denck, *Vom Gesetz Gottes*, 1526, QFR, Band XXIV, 2 Teil, 55.
115 Hubmaier, *Von der Freiheit des Willens*, Nikolsburg, 1527.
116 *Ibid.*

the flesh under angelic forms and thrust all their "sins and guilt upon God, as Adam upon his helpmeet and Eve upon the serpent."[117] It is in order to root out such tares (*unkraut*) which makes God responsible for all our blasphemies, and is, therefore, the highest blasphemy of all, that Hubmaier says he has written his little book "and therein shown what man is *in* and *apart from* the grace of God in Christ and what is possible for him."[118] Thus, for Hubmaier, as well as for Denck, the claim to the experience of grace is nullified if one does not seize the new possibilities that are opened up for him through the grace of God in Christ.

Melchior Hoffmann in the latter phase of his Lutheran ministry was expelled from the city of Dorpat by the Lutheran clergy there, because he taught that holiness of life was necessary for salvation.[119] Hoffmann on his part looked upon their reformation as one from which the fruits of faith were absent and said of it that "a new devil had appeared which was worse than the first one which had been routed by the grace of God."[120] Hoffmann meant by the first devil the Roman Catholic hierarchy with the Pope at its head as the Antichrist. The new devil was the Lutheran clergy, who had taught the whole world to cry, "Believe, believe; grace, grace; Christ Jesus,"[121] without getting the world to take on the fruit of a new and better life.

The works of Menno Simons and Dirk Philips abound with similar expressions directed toward the Magisterial Reformers and their followers who talk much about grace but do not manifest the fruits of the new life in Christ.

> Some [says Menno] cry nothing but grace, Spirit, and Christ, but trample daily on Thy grace, grieve They Holy Spirit, and crucify Thy Son with their vain and carnal life, as is evident.[122]

As he wrote of the new birth, Menno declared there were many who boast of the grace of the Lord, his merits, death, and blood, but that there was not found among them "the irreproachable godly life to which the Scriptures admonish."[123] Menno says that many who with boldness boast of the grace of the Lord actually engage under Christ's name in blind and bloodthirsty tyranny against the children of God.[124] Perhaps one of Menno's severest criticisms against the other Protestant Reformers, because of the lack of disciplined and Christlike living among their followers, was made in *The True Christian Faith*, first written in 1541 and revised in 1556. Menno writes that those who have deserted Catholicism and joined the Reformation movement say

---

117 *Ibid.*
118 *Ibid.* Italics are mine.
119 Friedrich Otto zur Linden, *Melchior Hoffmann ein Prophet der Wiedertaufer* (Haarlem: De Erven F. Bohn, 1885), p. 38.
120 *Ibid.*, p. 76.
121 *SAW*, p. 201. The quotation is from Hoffmann's *Die Ordonnantie Godts*, and the original appears in *BRN*, V, 165.
122 Menno Simons, *Meditation on the Twenty-Fifth Psalm*, ca. 1537, *CWMS*, p. 68.
123 Menno Simons, *The New Birth*, ca. 1537, *CWMS*, p. 89.
124 *Ibid.*

> how miserably the priests have had us poor people by the nose, robbing us of the blood of the Lord, and directing us to their peddling superstitions and transactions. God be praised, we caught on that all of their works avail nothing, but that the blood and death of Christ alone must cancel and pay for our sins. They strike up a psalm, *Der Strick ist entzwei und wir sind frei*, while beer and wine verily run from their drunken mouths and noses. Anyone who can but recite this on his thumb, no matter how carnally he lives, is a good evangelical man and a precious brother. If someone steps up in true and sincere love to admonish or reprove them for this, and point them to Jesus Christ rightly, to His doctrine, sacraments, and unblamable example, and to show that it is not right for a Christian so to boast and drink, revile and curse; then he must hear from that hour that he is one who believes in salvation by good works, is a heaven stormer, a sectarian agitator, a rabble rouser, a make-believe Christian, a disdainer of the sacraments, or an Anabaptist.[125]

For Menno it is vain to boast in the grace of Christ, if the old undisciplined carnal life remains and the new life in Christ is absent.

(b) The Theologians and Ministers are Hucksters of "Cheap Grace"

Both in South Germany and in Holland the leaders of the Radical Reformation placed the blame for the lack of moral earnestness within the Magisterial Reformation upon the theologians and ministers of that movement. Also they felt that this lack of moral earnestness was the direct result of the forensic concept of grace which prevailed among the other Protestants.

Hans Denck in *Vom Gesetz Gottes* maintained that the effect of this doctrine had led to a condition

> where the whole world was full of people whose fruits and lives were somewhat better before they had boasted of faith than afterward. And this shall be the people through whose good works the heathen shall be moved to praise God, the Father in heaven![126]

Denck concludes that no converts will be won from the heathen by those who do not manifest the fruits of grace in their daily lives. Rather, the heathen will look upon the Christians, and they will either say that God is not merciful as the Christians portray Him, since He allows them to err so badly, or else that He is not righteous, since He tolerates such evil among them, or finally that He is impotent and can neither help nor punish His people.[127]

Menno Simons and Dirk Philips both felt that the lack of moral earnestness within the churches of the Magisterial Reformation was due to the fact that the preachers preached grace and forgiveness without the demand for repentance and new life. Menno says that these preachers tell their people that they may advance the Gospel by force of arms, that faith is all that matters, that we are poor weak sinners and cannot keep the commandments, and that they comfort their people with similar easygoing consolations.[128] By such preaching, says Menno,

---

125 Menno Simons, *The True Christian Faith*, CWMS, p. 334.
126 Hans Denck, *Vom Gesetz Gottes*, 1526, QFR, Band XXIV, 2 Teil, 52.
127 *Ibid.*, p. 52.
128 Menno Simons, *Reply to Gellius Faber*, 1554, CWMS, p. 631.

> they turn the grace of God into lasciviousness, as Jude has it, because they continue unchanged in the old state of sinfulness without any fear of God, as if they never in their lives have heard one syllable of the Word of God, and as if God would not punish ungodliness and unrighteousness.[129]

Menno declares that the whole Germanic nation has come to "a wild and reckless freedom by the preaching of their free Gospel."[130] Yet, those who undertake to reproach men for unchastity, carousing, pomp and splendor, cursing, swearing, and the use of unchaste and foul words must immediately hear that they are vagabonds, fanatics, heaven stormers, or Anabaptists.[131]

Both Menno and Dirk said that the preachers of the other Protestant churches were preachers of the world, who were not regenerate and who hence walked according to the flesh themselves. As a result they converted no one from drunkenness, avarice, or pride. They preached only what the people wished to hear, and as a result their hearers were strengthened in their vices rather than helped to the new and better life. Such preaching, said they, is like placing pillows under people's arms and throwing down cushions for them to walk upon.[132] Ministers, themselves, said Dirk, must lead blameless lives and be proved by the cross.[133] Ministers and lay people alike, who boast of faith without love and good works, have an idle boast, and their faith is vain. They are those who at the last judgment must hear the words, "Depart from me, you evil doers, for I have never known you."[134]

C. Freedom of the Will as Opposed to the Bondage of the Will

The Magisterial Reformers arrived at their concept of grace through an anthropology that centered in the bondage of the will and the doctrine of predestination. In Lutheranism, as well as within Calvinism, predestination was the solution to the problem posed by the bondage of the will. It is perhaps true that Calvinism stressed more the absolute sovereignty of God in the eternal decrees of divine election, while the stress within Luther at least was more upon the absolutely gracious character of that election. But to both systems the bondage of the will was the necessary safeguard to the sovereignty of God in grace. Luther in his reply to Erasmus called the bondage of the will "the hinge upon which all turns," and thanked him that he had aimed for the vital spot.[135]

---

129 *Ibid.*
130 *Ibid.*, p. 660.
131 *Ibid.*
132 Menno Simons, *Confession of Distressed Christians*, 1552, *CWMS*, pp. 508–09. Also, Dirk Philips, *Van der Sendinge der Predicanten oft Leeraers, BRN*, X, 217. In this work Dirk discusses among other things the signs of an effective calling to the ministry. A sign that the preachers of the Magisterial churches are not called is the fact that by their preaching they convert no one.
133 Dirk Philips, *Van der Sendinge der Predicanten oft Leeraers, BRN*, X, 233.
134 Dirk Philips, *Bekentenisse vander scheppinge, verlossinge, ende salichmakinghe, BRN*, X, 67.
135 Luther, *The Bondage of the Will*, p. 319.

The Radical Reformers, on the other hand, felt that bondage of the will, predestination, and invincible grace had to be rejected both to safeguard God's eternal goodness and man's moral responsibility. All of the Radical Reformers developed an anthropology that centered in the freedom of the will, and this fact was also of primary importance in the development of their concept of grace. No matter whether a doctrine of the freedom of the will is arrived at through the conviction that the consequences of the fall and original sin were partially eliminated by the universal effects of Christ's atonement as in Melchior Hoffmann, or by maintaining that man was tripartite, body, soul, and spirit, and that in the fall only the first two entities had been affected, while a third remained whole, as in Balthasar Hubmaier, or by positing a doctrine of natural law or revelation, as in Pilgram Marbeck. It is obvious that from the viewpoint of systematic theology alone, an anthropology that is centered in the freedom of the will rather than in the bondage of the will will result, if not in a different concept of grace, then at least in a different opinion as to the manner in which grace is appropriated.[136]

136 See Chapter II for a discussion of the various routes by which different Radicals arrived at their freedom of the will anthropology.

CHAPTER II

ANABAPTIST OR RADICAL ANTHROPOLOGY

A. The Creation and Fall of Man

The point of departure for the anthropology of all of the Radical Reformers is the concept of man as originally created in the divine image. In this they do not differ either from the Magisterial Reformers or from historic Christianity. Creation in the divine image involved the assurance of eternal life,[1] man's wisdom, righteousness, and his lordship over all creatures[2] in an eternal paradise, on condition that he obey the command of God "in which all things have and must have their being."[3] Pilgram Marbeck was emphatic in his insistence that man's fleshly or human nature as originally created by God was completely good, and that any view to the contrary would make God Himself the author of sin.[4] Hubmaier saw man's tripartite nature consisting of body, soul, and spirit, as the reflection of the divine image or the holy Trinity. Hubmaier maintained, on the basis of John 1:13, that as originally created by God each *substantiae* or *ousia* in man had a will of its own, and that all three substances in man were good and entirely free to choose good or evil, life or death, heaven or hell, and he had the power to distinguish between good and evil, even as God does.[5] Hans Denck, Melchior Hoffmann, and Caspar Schwenckfeld did not elaborate on man's original condition in creation. However, it is plain from what they have to say concerning the fall, that they did not differ essentially at this point from the lines drawn by historic Christianity, which saw man created in the image of God as a being endowed with reason in order that he might decide in favor of the good and enjoy eternal life.[6]

Nor can it be maintained with any degree of accuracy that the Radicals denied the fall and original sin as a consequence of the same. Hans Denck, alone among the representatives of the left wing of the Reformation included in this study, fails to deal seriously with the fall. But even he can say that Christians seek the perfection which Christ never lost,[7] and all the others outline in rather full detail the deprivation of the original blessedness, which Adam lost through the fall and the curse which fell upon his descendants as a consequence of the same.

Melchior Hoffmann believed that through the transgression and disobedience of the first Adam the whole human race was delivered into the bondage of Satan,

---

1 Dirk Philips, *Bekentenisse vander scheppinge, verlossinge, ende salichmakinghe*, BRN, X, 65.
2 Menno Simons, *The Incarnation of Our Lord*, 1554, CWMS, p. 804.
3 *Ibid.*, p. 816.
4 Marbeck, *Verantwortung*, pp. 192–94. This affirmation is made by Marbeck in his refutation of Schwenckfeld's Celestial Flesh Christology. See Chapter III for details.
5 Hubmaier, *Von der Freiheit des Willens*. See also the translation in English in SAW, pp. 112 and 121.
6 Adolf Harnack, *Outlines of the History of Dogma*, trans. Edwin Knox Mitchell and introduction by Philip Rieff (Boston: Beacon Press, 1957), p. 229.
7 Hans Denck, *Was geredt sei, dass die Schrift sagt*, 1526, QFR, Band XXIV, 2 Teil, 37.

which was so complete that no hope of nor desire for redemption remained in any human creature.[8] Dirk Philips said that as a result of Adam's transgression of God's command he with all his descendants came into corruption and damnation, are sinners, and are of a sinful nature.[9] Menno Simons spoke of the transgression of God's command by Adam and Eve when they were led astray by the serpent, and declared that as a result of this transgression man fell through the justice of God "into the threatened curse, condemnation, and death."[10] This curse extends to all of Adam's descendants, so that all who are now born of Adam are as a result of the corrupt nature which they have received from him, carnally-minded, unbelieving, disobedient, blind to divine things, "deaf and foolish, and bound for damnation and eternal death, if not renewed by the Word."[11] Hubmaier bluntly said that as a result of Adam's transgression he lost not only the knowledge of good and evil but also the capacity or power to desire the good, and that as a result of the fall every man is born in original sin and wrath[12] and is destined from the moment of his birth for death and dust.[13] Pilgram Marbeck, though accused by Schwenckfeld of denying the fall and original sin, felt that Schwenckfeld had misunderstood him. He did not deny either the fall or original sin as a consequence of the same, but rather located the latter in the mature person's ability to distinguish between good and evil. Because of the fall natural reason always wishes to know more than it is possible for it to know. It is this reason which must be buried in the small stream of water baptism, because it is in her that the devil has his rule (regiment) over humanity. This reason has the appearance of wisdom, but she is, in fact, the highest enemy of God, and as a thief and a robber she steals God's glory.[14] Caspar Schwenckfeld, as already noted in Chapter I, believed that in the fall the ruin of man was so complete that from the fleshly or creaturely nature of the first Adam no children of God could be born.

1. The Extent of the Fall

Between Radical and Magisterial Reformers there is no quarrel over the doctrine of creation in the divine image, nor do the Radicals deny that a fall of man has in fact occurred. The point at which real differences appear in the two Reformations is rather on the question of the degree in which the divine image was destroyed by the fall. Was the destruction of the divine image total or only partial? The debate over this question between these two groups in the sixteenth century Reformation period was, in some respects, not unlike the contemporary debate between Karl Barth and Emil Brunner on the same issue.[15] In the sixteenth century Reforma-

---

8 Hoffmann, *Verclaringe van den geuangenen ende vrien wil*, BRN, V, 184.
9 Dirk Philips, *Bekentenisse vander scheppinge, verlossinge, ende salichmakinghe*, BRN, X, 65.
10 Menno Simons, *The Incarnation of Our Lord*, 1554, CWMS, p. 816.
11 Menno Simons, *A Kindly Admonition on Church Discipline*, 1541, CWMS, p. 416.
12 Hubmaier, *Von der Freiheit des Willens*. See also SAW, pp. 117 and 119.
13 SAW, p. 120.
14 Marbeck, *Verantwortung*, p. 133.
15 Karl Barth, *Natural Theology: Comprising "Nature and Grace" by Emil Brunner and the Reply "No" by Barth*, trans. Peter Fraenkie (London: Geoffrey Bles, 1946).

tion era the Radicals on the whole had a more optimistic view of man than the one which prevailed on the Magisterial side.

The fall, as interpreted by the Radicals generally, left some vestige of the divine image which could serve as a point of contact for God's approach to man in the experience of redemption through Christ. In the thought of Hans Denck it is the Neoplatonic *Logos* or the inner Word, which dwells within us, but is not from us.[16] Hubmaier posits the unfallen will of the unfallen spirit of his trichotomous man as the point of contact for the work of Christ in the redemption of man,[17] and Marbeck, on the basis of Rom. 1, proposes what amounts to a doctrine of natural law, the good light which shines in every man and gives him a natural knowledge of good and God.[18] Marbeck held that since all mankind has descended from Adam, every individual has received from Adam not only original sin but also original grace, inasmuch as Adam had received the inbreathed breath of God (*der einblasen athem Gottes*) before the fall, he passed the consequences of this as well as the consequences of his transgression on to all his descendants.[19] This is the good light which shines in every man and is sufficient to bring him to the knowledge of his need for Christ, provided he lets it shine at full strength.[20]

Melchior Hoffmann did not solve the problem of the fall by positing some vestige of the divine image left in man despite the fall, but rather in a view of the atonement which restored in a measure the image which was completely lost through the fall and which was universal in its effects.[21] Dirk Philips and Menno Simons to some extent follow Hoffmann at this point, though both of them also show independence from Hoffmann. The manner in which the thought of each was developed in relation to this problem is discussed fully under Sections B and D of this chapter.

B. *Original Sin and Its Consequences*

Within the Magisterial Reformation original sin was viewed primarily in its Augustinian character as the bondage or the servitude of the will. At least it is in the bondage of the will that the total depravity inherited by all men through Adam's fall manifests itself most sharply. Within the Radical Reformation it was more often viewed either as a sickness (Hans Denck)[22] or as the loss of the capacity to distinguish between good and evil (Hubmaier)[23] or as a poison which introduced an alien corruption into the nature which was originally good and incorruptible (Menno Simons).[24] In Pilgram Marbeck's thought original sin manifests

---

16 Hans Denck, *Bekenntnis für den Rat zu Nürnberg*, 1525, *QFR*, Band XXIV, 2 Teil, 21.
17 Hubmaier, *Von der Freiheit des Willens*. See also *SAW*, p. 120.
18 Marbeck, *Verantwortung*, p. 231.
19 *Ibid.*
20 *Ibid.*, pp. 231 and 233.
21 Hoffmann, *Verclaringe van den geuangenen ende vrien wil*, *BRN*, V, 184–85.
22 Hans Denck, *Bekenntnis für den Rat zu Nürnberg*, 1525, *QFR*, Band XXIV, 2 Teil, 20. Denck does not use the term, original sin, but he speaks of "*dise angeborne kranckhayt oder armutseligkayt*," which only increases the more he seeks to cleanse and rid himself of it.
23 Hubmaier, *Von der Freiheit des Willens*. See also *SAW*, p. 122.
24 Menno Simons, *Meditation on the Twenty-Fifth Psalm*, *CWMS*, p. 73.

itself only, or is located only, in the natural reason (*vernunft*) of the mature person in the sense that it wishes to know more than is possible for it to know.[25] And in the thought of Dirk Philips, also, original sin comes to life only as the individual reaches the stage of maturity that makes it possible for him to distinguish between good and evil.[26] Both Dirk Philips and Menno Simons speak of the "sinful nature" which humanity has inherited from Adam because of the "poison of the serpent." All descendants of Adam are as a result of this poison of the serpent from the moment of their birth burdened with an inclination toward evil. But the inclination itself is not sin, except in the mature person who has reached the capacity to distinguish between good and evil.[27]

It is thus possible to distinguish within the Radical Reformation four distinct concepts of what original sin is. It is described as an inborn incurable sickness, as the loss of the power to distinguish between good and evil, as a poison which has wrought a corruption within a nature originally good, and as the natural reason of the mature man which over-extends itself into the realm of the supernatural. Original sin was not denied by any of the Radical Reformers, but none of them saw it as it was seen within the Magisterial Reformation, primarily in its Augustinian light, as the bondage of the will.[28]

It was exactly this location of original sin within the reason of the mature person that brought from Schwenckfeld the declaration that the writers of the *Vermanung* had taught a doctrine of original sin, which bordered on Pelagianism. Schwenckfeld saw the location of original sin in the reason of the mature man as a departure from the position of the Christian Church, which with the support of Holy Scripture taught that a genuine corruption had been introduced into human nature through Adam's fall in "which nature all human beings are conceived and born."[29] Schwenckfeld saw the location of original sin in the knowledge of good and evil as "an old Pelagian error in which all men are declared as innocent as Adam was before the fall, which error was at some time or other anathematized by the Church."[30]

Marbeck replied that to locate original sin within the fleshly or creaturely nature of man as Schwenckfeld wished to do would make God the author of sin. Since

---

25 Marbeck, *Verantwortung*, pp. 133 and 217. Marbeck states that he does not seek sin only in isolated acts of sin, but in the fallen nature of the reasonable man, and not only seeks it but finds it!
26 Dirk Philips, *Vander Doope*, BRN, X, 74, 75, 91, and 92. Also *Van der wedergeboorte ende nieuwe Creatuere*, BRN, X, 331.
27 *Ibid.*, p. 331. Also Menno Simons, *Confession of the Distressed Christians, CWMS*, p. 504. Menno attributes the sinful nature of Adam to the poisonous bite of the Satanic serpent. Also, *Reply to False Accusations*, 1552, pp. 563–64, and *Foundation of Christian Doctrine*, 1539, p. 134. One of the "false accusations" to which Menno sought to reply was the accusation that the Dutch Anabaptists denied the possibility of forgiveness for postbaptismal sins. In the reply Menno speaks of the corrupt sinful nature, the lust and desire of the flesh, which all inherit at birth from corrupt sinful Adam, as original sin.
28 Robert Friedmann, "The Doctrine of Original Sin as Held by the Anabaptists of the Sixteenth Century," *MQR*, XXXIII, No. 3 (July, 1959), 206–14.
29 Caspar Schwenckfeld, *Judicium, Corpus Schwenckfeldianorum*, ed. Chester David Hartranft, *et al.* (Leipzig: Breitkopf & Härtel, 1927), VIII, 189.
30 *Ibid.*, pp. 189–90.

flesh and blood, by which Marbeck meant human nature, are a good creation of God, original sin cannot, reasons Marbeck, be inherited through the procreative act itself. Therefore, original sin is inherited in all men, as it was in Adam and Eve at the point where they arrive at the knowledge of good and evil.[31]

Yet, while there is a doctrine of original sin within the Radical Reformation, it is true these Reformers did not believe that the guilt of original sin could be attributed to either infants or children. This was not due to the fact that children themselves were regarded as innocent or free from the taint of original sin, but rather due to the fact that so far as children were concerned, original sin had in principle been eliminated through the atonement. Children were for Christ's sake in grace, and this grace was considered universal in its outreach. This view appears repeatedly in the thought of Menno, Dirk, and Marbeck, and traces of it appear also in the thought of Denck, Hoffmann, and Hubmaier, though in a less developed and somewhat modified form. Since it is in the thought of the first three men mentioned above that abolition of original sin for children by the universal grace of Christ's atoning death is most clearly outlined, it is to their writings that we shall first turn in order to substantiate what was said above.[32]

In his treatise on Christian baptism Dirk Philips maintains on the basis of John 1:29[33] that so far as original sin is concerned Christ has taken away both the sin of Adam and that of the whole world. Dirk continues as follows:

> Therefore, the sin of Adam and Eve may now neither condemn nor judge anyone, because Christ has taken this away through his death and blood (Rom. 5:6), as we with God's help will further indicate. But as sin had its origin and inception in Adam and Eve in disobedience and in the knowledge of good and evil, so in the same way it occurs with children. For while they are, of course, descendants of a sinful Adam, yet original sin, as man calls it, is not reckoned to their account for the sake of Christ. For they are in this respect even as Adam and Eve were before the fall, in that they are innocent of either right or wrong and understand neither good nor evil.[34]

In the same work Dirk argues for the universality of Christ's grace with reference to original sin in children on the basis of Matt. 19:13–14.[35] Dirk reasons that since Christ through his death has taken away the sin of the whole world, no guilt may be attributed to children because of Adam's sin. To regard children as

---

31 Marbeck, *Verantwortung*, pp. 190–93. See also p. 217 where Marbeck says that he does not seek to locate sin alone in isolated individual acts, as Schwenckfeld says he does, but "*in der verfallenen natur der vernifftigen menschen suchen, ja nit allein suchen sondern auch finden.*"
32 The thought of the other three men is more closely related to the repudiation of infant baptism within the Radical Reformation, and, therefore, is more fully discussed in Chapter IV, Section B.
33 The text of the Scripture reference reads as follows: "The next day he saw Jesus coming toward him and said, 'Behold, the Lamb of God, who takes away the sin of the world.' "
34 Dirk Philips, *Vander Doope*, BRN, X, 74–75.
35 The full text of the above reference reads as follows: "Then children were brought to him that he might lay his hands on them and pray. The disciples rebuked the people; but Jesus said, 'Let the children come to me and do not hinder them; for to such belongs the kingdom of heaven.' "

guilty on account of original sin would be to deny them the death, blood, and merits (*verdiensts*) of Jesus Christ.

> For if children may be damned through Adam and because of his transgression, then Christ has died in vain for them. Then the guilt of Adam has come upon us, and it was not paid for through Jesus Christ. If this be the cause, then the guilt of Adam has come upon us, and it was not paid for by Jesus Christ, and grace has not overcome sin, nor has life overcome death through Jesus Christ. This be far hence![36]

Dirk regards this doctrine of universal grace purchased for children through the death and blood of Christ as both Scriptural and apostolic. The entire Holy Scriptures and the apostles teach that "original sin has been paid for and taken away in the measure that children may neither be judged nor condemned by Adam's transgression"[37]

As early as 1539 Menno Simons stated his conviction, also based in part on the Matt. 19:13–14 passage and the parallel passages in Mark 10:14 and Luke 18:16, that the atoning death of Christ had made available to infants and young children a grace that was universally efficacious. Life is promised them by pure grace through the death and blood of the Lord.[38] In the same year in his work on baptism Menno wrote those who die in childhood and before they have discretion or faith, die under the promise of God and the generous promise of grace given through Jesus Christ.[39]

In the *Confession of Distressed Christians* of 1552 and in the *Reply to Gellius Faber* of 1554 Menno repeats these same affirmations without any essential change. The promise of grace is a generous promise, because it extends even to the children of unbelievers.[40] Innocent children, as long as they live in their innocence, whether they are the children of believers or unbelievers, are in grace through the merits, death, and blood of Christ.[41] In the work on Christian baptism of 1539 he calls this grace in which little children are included "a peculiar promise," and indicates that at this point the children of Christian parents may possibly have some advantage.[42]

Pilgram Marbeck, too, held a doctrine of universal grace for all children of all men, and he connected this in some way with the atonement. Christ had come to restore all things and to bring all things to right again.[43] Yet Marbeck's doctrine of universal grace is also at times the grace which all men have received from Adam by virtue of being his descendants. They share not only in the original sin, since they are descended from Adam's loins, but also, and in the same measure, they

---

36 Dirk Philips, *Vander Doope, BRN*, X, 91–92.
37 *Ibid.*, p. 92. Another of the biblical texts which Dirk quoted in support of the universal grace which was purchased through the atonement was Gen. 22:18, the divine promise to Abraham that through his seed all nations of the earth should be blessed.
38 Menno Simons, *Foundation of Christian Doctrine, CWMS*, p. 131.
39 Menno Simons, *Christian Baptism, CWMS*, p. 241.
40 Menno Simons, *Reply to Gellius Faber, CWMS*, p. 707.
41 *Ibid.*, p. 708.
42 Menno Simons, *Christian Baptism, CWMS*, p. 280.
43 Marbeck, *Verantwortung*, p. 206.

share in original grace, since the promise was made to Adam when as yet no child was born from Adam and Eve.[44] Marbeck's stress is not so much on the removal of original sin through the atonement, as on the affirmation that original sin does not become hereditary in children before they can distinguish between good and evil.[45] There is at least no activity of original sin which leads to damnation before the knowledge of good and evil.[46] And as Adam and Eve were in grace before the fall, so are children while in the years of their innocence.[47] Yet, while Marbeck at this point associates the universal grace in which children stand with the original grace which all men received from Adam, he also says that children are in grace because of Christ. The two graces which are both universal appear to be interchangeable in Marbeck's thought.

Marbeck also expresses himself somewhat less surely than do Menno and Dirk on the fate of the children of unbelievers who die before reaching maturity, which enables them to distinguish between good and evil. He shows concern for the fate of the children of both Turks and Jews, but says that whether either these children or those who died in Sodom and Gomorrah and similar catastrophes are saved or not is not a matter for men to decide. This is a matter which belongs in the secret councils and judgments of God. For men to attempt to decide the fate of such children, before Christ has revealed it, is to run ahead of Christ.[48]

On the whole, it may be said that while the Radicals regarded original sin as the tragic consequence of the transgression of the first Adam and looked upon his one act of disobedience as the tragic event that had altered the whole human situation for the worse, so they regarded the obedience unto death of Christ as the second Adam, as the blessed event which radically altered the whole human situation for the better. Through the obedience of Christ, the second Adam, the universal tragedy which resulted from the disobedience of the first was at least in part already ameliorated. Indeed, Menno Simons can say, "Jesus Christ through his obedience undid the disobedience of Adam and all his seed and by his painful death restored life."[49]

With this concept of a universal grace, which in principle either removed the consequences of original sin or at least greatly ameliorated them, the Radical Reformers practically eliminated the *massa perditionis* of Augustine, which still reigned within the Magisterial Reformation and was the necessary presupposition for its doctrine of invincible grace through the eternal decrees of divine election. The universal grace which bestowed upon children in their innocence the benefits

---

44 *Ibid.*
45 *Ibid.*, p. 193.
46 *Ibid.*, p. 194.
47 *Ibid.*, p. 195. On the basis of this position, Schwenckfeld's remark in the *Judicium*, that the authors of the *Vermanung* teach that original sin should not be attributed to children, because they are like Adam and Eve before the fall, is, of course, justified. See *CS*, VIII, 189–90, and *Vermanung*, p. 242.
48 Marbeck, *Vermanung* in *Gedenckschrift zum 400 Jährigen Jubiläum der Mennoniten oder Taufgesinnten, 1529–1925*, ed. Christian L. Neff (Ludwegshafen: Konferenz der Süddeutsche Mennoniten E.V., 1925), pp. 271–72.
49 Menno Simons, *Foundation of Christian Doctrine, CWMS*, p. 145.

of Christ's death and blood broke the solidarity of humanity as a solidarity in sin, and in its place postulated a large portion of humanity as a solidarity in grace. The transition from the period in life during which one was a part of this humanity, which by virtue of the universal efficaciousness of the atonement was constituted as a solidarity in grace to the period of responsible adulthood, tended to make each individual stand alone as an isolated and individual sinner at the point where he himself acquired the capacity to distinguish between good and evil.[50]

C. Actual Sin

Not all of the representatives considered in this study make a sharp distinction between original sin, on one hand, and actual sin, on the other. Among those who attempt some sort of distinction are Pilgram Marbeck, Caspar Schwenckfeld, Menno Simons, and Dirk Philips. Their statements concerning the distinction will be considered in the order in which their names here appear.

---

50 Several historical antecedents within the contemporary situation are suggested as possible sources for this concept of universal grace, which nullifies the consequences of original sin for children and ameliorates them for adults. In the *Verantwortung*, which was begun about 1544, Marbeck refers to a Church of Christ in Moravia, which several years ago drew up sixteen articles of faith, one of which had to do with the question of original sin in children. The decision of this church on this point was that "children have before the practice of understanding no sin, for what is inherited in them does not endanger their salvation until it breaks out in actual sin." p. 268. In a footnote on this statement by Marbeck, Johann Loserth comments that no other source for this decision by the Moravian Church had been found, but he thinks that Marbeck may have learned of the decision through Leopold Scharnschlager, who had lived for a while in Moravia. p. 268.

Another possible source for the concept of a universal grace, which was assigned to children in their innocence, particularly for the Dutch Anabaptists, was the influence of the Sacramentarians, or Sacramentist, as they are called in the *ME*, IV, 398–99. These groups arose as early as 1530, and by 1535 many of them had joined newly formed Anabaptist congregations. William Keeney in his doctoral dissertation on the Dutch Anabaptists has pointed out that during the torture of one of these Sacramentarians, who was later martyred, the priests who had been assigned to interrogate her disagreed with each other on the fate of children who died without receiving baptism, one holding that such infants were damned; the other, more closely in agreement with the heretic, holding that infants were not contaminated by original sin to the extent that their salvation was endangered by it.

A third possible source for this concept of a universal grace made available through the atonement is the direct influence of Melchior Hoffmann, who saw the atonement of Christ as the second Adam, as the event which broke the bondage which resulted from the transgression of the first Adam. The route over which Hoffmann traveled to arrive at this position is fully discussed under Section B of this chapter. It is possible that Menno Simons and Dirk Philips borrowed from Hoffmann at this point as well as at the point of Christology. But if they did, they show independence in the way they develop and apply the doctrine of universal grace. For Hoffmann the universal grace released through the atonement was primarily the restoration of the freedom of the will. For Menno and Dirk it was primarily the imputed righteousness, the benefits of Christ's merits, death, and blood to all infants and young children, who were for Christ's sake in a state of grace, and the guilt of Adam's sin was not reckoned to their account.

In any case, whatever its origin, the conviction that children were through Christ universally freed from the crippling effects of original sin prevailed among the Anabaptists of the Radical Reformation, both in Holland and South Germany right on to the end of the formative period of the movement.

Pilgram Marbeck's concept of actual sin in distinction from original sin, as well as that of Caspar Schwenckfeld, comes to light in the course of the controversy between Marbeck and Schwenckfeld, which began with Schwenckfeld's *Judicium* of the *Vermanung* in 1542, and continued until Marbeck's completion of the *Verantwortung* about 1550.[51] The first part of the *Verantwortung* was completed as early as 1544 and was drawn up as a rather hasty reply to the *Judicium* with the promise that the second part would be a fuller reply to Schwenckfeld. Between 1544 and 1550 Marbeck evidently wrote the *Testamentserläuterung*, because this work is often cited by specific chapters in the second part of the *Verantwortung*.

Schwenckfeld in the *Judicium* had maintained that the authors of the *Vermanung* had no proper knowledge of original sin, and, therefore, they could have no proper knowledge of actual sin either. These authors, said Schwenckfeld, are deficient in judgment, because "they judge sin with human understanding and see it in the light of worldly evil only, and not in the nature of the inward uncleanness of the heart."[52] The failure of the Anabaptists to make the proper distinction between *sin* and *sins* was due, said Schwenckfeld, to the fact that they did not distinguish either between the righteousness of deed and that of faith, nor between the *new* and the *old* man.[53] The consequence of this is, according to Schwenckfeld, as follows:

> Sins, say I, they judge alone according to outward deeds. What is still worse, alone according to the knowledge of him who sins, and not according to the knowledge of God, or according to the ground of an evil and corrupt heart. They can also not rightly distinguish between sin which we have by nature and sins (which we commit). They even think that he who does not recognize his sins has none; that they are not reckoned to his account. All of which is a serious error against the grace of God and against Christ, who is the only justifier [rechtmacher] of men.[54]

One must learn that there are two kinds of sin. One is the *act* of outward transgression; the other, *inward desire* of the heart.[55] Actual sin, or the *sins* which men commit, are simply the deeds by which they reveal, as did Adam and Eve in the actual eating of the forbidden fruit, the corrupt impulse of their hearts.[56] The logical consequence of the Anabaptist position that there is no sin where there is no knowledge of sin would be that he who is born a fool or a crazy man is no sinner before God but innocent and righteous, and Paul before his conversion was no sinner when he persecuted Christians in ignorance and did it with a good Pharisaic conscience.[57] The need of the Anabaptists, as Schwenckfeld sees it, is that they should go to school a while longer in order that they may learn how to distinguish between a good Pharisaic conscience and a good Christian conscience. Those who wish to teach others must first learn to know themselves or they will

---

51 *ME*, III, 494–96.
52 *CS*, VIII, 190.
53 *Ibid.*, p. 190.
54 *Ibid.*, pp. 190–91.
55 *Ibid.*, p. 192.
56 *Ibid.*, pp. 192–93.
57 *Ibid.*, pp. 190–91.

make new Pharisees out of those whom they teach, i.e., "such people who do not guard against sin other than sinful acts, and have, so far as their inward desires are concerned, considered themselves innocent and righteous."[58]

Marbeck replies in the *Verantwortung* that Schwenckfeld's accusation that the *Taüfer* restrict sin to the outward act alone is false. They know very well that all outward sin, i.e., sin which reveals itself in sinful act, has its origin in inward desire, even as the actual transgression of Adam and Eve began from the moment that they desired to be like God.[59] Yet, while all sin which eventuates in the actual expression of a sinful act, has its origin in the inner temptation of the devil's spirit with a human spirit, such temptation cannot occur before the dawn of reason (*vor der zeit der vernunft*). Children are, therefore, not included in the curse of original sin before they arrive at this point, but remain innocent and unspoiled until they reach this degree of maturity. "Nothing outward," says Marbeck, "can or may be called sin without the inner, and no flesh or body or person can sin without the previous corruption [*verkerung*] of his human spirit."[60] The child remains unspoiled in his human spirit until he reaches maturity for the reason that the devil, who is an evil spirit, cannot previously get to the mind to falsify it. If he, the devil,

> wants to bring a sin to the point of outward expression, so that it can be called a sin, then he must first begin in man's mind or spirit to falsify man's mind and spirit, to change it and to lead it astray, so that the human mind becomes one with the mind and spirit of the devil, prepared for all evil. Only then follows the outward work of sin, through the flesh and blood and body of a man, and, therefore, no sin may take place without the devil's corrupted spirit; just as little as the fruit and work of the spirit and faith to eternal life can follow without the activity of the Spirit as the Holy Spirit of Christ. The Spirit of Christ must first convert the spirit of man, make him alive to every good work, regenerate him, assure him, and keep him in the new birth, so that he neither sins nor is deceived, and as a consequence brings forth the good works of faith.[61]

Yet, according to Marbeck, the natural man has even before his conversion and rebirth as a child of God the capacity to resist the inner temptation of the devil and to fight against it because of the first grace which he received in creation. This first grace is the "light of nature," which shines and works in a man so that it is possible for him to turn away from temptation and not do the outward thing.[62] Actual sin has, therefore, for Marbeck two aspects. One is that of refusing to walk in the light of nature, which is the first grace and thereby to extinguish the light. The other aspect is that of refusing to accept the second grace, which is the regenerating and sanctifying power of the Holy Spirit and makes possible both the new life in Christ[63] and the supernatural knowledge of spiritual things.[64]

Dirk Philips and Menno Simons approach the problem of actual sin from a dif-

---

58 *Ibid.*, pp. 190–91.
59 Marbeck, *Verantwortung*, pp. 249–50.
60 *Ibid.*, p. 251.
61 *Ibid.*
62 *Ibid.*, p. 254.
63 *Ibid.*, p. 251.
64 *Ibid.*, pp. 233–34.

ferent angle, because Menno in particular had a different concept of original sin. For Menno, as previously seen, original sin was a corruption of the fleshly or human nature of man, which had been introduced through the poisonous bite of the serpent, while for Dirk original sin in children was atoned for and removed through Christ's death and, therefore, could not endanger their salvation before the dawn of reason. Dirk, as well as Menno, could speak of the poisoned flesh of Adam. Once children become mature enough to have a knowledge of good and evil they must of themselves confess that they are poor sinners "born out of the flesh out of Adam, which was bitten and poisoned by the serpent, and that all who descended from him became participants of his sinful character [aert]."[65]

Menno speaks of original sin in exactly the same way in the *Reply to False Accusations* of 1552. Original sin is the corrupt sinful nature, the lust and desire of our flesh, contrary to God's law and original righteousness, which is inherited at birth by all descendants of corrupt and sinful Adam.[66] Actual *sins* are for Menno the fruit of the first or original *sin*. Menno divided actual sins into two classes. The first class may be called the "works of the flesh," because they have their origin in the flesh of Adam, which is corrupt and sinful. These sins include adultery, fornication, avarice, dissipation, drunkenness, hatred, envy, lying, murder, theft, and idolatry. These actual *sins* of the flesh are in a sense the most deadly in Menno's eyes, because they spring from the very source of corruption in fallen man. Menno writes:

> Wherever original sin, which is the mother, and actual sin, which is the fruit, are connected together, there is no forgiveness nor promise of life; but there wrath and death abide unless these sins are repented of, as the Scriptures testify.[67]

The power of original sin can be broken only by the new birth, which is grace as God's regenerating act. Through the new birth and true repentance one can both resist original sin and die to actual sin.

> For as the natural birth which is of Adam is unclean and sinful, and begets all evil and unrighteousness unto death according to the will of the devil, so on the other hand the heavenly birth which is of God is clean and pure, and begets all righteousness and piety unto life according to the will of God. Rom. 5; I John 3:5.[68]

The second class of actual *sins*, which Menno notes as being distinct from original *sin*, is what he calls "human frailties," errors, and stumblings, such as careless words and unpremeditated lapses in conduct, which are daily found among the saints as well as among the impenitent and unbelieving. There is, however, a difference in the way the impenitent and the saint commit these actual sins of human frailty. The impenitent do it with boldness and without hesitation, because they are yet in the blindness of their first birth and do not know the

---

65 Dirk Philips, *Van der wedergeboorte ende nieuwe Creatuere, BRN*, X, 331.
66 Menno Simons, *Reply to False Accusations, CWMS*, p. 563.
67 *Ibid.*, p. 563.
68 *Ibid.*

ugliness of their sins. Those who are born from above, i.e., of God, know both the ugliness and the seriousness of sin, and through the grace of the new birth

> fight daily with their weak flesh in the Spirit and in faith. They sigh and lament about their errors, which they with Paul sincerely abhor and to which they do not consent. They know them to be contrary to original righteousness and God's law, and are therefore sinful. They approach the throne of grace daily with contrite hearts and pray, Holy Father, forgive us our trespasses as we forgive those that trespass against us.[69]

One finds exactly the same classification of actual sins into categories of sins of the flesh and sins of weakness in the thought of Dirk Philips. Open works of the flesh are sins of darkness that separate men from God[70] and can, therefore, not be tolerated in the Church of Christ.[71] Sins of weakness, on the other hand, are forgiven and covered through the righteousness of Christ.[72] Christians often sin blindly and ignorantly and have need of the grace and mercy of God.[73]

Thus, while Menno and Dirk tend to see actual sin in terms of isolated or individual sinful acts, it cannot be said that their view of sin is in any sense Pelagian. Even these individual acts of sin spring from the sinful nature. The first is not overcome by the sheer force of the human will but by grace as God's act of regeneration. It is by virtue of this that one is able to fight against actual sin, and even so one needs daily God's mercy as a grace of forgiveness for those sins that are committed in frailty and ignorance.

D. The Freedom versus the Bondage of the Will

At no other point did the Radical Reformers differ so strongly with the Magisterial Reformers as on the question of the bondage of the will. Although the Radicals formulated their doctrines of the freedom of the will in different ways, behind every way there lies a resolute and outright rejection of the fundamental presuppositions of the Magisterial Reformers in regard to predestination and the bondage of the will. The Radicals rejected these doctrines on the ground that, first, it was unworthy of God that He should predestine some to eternal bliss and others to eternal damnation; second, that behind it men found excuses for their profligate lives. The Radicals rejected the doctrine of predestination, because they sensed that the doctrine pushed to its logical conclusions laid the ultimate responsibility for the moral evil present in the world upon God as the predestinator. Unable to accept such a conclusion, the Radicals sought for a solution that would exonerate God and confront man with the unavoidable responsibility of making his own decision, either for or against Christ.

Not all of the representative leaders of the Radical Reformation considered in this study developed in a systematic way their doctrines of the freedom of the

---

69 *Ibid.*, p. 564.
70 Dirk Philips, *Vanden Ban, BRN*, X, 255.
71 *Ibid.*, pp. 258–59.
72 *Ibid.*, p. 260.
73 *Ibid.*, p. 264.

will. Those who did were Hans Denck, Balthasar Hubmaier, and Melchior Hoffmann. The other four representatives included often imply that they have a doctrine of the freedom of the will, and both Menno Simons and Caspar Schwenckfeld deplore the opposite doctrine within the Magisterial Reformation as the source of much evil and mischief, but neither of them develop their own views systematically at this point.[74]

All three of the men who did develop at least a well reasoned argument against the bondage of the will, if not a systematic doctrine of the freedom of the will, did so in reaction to this doctrine as set forth in Luther's *De Servo Arbitrio*. Denck and Hoffmann react directly to Luther's work. Hubmaier's reaction may be influenced by Luther's position as interpreted by Zwingli. All three men – Denck, Hubmaier, and Hoffmann – wrote within a few years of each other; Denck in 1526, Hubmaier in 1527, and Hoffmann sometime between 1530 and 1531; yet, each man found his own unique solution to the problem.

Hans Denck gave expression to his conception of the freedom of the will in *Was geredt sei, dass die Schrift sagt*, 1526; in *Ordnung Gottes*, 1527; and in the so-called *Widerruf*, 1528. In the first work Denck approaches the problem from three sides: (1) the fact that God created the will good and free,[75] (2) the disciplinary value of evil for one who comes through the effects of sin to recognize sin as sin and therefore to abandon it,[76] (3) the love of the creaturely, which one must forsake in order to obtain salvation.[77] These same emphases are repeated in a somewhat different manner in the other two works, and Denck's three works on the freedom of the will are, therefore, treated as one unit.

---

74 Schwenckfeld, for example, states that at one time he thought that the spirit which taught the doctrine of the bondage of the will was from God. Now he knows that it was not from God, and asks forgiveness for his previous errors, and sees this doctrine as the source of much mischief in the world. *CS*, IV, 697.

Menno Simons in the *Meditation on the Twenty-Fifth Psalm*, written as early as 1537, rejected vigorously the notion that some were ordained by God to wickedness on the ground that this would make God, who is eternally good or has created all things good, into a cruel devil. P. 75. In two other works, *The Incarnation of Our Lord* and *Reply to Gellius Faber*, Menno makes statements that imply a doctrine of the freedom of the will. In the first work, p. 816, Menno says that when God created man "he was left in the hands of his own will, as Sirach says." In the second, p. 760, he calls Zwingli's position on the bondage of the will an "abomination of abominations," since, as Menno understood it, this implied that God caused the thief to steal and the murderer to kill, and yet their punishment was also brought about by God's will.

So far as Dirk Philips and Pilgram Marbeck are concerned, there is no developed doctrine of the freedom of the will in the thought of either one. Yet, it is implied in what they have to say about voluntary entrance into the Church. Philips, like Hoffmann, uses the image of Rebecca, who voluntarily became the bride of Isaac, as an illustration of the relationship which God desires between himself and his people. *Vande geestelijcke Restitution, BRN*, X, 350. Marbeck, both in the *Vermanung* (p. 250) and in the *Confession of Faith*, prepared for the Strasbourg Council in 1531 (*MQR*, XII, No. 4 (October, 1938), 190–91), objected to infant baptism on the principle that this brought people into the Church by compulsion.

75 Hans Denck, *Was geredt sei, dass die Schrift sagt, QFR*, Band XXIV, 2 Teil, 31.
76 *Ibid.*
77 *Ibid.*, p. 35.

> We know [says Denck] that God is good in truth, and if He were not good (this be far from him!), then He would not be God, and because He is good, He has also made and created everything good.[78]

Those are, therefore, false Christians who say that they can do nothing but what God works in them,[79] for every individual has received from God the soul which He pours into man at creation in order that he may recognize God's mercy and not despise it.[80] Denck declares that the devil could not have better messengers than those who say that God works evil in the wicked as well as good in the elect.[81] A person who says that he can do nothing, either good or evil, "steals from God the will which He has created good and free and sets his own will against God."[82]

Since God is good, all that He created is good. Insofar as man is evil, he is evil without God and out of his own property (*eygenthumb*).[83] God does not compel anyone to do evil. On the contrary, He remains good, even though man has through his own fault cast himself into death which God did not create.[84] Because God is eternally good, "He allows His sun to shine on the evil and on the good, Matt. 5, and gives every man grace and reason to repent, . . . and no one reason to sin."[85] Denck allegorizes the Matt. 5 passage, so that the light which shines on the evil and the good is not the sun, but the light by which Denck means the inner Christ shines in all men and gives them free power (*gewalt*), so that whoever receives this light may become a child of God and enter his Father's kingdom.[86] For him who does not desire this light it nevertheless shines

> unto his judgment and damnation, John 1:9. For it would not be fitting for him who desires voluntary service to compel anyone to serve against his will. God desires that every man shall be saved, but He knows very well that many will damn themselves.[87]

If someone should ask what is the real difference in whether God is the cause of evil or whether He permits evil, are they not one and the same thing? Denck replies the difference is that through the disciplinary value of evil, God can lead men to reject it *voluntarily*. If God had ordained things otherwise, He would have "forced and driven men like a stone or a block."[88] Of course, if God had created nothing, there would be no sin, but if there were no creatures, then there would be none to render praise to the Creator, and this would be detrimental both to the

---

78 Hans Denck, *Ordnung Gottes*, 1527, *QFR*, Band XXIV, 2 Teil, 90.
79 Hans Denck, *Was geredt sei, dass die Schrift sagt, QFR*, Band XXIV, 2 Teil, 31.
80 *Ibid.*, p. 35.
81 *Ibid.* The polemic is directed against Luther.
82 *Ibid.*, p. 31.
83 Hans Denck, *Ordnung Gottes, QFR*, Band XXIV, 2 Teil, 90.
84 *Ibid.*
85 *Ibid.*
86 *Ibid.*
87 *Ibid.* This shows that Denck did not, as Bucer maintained, teach a doctrine of universal salvation.
88 Hans Denck, *Was geredt sei, dass die Schrift sagt, QFR*, Band XXIV, 2 Teil, 29.

creatures and to their Creator.[89] And if God had prevented sin, i.e., made it impossible for man to sin when He created him, then His mercy would not have been mercy, because it would not have had any object (*gegenworff*). On the other hand, if it is not now possible for God to overcome sin, then argues Denck, God is not Almighty, and His enemy, sin, stands eternally beside and against Him, as powerful as God is.[90] According to Denck, sin is as nothing before God, because He can use it as a punishment to lead men away from sin. "To him who recognizes it as a punishment in truth, to him it is no more sin, but it is rather a wonderful encouragement to him to recognize the real good and to love it."[91] One can only say, however, that sin is good, when he recognizes it as a punishment and does it no more. Such a man who recognizes sin as the darkness and discord which he has deserved is already in part in the light and peace into which God has led him.[92]

God overcomes sin in us in this way, because He desires no one in His service by compulsion. Denck speaks much about *gelassenheit*, and the term, as he uses it, means surrender of one's own will to the will of God. Both he who surrenders and he who does not are free, but the former is blessedly free (*wol frei*) and blessedly bound, while the latter is free in an evil manner (*ubel frei*).

> The one whose servant one is, he makes him free to that which he wills in his service. God compels no one to remain in His service, for love does not compel. But the devil cannot compel anyone to remain in his service, who has once known the truth.[93]

In order to obtain salvation, however, one must abandon his love of the creaturely. The "love of the creaturely" was an expression which Denck borrowed from the *Theologia Germanica*. God has made the creatures so that they might praise Him, and one must exercise care not to love the creature more than the Creator. One must not say that it is impossible to forsake this love of the creaturely, which in a sense is also self-love, because it is possible with God for whom nothing is impossible, and God is always prepared to do the best insofar as man is willing to allow it.[94] The nearer one approaches to and is in harmony with the source of creation, the more he will be free; the more he has sunk into damnation through excessive love of the creaturely, the more he will be bound.

> But no matter how free he is, yet he cannot do the good otherwise than in a suffering manner, Philippians 2, and no matter how much he is bound, he can yet freely suffer what the Word does in him, and whoever says that he has not received grace from God to become pious is a liar as all men are.[95]

In Denck's thought then, there are three primary reasons why one should hold to a doctrine of the freedom of the will, as opposed to the bondage of the will:

89 *Ibid.*
90 *Ibid.*
91 *Ibid.*, p. 30.
92 *Ibid.*
93 Hans Denck, *Widerruf*, 1528, *QFR*, Band XXIV, 2 Teil, 107.
94 Hans Denck, *Was geredt sei, dass die Schrift sagt*, 1526, *QFR*, Band XXIV, 2 Teil, 35.
95 Hans Denck, *Ordnung Gottes*, *QFR*, Band XXIV, 2 Teil, 96.

(1) such a doctrine alone safeguards the absolute and eternal goodness of God, (2) such a doctrine is the only safeguard for the personal and completely voluntary character of Christian-salvation, (3) such a doctrine alone will confront man with the responsibility of exercising the freedom in which he was created by God and prevent him from shifting the blame for his own faults from himself to God.

Balthasar Hubmaier formulated his doctrine of the freedom of the will in a very different manner from that of Denck; yet, the reasons he gives for rejecting the doctrine of the bondage of the will are essentially the same. Hubmaier states his reasons clearly in the *Vorred* of his treatise on free will.[96] Hubmaier wrote this treatise at Nikolsburg in 1527 and addressed the preface to Duke George I (1493–1531). In it he says that the condition of the world is now worse than it has been for a thousand years. Hubmaier attributes the low state of morals to two emphases in the Magisterial Reformation, which he says are in themselves but half-truths. One of these emphases is, "We believe; faith saves us." The other is, "We cannot do anything good. God works in us the willing and the doing [*Vollbringen*]. We have no free will."[97] Hubmaier says in the preface that it is for the purpose of rooting out such tares (*unkraut*) as these half-truths that he wrote his book on free will to show "how and what man is in and outside of God's grace and what he can do."[98]

Hubmaier begins with a discussion of what man is in three different states, as he was before the fall, as he became after the fall, and as he should be when restored. Hubmaier uses scholastic categories and relies heavily upon the Pauline distinction between flesh, soul, and spirit in the development of his argument for the freedom of the will.

According to Hubmaier, God created man a corporeal and reasonable creature, consisting of body, spirit, and soul with each *substantiae* or *ousiai* having a will of its own. Hubmaier finds Scriptural support for the three separate wills within man in the John 1:13 passage.[99] As man was before the fall, all three substances were good, and every will was free and capable of a free choice of good and evil,[100] but after the fall it was different.

Through the fall the flesh lost both its goodness and its freedom. It is now utterly worthless and helpless; it can do nothing except sin, resist God, and hate His commands. Hubmaier makes use of such passages as Rom. 7:5ff., Gal. 5:13ff., I Cor. 11:27, I Cor. 15:50, and Matt. 16:17, as support for his argument that since the fall the flesh is worthless.

The spirit of man, however, as Hubmaier uses the Hebrew term, *nephesh*, has

---

96 The full title of this work in German is as follows: *Von der Freyhait des Willens, die Gott durch sein gesendet wort anbeüt allen menschen, und jnen dar jn gwalt gibt seine Khinder ze werden, auch die waal guttes ze wöllen und ze thon ... oder sj Khinder des Zorns, wie sy denn von natur seine ze bleiben lassen.*
97 Hubmaier. This work is also available in an English translation by George H. Williams in *SAW*, pp. 114–131. Pp. 131–35 of the translation are from Hubmaier's second work, *Das ander Biechlen von der Freywilligkait des menschens*, which he promised Duke George I in the introduction to the first book.
98 *Ibid.* See also *SAW*, p. 115.
99 *Ibid.* See also *SAW*, p. 117.
100 *Ibid.* See also *SAW*, p. 119.

not fallen. It remains in man as good and upright and whole as it was before the fall, for it did not consent either by the will, counsel, or act to the eating of the forbidden fruit by the flesh. The spirit was forced against its will to participate in the eating (*mitessen*) as a prisoner in the body.[101] The spirit is, therefore, without guilt (*schuld*). The guilt and sin is that of the flesh and of the soul, which through the fall also became flesh or, as Hubmaier puts it, an Eve. Hubmaier finds support for his tripartite view of man and the wholeness of man's spirit after the fall in I Thess. 5:23: "May your whole spirit and soul and body be kept sound and blameless at the coming of our Lord Jesus Christ." As both Vedder and Williams have pointed out, Hubmaier used the Latin Vulgate text, and he improperly construed the *integer* in the sentence which reads: *"Ipse autem Deus pacis sanctificet vos per omnia, ut integer spiritus vester, et anima, et corpus sine querela in adventu Domini nostri Jesu Christi servetur"*[102] to apply only to *spiritus*.[103] Hubmaier says that Paul in this text shows the wholeness (*gantzhait*) and uprightness (*auffrichthait*) of the spirit of man even after the fall.[104]

The soul, however, which is the third part of man did not fare as well as the spirit. Through the disobedience of Adam it was sorely wounded in the will (*in dem willen der massen verwundt*) and became ill with a sickness unto death, so that it can of itself neither choose the good nor avoid the evil, inasmuch as through the fall it has lost the knowledge of good and evil and can do nothing except sin and die. Insofar as the ability to accomplish the good is concerned, the soul has become powerless and without works (*werklos*).[105]

The impotence of the soul and its will in the fallen state is due to the worthlessness of the flesh, which is the implement of the soul. Even though the soul might wish to do good and make every possible effort to do so, its effort would be in vain, because the flesh, the implement through which the soul must act, has become worthless, and the damage done to it is partly irreparable in this life.[106]

The fall of the soul is not, however, so irreparable as that of the flesh. The soul or its will can be partially restored here on earth for the reason that Adam, who is a type of the soul as Eve is of the flesh, would have preferred *not* to eat of the forbidden fruit, and did eat *against* his own conscience, because he was more obedient to Eve, his flesh, than to God.[107]

The soul can be restored again, because God will receive all men who hunger and thirst after piety and who very much wish to do what is right. That man has this power of desiring what is right and good is assured through the unfallen spirit. It is the vestige of the image in which God created man, and though the old serpent (Gen. 3:1–6) has obscured it and almost blacked it out through sin, he has not been able to extinguish God's breath (*nephesh*) in us entirely. Though both the soul and the flesh have been sorely wounded, the spirit has retained its original

---

101 *Ibid.* See also *SAW*, p. 120.
102 Biblia Sacra (Romae, Tornaci, Parissis: Desclee et Socii, 1947), N. T. Sec., p. 223.
103 *SAW*, p. 120, footnote.
104 Hubmaier, *Von der Freiheit des Willens*. See also *SAW*, p. 120.
105 *Ibid.* See also *SAW*, p. 121.
106 *Ibid.* See also *SAW*, p. 121.
107 *Ibid.* See also *SAW*, p. 121.

righteousness (*erbgerechtigkait*) in which it was first created. Hubmaier says that

> the proud thinkers who speak of the higher and lower faculties [*portionen*] of man have been led astray by the heathen Aristotle, who knew of nothing and postulated nothing in man except soul and body. The spirit was too heavenly for him. With his natural and human comprehension [*verstand*] he could not comprehend the breath of the living God.[108]

This freedom of the will of the unfallen spirit is, however, not true freedom. As long as the spirit is imprisoned within the completely fallen flesh and the unrestored soul, it would gladly will and do, but it cannot accomplish anything except that it give inward testimony *to godliness* and *against sin*, while it cries out to God without ceasing, like a prisoner in unspeakable groaning.[109] True freedom of the will is experienced only when the fallen will of the fallen soul is restored through Christ, who is the sent Word of God and brings the *new grace* without which man cannot be restored after he has lost the *first grace*, in which he was originally created.[110] After the soul has been restored from the fall (*demnach nun die sel nach dem widerbrachten fall, durch das gesendet wort gesund und recht frey gemacht ist*) through the sent Word, it is again truly made free and can will and do the good to the extent that this is required of it.[111]

> The soul is now able to dominate completely the flesh [*dermassen gebietten*] to tame it and to master it, so that it must, contrary to its nature, go with the spirit and the soul even into the fire for the sake of the name of Christ.[112]

Hubmaier at an earlier point in the argument had characterized the three wills within man as the will of the flesh which does not desire to suffer, the will of the soul which would gladly suffer but yet on account of the will of the flesh would rather not suffer, and the will of the spirit which is desirous to suffer (*den willen des geysts, der da will begirig leyden*). One of the effects of the soul's restoration from the fall is that the will of the soul is freed from domination of the will of the flesh and thus regains its desire to suffer.[113]

In Hubmaier's second book on free will he made a distinction between the absolute will of God (*voluntas absoluta*) and the revealed will of God (*voluntas revelata*). Confusion in the interpretation of Scriptural texts, such as Rom. 9:18, "God has mercy on whom He will; whom He will He hardens," and I Tim. 2:4, "God wills that all men be saved," is the result of failing to distinguish between two wills. According to God's absolute or hidden will, says Hubmaier, He could consign Peter to hell and conversely raise Judas or Caiphas to heaven, and in so

---

108 *Ibid.* See also *SAW*, p. 124.
109 *Ibid.* See also *SAW*, p. 123
110 *Ibid.* See also *SAW*, pp. 123, 126, and 128.
111 *Ibid.* See also *SAW*, footnote, p. 126, where the reference observed is clearly to the stake of martyrdom.
112 *Ibid.*
113 *Ibid.*

doing He would do no evil, since men are in His hands.[114] Yet, according to His revealed will God desires that all men should be saved, for He has commanded that the Gospel should be preached to all creatures.[115] It is the latter will only, says Hubmaier, that need concern men. They can let the hidden will of God alone in its worthy majesty and turn their attention to the will of God, which wills that all men should be saved. This will which Hubmaier refers to as an attracting (*Zukherenden*) will, in distinction from the absolute will of God, which is a repelling (*Abkherenden*) will, desires that all men be saved. It wills and draws men to salvation, yet choice is still left to man, since God wants him without pressure, unconstrained, under no compulsion. Only those who resist God's attracting will experience His repelling will as one of justice and punishment. There are, of course, says Hubmaier, not two wills in God but one; yet, man because of his poor understanding has to speak of God in a human way. And when man encounters God's will as a repelling will, it is man with his sins that is guilty before this will and not God.[116]

Thus, Hubmaier, in his development of a doctrine of the freedom of the will, shows concern not only for man's moral responsibility but also for the personal and voluntary character of Christian salvation with the implication that compulsion would be a violation of grace and for the protection of the moral character of God.

Melchior Hoffmann develops his doctrine of the freedom of the will in a manner that is different from that of either Denck or Hubmaier, although there are indications that some of his basic presuppositions were borrowed from Denck. At an earlier point in Hoffmann's career he had been what George H. Williams calls the "Protestant apostle to the Baltic."[117] He had traveled the Baltic regions as a Lutheran with Luther's approval[118] and in 1526 had written a commentary on the twelfth chapter of Daniel, in which he expressed Lutheran views on the bondage of the will.[119] Sometime between 1531 and 1532, while Hoffmann was in Strasbourg for a third time, he wrote a treatise on the freedom fo the will.[120] The editors of the *Bibliotheca Reformatoria Neerlandica* state that

> what gave Hoffmann the occasion to write about free will just in the years, 1531–1532, we do not know. He was, of course, not unfamiliar with Luther's *De Servo Arbitrio*, which had recently appeared in a German translation, and certainly at Strasbourg he would have become aware of Zwingli's deterministic thought patterns.[121]

Whether Hoffmann was now motivated by a reaction against Luther or by the rigid predestinarian position of the Strasbourg Reformers, his new work was a repudiation of both.

114 *SAW*, p. 133.
115 *Ibid.*, p. 132.
116 *Ibid.*, p. 132.
117 *Ibid.*, p. 182.
118 *ME*, II, 779.
119 *Ibid.*, p. 782. The *Commentary on Daniel* is unfortunately not available in this country.
120 Hoffmann, *Verclaringe van den geuangenen ende vrien wil, BRN*, V, 183–98.
121 *Ibid.*, p. 174.

However, having begun his Protestant pilgrimage which at least approached that of Luther on the bondage of the will, Hoffmann was forced to work his way out of that position. Hoffmann in his new work emphasized the eternal goodness of God, who is, therefore, in no sense the source or the cause of evil, and God's desire to have people in His service voluntarily rather than by compulsion.[122] Hoffmann argues that as the transgression of the first Adam resulted in universal bondage for the human race and delivered the race into the hands of Satan as his rightful property, so that every human creature was so completely bound that through its own power, it could neither become free or even desire to be redeemed,[123] so Christ, the second Adam, by his obedience and death has liberated man from this universal bondage into which he was cast by the first Adam.

Hoffmann writes:

> The noble and high testimony of God is this: that God is no respecter of persons or should be. But as is written in Ecclesiasticus, the fifteenth chapter [verse fourteen], He made man from the beginning, that is, he has born him out of the death of the first Adam again to life through His Word, Jesus Christ, and has brought him true enlightenment and knowledge, and has placed his will again in his hands, so that it comes to pass that from then on man became a truly free creature; John, in the eighth chapter [verse thirty-six], that he from this time on may be prepared to have his own choice or election, whether he will now taste of good or evil, whether he will choose life or death, whether he will walk in the way of God or remain the property of Satan. And what he accepts or chooses, that is also given to him.[124]

This act of placing man's will again in his own hands is for Hoffmann an act of utter grace on God's part. God pays the purchase price for man, who became the property of Satan through the transgression of the first Adam in and through the death of Christ as the second Adam. Thus, through the payment of a debt which man owed, but could not pay, God shows Himself gracious.[125] For Hoffmann, God's act of placing man's will again in his own hands, whereby he who was bound becomes again a truly free creature, is the first, but also the absolutely necessary, step in the whole process of redemption. Man's will has been placed in his own hands, but salvation is now possible only as man exercises his restored freedom of the will in the choice of good rather than evil in the decision to walk in the way of God rather than to remain the property of Satan.[126]

---

122 W. I. Leendertz in his *Melchior Hofmann* (Haarlem, 1883), pp. 239ff., sees in these new emphases of Hoffmann the influence of Hans Denck. If so, the influence was mediated indirectly. Denck was banished from Strasbourg on Christmas Day, 1526, and Hoffmann did not arrive there until June of 1529. Denck died in Basel in November of 1528.
123 *BRN*, V, 184.
124 *BRN*, V, 194. Hoffmann maintained that the effects of Christ's atonement were universal, because it was only at this point in history that God could keep His promise to Abraham, that in his seed all nations of the earth should be blessed. Since God is absolutely good, He may not change or break His promise in all eternity. See *BRN*, V, 188.
125 See Chapter III for a fuller discussion of Hoffmann's view of the atonement, which here comes to light as being near to the ancient theory which held sway in the Western Church until the time of Anselm of Canterbury.
126 One should note the sharp difference between Hoffmann's position and that of the

It is not only because God is gracious that He places man's will again in his own hands, but also because

> God will and shall save no human creature without its will, but voluntarily, without compulsion, through His wisdom and loving call, as is written in Rev. 3:20, Behold I stand at the door and knock, if any man shall hear my voice and will open the door, I will come in to him. Here there is no compulsion at all, but all is voluntary. Those who desire to hear God's Word and desire to seek Him in their hearts, to them the precious wisdom of God will enter and satisfy [him][127] with the bread of understanding and cool him with the water of life. Prov. 1:9, Matt. 22, Luke 14, John 6.[128]

Much confusion in the interpretation of Scripture comes about, says Hoffmann, because men do not make a proper distinction between *compulsion* and *constraint*. Hoffmann sees in the story of Isaac and Rebecca in Genesis 24, and the instructions to Abraham's servant to seek a bride that would come *willingly*, evidence that God desires men to enter His service voluntarily.[129] The parable of the banquet in Luke 14, in which the invited guests refused to come and the lord of the banquet sent his servant into the highways and byways to *compel* men to come in so that the banquet hall might be filled, was evidently used by Hoffmann's opponents in support of their doctrine of predestination and bondage of the will.

One should note, said Hoffmann, that *urging* others to come to the banquet was not *compelling* them to come.

> This urging is not compulsion but constraint, such as that with which a good friend constrains another to eat with him or to remain overnight. The other makes up his own mind whether he wishes to remain or not, even as the two disciples constrained Christ to go with them after his resurrection in the last chapter of Luke, and as Jacob constrained Esau to take the cattle which he presented to him in Gen. 33, and as also Naaman, the Syrian, constrained the prophet, Elisha, to take his presents, but he did not wish to at all.[130]

Hoffmann uses two other Scriptural references to make his point on the difference between *constraint* and *compulsion* — Lot, constraining the two angles to come into his home in Gen. 19, and the parable of the supper in Luke 14. One must not suppose, he says, that those who did not wish to come at the invitation of the holy apostles were bound and carried by force.[131]

> So it is of the greatest necessity that everyone should take care, for he should know during these hard times how necessary it is to distinguish between these mistaken spirits who do not wish to see the difference.[132]

Magisterial Reformation, where the possibility of salvation lay not in man's exercise of a restored free will but in God's electing an invincible grace as the overcoming of a will that remained in bondage.
127 Change of number in text.
128 *BRN*, V, 195.
129 *BRN*, V, 193–94.
130 *Ibid.*, p. 194.
131 *Ibid.*
132 *Ibid.*

The "difference" to which Hoffmann refers is between *constraint* as he defined it, on the one hand, in which the decision to respond in faith to God's approach in Christ is left in the hands of man, who has had the freedom of his will restored; and *compulsion*, on the other hand, where man's fate is sealed in the eternal decrees of divine election, quite apart from any decision to respond by man himself. Hoffmann regarded the latter alternative as a denial of the universal efficacy of the atonement and of that grace, whereby God had placed man's will again in his own hands and made him a truly free creature. As Friedrich Otto zur Linden observes, Hoffmann resisted as the grossest blasphemy those doctrines of the Reformation, which in their consequence had to lead to the conclusion that God was either the mediate or the immediate source of sin.[133] His first concern in the development of a doctrine of the freedom of the will was to safeguard the honor and eternal goodness of God; his second, to retain the personal and voluntary character of Christian salvation.

It should be noted that although Hoffmann lays much stress on man's ability to choose the good and desire it, now that the freedom of his will has been restored, the initiative remains with God, who through Christ is the Renewer. "And God is more desirous to receive heart, mind, and spirit through his Word, Jesus Christ, than man is to give it."[134]

E. Man in the Eschatological Framework

1. The "Age of the Spirit"

Not only did the anthropology of the Radical Reformers, as outlined above, have a profound effect upon their concept of grace. Of almost equal importance was the eschatological framework within which this anthropology was set. As was the case with the doctrine of the freedom of the will, not all the representatives of the Radical Reformation considered in this study developed their eschatology in the same manner or to the same extent. The eschatologies that were developed fall into two fairly distinct categories: (1) the "age of the Spirit," (2) the "time of grace."

The former was most fully developed by Melchior Hoffmann in *Auslegung der heimlichen Offenbarung Joannis des heyligen Apostels und Evangelisten*, which was printed at Strasbourg in 1530. The book is not available in this country, but a brief summary of it appears in Volume II of the *Mennonite Encyclopedia*, and Peter Kawerau in his work on Hoffmann as a religious thinker makes extended use of Hoffmann's commentary on Revelation.[135] According to the summary of Hoffmann's interpretation of Revelation published in the *Mennonite Encyclopedia*, Hoffmann divides church history into three periods. The first period is from apostolic times to the reign of the popes; the second period is the period of unlimited papal power; while the third period, prepared for by Huss, begins with the

---

133 Zur Linden, pp. 274–75. See also Peter Kawerau, *Melchior Hoffmann als Religiöser Denker* (Haarlem: De Erven Bohn N.V., 1954), p. 46.
134 *BRN*, V, 195.
135 Kawerau, pp. 75–114. The chapter is titled, "Geist und Geschichte."

Reformation. In this period the Pope is deprived of all power, and the office of the letter is turned into spirit. When this has taken place, the two witnesses of the last day appear, and in order to destroy them the adherents of the letter and the papists will join forces. The two witnesses will be killed, and spiritual Jerusalem, which is the true church, will be destroyed by the Turks. The prostration of the church will last for three and one-half years, after which Christ will appear, hold judgment, and renew heaven and earth.[136]

The significance of the "age of the Spirit" lay for Hoffmann not so much in the characteristics of this age itself, although these were unimportant, particularly with reference to finding the right hermeneutical method.[137] The real significance of the "age of the Spirit," however, was that it became the period of preparation for the eschaton itself. Hoffmann saw himself as one of the two witnesses of the end time, therefore, as one appointed of God to prepare the world for the eschaton. It was on the strength of this conviction that Hoffmann ventured twice to predict that Strasbourg would be the scene of the last judgment, once in 1534 after being imprisoned for nearly a year, and again in 1535.[138]

Without doubt there lies behind this threefold periodization of history in Hoffmann's thought the influence of Joachim, Abbot of Floris (1131–1202), and his use of the book of Revelation as a means of interpreting history in three dispensations, based upon the doctrine of the Trinity. Joachim represented the three ages of Father, Son, and Spirit, in terms of three circles, each of which overlapped into the other.[139] The three ages, as indicated by the overlapping circles, are not distinctly separate from each other. As Harold O. J. Brown has observed, "Each of the ages can be subdivided into preparation and fruition, and there is no clear dividing line between them; they blend into one another.[140]

One of the schemes under which Joachim portrayed his tripartite division of history was the following:

The Time before the Law
First Age: *The time under the Law, Age of the Father*
Second Age: *The time under grace, Age of the Son*
Third Age: *The time under spiritual intelligence, Age of the Holy Spirit*[141]

It seems obvious that Hoffmann saw himself as one who lived near the close of this third age, and, therefore, as one who could help to prepare the world for the coming of the eschaton itself. In Joachim's scheme of providential progress it is Elijah who reappears, as the "age of the Spirit" draws to a close at the end of the

---

136 *ME*, II, 781. See also Zur Linden, pp. 195–202.
137 See Chapter V of thesis.
138 *ME*, II, 783–84. It was this chiliastic element in Hoffmann's thought that later led to the debacle of Münster.
139 Joachim, Abbot of Floris, *Exposito in Apocalypsim* (Venice: F. Bindonus and M. Pasimus, 1527), p. 38.
140 Harold O. J. Brown, "Joachim of Floris and the Third Age in History" (unpublished S.T.M. thesis, Harvard Divinity School, 1959), p. 33.
141 Joachim, Abbot of Floris, p. 5.

world. Just prior to Hoffmann's imprisonment in Strasbourg Hoffmann became increasingly obsessed with the notion that he himself was either Elijah or Enoch.[142] There are also some echoes of this tripartite division of history, with the final age being that of the Spirit among the other Dutch Anabaptists. The Holy Spirit has a very significant role in the thought of Dirk. The Holy Spirit is the agent of regeneration in the experience of the new birth.[143] It is the Holy Spirit, who writes the new covenant of Jer. 31:33 upon the hearts of believers.[144] It is the Holy Spirit, who through His power and nature (*eygenschap*) makes the believer in the experience of the new birth become a participant in the divine being (*wesens*) of Jesus Christ.[145] The Holy Spirit is the earthly presence and power of Jesus Christ, who is now bodily in heaven.[146] It is the first requirement of ministers who are called of God that they should be taught by the Holy Spirit, for He is the real schoolmaster, and those who are not taught by Him do not understand the Scriptures.[147]

2. *The Brevity of the "Time of Grace"*

In the scheme of history, which Hoffmann borrowed from Joachim and adapted to his own views, the interval of time between the appearance of the witnesses of the last day and the coming of that day itself was at one and the same time both the "time of grace" and the "last and perilous time."[148] It was a "time" or a "day" of grace, because during this interval, which might end at any moment with the coming of the last day, man was still confronted with the possibility of choice. The interval was also a perilous time, not only because it might end at any moment, but also because men who did not exercise their power of choice during

---

142 See Karl Löwith, *Meaning in History, the Theological Implications of the Philosophy of History* (Chicago: University of Chicago Press, 1949), for an excellent chapter on Joachim and the theological implications of his view of history. Dr. Löwith makes a more definite break between each separate age than does Joachim, and he does not refer at all to Joachim's influence upon the Radical Reformers. Yet, he does point out that the Franciscan movement recovered for the Church, whose primary concern had become that of making her own position in the world secure, the eschatological passion of the early Christians "who were heroically unconcerned with the continuous history and civilization of this world." P. 156. This radical eschatology, which looked forward with eager anticipation to the end of this present evil world, was also typical of the Radical Reformation.

Franklin H. Littell has suggested that the Joachimite ideas in relation to the restitution of the Church were transmitted to the Anabaptists by George Witzel. See Littell, p. 73. But there are occasional phrases of rather corrupt Latin in Hoffmann's writings, and it is possible that Hoffmann read Joachim in the original.

143 Dirk Philips, *Vander Doope, BRN*, X, 95.
144 Dirk Philips, *Van der Menschwerdinghe ons Heeren Jesu Christi, BRN*, X, 126.
145 Dirk Philips, *Van der wedergeboorte ende nieuwe Creatuere, BRN*, X, 315.
146 *Ibid.*
147 Dirk Philips, *Van der Sendinge der Predicanten oft Leeraers, BRN*, X, 208 and 212. For other examples of the work of the Holy Spirit in the thought of Menno and Dirk, see Chapter VII of thesis.
148 W. I. Leendertz, *Melchior Hofmann* (Haarlem, 1883), p. 374, Bijlage VI. Taken from a microfilm copy, 4282C-48, Widener Library, Harvard University.

the "day of grace" would find their destiny in the lake of fire, which is the second death.[149]

This same concept of an interval of time, which is both a "time of grace" and the "last and perilous time," appears also in the thought of Menno and Dirk, though not as a part of their view of history. Dirk, for example, sees evidence of the "last and perilous time" of which the apostles spoke in the ministers who preach the Gospel without the law and hence bring no one to repentance. They are the "false teachers" who are "signs of the last and fearful time."[150] The "last and perilous time" is also attested to by those who themselves undertake the restitution of God's kingdom on earth when this role has been assigned to Jesus Christ alone.[151] The "last and perilous time" is a time when men engage in all kinds of idolatrous practices and, therefore, a time when one needs in a particular way the gift of the Holy Spirit, so that one may be able to distinguish between good and evil and between true and false forms of worship.[152]

Yet, side by side with this "last and perilous time" and coterminus with it is the "day of grace." With Christ the "time of the law" has come to an end, and the "time of grace" with its comforting Gospel is here.[153] The present time is the time of God's proffered grace (*tijt de sengheboden genade Godts*), which can idle away and as a consequence fall under God's judgment.[154]

Similar notes on the relationship between eschatology and the "day" or "time" of grace are sounded by Menno Simons. One of the most explicit and fully developed of Menno's views on the relationship between the "day of grace" and the eschaton is found in *Foundation of Christian Doctrine*, 1539. In this work also a sense of imminent and impending disaster appears side by side with an urgent call to decision, while time remains in which men may make decisions. Menno's appeal to his contemporaries to avail themselves of the opportunity provided by the "day of grace" appears to have been directed in part against those who advocated waiting to reform the Church until some new revelation would give specific directions for reform, or until a greater spirit of tolerance would make the needed reform easier. He writes:

> Therefore comfort not one another with senseless comfort and uncertain hope, as some do who think that the Word will yet be taught and observed without the cross. I have in mind those who know the Word of the Lord, but do not live according to it. Oh, no! it is the Word of the cross and will in my opinion remain that unto the end.[155]

After a brief passage in which Menno reminds his readers that Christ and all the

---

149 Kawerau, pp. 75–111.
150 Dirk Philips, *Van der Sendinge der Predicanten oft Leeraers, BRN*, X, 207.
151 Dirk Philips, *Vande geestelijcke Restitution, BRN*, X, 342–43. The thrust is against Rotmann, who wrote his *Restitution* in support of the Münsterite kingdom. The date of this work by Philips is ca. 1559.
152 Dirk Philips, *Voorrede, Verantwoordinghe ende Refutation op twee Sendtbrieven Sebastiani Franck, BRN*, X, 489–90.
153 Dirk Philips, *Vande geestelijcke Restitution, BRN*, X, 367.
154 Dirk Philips, *Vande Gemeynte Godts, BRN*, X, 379–80.
155 Menno Simons, *Foundation of Christian Doctrine, CWMS*, p. 109.

apostles had to suffer for their faith and that the disciple must never expect to be above his Lord, Menno continues:

> Therefore, tear from your hearts the harmful thought that you may hope for another time, lest you be deceived by your vain hopes. I have known some who waited for a time of freedom, but did not live to see it. Had the apostles and fathers waited for it, the Gospel of the kingdom would to this day have been silent, and the Word of the Lord unpreached.[156]

Menno then urges his readers not to "wait for a different time," since we have already received "the acceptable time of grace," and the angel of *Revelation* has sworn that "after this time there shall be time no more."[157] This time is for Menno "the promised day of grace," the "time of the appearance of the promised seed," the "time of redemption," the "time of the sacrifice," by which all things have been reconciled in heaven and on earth; the time for the fulfillment of all the figurative transactions into a new and spiritual reality and abiding truth, in contrast to the promises of these realities which the fathers hoped for but had to see from afar.[158]

Although the scheme of history in three distinct epochs or periods is not present in the writings of Menno and Dirk, the sense of the radically new situation in which man stands since the atoning work of Christ, as the second Adam, is. This radical newness divides history sharply into B. C. and A. D., and there is an underlying conviction that there is a real difference in the manner in which God dealt with man before and after the incarnation and the atonement of Christ.

It is at this point that the Dutch Anabaptists approach closely the thought of Pilgram Marbeck. For Pilgram, too, history is divided into three different periods or epochs, but the center from which all history is dated, both backward and forward, is not the eschaton, as it was for Hoffmann, but rather the incarnation. The time before Christ is designated by Marbeck as the "grace of yesterday"; the time since Christ as the "grace of today"; and the future age which will be ushered in by Christ's return as the "grace of tomorrow." Marbeck did not attempt to say when the return of Christ would take place or when the "grace of today" would be displaced by the "grace of tomorrow." His main concern was not with the future but with the atonement, which he viewed as the payment of a debt which made possible real forgiveness (*wesentliche*) of sins, while the patriarchs who died before Christ's death had only the promise of forgiveness.[159]

156 *Ibid.*, p. 110.
157 *Ibid.*
158 *Ibid.*, p. 108.
159 Marbeck, *Verantwortung*, p. 318. This same emphasis appears again and again in Marbeck's *Testamentserläuterung*, which in effect is the content of the entire Bible systematically arranged under the categories of "Yesterday" and "Today". This distinction was already present in the *Vermanung* of 1542 and was further developed in the controversy with Schwenckfeld in the *Verantwortung* of 1544–1550. Schwenckfeld in the *Judicium* had criticized Marbeck for saying that Abraham and the other patriarchs who had lived and died before the time of Christ had not experienced real forgiveness of sins, and, therefore, could not be considered Christians or children of God before the atonement and Christ's descent into Hades to preach to the spirits who were in prison. Schwenckfeld maintained, in opposition to Marbeck, that Abraham was a Christian before he became a Jew. *CS*, VIII, 198.

Neither Hans Denck nor Balthasar Hubmaier made any systematic connection between the doctrine of grace and eschatology. Their attention was centered rather in the new situation in which man stood because of the incarnation and the atonement, and for Hubmaier the new situation involved a partially restored human nature.[160] Schwenckfeld, as was characteristic of all the Spiritualists, tends to disregard the historical and is not greatly concerned with the eschatological. Insofarpas Schwenckfeld thought historically at all, he looked toward the glorified Christ rather than to the Crucified One as the center for a meaningful interpretation of history. And here it was not so much *Heilsgeschichte* that concerned him as the personal piety of the individual Christian. His concern was not so much with an imminent eschaton but with a new revelation in a future age of the Spirit.

---

160 *SAW*, p. 131.

CHAPTER III

THE GRACE OF GOD IN CHRIST

A. *The "Time of Grace" in Contrast to the "Time of Law"*

The preceding chapter has emphasized the fact that for the representatives of the Radical Reformation considered in this study the situation in which mankind had stood since the transgression and fall of the first Adam was radically altered with the advent of Christ as the second Adam. Both in the Netherlands and in South Germany this difference was described in terms of the "time of grace" and the "time of law." The period of history from the fall to the advent of Christ was designated as the "time of law," while the period of history from the incarnation to the second advent and the eschaton was designated as the "time of grace."

This periodization of history can best be illustrated by means of a straight line bisected at two points, the first section representing the fall of man and the second, the advent of Christ.

In general it may be said that the "time of law" was regarded as a dispensation in history when God's way of dealing with guilty sinners was either much more severe, or else far less adequate, than was the case during the dispensation designated as the "time of grace." The event which separated the two dispensations from each other was, of course, the incarnation and the atonement of Christ. The difference between God's greater severity *with* the sinner during the "time of law" on the one hand, and an inadequate remedy *for* him on the other, indicates the difference between the way in which the Dutch and South German Anabaptists regard the dispensations of law and grace. Menno Simons and Dirk Philips emphasize the greater severity of God with sinners during the "time of law," while Pilgram Marbeck emphasizes much more the inadequacy of the law to meet the needs of sinful and fallen man.

Among the Dutch Anabaptists the concept of a difference between the "time of law" and the "time of grace" appeared to have originated with Melchior Hoffmann. Hoffmann was a gifted, though an uneducated, man, and he used his literary talent with great skill to show the disparateness of the dispensations. During the "time of law" man is in bondage to Satan as a result of Adam's fall, but he is nevertheless sustained by the "moonlight" of divine faith and the precious promise of God's intervention (*ontferminge*) of grace.[1] The difference between the light of the moon and the light of the sun is elsewhere described in Hoffmann's thought as the difference between a promise and the fulfillment of that promise. In addition Hoffmann used also the terms, "letter" and "spirit," to differentiate between the dispensations of law and grace. This contrast appears in a brief work written by Hoffmann from Strasbourg in 1533.

In the abovementioned work Hoffmann finds in the design of the tabernacle the key to the correct interpretation of both Old and New Testaments, as well as the key to the door of the "time of grace." The courtyard of the tabernacle represents

---

1 Melchior Hoffmann, *Verclaringe van den geuangenen ende vrien wil, BRN,* V, 184.

the Old Testament and the "time of the letter," while the holy place represents the New Testament and the acceptable year or the "time of grace."[2]

In *The True Christian Faith* Menno Simons speaks of the fate of the fallen angels, of the antediluvian world, of Sodom and Gomorrah, of those who worshipped the golden calf, and of the children of Israel, who rebelled under the leadership of Moses during the wilderness wanderings. God dealt with such sinners during the "time of law" by destroying them.

In the "time of grace" God spares sinners through His great mercy. He leads them by His right hand, renews them by His Word, begets them as His children by the Holy Ghost, and enlightens them by the clear word of His truth.[3] Menno writes:

> Thus by His grace we bade farewell to the world, flesh, devil, and all and freely entered upon the path of peace, beneath the easy yoke of the Gospel. Methinks this is grace, if ever there was any.[4]

Dirk Philips in his *Vande geestelijcke Restitution*, ca. 1559, makes a similar, though yet different, emphasis, utilizing the imagery of the *Song of Solomon*. The "time of law" has expired (*verloopen*), the wrath of God has been stilled, and the joyful "time of grace" has come.[5] During the "time of law" Achan and all his household were stoned to death for an offense which was his alone (Josh. 7: 24—26). Sodom and Gomorrah were destroyed by fire, and the people who worshipped the golden calf, which Aaron erected for them, were slain with the sword. In contrast to God's severity with sinners during the "time of law," the "time of grace" involved the proclamation of the Gospel, which brought forth in those who believed the fruits and flowers of righteousness. The land is now fruitful in faith and in the knowledge of God, the plantings of the Lord spring forth, and the branches on the vine, Jesus Christ, produce clusters, and give forth the sweet odor of life through the power of Jesus Christ, which is in them. This, says Dirk, happened in the time of the first apostles and happens daily in his own time among those who believe.[6] In the thought of Dirk the difference is closely related to the manner in which God now deals with people. The emphasis is on the contrast between the effects of law and grace upon the nature of man. However, in Menno's thought the difference between the dispensations is pushed back so far that it almost becomes a difference within the nature of God Himself.

Both Menno and Dirk warn men not to interpret the patience and longsuffering of God during the "time of grace" as indifference. Menno especially reminds his contemporaries that should one fail to repent during the "time of grace," which

---

2 Melchior Hoffmann, *Der Leuchter des alten Testaments ussgelegt, welcher im heyligen stund der hütten Mose mit seinen siben lampen, blumen, knöpffen... Und alles das such reicht uff die siben versamling des nuewen Testaments*, printed by Leendertz as one of the bijlagen from Hoffmann's work on p. 374.
3 Menno Simons, *The True Christian Faith*, CWMS, p. 327.
4 *Ibid.*, p. 328.
5 Dirk Philips, *Vande geestelijcke Restitution, BRN*, X, 367.
6 *Ibid.*

expires for individual man at the time of death and for the race at the eschaton, he would fall again under the dreadful wrath of God.[7] A similar though somewhat modified contrast between the dispensations of law and grace appears also in the thought of Pilgram Marbeck. Marbeck uses the terms, the "grace of yesterday" and the "grace of today," to give expressions to his view of the disparateness of the dispensations. This distinction was already present in the *Vermanung* of 1542 and was one of the points challenged by Schwenckfeld in the *Judicium* of the same year. Marbeck replied to this aspect of Schwenckfeld's criticism in the first part of the *Verantwortung*, which was completed around 1544, and in the *Testamentserläuterung*, which was completed about 1550.[8] In the later works Marbeck does not develop anything essentially new with respect to the "grace of yesterday" and the "grace of today," but simply reiterates in a more forceful way what had been previously stated. In the *Testamentserläuterung*, particularly, Marbeck supports with numerous proof texts the position already taken in the *Vermanung* of 1542. Marbeck had then maintained that Abraham and all the patriarchs who lived and died before the time of Christ were not Christians or God's spiritual children. They had received neither actual (*wesentliche*) forgiveness of sins, nor the gift of the Holy Spirit, nor eternal life, but were believers in *hope only* until the time of the incarnation and atonement. Under the "grace of yesterday" the believing ones who lived before Christ were given a grace that was effective in temporal affairs only. The children of Israel found grace (favor) in the sight of the Egyptians at the time of the Exodus, so that they were not sent empty away. The remnant of Israel in the wilderness found grace in the sight of God, so that they were not destroyed along with those who had felt the fierce anger of the Lord. Joseph found grace in the sight of Potiphar, captain of the guard (Gen. 41:38), and God gave Daniel grace in the sight of King Nebuchadnezzar (Dan. 1:19–20).

The temporal character of the "grace of yesterday" was thus either the indirect action of God, whereby He caused others to act favorably toward those who were believers in hope, or it was God Himself acting favorably toward His people rather than visiting upon them the full fury of His wrath. The temporal grace saved one from temporal punishment of sin, but it could grant neither forgiveness for sin nor eternal life. The "grace of yesterday," which was *only a temporal grace (nur zeitlich)*, left all men, pious or impious, locked up under the curse of the law until the "grace of today" appeared in Christ.[9]

7 Menno Simons, *Epistle to Martin Micron*, 1556, *CWMS*, p. 921. Menno here argues against capital punishment on the ground that this would take from the impenitent his "time for repentance" of which, in case his life were spared, he might yet avail himself.
8 Marbeck also speaks of the "grace of tomorrow," which will begin with Christ's second advent and the eschaton, but he does not venture to predict when this will occur. Therefore, it plays no major role in his thought. *Verantwortung*, p. 328.
9 Marbeck, *Testamentserläuterung*, p. 45. No date or place of publication given. From a microfilm copy of the original now in the Berlin Library, Berlin, Germany, secured through the courtesy of Dr. William Klassen, Mennonite Biblical Seminary, Elkhart, Indiana. Through the interest of Mr. James Tanis, librarian at Harvard Divinity School, the services of Widener Library were engaged to make a negative copy from Mr. Klassen's microfilm, which is now available at Andover-Harvard Library of the Harvard Divinity School.

Marbeck found in Heb. 9, 10, and 11, with their emphasis upon the new and better covenant, and in I Pet. 1:5, with its reference to a "salvation ready to be revealed at the last time," the Scriptural support for the inadequacy of the "grace of yesterday." The grace of which the prophets spoke, says Marbeck, was always referred to in the future tense. They urged people, according to I Pet. 1 and Heb. 10 and 12, not to place their hope in the "grace of yesterday" but wholly and entirely (*gantz und gar*) upon Christ.[10]

Of course, those who lived during Old Testament times *hoped* for the eventual forgiveness of their sins, because the "grace of today" was already promised yesterday. Yet this grace was not really received until the incarnation had taken place, the atonement made, and the ascended Lord had poured out the Holy Spirit in His fullness. Not until this had taken place could God grant real forgiveness for the sins committed during the "time of yesterday" under the divine patience.[11]

The contrast between the "grace of yesterday" and the "grace of today" is for Marbeck not a contrast between God's greater severity during the first dispensation and His greater leniency during the second, as it was for Menno and Dirk. The contrast is rather between inadequacy and adequacy, between a prophecy and the fulfillment of that prophecy or between shadow and reality. The whole period of the first dispensation is characterized by the fact that the "time of yesterday" was a time of blindness, a time of lack of wisdom, understanding, and revelation, while in the second dispensation the enmity (*zorn*) between man and God has been removed. Man who had been hitherto locked up under the wrath of God is now released and has blessing and life instead of curse and death.[12] The "grace of yesterday" was equivalent to the law, which could do no more than to reveal to men the fact of their sinfulness before God and their need of Christ, the Physician.[13]

There is one important exception to this generalization of the contrast between the Dutch Anabaptists and Pilgram Marbeck on the difference between the "time of law" versus the "time of grace." This is found in a brief passage from Dirk Philips in *Vande Gemeynte Godts*, ca. 1560. Dirk speaks of the congregation of God which existed outside of Israel and was made up "of those who honored God and lived according to His will by the law of God inscribed in their hearts.[14] The congregation of God outside of Israel consisted of all among the heathen who have believed in Jesus Christ and are, therefore, in their uncircumcision of the flesh (Rom. 2:26) and in their heathendom counted as the spiritual seed of Abraham and of the Promise, and from this it follows that they have been of God and of Christ.[15] Not only does Dirk regard Abraham as a Christian before the time of the incarnation and the atonement, but those outside Israel who follow the law of God written on their hearts are Christians as well.

10 *Ibid.*, p. 47.
11 *Ibid.*, p. 138.
12 *Ibid.*, pp. 346–50.
13 Marbeck, *Verantwortung*, pp. 233–34.
14 Dirk Philips, *Vande Gemeynte Godts,* BRN, X, 385. See also *SAW*, pp. 332–33.
15 *Ibid.*, p. 385.

Neither Hans Denck nor Balthasar Hubmaier developed their thought regarding the grace of God in Christ in terms of a periodization of history, or in terms of a more severe or more gracious attitude toward sinners on God's part before and after Christ, but rather in terms of the new possibilities which the coming of Christ has opened up for mankind. Denck insists that those who know and love Christ can now keep the law and yet they have no room before God to boast of their own merit. For it is through God's grace in Christ that a way has been opened up which before was impossible for the whole world. To say that the law was given *only* so that through it men might learn to know themselves as sinners is to make God a liar, who both gave the law that it should be kept and in Christ gave also the possibility of keeping it to those who know and love Christ.[16] Through Christ, God in His almighty power, has made possible what was previously impossible. Men may cast God aside as they will; in Christ the Mediator is now near, through whom they may turn again to God.[17]

Hubmaier develops his thought concerning the new situation in which man stands with the coming of Christ in connection with his trichotomous anthropology.[18] Hubmaier speaks of a *first* grace as the state in which man was originally created in which it would have been possible for man to maintain his innocence and continue in it until he had obtained eternal life. The possibility also existed that man might cast aside this first grace through disobedience and so lose the freedom in which he was first created, together with it the opportunity of gaining eternal life. This did, in fact, occur in the fall of Adam. Through the fall the first grace and freedom in which man was created was darkened and lost, so that without *new grace* from God man can now neither know what is good or evil, nor can he desire that which is good. But after the fallen soul has been restored to health again through the new grace that is now available in Christ, man can again know what is good or evil, and he can resist evil and desire the good. The restored soul, together with the unfallen spirit of man, constitutes the man as he is when restored through the new grace that is now available in Christ. Man who was previously lost can now be saved, if he will, through this grace. If man does not avail himself of this grace, he will be damned, but the fault is now his own, not that of God.[19] The full title of this work by Hubmaier is significant in itself, in that it indicates that Hubmaier thought of Christ as the sent *Word* and the bearer of this *new grace* through whom God gave power *to all men to become His children* or *to remain children of wrath*, such as they were by nature.[20]

Regardless of the exact manner in which the Radical Reformers developed their convictions that the grace of God in Christ had brought a new age or a new era, they were, with the exception of Schwenckfeld, in agreement that the coming of Christ had placed hitherto fallen man in a radically new situation. The "time of grace," the "grace of today," and the new grace all speak of the new possibilities

---

16 Hans Denck, *Vom Gesetz Gottes*, 1526, *QFR*, Band XXIV, 2 Teil, pp. 57–58.
17 Hans Denck, *Was geredt sei, dass die Schrift sagt*, *QFR*, Band XXIV, 2 Teil, p. 38.
18 For details see Chapter II of thesis.
19 Hubmaier, *Von der Freiheit des Willens*.
20 *Ibid.*

that are opened up for man in Christ. Man must now no longer be viewed as he is in Adam but as he may become in Christ, who is the second Adam.

B. *The Appropriation of Grace through Conversion*

The Radical Reformers, both in South Germany and in the Netherlands, thought of grace as operative on more than one level. Leonhard Schiemer, as noted in Chapter I, pages 41–44, spoke of three levels of grace. In general, however, the whole mosaic of radical thought concerning the various aspects of the concept of grace is brought into sharper focus, if we limit the levels to two and designate the first as the grace of natural law, while the second is designated as the grace of supernatural regeneration. The first is sufficient to enable fallen man to turn toward Christ but not sufficient to restore or recreate the divine image. For the sake of greater clarity the presentation of these two aspects of grace is here made in chronological order, beginning with the leaders of the Radical Reformation in South Germany.

It should be noted, first of all, that Balthasar Hubmaier's tripartite anthropology had far-reaching effects upon the concept of grace which developed within the South German wing of the Radical Reformation. This is most evident in the thought of Leonhard Schiemer and Pilgram Marbeck and appears to have been appropriated by Schiemer directly from Hubmaier. In the autobiographical sketch on Schiemer, which is found in the *Glaubenszeugnisse*, edited by Dr. Lydia Müller, Schiemer states that he had served for a time as a priest in Austria, and then because of disappointment at the low level of the spiritual life within the priesthood he left it to become a barefoot friar. Here he remained for six years, being shifted from cloister to cloister, but at the end of this period Schiemer states that he abandoned the monastery for the same reason that he had earlier left the priesthood. After leaving the monastery Schiemer wandered to Nürnberg, where he learned the tailor's trade, and thence to Nicolsburg, where he came into direct contact with Hubmaier. He states that at Nicolsburg he heard Hubmaier speak of baptism and (other) doctrine to which he was at first hostile, and that he persecuted the same.[21] At the present time it is not known how extended Schiemer's contacts with Hubmaier were nor how personal they became. What is plainly evident is the fact that despite Schiemer's one time hostile attitude toward Hubmaier and his doctrine he, nevertheless, learned much from him. The traces of Hubmaier's tripartite anthropology are plainly visible in the doctrine of grace as developed by Schiemer. Where Hubmaier posits the unfallen spirit of fallen man as that which gives fallen man limited freedom and, therefore, makes him morally responsible for his own destiny, Schiemer speaks of the light of conscience which shines in all men to give them a knowledge of what is good or bad. Schiemer declares that all men have this light despite the fall, since God shows no partiality, and that every man is, therefore, responsible for the degree to which he allows this light to shine or for the extent to which he darkens it.[22] The probable effect of

---

21 Schiemer, "Von Drierlei Gnad," *QFR*, XX, 80.
22 *Ibid.*, p. 62.

this aspect of the thought of Schiemer upon that of Pilgram Marbeck has already been noted. Genetically the line of influence seems to run from Hubmaier to Schiemer to Marbeck. It is unlikely that either of the latter two men were sufficiently aware of the subtleties of Scholastic theology to arrive at such distinctions on their own. Their view of the concept of grace must now be more fully explored.

Schiemer and Marbeck both refer to the light of conscience, or the natural knowledge of good and evil, as the first grace. This first grace, however, even when allowed to shine at its full strength, is sufficient only to show fallen man how sinful he really is and how great his need of Christ as redeemer actually is. When the light of this first grace is fully heeded, says Schiemer, "then it is our schoolmaster to bring us to Christ."[23] Grace on this first level is able to bring about conversion when this term is used in its Latin sense of *converso*, to turn around and face in a different direction, but it is not able to effect regeneration as an ontological change within the individual. In the thought of Pilgram Marbeck the *lux naturalis*, which still shines within fallen man, is, as Torsten Bergsten has pointed out,

> the counter-inheritance which is the opposite and positive side of the concept of original sin. Original grace has in the same manner gone out from Adam's loins over all his descendants. The entire future race rested according to this view in Adam's loins, and there received a double inheritance. The negative inheritance, original sin, God in His mercy restrains through original grace.[24]

Although Marbeck's representation of the *lux naturalis*, as the original or first grace which can lead to natural righteousness, seems to include a Church of God before and outside of Christ, Marbeck, as Bergsten has indicated, never treats these two as identical. Because of sin the natural righteousness is destined to be imperfect, and the natural light can do no more than to reveal to man the fact that he is stricken, wounded, and ill and in need of Christ, the true physician.[25] Although Marbeck develops his tripartite anthropology in his own way, his indirect dependence upon Hubmaier at that point is so obvious as to be almost beyond question. A summary statement to the effect that for Radical Reformers in South Germany the first level of grace had an anthropological rather than a soteriological base would, in my judgment, be fairly accurate.

Among the leaders of the Radical Reformation in the Netherlands grace was also conceived as operative on two levels with the difference, however, that here both levels were soteriologically based. In the Netherlands the genetic line of influence

---

23 *Ibid.*, p. 66.
24 Torsten Bergsten, "Pilgram Marbeck und Seine Auseinandersetzung mit Caspar Schwenckfeld," *Kyrkohistorisk Arsskrift* (Uppsala: Utgiven av Svenska Kyrkohistoriska Foreningen, 1957), p. 79; Marbeck developed this view of original grace in his reply to Schwenckfeld, who had accused him of having Pelagian tendencies and of denying original sin. For a complete and competent analysis of Marbeck's thought on this point see pp. 75–80 of the above mentioned article by Bergsten and pp. 201, 195, 218, 222, 223, 231, and 266 in Marbeck's *Verantwortung*.
25 Marbeck, *Verantwortung*, p. 234.

appears to run from Melchior Hoffmann to Dirk Philips and Menno Simons. Melchior Hoffmann, as we have seen in Chapter II, saw the atonement of Christ as the cause of a universal grace by means of which Christ, as the second Adam, had liberated mankind from the universal bondage into which it was cast by the transgression of the first Adam.[26] Through the atonement the will of man, hitherto in bondage, is again set free, so that man's will is, in Hoffmann's words, again placed in his own hands. Since God through Christ has now restored man's ability to make a real decision, he must now use this ability and repent of his sins before he can experience the grace of regeneration.

It is in this light that Hoffmann must be understood as he writes:

> No one has part in the paschal lamb [which is Christ], or may eat of it, except those who are circumcised, that is, those who on a true and better life abstain from sin and are circumcised in the foreskins of their hearts.[27]

The unrepentant sinner has his face turned away from God's proffered grace in Christ. Hence, the need for preaching the Law first to bring man to an awareness of his estrangement from God, so that he may utrilize the *common* or universal grace, which God in Christ offers to all men and not, as the Lutheran and Reformed clergy imagine, only to the elect, who are predestined to be saved by means of the eternal decrees of divine election and invincible grace. The Strasbourg Synod of 1533 was aware of these two levels of grace within Hoffmann's thought and condemned it along with three other aspects of his teaching, as being among the most damnable of errors.[28]

While Dirk Philips and Menno Simons do not, as indicated in Chapter II, explicitly connect the freedom of the will in otherwise fallen man with the universal grace which Christ, as the second Adam, has won through the atonement, such a view is implicit in many of their statements. A strongly voluntaristic tone colors all of their writings and forms the background of all of their thought. Dirk and Menno do see the universal grace of Christ's atonement as efficacious for all infants and children, so that none may be condemned because of Adam's sin. This universal grace of the atonement removes all the guilt of original sin and leaves only an evil inclination. This evil inclination is for Christ's sake not regarded as sin until it breaks out in the actual sin of the mature person.

Actual sin implies the consent of the will in the mature or adult person. Since he is ethically and morally responsible for his own destiny, the Law must be preached first, so that the will may be motivated to choose what is right in God's sight. Through the Law men learn God's severe judgment against sin and have their hearts smitten, so that they may be afterwards comforted by the Gospel.

---

26 The two texts which the Dutch Radical Reformers most often appealed to in support of this view of the universality of grace were John 1:29b, "Behold the Lamb of God that takes away the sin of the world," and I Cor. 15:22, "For as in Adam all die, so also in Christ shall all be made alive."
27 Hoffmann, *Verclaringe van den geuangenen ende vrien wil*, BRN, V, 190.
28 *Handelinge van der disputacie in Synodo te Straesburch teghen Melchior Hoffman door die predicanten derseluer stadt*, BRN, V, 228.

The insistence, found within the writings of both Menno and Dirk, that man must repent before he can receive forgiveness and regeneration implies that man has this ability, either in spite of the fall or in consequence of a partial restoration from it. Cornelius Krahn has noted that if Menno's concept of repentance were expressed in modern terms one would say of it, that it is an *anknüpfungspunkt* for the grace of God, which then leads man to the new birth.[29]

This is one way of expressing Menno's thought at this point and not the least happy one, but in *The True Christian Faith*, written in 1541, and in the *Reply to Gellius Faber* of 1554 Menno hints that he thinks of repentance itself as being the result of the reception of God's grace. In the first he warns his readers against the assumption that men can receive faith, repentance, sorrow for sin, and the grace of God whenever it is convenient for them.[30] In the second work Menno warns against the danger of willful sinning. "For who knows whether he who thus willfully sins against his God will ever again in all his days receive grace and come to true repentance."[31]

The question must, therefore, be raised whether Menno and Dirk, as well as Hoffmann, saw man's ability to repent in the presence of the proclamation of the law as the result of an initial or common grace which God through Christ had imparted to all men. If so, they have moved one step further beyond their *nomos* standpoint, yet it still remains true that the grace of repentance or conversion precedes the grace of regeneration. Both in South Germany and in the Netherlands, therefore, grace on the first level represents only the first step on the way of salvation. While the Radicals were all insistent upon repentance or conversion as the necessary *first step* for the beginning of the new life in Christ, they did not imagine that man could bring this about by himself. Where repentance or conversion occurred, they were more often than not regarded as the result of man's response to an initial or common grace which God granted to all men; sometimes through the grace of natural law as in Schiemer and Marbeck; at other times through the universal grace of the atonement as in Hoffmann, in order that they might be able freely to appropriate the grace of regeneration.

C. *The Appropriation of Grace through Regeneration*

It was noted in Chapter I that the concept of salvation which prevailed within the Radical Reformation was predominantly the Johannine concept of salvation as the divinization of man. This was true for all but two of the representatives of that Reformation considered in this study. Whereas in the Magisterial Reformation grace was looked upon from man's side as God's act of forensic justification in which the sinner is declared righteous without actually being made so, in the Radical Reformation grace was rather regarded as the act whereby God through the agency of the Holy Spirit brought about an actual ontological change within the nature of man himself. Through the Holy Spirit the image in man which was

---

29 Cornelius Krahn, *Menno Simons (1496–1561)* (Karlsruhe i.B.: Heinrich Schneider, 1936), p. 129.
30 Menno Simons, *The True Christian Faith*, CWMS, p. 373.
31 Menno Simons, *Reply to Gellius Faber*, CWMS, p. 715.

lost through the fall is restored, and the believer is made a participant in the divine nature itself. Thus, the result of grace in man is a reversal of the incarnation in which the eternal Word becomes man in order that man may become God.[32]

Even for the two representatives included in this study who do not make the Johannine concept of salvation their own, grace is still thought of as effecting an ontological or metaphysical change within the believer himself, rather than merely a change in status before God as expressed in the *simul iustus et peccator* formula. It would, I think, not be incorrect to say that grace understood as the act whereby God renews the divine image in man and makes the believer a participant in the divine nature held the same centrality within the Radical Reformation as did the concept of grace as God's act of forensic justification within the Magisterial Reformation.

It was noted in Chapter II that within the Radical Reformation the primary emphasis in the doctrine of original sin was not on the bondage of the will as was the case in the Magisterial Reformation, but rather upon the corruption of man's physical nature or upon the loss of his ability to distinguish between good and evil. The concept of grace as a restoration of man's original nature and the renewal of the lost faculties and virtues through participation in the divine nature is not unrelated to this concept of original sin.

Hans Denck, in whose thought both medieval mysticism and Augustinian Neoplatonism are combined, specifically states in two of his major works that his concept of salvation is that of the divinization of man. In Denck's thought, however, it is not so clear that the whole process of divinization is dependent upon grace as God's initial act of regeneration. This is due to the fact that Denck felt within himself not only the *angeborne kranckhayt* (his term for original sin), but also the inner Word. He announces in his earliest work his intention to follow that Word wherever it may lead him.[33]

In his *Was geredt sei, dass die Schrift sagt* of 1526 Denck says that the reason the Word dwells within us is that it may divinize us,[34] and in the *Ordnung Gottes* of 1527 Denck calls the activity of this inner Word the grace of God.[35]

> Whoever says that he does not have grace from God to become righteous [fromm zu werden], he is a liar as all men are, Ps. 116, because he lies against God, who pours out His mercy upon all men, Ps. 119, 145, Jer. 18:33, etc., as well as His wrath. Yes, much more abundantly, Rom. 5, Ex. 20, for else the godless would be innocent as they wish to be, but they cannot maintain this with truth, John 9, Rom. 3, Ps. 57.[36]

In Denck's thought it is the function of grace understood as the prompting of the inner Word to lead man ever nearer to his original condition in creation. The nearer man approaches this condition the more it becomes possible for him to do the good. And yet man, because he must still seek the perfection which Christ never lost, cannot make this return journey in his own strength. He can only allow

---

32 See pp. 158–61 of thesis.
33 Hans Denck, *Bekenntnis für den Rat zu Nürnberg*, QFR, Band XXIV, 2 Teil, 20–21.
34 Hans Denck, *Was geredt sei, dass die Schrift sagt*, QFR, Band XXIV, 2 Teil, 39.
35 Hans Denck, *Ordnung Gottes*, QFR, Band XXIV, 2 Teil, 96.
36 *Ibid.*

this inner Word to bring about a gradual transformation within himself. He cannot create the transformation by himself. This gradual transformation is in effect a renewal of the divine image, but in fairness one must say that here renewal comes by imitation rather than by regeneration. In Denck's thought the inner Word is the universal *Logos*, by reason of which God is present in all His creatures and still present to a greater degree in mankind than in any other creature, even though man is fallen.

It is the inner Word which has now become incarnate in the historic Jesus, who now serves man as both mediator and example.[37] Men who were given free will in creation are now without excuse if they do not go on to receive righteousness out of grace through the mediator and through his example improve their lives.[38]

It cannot be maintained, as noted in the beginning of this section, that Balthasar Hubmaier and Pilgram Marbeck make the Johannine concept of salvation their own. Yet they, too, each in his own way, put more stress on the ontological change that is wrought by God's grace within man's nature than upon the change in status before God through forensic justification. Hubmaier, like Denck, developed his concept of what grace is and of what it enables hitherto fallen man to do in connection with his conscious and vigorous rejection of the Lutheran doctrine of the bondage of the will. In Hubmaier's treatise on the freedom of the will, which is dealt with in its completeness in Chapter II, he mentions the soul as one of the three entities in man that was sorely wounded through the fall. Through the new birth of which John spoke in John 3, however, the soul is again restored to its original condition in creation. It is this reëstablished primeval man that Hubmaier has in mind as he writes that it is his intention to show man what is possible for him in the grace of Christ.

Grace is thus again the act of God, whereby He brings about an ontological change within the nature of man himself. The lost image of God is restored, and a divine power indwells the life of the believer, thus making it possible for him to accomplish what was previously impossible.

Walther Koehler is of the opinion that Hubmaier developed this concept of grace in direct opposition to the forensic concept as found in Luther's doctrine of justification by grace through faith alone, as expressed in the *simul iustus et peccator* formula.[39] Grace so understood, says Hubmaier, allows one to change Christian liberty into fleshly liberty and makes carnal Christians rather than those who carry the cross.[40]

The influence of the thought of Leonhard Schiemer upon that of Pilgram Marbeck, with respect to grace as natural law, has been previously noted. This influence is also discernible as we consider grace on its second and highest level as God's act of regeneration. Schiemer states the case for what he calls the "second grace" in the following manner.

37 Hans Denck, *Was geredt sei, dass die Schrift sagt, QFR,* Band XXIV, 2 Teil, 35.
38 *Ibid.*, pp. 38 and 43.
39 Koehler, p. 358.
40 *Ibid.* There is a play on words in the German, which is missed through the English translation, *"Christliche freiheit in fleischliche freiheit"* and *"Kreutz Christen"* as opposed to *"Fleisch Christen."*

> It is a great work of God to create a human being out of nothing, and it is just as great a work to justify a sinful man. But this may not take place apatr from Christ, who is our righteousness ... through his conception, birth, death, and resurrection within us.[41]

According to Schiemer, two conditions must be met before men can obtain this second grace. The first condition is that they utilize the first grace through which sin is revealed,[42] and the second is that there must be a genuine sorrow for sin. The purpose of this sorrow is that through it God seeks to wean men away from all love of the creaturely in order that they may truly love Him as the only God. When God has accomplished this within us, He "places us naked and bare into the second birth, and gives us His Spirit and teaches us to love Him."[43]

This new birth is the restoration of the fallen soul, which again gives one who has experienced grace as regeneration the power, not only to know and desire the good but also to accomplish it.[44] The similarity of the thought of Schiemer to that of Hubmaier is again obvious, and the dependence of both Schiemer and Marbeck appears to be beyond question. Marbeck, like Schiemer, stresses the ontological change that is wrought within the believer through grace as regeneration more than he stresses grace as God's act of forensic justification. The *lux naturalis*, which Marbeck called original grace, could in his thought lead one either to Christ or to natural righteousness. The believer, however, who through faith in Christ has experienced grace on the level of regeneration, is lifted above the realm of natural into that of supernatural righteousness. The structure of Marbeck's thought here is clearly outlined by Torsten Bergsten as follows:

> The person who comes to Christ receives through the Holy Spirit a supernatural knowledge of good and a supernatural righteousness. Through faith in Christ it becomes possible for man to fulfill God's revealed law in a spiritual way and to accomplish what was previously impossible. Man is brought out of nature into super nature.[45]

Marbeck, as Horst Quiring has noted, made a very careful distinction between the *"unsterblichen Geist,"* which all men have as a result of their creation by God and the Holy Spirit, which alone can transpose one from the order of nature into the order of super nature.[46]

---

41 Schiemer, "Von Drierlei Gnad," *QFR*, XX, 66.
42 *Ibid.*
43 *Ibid.* p. 65.
44 *Ibid.*, p.63.
45 Bergsten, p. 77. See also Marbeck, *Verantwortung*, pp. 201, 231, 234f.
46 Horst Quiring, "The Anthropology of Pilgram Marbeck," *MQR*, IX, No. 4 (October, 1935), 161–62.
It is possible to discern in the distinction which the Radicals here make between nature and super nature, between a first or common grace which moves man to repentance but does not save him, and a second or even a third grace which is in effect a justifying grace, the substructure of scholastic theology, as it came to flower in the thought of Thomas Aquinas and Duns Scotus. See Question 109, Article 1 of *The Summa Theologia,* where Thomas says:
"Now every form bestowed on created things by God has power for a determined act, which it can affect in proportion to its own proper endowment; and beyond this act it is

The term, new birth or "birth out of God," was the term most often employed by the Dutch Radicals to define what they primarily understood by grace. Behind this term in English there lies a very conscious and deliberate choice of Dutch prepositions which are used in converse manner from those employed by Menno and Dirk in their incarnation formula. In this manner they avoided any possibility of pantheism, where man is absorbed into God.

> Man [through the appropriation of grace in the new birth] is born out of [*uit*] and not from [*van*] God, so that man's divine nature can only be created or conferred. On the other hand, Christ and the Holy Spirit are begotten from [*van*] God, so that their divinity is uncreated.[47]

Among the Dutch representatives considered in this study Melchior Hoffmann appears to have been the first to use these prepositions to indicate the source of Christ's humanity on the one hand and the source of regenerate man's divinity on the other. In eternity the eternal Word is begotten from (*van*) God;[48] in time man is born out of (*uit*) God, and this participation in the divine nature through grace understood as regeneration is what makes possible the life of victory over sin.[49]

Dirk Philips and Menno Simons take over the term, "birth out of God," to give

---

powerless, except by superadded form, as water can heat only by fire. And thus the human understanding has a form, viz., intelligible light itself, which of itself is sufficient for knowing certain intelligible truths, viz., can come to know through sensible things. Higher intelligible truths the human intellect cannot know, unless it be perfected by a stronger light, viz., the light of faith or of prophecy, which is called the *light of grace,* inasmuch as it is added to nature." (Quoted in *Introduction to Saint Thomas Aquinas,* ed. Anton C. Pegis (New York: The Modern Library, Random House, 1948), p. 653.

One can see also traces of the distinction between *attrition* and *contrition,* as it is developed in the thought of Thomas and Duns Scotus. It may be briefly said that *attrition* came to be regarded as a purely human inclination toward the reception of grace, which marked a *certain* but not a *perfect* displeasure toward sin and, therefore, did not merit forgiveness, while contrition was brought about by infused grace, and, therefore, made forgiveness possible through absolution.

Duns Scotus could speak of attrition and contrition as the two ways of justification. When attrition had endured long enough, or had reached a sufficient height of intensity, it establishes a (*de congruo*) or claim to the favorable regard of God. When the penitent makes his confession, grace is infused and sin destroyed by the impartation of love and the conversion of *attritio* into *contritio.* Since man cannot know when contrition has endured long enough or reached sufficient intensity to be regarded *de congruo* and only God in His freedom decides, attrition as the extra-sacramental way of justification is beyond the reach of most Christians.

For a full discussion of the distinction between *attrition* and *contrition* as developed in the thought of Thomas and Scotus see Gordon J. Spykman, *Attrition and Contrition at the Council of Trent* (Kampen: J.H. Kok, N.V., 1955), pp. 59–79, and Reinhold Seeberg, *Textbook of the History of Doctrines,* trans. Charles E. Hay (2 vols.; Grand Rapids, Michigan: Baker Book House, 1958), pp. 135–137. The Radicals did not follow the Scholastic pattern exactly. They had learned too much from Luther to depend in any way upon sacramental justification. Yet, insofar as they made repentance an *anknüpfungspunkt* for the grace of regeneration, they were closer to the Scholastics than to the Magisterial Reformers.

47 William Keeney, "The Development of Dutch Anabaptist Thought and Practice from 1539–1564," (unpublished Ph. D. thesis, Hartford Theological Seminary, May, 1959), p. 106.
48 Hoffmann, *Die ... sendebrief to den Romeren ... verclaert, BRN,* V, 310.
49 Hoffmann, *Die Ordonnantie Godts, BRN,* V, 151.

expression to their conviction that the new birth results in a new nature. Wherever the term appears in English one may safely assume that behind it lies the use of the Dutch (*uit*). This will simply be assumed in the remainder of the discussion of this section. The ontological change wrought in man's nature by God's grace is the new creature in Christ. The birth out of God, which forms the new creature through the renewal of the divine image and causes the believer to participate in the divine nature, both Menno and Dirk looked upon as an utterly gracious act of God. It does not originate *in* nor is it based *upon* human merit. The means (middle) through which God effects this ontological result of grace is faith, and faith is awakened through the hearing of the Gospel. Those who through the hearing of the Gospel and the cooperation of the Holy Spirit come to believe that Jesus Christ is the eternal Son of God, these are born out of God.

> From all this [says Dirk] it is clear that the new birth is verily the work of God in man through which he is born anew out of God together [*overmits*] with faith in Jesus Christ and the Holy Spirit. For the Heavenly Father generates or bears the new creature, but the Word of the Heavenly Farther is the seed from which the new creature is born, and the Holy Spirit renews, sanctifies, and keeps the new creature in the divine being [*wesen*]. Therefore, such a new birth is a mighty and fruitful work of God which comes through the Almighty and Most High God through Jesus Christ and the Holy Spirit.[50]

Participation in the divine nature did not mean for Dirk that the line of demarcation between God as creator and man as creature was ever eliminated either in time or eternity. He writes:

> Now although men become participant in the divine nature, gods and children of the Most High, they yet do not become in being and person what God and Christ alone are. Oh, no! The *creature* will never become the *Creator*, and flesh will never become eternal Spirit, which God is, for this would be impossible. But the believers become gods and children of the Most High through the new birth, the impartation and fellowship of the divine nature, righteousness [*vromicheit*], glory, purity, and eternal life. They will be glorified as God is glorified, shine as God shines, and live as God lives eternally. And even as God is a spirit, so they will become spirits and spiritual; these who according to their outer bodies are earth and flesh, or have been, will be taken up into glory even as God is in glory. But men are and remain there as creatures, and God alone [is] creator and ruler. Nevertheless, they are one and God is all and in all. I Cor. 15:28.[51]

Dirk did not believe that the experience of grace as the birth out of God would make it possible for the believer to live a sinless life in this world. As long as the new creature in Christ must live in the body derived from the flesh of the sinful and corrupt Adam, they are subject to sin which can only be covered by the *imputed passive righteousness*, which Christ has won for them through the atonement. But even though the believer who has through faith by grace been reformed, so that he is now a new creature in Christ, the fact that he still lives within a body which will eventually die and see corruption is not reckoned unto

---

50 Dirk Philips, *Van der wedergeboorte ende nieuwe Creatuere*, BRN, X, 317–18.
51 Dirk Philips, *Van der Menschwerdinghe ons Heeren Jesu Christi, BRN,* X, 148–49. Italics mine.

him as sin, so long as he remains within the new nature which he has received from Christ, the second Adam.⁵²

Menno Simons also intended to convey the ontological result of God's grace as a change within man's nature by his use of the expression, "birth out of God." As he used it, however, it stands in a somewhat closer relationship to his own peculiar notion of <u>original sin as a corruption in the physical substance of man</u>, which was caused by the poison of Satan, the old crooked serpent, and then transmitted by Adam to the whole human race. If man is to be saved, he must be delivered from the corruption that is in him by reason of his first birth through the experience of the new birth.⁵³ Man by his first birth is out of the first and fleshly Adam; his nature, therefore, earthly and Adam-like. The natural man is carnally minded, blind, unbelieving, disobedient, deaf, and foolish. His end, if not renewed by the Word, will be damnation and death.⁵⁴ Man, therefore, has hope of salvation only if he is born anew out of God. "For the regenerate are in grace and have the promise as you have heard."⁵⁵ While sin and wickedness are the natural fruit of the first birth from the first corrupt Adam, the natural fruit of the new birth from Christ as the second Adam is a life of peace and righteousness. Christians are baptized with the Holy Spirit into the spotless holy body of Christ. "They put on Christ and manifest his spirit, nature, and power in all their conduct."⁵⁶

The same contrast between the nature which is inherited from the first birth and the evil that flows from this nature, and the new nature that is the ontological result of God's grace bestowed through the new birth is found in Menno's *Reply to False Accusations* of 1552. Here Menno calls the birth out of Adam <u>the natural birth</u>. This birth is unclean and sinful, and its fruit, according to the will of the devil, is evil, unrighteousness, and death.⁵⁷ On the other hand, <u>the heavenly birth</u>, or the birth out of God, begets the fruit of righteousness, piety and life, according to the will of God.⁵⁸

Menno, like Dirk, stresses <u>the gracious character of the grace of regeneration</u>. God bestows it upon miserable sinners in their awful blindness.⁵⁹ It is a gift given by the Father of light and grace.⁶⁰ Those who have received this gift are again created in God's image⁶¹ and share in the nature of Christ, the second Adam, in a quasi-physical way. Christians are bone of Christ's bone and flesh of Christ's flesh.⁶²

Menno carries <u>the analogy of the new nature</u> which Christians receive from the birth out of God so far, that he can say that through it Christians are conformed

---

52 *Ibid.*, p. 150.
53 Menno Simons, *The New Birth, CWMS*, p. 92. See also *Opera Omnia Theologica*, ed. Hendrick Jansz Herrison (Amsterdam: Joannes van Veen, 1681), p. 125B.
54 *Ibid.*, p. 92. Also *Opera*, p. 125B.
55 *Ibid.*, p. 92. Also *Opera*, p. 125B.
56 *Ibid.*, pp. 93, 96–97. Also *Opera*, pp. 125B and 127B.
57 Menno Simons, *Reply to False Accusations, CWMS*, pp. 563–64.
58 *Ibid.*
59 Menno Simons, *The True Christian Faith, CWMS*, pp. 325–26.
60 Menno Simons, *A Kindly Admonition on Church Discipline, CWMS*, p. 416.
61 *Ibid.*
62 Menno Simons, *Foundation of Christian Doctrine, CWMS*, p. 148.

to the nature and image of Christ, even as he was conformed to the nature and image of God.⁶³ Through the virtue of the new birth Christians are

> so joined to Christ, are become so like unto him, so really implanted into him, so really converted into his heavenly nature... [that the relationship between Christ and the Christian is as close as that between the twig and the vine]. For how can the twig of the vine bear fruit different from that of the vine from which it springs.⁶⁴

The "learned ones," says Menno, (a term both Menno and Dirk used with reference to the theologians and ministers of the Magisterial Reformation) are unjust when they say that the Dutch Anabaptists seek their salvation in works, words, or sacraments. The Radicals know very well that those who accept Christ by a true faith are in a state of grace for Christ's sake, and have God as their Father, who grants them Jesus Christ with all his merits, fastings, prayers, tears, sufferings, cross, blood, and death, together with his spirit, inheritance, kingdom, glory, joy, and life. "And all this we say, not by our own merits and works, but by grace through Jesus Christ."⁶⁵

From the utter seriousness given by Menno to the new creature in Christ as the ontological reality which by grace made the believer a participant in the divine nature, it might be assumed that he held to the possibility of sinlessness in this life. Such, however, is not the case, although there is a strong perfectionist strain in his thought. Menno asks his readers not to think that they, the Dutch Anabaptists, boast of being perfect and without sin. So far as he is concerned he confesses often that his prayer is mixed with sin and his righteousness with unrighteousness.⁶⁶ Like Dirk, Menno is aware that along with the new nature which he has received through the birth out of God, he must still struggle with the old corrupt nature which he has received from Adam and will remain with him to the end of his days. All Christians "daily sigh and lament over their poor unsatisfactory evil flesh, the manifest errors and faults of their weak lives."⁶⁷ Yet it is because of this new nature which is the ontological result of grace, that the Christian can fight against his evil flesh, prove by his actions that he believes the Word of the Lord, that he knows and possesses Christ in power, and that he is born of God and has God as his Father.⁶⁸

Caspar Schwenckfeld's concept of grace was also related in a most intimate way to the concept of salvation as the divinization of man. One of the clearest explanations of his understanding of salvation, and in connection with it, of his idea of the "new man" as the ontological result of grace, is found in a brief work entitled *Ain Kurtze und nutsse underwehsung aines waren Christen Menschens vom alten und neuen Mensch.*⁶⁹ In this work Schwenckfeld starts with the assumption that due to the fall

63 Menno Simons, *A Kindly Admonition on Church Discipline*, CWMS, pp. 409–10.
64 *Ibid.*
65 Menno Simons, *Confession of Distressed Christians*, CWMS, pp. 504–05.
66 *Ibid.*
67 Menno Simons, *The New Birth*, CWMS, p. 95. See *Opera*, p. 125B.
68 *Ibid*, See *Opera*, p. 125B.
69 *CS*, VIII, 47–49.

Christians do not derive from the first birth out of Adam and Eve, but that they must after the first birth in the flesh be born again through a new birth in the Spirit through Jesus Christ.[70]

Schwenckfeld makes use of a distinction between God as Creator and God as Father to show that the source of the divine in him, in whom the new man has been formed, is from God rather than from man. On the level of the first birth all men, believers and unbelievers alike, have God as their creator. On the level of the second or new birth, which takes place within the old man through the regenerating power of the Holy Spirit, a new man is born who has God as his Father, because he has been *begotten of God* through the Holy Spirit in Jesus Christ.[71] God is not in this sense the Father of all men whom He has created, but only of those whom He has *begotten* in Jesus Christ,[72] who is himself the grace of God and the mercy of God.[73] The new man is thus the ontological result of God's grace within the old nature of the old man, even as is the new creature in Christ, in the thought of Menno and Dirk. Through Christ God, the Almighty Father, places within the heart of man the kernel of an eternal seed, through which He makes the flesh of man participate in His own divine nature on account of the flesh of Christ.[74]

Salvation is for Schwenckfeld also a process of the gradual deification of man, which begins in this life and ends only after death when the redeemed man is elevated to the presence of the glorified Christ. The whole process of sanctification depends, however, upon God's initial act of grace in regeneration. In this life the new man grows gradually, and the old man is gradually subdued, so that within the present life one lives at one and the same time within the order of nature and within the order of grace.[75]

One is able to judge whether he lives within the order of nature or within the order of grace by the degree to which he is able to renounce all godlessness and live an upright and godly life in this present world. Schwenckfeld says:

> We are under grace when we are in the faith of Jesus Christ, when a little strength or spark or light allows itself to be cast into our hearts out of heaven, in order that Christ may become known to us and his redemption assuring [tröstlich].[76]

Grace has the upper hand in us when we love God, acknowledge Christ as our Redeemer, fear his judgments, and "when we begin not to allow sin to reign in us unto death and never again follow the urge of sin so willingly or are obedient to it."[77]

Thus for Schwenckfeld grace embraces both the regenerating act which creates

---

70 *Ibid.*, p.47.
71 *Ibid.*, pp. 55–57.
72 Schwenckfeld, *Von der Sund und Gnad. Adam und Christo, CS*, VI, 619.
73 *CS*, VIII, 57.
74 *Ibid.*
75 *Ibid.*, VI, 631.
76 *Ibid.*, p. 632.
77 *Ibid.*

the ontological change of the new man with the nature of the old man, as well as the continuing work of the Holy Spirit in the gradual sanctification of the believer. The concept of grace as the imputation of Christ's righteousness through forensic justification plays a very minor role in the thought of Schwenckfeld.[78]

D. The Significance of the Celestial Flesh Christology

Of the seven representatives of the Radical Reformation considered in this study only four held the doctrine of the Celestial Flesh of Christ. These four, however, include all three of the Evangelical Dutch Anabaptists, and the Evangelical Spiritualist, Caspar Schwenckfeld. Schwenckfeld himself held this doctrine at an early point in his career, and he claimed to have revived it from antiquity. He read the Greek Fathers, and among them Hilary of Poitiers and Athanasius were his favorites.[79] George H. Williams thinks that Schwenckfeld may have come upon his particular form of the Celestial Flesh Christology through the doctrine associated with Appollinaris and Appelles.[80] In any case, whatever the origin of his views on the humanity of Christ, Schwenckfeld expressed them as early as 1528 and perhaps earlier. He complains in one of his many documents that in that year Zwingli had published at Zurich, without Schwenckfeld's knowledge or consent, a treatise of his on the Lord's Supper, in which his views on Christology were also expressed.[81]

Schwenckfeld was of the opinion that both Melchior Hoffmann and Sebastian Franck had borrowed their Christologies from him, but that in the process of borrowing they had also distorted the doctrine. He said of both men that they drew "error from his truth as a spider draws poison from a lovely flower."[82] Schwenckfeld was undoubtedly correct in seeing a difference between his own Christology and that of Melchior Hoffmann, for Hoffmann, too, saw the difference.

The full outlines of Schwenckfeld's Christology are complex, and in their fullness they are beyond the scope of this study. In the main, however, it is correct to say that Schwenckfeld believed that Christ received his flesh from Mary, but in such a way that both in his humanity and in his divinity Christ was the Son of God and had God as his Father. Schwenckfeld expresses this many times and seems pained by the fact that neither the Anabaptists nor the other Protestants understand his point of view. He felt that the other Protestants regarded "Christ, the man, as a creature, not only according to his first birth when he walked here

---

78 For a further discussion of the way in which Schwenckfeld understood grace in relation to justification see Koehler, pp. 356–57.
79 *ME*, IV, 1122.
80 *SAW*, p. 162.
81 *Ein Christlicher Sendbrieff vom span und rechten Mittel zwischen der Luthrischen und Zwinglischen opinion im Artickel des Herrn Nachtmals...*, *CS*, XIV, 106. Schwenckfeld says that it was because of this document published by Zwingli that he had to leave his Fatherland and that Zwingli published it, because it agreed with him against the Lutherans and their idolatrous interpretation of impanation, without knowing of the document's Christological teaching, though this was also clearly expressed in it.
82 *ME*, IV, 1121.

upon earth, but also after his glorification and deification,"[83] and that they thus robbed God of his fatherly office in the humanity of Christ and Christ of his divine sonship.[84]

On the other hand, Schwenckfeld said that there were

> certain Anabaptists whom one may designate as Hoffmannites, who say that Christ did not take his flesh from Mary, but that the Word created for himself a flesh in Mary without the aid of the Virgin and her flesh. The others say that he brought it from heaven as the heretic, Valentinus, at one time taught.[85]

Schwenckfeld did not think that the doctrine of the Celestial Flesh of Christ, as he taught it, left him open, either to the charge of the Valentinian or Eutychian heresy of denying that Christ had a human nature and teaching that he had a divine nature only,[86] though this is what opponents accused him of.

The correctness of Schwenckfeld's criticism of Hoffmann's Christology comes to light in Hoffmann's own criticism of the Christology of Schwenckfeld. T. W. Rörich records Hoffmann's express desire to be heard in Strasbourg in 1533, before Schwenckfeld and all others, who teach that Christ received his flesh from Mary, the virgin. Hoffmann says that Schwenckfeld has both written and taught such errors, while he (Hoffmann) had resisted all such teaching for the past four years.[87] Rörich also gives Hoffmann's statement of his own Christological views in regard to the origin of Christ's humanity, which are as follows:

> Jesus Christ is alone the Word of God, who himself became flesh through his divine power, and received nothing from the Virgin Mary; else she would not have remained a virgin. He is alone [from] the seed of the Spirit. Even as the water in the jars at the wedding of Cana became wine through divine power, and took unto itself no wine from the jars nor from any other wine. As the Bread from heaven, he [Christ] fell from heaven and became himself a seed [corn], but received nothing from the earth.[88]

Rörich goes on to say that Hoffmann found support for these views in his interpretation of John 6 and I Cor. 15, maintaining that the Scriptures were full of such passages which testify that Christ alone is the Word of God.[89]

The origin of Hoffmann's particular type of the Celestial Flesh Christology remains obscure at present, but it was no doubt he who transmitted it to Dirk Philips and Menno Simons. They reproduce it in almost identical form and use the same Scriptures, John 6 and I Cor. 15:22–24, in support of it.

The reason for the difference between the Christologies of Hoffmann, Menno, and Dirk, on the one hand, and that of Schwenckfeld, on the other, lay in the fact

---

83 *CS,* VI, 512.
84 *Ibid.,* XV, 314–15.
85 *Ibid.,* p. 513.
86 *Klari zeugnuss auss den Büchern dess Neuen Testaments von der göttlichen herrligkait der Menschhait Christi in der Glorien,* ca. 1541, *CS,* XII, 578.
87 T.W. Rörich, "Strassburgische Widertaüfer," *Zeitschrift für Historische Theologie,* ed. C.W. Riedner (Gotha: Frider And. Porthes, 1860), p. 69.
88 *Ibid.* See also *BRN,* V, 311.
89 Rörich, p. 69.

that for the first three men the significance of the Celestial Flesh of Christ was attached to his work as Redeemer in the incarnation and the atonement, while for Schwenckfeld it was related to the work of the reigning Christ in glory. It is now our task to clarify the part played by the Celestial Flesh of Christ in each of these roles and to show how in each instance this is related to the concept of grace. Although from the standpoint of the time of origin Schwenckfeld appears to have been the earliest to advocate this type of a Christology within the Radical Reformation, for the sake of logical presentation it will be better to begin with Hoffmann, Dirk, and Menno.

Their interest in and concern for the Celestial Flesh of Christ, from the standpoint of the incarnation, stems from their desire to keep the eternal Word unspotted by this present evil world. A significant part of Hoffmann's booklet, *Von Fleisch Christi*, has been reproduced in the so-called *Bijlagen* in the work on Hoffmann by W. I. Leendertz, pp. 387–91. Page 385 also contains a brief excerpt from Hoffmann's *Von der wahren hochprächtlichen einigen Maijestat Gottes und von der warhaftigen Menschwerdung des Weigen worts und Sohns des allerhögsten.*

In both works Hoffmann gives expression to his conviction that due to Adam's fall the whole seed of Adam was in corruption,[90] and that Christ, therefore, would have been an inadequate Redeemer if he had received his flesh from Mary, who was also of Adam's seed. Hoffmann argues that if man had been pure, then it would not have been necessary for the whole bloody mass (of humanity) to be purified by the Holy Spirit. If man had been pure, then men like Melchizedek, Enoch, Joseph, and Solomon "would have been sufficient to bring about the redemption which dwells alone in Christ, the eternal Wisdom of God."[91] Such, however, was not the case, and, therefore,

> if redemption was to be brought about, then God must send His pure, clear, and spotless Word, and allow this to become a visible and palpable [*greiflich*] person [*mensch*] which eternal Word is also the eternal life of all men.[92]

Hoffmann writes, "*Dicit eitam pelle omnia id est Christo agno fuisse inditas primas homines ut nuditas tegretur.*"[93] (He says all skin, meaning that men were all clothed with Christ, the Lamb, so that their nakedness might be covered.)

Hoffmann's concern for a pure Christ, uncontaminated with Mary's sinful flesh through his incarnation is to safeguard his adequacy as Redeemer in his atonement. Dirk and Menno follow him at this point, though they view the atonement somewhat differently. Dirk expresses his views on the incarnation as follows. He argues, as did Hoffmann, on the basis of I Cor. 15:47 that there is a distinct difference between Christ and Adam, and that "if the body of Christ had been formed by Mary, as the world foolishly says, then there would be no difference between Christ and Adam."[94] For while Adam was created out of earth by God

90 Leendertz, pp. 385 and 387.
91 *Ibid.*, p. 385.
92 *Ibid.*
93 *Ibid.*
94 Dirk Philips, *Van der Menschwerdinghe ons Heeren Jesu Christi*, BRN, X, 140.

and had no other Father than God, even as Christ was conceived in Mary through the Holy Ghost and also had no other Father than God, the whole earth is now contaminated with sin. All men are according to nature dust, and if Christ would have received his body from Mary, it would have been made from human seed which is unclean.[95]

Therefore, says Dirk, the Word which *became* flesh in Mary was holy, pure, and undefiled, and has not seen corruption, but it is the living bread which gives life to the world.[96] Dirk says that while Christ partook of flesh and blood and thus became in a measure like his brethren in all things, sin excepted, "nevertheless in his *being* he is the Word that became flesh, the second Adam, that is the second man, the Lord himself from heaven."[97] Dirk infers that the question most commonly asked by those who oppose his Christology is how it was possible for Christ to suffer and die if he did not receive his flesh and blood from Mary. He states that the question in reply is, "If the flesh of Christ is from the earth and earthy, yes, from Adam and his seed, which was of a sinful nature and cast under the curse, how could Christ have made an eternal atonement for our sins and paid for them."[98]

Dirk's concern in the manner of the incarnation of Christ as the eternal Word, like that of Hoffmann, is to keep the Redeemer free from the contamination, so that in his death he may make an adequate atonement. Menno's argument for the Celestial Flesh of Christ in relation to his incarnation is almost identical. He expresses this in three different works with somewhat varying emphasis but without significant changes.[99] Menno maintains that through the fall Adam and all his seed entered into the death announced by the Word, who created him in the event of his disobedience. Because Adam sinned it is altogether righteous that he and his descendants had to die, since they now have nothing with which to pay their debt.[100] God cannot reconcile the world unto Himself by Adam's flesh, which by God's righteousness is subject to wrath and curse.[101] Therefore, Christ's flesh cannot be from our sinful and death-guilty flesh.[102] If, says Menno, the man Christ were of the natural seed and flesh of Adam, then he would be an impure and sinful Christ.[103] Those who deny the Celestial Flesh of Christ blaspheme and rob Christ of his holy humanity.[104] Therefore, one must say of the eternal Word, not that it *took on* flesh, but that it "became a poor miserable mortal man and died a bitter death for us."[105] It is only the *pure* Christ whose death can be payment for our

---

95 *Ibid.*
96 *Ibid.*, p. 150. The reference to John 6 is obvious here, though it is not cited in the text after the usual custom of Dirk.
97 *Ibid.*, p. 149. The Scriptural reference here is I Cor. 15:47.
98 *Ibid.*, p. 150.
99 These works written in 1544 were *Brief and Clear Confession, The Incarnation of Our Lord,* and *Reply to Gellius Faber.*
100 Menno Simons, *Brief and Clear Confession, CWMS,* p. 428.
101 *Ibid.*
102 Menno Simons, *Reply to Gellius Faber, CWMS,* p. 764.
103 Menno Simons, *The Incarnation of Our Lord, CWMS,* p. 807.
104 Menno Simons, *Reply to Gellius Faber, CWMS,* p. 764.
105 Menno Simons, *The Incarnation of Our Lord, CWMS,* p. 800.

sins. Consequently, it is not those who teach the Celestial Flesh Christology who rob man of their Redeemer but rather those who deny it.[106]

It is obvious from what has been said above that all three of the Dutch Anabaptists thought of Christ's atonement as the purpose of his incarnation and of the atonement as the payment of a debt which man owed but could not pay. They differ on the question as to whom the debt was paid. Melchior Hoffmann held to the ancient theory that Christ's death was a ransom paid to the devil. Hoffmann, however, developed the theory in a rather unique way. He argues that through the fall all of Adam's seed became the property of Satan, and that Satan cannot be paid with that which is already his own;[107] hence, the necessity of the Celestial Flesh of Christ. If his flesh is from the seed of Adam, he may not introduce grace (*mag er die Gnad nit ein führen*),[108] and were it not for the Celestial Flesh of Christ, then, says Hoffmann, it would follow that

> righteousness came into existence through unrighteousness, and that life was introduced by death, the blessing by the curse, holiness by lack of holiness [*unheilkeit*], peace by discord, cleanness by uncleanness, and grace by lack of grace [*ungnad*].[109]

Within this frame of reference grace becomes the satisfaction of a debt which man owes to the devil but which he cannot pay, because the fall and original sin have left him bankrupt.

Dirk and Menno make the same emphasis on Christ's death as the satisfaction of a debt which he could not have made without the Celestial Flesh, but in their thought the satisfaction is made to God rather than to the devil. Dirk says that in order to be the Mediator between God and man, Christ had to be truly God and man. According to Christ's divinity he is fully able to help us eternally, reconcile the Father, and accomplish His will, since the will of the Father and the will of Christ are one.[110] It is in Christ's humanity, however, that "he was able to offer himself as a pure, holy, and acceptable sacrifice ... because he died guiltless for us, and human nature in him is uncontaminated and without sin."[111] Menno Simons maintains that God could not have reconciled the world to himself by Adam's flesh without compromising His righteousness, since by God's righteousness all of Adam's race was subject to wrath and curse. God's act of reconciliation through the Christ of the holy humanity is, therefore, an act of sheer grace. God has reconciled us with this pure Christ, "who became like unto the first Adam in all things, unrighteousness, disobedience, and sin excepted, in order that all honor and praise should belong to God and not to us or to Adam."[112] Menno sees it as altogether right that Adam and his seed should die, since Adam had disobeyed the Word that created him. Mankind is now bankrupt and has nothing to pay for its sin of disobedience. If man now lives at all, it must be solely by grace, mercy, and

---

106 Menno Simons, *Reply to Gellius Faber, CWMS*, p. 764.
107 Leendertz, p. 385. See also *BRN*, V, 313.
108 *Ibid.*, p. 385.
109 *Ibid.*
110 *Van der Menschwerdinghe ons Heeren Jesu Christi, BRN*, X, 139.
111 *Ibid.*
112 Menno Simons, *Brief and Clear Confession, CWMS*, pp. 428–29.

love.¹¹³ It cannot, however, be grace, if Christ's flesh is of our own sinful and death-guilty flesh, for "then the sin with which He was tempted must have dwelt in His flesh, and then He died in just recompense and not for grace."¹¹⁴

In Schwenckfeld's thought the significance of Christ's Celestial Flesh was not centered in the atonement. In fact, the atonement plays a rather minor role in Schwenckfeld's Christology. He does speak of the office of Christ's suffering, but it has more the nature of the heroic example than the sometimes crass substitutionary atonement, which is characteristic of Hoffmann, Menno, and Dirk. Schwenckfeld does speak of the death of Christ as the event in which he was made a curse for us and through which he removed the handwriting that was against us. And he does say that

> even as mothers lead their children to the graves of their fathers, or show them their father's tokens of victory [*siegzaichen*], so the newborn child of God should be led first of all to the crucified Christ, who died and was buried for sinners.¹¹⁵

Yet that which fills the whole horizon of Schwenckfeld's thought and kindles the flame of his devotion is the glorified humanity of the glorified Christ, which is somehow communicable to Christians. Christ's body which now stands before God in eternity "is the food of our souls to eternal life."¹¹⁶ It is the glorified Christ, who is the source of grace, and who communicates his grace directly to the soul of the believer through the Holy Spirit.¹¹⁷

Although the Christologies of Hoffmann, Menno, Dirk, and Schwenckfeld have Gnostic tendencies, they did not, as did the Gnostics, wish to deny that Jesus had a truly human nature. The problem for them was rather what was the source and substance of that humanity. Since humanity was corrupted through the fall and the corruption was passed on to all succeeding generations, how can Jesus be an adequate Redeemer if he partakes of our own sinful nature? At the time that these men wrote, the dogma of the immaculate conception of Mary, which removes the problem one generation, was not yet accepted even in the Roman Catholic Church. Proposed by Pope Sixtus IV, whose reign extended from 1471 to 1484, the immaculate conception was not declared a dogma until December 8, 1854.

In an attempt to solve this problem both Menno and Dirk used an incarnation formula, which they apparently borrowed from Hoffmann. The formula in English is Jesus Christ conceived *in* Mary *by* the Holy Spirit but born *out of* Mary rather than *from* Mary. The intent of this formula was to show that as the eternal Word in his divinity is begotten of God (*van God gheboren*) in eternity before all worlds began, so in his incarnation his humanity is begotten of God through the

---

113 *Ibid.*, p. 438.
114 Menno Simons, *Reply to Gellius Faber, CWMS*, p. 764. It should be noted that it was easier for Menno to accept the Celestial Flesh Christology, because he believed that the woman's role in normal reproduction was an entirely passive one.
115 *CS*, XIV, 112.
116 For a fuller treatment of this phase of Schwenckfeld's thought see Chapter IV.
117 *CS*, VIII, 238.

Holy Spirit.[118] The human nature of Jesus is nourished in Mary's body but does not receive its substance from her. It is, therefore, similar to the nature which Adam had before the fall.

The English translation of this formula partially hides a very careful distinction between the Dutch prepositions, *door, uit,* and *van,* which was already present in Hoffmann and later taken up by Menno and Dirk, where it was used with even greater care. The distinction between *van* and *uit* was particularly crucial for their understanding of the incarnation. According to their view Jesus is born out (*uit*) of Mary but not from (*van*) Mary.[119]

Schwenckfeld wished to make essentially the same distinction when he insisted that both in his humanity and in his divinity Christ was the Son of God. Where Menno and Dirk used the Dutch prepositions, *uit* and *van,* however, Schwenckfeld made use of the concepts of God as Father, on one hand, and as Creator, on the

---

118 Hoffmann, *Die ... sendebrief to den Romeren ... verclaert, BRN,* V, 311–12.
119 See the following works by Menno, together with references to specific pages, where the prepositions *uit* and *van* are used in this manner:
   Foundations of Christian Doctrine; CWMS, pp. 115, 144.
   Dat Fundament der Christelycker Leere, Opera, pp. 9B, 25A.
   Brief and Clear Confession, CWMS, pp. 428, 433, 434, 435, 436.
   Een Fundament en Klare aenwysinge van de salighmakende Leere Jesu Christi, Opera, pp. 525B, 527A, 529A, 530A, 531A.
   Reply to Gellius Faber, CWMS, p. 766.
   Een klare Beantwoordinge over een Schrift Gellii Fabri, Opera, p. 315.
   The Incarnation of Our Lord, CWMS, pp. 807, 828, 832.
   Een klare onwederspreekelyke Bekentenisse en Aenwysinge ... dat de geheele Christus Jesus, Godt en Mensche, Mensche en Godt, Gods eengeboren en Eerstgeboren eygen Sone is ... Met een grondelijke Confutation, Beantwoordinge en Oplossinge der voornaemster Tegenspreuken van Johanne a Lasco, Opera, pp. 367B, 379B, 382A.
   Reply to Martin Micron, CWMS, pp. 866, 884, 886, 907, 909;
   Een gantsch duidlyk ende bescheyden Antwoordt ... op Martini Microns, Opera, pp. 566A, 577A, 579A, 593A, 595A.
Following are the works of Dirk Philips, together with the page references in *BRN,* X, in which the prepositions, *uit* and *van,* are used in the incarnation formula in the same manner in which Hoffmann and Menno also used them:
   Bekentenisse onses gheloofs, BRN, X, 63.
   Van dat Auontmael, BRN, X, 115.
   Van der Menschwerdinge ons Heeren Jesu Christi, BRN, X, 139.
   Vande rechte kennisse Jesu Christi, BRN, X, 165, 166.
   Vande Gemeynte Godts, BRN, X, 383, 391.
   Een Lieffelijcke Vermaninge, BRN, X, 447.
For a complete and very competent analysis of the use which Menno and Dirk made of the Dutch prepositions, *uit* and *van,* in their theory of the incarnation, as well as in their soteriology, see the unpublished thesis of William Keeney, Appendix II, pp. 333–351. Keeney is the first modern scholar to see the vital connection between Christology and soteriology in Menno and Dirk. Perhaps he has seen the connection even more clearly than Menno himself saw it, for Menno said that he never preached about this theory of the incarnation before the congregation and that there were some brethren who had never heard it. From its soteriological side, however, they must have heard it every time they heard Menno preach. See Menno's introduction to *Brief and Clear Confession, CWMS,* pp. 427–30.
   John C. Wenger, who edits the *Complete Writings of Menno Simons,* is embarrassed by the Christological arguments and suggests that there is little profit in them for the average reader. *CWMS,* pp. 836–37.

other hand. God, the Father, begets the humanity of Jesus in and from Mary through the Holy Spirit in such a manner that original sin is eliminated from him. Mary is, therefore, not the beginning, ground, and origin of this man.[120] In the experience of salvation this formula is reversed, so that God through regeneration becomes the Father of the new man, while He is the Creator of all men.[121]

---

120 *CS,* VI, pp. 236, 237, 239.
121 See pp. 70–72 above.

CHAPTER IV

THE GRACE OF CHRIST AND THE CHURCH OF CHRIST

*A. The Church as the Community of the
New Covenant of Grace*

The recent contributions of several scholars in the field of Radical Reformation thought have helped to clarify the history of the period by showing that two different concepts of the nature of the Church prevailed between the Radical and Magisterial Reformation groups of the sixteenth century. The latter accepted in essence the view of medieval Catholicism in which the Church as the *Corpus Christi* was regarded as coextensive with society as the *Corpus Christianum.* The Magisterial Reformers modified this concept of the nature of the Church only very slightly with their concept of the *folkskirche*, in which Church and society were also regarded as coextensive.

The Radicals rejected both these views of the nature of the Church and developed in their stead a view which emphasized what might be called the *otherness* of the Church. The aim of the Radical Reformers in general, and of the Evangelical Anabaptists in particular, was to recapture the New Testament ideal of the Church as it had existed during the *golden age* of the Church's life during the apostolic period. Behind this consciously chosen aim to recover the Church's golden age there lies an almost universal conviction among the Radicals that either at some particular *point in history*, or during a period of time sufficiently far removed from the apostolic age to allow abuses to creep into the Church's life, she had fallen either *abruptly* or *gradually* from her apostolic foundations.[1]

In this *gathered* Church or *rechte Kirche*[2] the necessary tension between the believing Church and the nonbelieving world was zealously guarded and maintained. The editors of the *Bibliotheca Reformatoria Neerlandica* note, for example, that in all of the writings of Dirk Philips there is a strong dualism between the Church and the world. The editors comment as follows:

---

1 For an excellent discussion of the various dates when the fall of the Church supposedly occurred, which is based upon primary sources, see James Leo Garrett, "The Nature of the Church According to the Radical Continental Reformation," *MQR*, XXXII, No. 2 (April, 1958), 112–13.

2 Littell, *The Anabaptist View of the Church.* Littell uses the term, *rechte Kirche*, and interprets the whole Anabaptist movement from the focal point of the fall and reconstitution of the Church.

Frank J. Wray in "The Anabaptist Doctrine of the Restitution of the Church," *MQR*, XXVIII, No. 3 (July, 1954), 186, sees the difference in the two Reformation groups in their approach to recovering the characteristics of the early Church. According to Wray the key to the Church concept of the Magisterial Reformers was *reformatio*, while that of the Radicals or Anabaptists was *restitutio*. Wray says, "In the point of view of the former a remnant remained within the Great Church and the task was to free the Great Church from the control of the papal Antichrist and to remove the abominations which had been introduced... The medieval church was beyond hope. The children of God must be recalled from exile. They must rebuild the true church upon apostolic foundations."

> The Church is always set over against the world. There is a complete difference between Christians and the world, between the world and Christ's disciples. Christians are to forsake all creatures and every earthly thing. Salvation can only take place in terms of being redeemed out of this evil world and out of this spiritual Egypt.[3]

What is here said of Dirk can equally well be said of all the other Evangelical Anabaptists whose names appear in this study. For them the true Church was always the Church of Christ *against* culture.[4] The true Church as viewed by the Evangelical Spiritualist, Caspar Schwenckfeld, was a church in the Spirit, which transcended all historical time and all external forms of worship.[5]

The Evangelical Anabaptists sought to maintain the Church as the "holy community" in separation from the evil world by making believer's baptism the door of entrance to the Church and the ban the door of expulsion from the Church, for those who manifested either by carnal life or false doctrine that they were no longer vitally joined either to the other members of the community or to Christ, its only Head. The Church so understood was a community made up of individuals who had availed themselves of the new opportunities that were now open to mankind because of the grace of God in Christ. The Church was indeed the community of the new covenant of grace, formed by God's regenerating act of grace and held together by the mystical union with Christ. The separation of the Church, so constituted, from the evil world was not an end in itself, but a means toward an end – that of safeguarding the *corporateness* of the Church *in* Christ.

It is the aim of this chapter to show that the corporateness of the *Church in Christ* is not unrelated to the Johannine concept of salvation and to the Celestial Flesh Christology, which was so prevalent throughout the Radical Reformation. Both ideas had far-reaching implications, as they were applied to the metaphors of the Church as the *bride of Christ* or the *body of Christ*. When these were used together with the Christ-mysticism with reference to the Church, the Church became nearly a quasi-physical extension of the body of her Lord.

Not all of the representatives of the Radical Reformation considered in this study stress with equal emphasis the *otherness* of the Church in its separation

---

3 *BRN*, X, Introduction, 50.
4 For a further elaboration of the "Christ against culture" stance of the Radical Reformers see H. Richard Niebuhr, *Christ and Culture* (New York: Harper and Bros., 1951), Chapter II. See also Hans J. Hillerbrand, "The Anabaptist View of the State," *MQR*, XXXII, No. 2 (April, 1958). Hillerbrand in his final summary calls attention to what he designates the Anabaptist dualism between the kingdom of Christ and this world. He describes it as a radical protest against the medieval synthesis of the kingdom of Christ and the world. He writes, "The world takes on almost sociological and geographical connotations and does not fall – as with Luther – into the inside of the Christian individual with the *simul iustus, simul peccator* doctrine. Or, to use Augustine's terminology, the *civitas terranee* becomes *civitas diaboli.*" Pp. 109–10. Dirk in his *Vande Gemeynte Godt* does speak of the emergence of two kinds of people with the birth of Cain and Abel, the former representing the synagogue of Satan; the latter, the Church of God. See *BRN*, X, 382.
5 See Schwenckfeld's *Judicium* of Pilgram Marbeck's *Vermanung* of 1542, *CS*, VIII, 169 and 184–85, where Schwenckfeld says that the *Taufbrüder* do wrong in that they equate their brotherhood with that of the apostolic church and objects to the phrase that "baptism is the narrow door of entrance to the Church," maintaining that this robs Christ of his glory.

from culture nor the corporateness of the Church in Christ in terms of the mystical union. Nor do they all feel that they are personally engaged in the task of reconstituting the fallen church. Hans Denck, as George H. Williams had indicated, was more the Contemplative Anabaptist,[6] whose chief concern was the development of the inner life, rather than the upbuilding of the Church as a disciplined brotherhood. Yet Denck was for a brief time the undisputed leader of the South German Anabaptist movement,[7] and as such he did develop a concept of the Church as a converted and disciplined brotherhood, separated from the evil world. It is clearly evident from what Denck writes of baptism, the Lord's Supper, and the ban, that he thought of the Church as a group of converted individuals who had separated themselves from the evil world and all uncleanness of the flesh in order that they might serve the Lord alone and turn their backs on the old sinful life.[8] Yet even as the Church was separated from the sinful world by conversion, it was united in a fellowship of love where the brethren were prepared to have their bodies broken for each other, even as the Lord's body was broken for them.[9] The members of the Church are "children of the covenant," who live in holiness and separation from the world,[10] and who, because they are in the service of love may not use force to resist evil, but must rather serve God and His grace.[11]

James Leo Garrett in the article referred to above found four ecclesiological types within the Radical Reformation, none of which seemed to fit exactly Balthasar Hubmaier's concept of the Church.[12] This Garrett attributes to the fact that Hubmaier was steeped by training in Catholic ecclesiology and to the fact that he took up the distinction of the universal and particular churches employed by the Magisterial Reformers, and joined it to Anabaptist distinctives.[13] Garrett thinks that the present social consequences of the corporateness of the Church as

---

6 *SAW*, p. 87.
7 Jan J. Kiwiet, "The Theology of Hans Denck," *MQR*, XXXII, No. 1 (January, 1958). Kiwiet states that the statements which appear in the court testimonies of the South German Anabaptists such as "Providence is not predestination," "God is not the originator of sin," "Baptism is the covenant of a good conscience with God," seem to stem from Denck's teachings. Kiwiet is here quoting from Sebastian Franck, *Chronica* (Strasbourg, 1536) Part III, 198. See p. 27, *MQR* article cited in this footnote. In the same article, p. 25, Kiwiet states that "Pilgram Marbeck and his friends were the continuation of Denck's ideas."
8 Hans Denck, *Von der wahren Liebe*, 1527, *QFR*, Band XXIV, 2 Teil, 81–82.
9 Hans Denck, *Ordnung Gottes*, *QFR*, Band XXIV, 2 Teil, 101.
10 Hans Denck, *Von der wahren Liebe*, *QFR*, Band XXIV, 2 Teil, 82–83.
11 *Ibid.*, p. 84–85.
12 These four types as defined by Garrett, pp. 115, 117–18, and 120, are paraphrased and condensed as follows:

a. The Church as a restored or gathered congregation or brotherhood of baptized believers under discipline and separated from the world and from the State. This type, says Garrett, was developed by the Swiss Brethren, the South German Anabaptists, and the Mennonites of North Germany, the Netherlands, and Prussia.

b. The Church-community as developed by the Hutterian Brethren. Hutterites shared with Anabaptists the ideas of a gathered, baptized, and disciplined congregation, separated from the world, but held also to the apostolicity and necessity of community of goods.

c. The Church-kingdom, which at Münster issued in a church-kingdom-state.

d. Schwenckfeld had the concept of the inward, invisible, universal, spiritual Church, ungathered without external sacraments or worship.
13 *Ibid.*, p. 122.

a body of the saved and forgiven did not attract Hubmaier's attention. It is true, as Garrett indicates, that Hubmaier kept more of the Catholic thought forms than any other of the Radical Reformers and that, therefore, the distinctions he made were between the universal and the particular church, rather than between the fallen and the restored church. "The particular church may err, but the universal Church is infallible."[14] Yet, it is fair to question whether Hubmaier was unaware of the present social consequences of the Church as a congregation of the newborn. It was after all through the new grace made available to men in Christ that men were born again through faith and admitted to membership in the Church by believer's baptism. It is only *within* the Church that is so constituted that "the conditions of paradise are restored. Outside it the will is in bondage to worldly flesh and there is no salvation."[15] This at least had implications for the manner in which the Church of Christ, formed by the grace of Christ, should conduct her corporate life, and these implications become clear in what Hubmaier had to say about the *manner* in which the Church should administer baptism, observe the Supper, and practice the ban. The discussion here is not concerned with what these *objectively are* but *how and by whom* they should be administered. In this Church the candidate who presents himself for baptism pledges that he will both participate in the discipline *of* the congregation and submit himself to discipline *by* the congregation. The Supper is properly observed only when it occurs at a meeting of the faithful who have gathered together at a previously specified time and place.[16] In the same work Hubmaier refers to the Church as the "holy community" (*die gemainschaft der heligen*), which has the key to ceasing (*ablassung*) from sin.[17] The Church as the holy community, formed by the new grace that has been offered to men in Christ, is also the bride of Christ, and it is her duty to keep herself pure. This is done through the use of the ban, and when the necessity to use it arises, it shall be the entire congregation (*die gantze Gemain*) which both hears the accusation and pronounces the sentence.[18] Certainly these aspects of Hubmaier's thought show that he was aware of the social consequences of his view of the Church so far as the Church's *corporate life* was concerned. It is true that he did not carry the Church's separation from the world so far as did his contemporaries within the Radical Reformation, but he was no more anxious than they to have the corporate life of the Church ruled by the state.[19]

It is, however, Melchior Hoffmann, Dirk Philips, Menno Simons, and Pilgram Marbeck, who in varying ways make the most of the Church as a community of the new covenant of grace. Hoffmann in his most important work, *Die Ordonnan-*

---

14 *Twelve Articles of Christian Belief*, trans. Howard Osgood, in Henry C. Vedder, *Balthasar Hübmaier* (New York and London: G. P. Putnam's Sons, 1905), pp. 134f.
15 *SAW*, p. 113.
16 Hubmaier, *Eine Form des Nachtmahles Christi*, 1527.
17 *Ibid.*
18 Hubmaier, *Vom christlichen Bann*, 1527.
19 In *Vom Schwert*, 1527, Hubmaier rejected the widely held Anabaptist position that a Christian should not hold office or wield the sword. (See Chapter VI for details.) But in the same work he makes it clear that he would not have the Church disciplined by the government. This the Church itself does through the use of the ban.

tie Godts, ca. 1530, refers to the Church as the Bride of Christ. Christ, who is the mouth of the spiritual Moses, is ever sending forth his apostolic emissaries who assemble for him his Bride out of the bonds of darkness and from the realm and power of Satan and to bring them (her) into the Kingdom of God and of the Lord Jesus Christ.[20] The apostolic emissaries of Jesus Christ gather the elect flock and call it through the Gospel from all corners of the earth.[21] The Church as the Bride of Christ is betrothed to him in the new covenant,[22] and individual believers are completely wedded to Christ by the grace of God.[23] Writing with reference to the Lord's Supper, Hoffmann said that "the many brides become *one* [italics mine] congregation,"[24] and thus the Church corporately, as well as individuals, becomes the "Bride of the Lord and he, the husband and bridegroom."[25]

The Church corporately is for Hoffmann also

> the brotherhood and heavenly band of all peoples who have been called wherever they are in the world that they might become the children of God and His Holy Spirit and heirs of His eternal kingdom.[26]

Hoffmann stresses the voluntary character of the newborn believer's entrance into the corporate Church. God compels no one to come, for compulsion would violate the gracious character of the new covenant. God's deliberate exclusion of some part of humanity from the community of the new covenant by means of predestination would be both a violation of man's restored freedom of the will and a defeat of God's desire that all men should be saved.[27]

Almost identical emphases are discernible in the thought of Menno Simons with regard to the nature of the Church. Menno, like Hoffmann, asks those who are members of the Church to remember that they "*voluntarily* accepted the covenant of the Most High, and that they *voluntarily* buried in baptism all that was not Christlike in them."[28] (Italics mine) The Church is, on the one hand, the *holy community* separated from the evil world, and on the other hand, it is the community which expresses in its corporate life the redeeming love and power of the crucified and risen Christ, both for its individual members and for the sinful world.

Menno asks his readers not to be alarmed at the term, *holy Church*. They must learn that not all who appropriate the name, Jesus Christ, and think themselves to be the true Christian Church are so regarded by him.[29] Those who are unbelievers,

---

20 *SAW*, p. 185. Also *BRN*, V, 148. Hoffmann in this selection is constantly shifting from the individual believer as the Bride of Christ to the Church or rather the congregation, which is collectively his Bride.
21 *SAW*, p. 185. *BRN*, V, 148.
22 *SAW*, p. 188. *BRN*, V, 153.
23 *SAW*, p. 188. *BRN*, V, 153.
24 *SAW*, p. 191. *BRN*, V, 159.
25 *SAW*, p. 196. *BRN*, V, 159.
26 *SAW*, p. 197. *BRN*, V, 160.
27 *SAW*, pp. 189 and 198. See also *BRN*, V, 150, or Chapter II, p. 54–55 above.
28 Menno Simons, *A Kindly Admonition on Church Discipline, CWMS*, p. 410.
29 Menno Simons, *Christian Baptism*, 1539, *CWMS*, p. 234.

or carnal and brazen sinners, are not the Christian Church, no matter what they may call themselves.[30] The door of entrance to the true and holy Church is so narrow that those who desire by grace to pass through it must leave hanging on its doorposts all gold and goods, all flesh and blood, and all evil inclinations.[31] Clearly, the true Church is for Menno the Church of those who have experienced God's act of regeneration, who are, as Menno says, "born out of God." He writes:

> They are not all Abraham's seed who are born of Abraham. Only the children of the promise are counted as the seed. Rom. 9:8. So also the holy Christian Church must be a spiritual seed, an assembly of the righteous, and a community of the saints; which is begotten of God, of the living seed of the divine Word, and not of the teachings, institutions and fictions of man.[32]

Menno's use of the two phrases, "The community of saints" and "begotten of the seed of the divine Word," with reference to the true Church carry special significance for his understanding of the corporate life of the Church. The first phrase, as James Leo Garrett has observed, has "no connotation of a relation between the 'church militant' and the 'church triumphant,' but is expressive of that corporate unity which now characterizes God's holy people."[33] This corporate unity was no hollow expression for Menno. Being a member of the community involved one in concern for the spiritual and material welfare of others, even to the point of the risk of one's own life and property. In *The True Christian Faith* Menno finds an example of the true faith in Abraham, who risked his life to rescue Lot, his kinsman, from the hands of his enemies. Gen. 14:13–24. So Christians should love their brethren who are with them "born of the incorruptible seed of the holy divine Word,"[34] that they will not only assist them with money and goods, but also when we see them

> driven forth for the Word of the Lord, then we should not close our doors to them, but receive them in our houses and share with them our food, aid them, comfort them, and assist them in their tribulations... In such a manner should risk our lives for the brethren, even if we know beforehand that it will cost us our lives.[35]

The relationship between Christ and the Christian was so close in Menno's thought, that to refuse shelter to a brother, who like oneself had been born of God, of the incorruptible seed of the divine Word, would have been equivalent to refusing it to Christ himself. This close relationship is brought about by the fact that those who with Christ are born of one Father (John 1:13) are flesh of Christ's flesh and bone of his bone. Eph. 5:30. Corporately the individual

30 *Ibid.*
31 *Ibid.*, p. 252.
32 *Ibid.*, p. 234.
33 Garrett, p. 125.
34 Menno Simons, *The True Christian Faith, CWMS*, p. 347.
35 *Ibid.*, pp. 347–48. After the outlawing of the Anabaptist movement by imperial decree at the Diet of Speyer in 1529, it became a crime punishable by death to give shelter to an Anabaptist. J. C. Wenger notes on p. 299 in a footnote in *CWMS* that more than 2,000 Dutch Anabaptists were martyred during the sixteenth century!

believers are Christ's "spotless, holy, and pure Bride, whom He in great love has wed."[36]

The phrase, "begotten of the seed of the divine Word," has special significance for Menno, as he uses it with reference to the Church as Christ's pure and spotless Bride. Both Menno and Dirk thought of the Church as the Bride of Christ, who is impregnated by Christ, her Bridegroom, with the seed of the divine Word, which in this case is the word of Scripture. If the Church bears children that originate from the doctrines, institutions, and fictions of man, then she is no longer a faithful bride, but an adultress, and the children she bears are not true children, but bastards.[37]

Thus, the pure Church without spot or wrinkle was for Menno, as well as for Dirk, a quasi-physical extension of the incarnation. The Celestial Flesh Christology of both men, noted in Chapter III, was not without its influence upon their concept of the Church. The Church so constituted is the community of the new covenant in grace. The covenant which God now makes with His people is not dependent upon any external signs, but is established by grace alone.[38]

Dirk Philips in his *Vande Gemeynte Godts* speaks of the seven ordinances of the true Church. These were the pure unadulterated doctrine of the Word, correct or true ministers, Scriptural use of baptism and the Lord's Supper, footwashing, and evangelical separation, including the ban, brotherly love according to Christ's command, the keeping of all Christ's commands, and suffering and persecution.[39] In the third section of this work Dirk compares characteristics of the true Church with the new Jerusalem described in Rev. 21. A comparison of the seven ordinances of the true Church with the characteristics of the new Jerusalem reveals the fact that for Dirk also the separation of the Church from the evil world, or the severing of the Church of God from the synagogue of Satan was but a means to the end of the corporateness of the Church in Christ as a community organized by the divine will, which the penitent enters at the door of grace through rebirth. As Garrett has observed, Dirk's interpretation of the Church as the new Jerusalem "is present rather than eschatological."[40] The emphasis in this section is on the corporateness of the Church in Christ. Only those who are born again of God and created anew in His image in their inner being can be members of this Church or congregation.[41] God founded His first congregation on earth with pure and holy people who had been made in His likeness and image, and, therefore, He still desires in His congregation people who are created in Jesus Christ and renewed by the Holy Spirit.[42]

Those who are thus born of God, created in Jesus Christ, and renewed by the Holy Spirit, are members of the household of God and citizens of the new Jerusa-

---

36 Menno Simons, *Christian Baptism, CWMS*, p. 285.
37 Menno Simons, *Foundation of Christian Doctrine*, pp. 164–65. Also Dirk Philips, *Vande geestelijcke Restitution, BRN*, X, 344.
38 Menno Simons, *Foundation of Christian Doctrine*, p. 125.
39 *BRN*, X, 393–406. For the English translation see *SAW*, pp. 228–60.
40 Garrett, p. 123.
41 *BRN*, X, 387.
42 *Ibid.*, pp. 386–87.

lem.[43] The Church may be appropriately called a city for the reason that in the Church as in a city there must be concord, which is achieved by the common consent of church members and citizens to be governed by the same law and polity.[44] Within the congregation of God this concord is achieved through the Holy Spirit, who is Christ's indwelling spiritual presence on earth, while he is bodily in heaven.[45] Christians, who are born of God, may rightly be called the new heaven and the new earth, for God dwells in the hearts of those who have received the seed of the divine Word and through the grace of God have been renewed through the power of the Holy Spirit.[46] The entrance to the congregation of God is the "door of grace," which is always open to penitent believers.[47]

Dirk, like Hoffmann and Menno, stresses the voluntary character of the penitent and newborn believer's entrance into the gathered congregation of God. Christ is the spiritual Isaac, who desires for himself a bride who comes voluntarily, even as did the literal Isaac.[48] Christ is also the second Adam, and the Church, his Bride, which has been taken out of his side, and is, therefore, bone of his bone and flesh of his flesh.[49] The Church in turn is the spiritual Eve, who is the mother of all Christians, "for from her have come and sprung the new earth, the new race, the new newborn children of God, who were born out of God's imperishable seed, that is from His living and powerful Word, and who issued from his Bride."[50]

The Church so constituted is in reality a quasi-physical extension of the incarnation. Christ is its Head, and its members are flesh of his flesh and bone of his bone, for they have become through the waterbath of the Word (Dirk means here the Word of Scripture), the Church without spot or wrinkle, and are actually made to participate in the divine nature.[51]

Repeatedly throughout his treatise on the Church, Dirk makes use of the covenant concept. When the first Church, which started with the angels in heaven, fell, God reconstituted it with Adam and Eve in Paradise. When they sinned and were driven from Paradise, God reconstituted the Church with the covenant and promise of the Redeemer, which was the first preaching of the Gospel. The covenant is renewed with Noah and again with Abraham.[52] Thus the Church is for Dirk in every age the covenant people of God, and it is always God, who takes the initiative in renewing the covenant.[53] Though Dirk does not speak of a fall of the Church within a distinctly Christian history, it is nevertheless clear that he thought of himself and his Anabaptist contemporaries as actively engaged in the

---

43 *Ibid.*, p. 409.
44 *Ibid.*, pp. 409–10. See *SAW*, p. 255, for the English translation.
45 Dirk Philips, *Vande geestelijcke Restitution, BRN*, X, 343.
46 *Ibid.*
47 *Ibid.*, p. 412.
48 *Ibid.*, p. 350.
49 *Ibid.*, p. 346.
50 *Ibid.*
51 *Ibid.*, p. 410. See *SAW*, p. 256, for the English translation. The conception of the Church here described rests upon Eph. 5:23; 1:22 and II Pet. 1:4.
52 *Ibid.*, pp. 381–84.
53 *Ibid.*, pp. 384–85. Dirk also speaks of a Church of God which existed from the beginning outside of the covenant relationship with Israel among those who followed the law of nature "inscribed by God in their hearts." See *SAW*, pp. 232–33, for the English translation.

task of reconstituting the Church upon its true apostolic foundations. Through their efforts Dirk believed that God would once again renew His covenant and reëstablish His Church as the community of the reborn children of God in the new covenant of grace.[54]

It is, however, in the thought of Pilgram Marbeck that the idea of the Church as the community of the new covenant of grace appears most clearly. Both Menno and Dirk found a large measure of continuity between Israel as the first covenant people of God and the Church as the new and spiritual Israel. For Marbeck there was no continuity, but rather a radical discontinuity. All that had gone before Christ was but a *shadow of the reality* of all the good that had come in Christ. Commenting on the great difference between the two covenants as he understood them, Marbeck points out that under the old covenant there was an element of compulsion. The command to Abraham to circumcise, which was the sign of the old covenant, involved the circumcision of children and slaves who could thus be included in the old covenant *without* their consent.[55] This cannot be under the new covenant.

> For in the New Testament, he who would enter into a covenant with God and desire to be comforted with His promise, he must (as must everyone) believe for himself. It matters not that he was born of people who were already Christians, for even as the light is differentiated from the lamp and the picture from reality, so much difference is there between Abraham's promise and race, and between Christians, as every reasonable person [*verständiger mensch*], who can distinguish between the Old and the New Testaments can easily comprehend.[56]

In the thought of Marbeck it is the "grace of today" in contrast to the "grace of yesterday," which makes possible the new covenant of grace. In all three of Marbeck's major works, the *Vermanung, Verantwortung,* and *Testamentserläuterung,* the difference between the old and the new covenants is determined by the new grace which is made available through the finished work of Christ. The old covenant, whether made with Noah or Abraham, involved only a temporal deliverance or a temporal inheritance.[57] The covenant with Abraham, instead of being one and continuous with Christ's new covenant, into which men entered voluntarily on the basis of their own faith in Christ, was the covenant of a promise not yet fulfilled.[58] The patriarchs, and all who lived before the time of Christ, were born into servitude (*knechtschaft*) and did not enjoy the actual (*wesentliche*) inheritance of what was promised under the old covenant until the new covenant or testament was established through the death of the one who made it.[59] No one, argues Marbeck, could become a Christian, or a spiritual child of God, until the

---

54 *BRN*, X, pp. 369–72.
55 Marbeck, *Vermanung*, p. 226.
56 *Ibid.*
57 Marbeck, *Testamentserläuterung*, pp. 133–34.
58 *Ibid.*, p. 134.
59 *Ibid.*, p. 132. Marbeck maintains that *covenant and testament* mean the same thing. His argument here rests largely upon Heb. 8, 9, and 10, where the supremacy of the new and better covenant established through Christ's perfect sacrifice, made once for all, is emphasized.

grace of God in Christ had arrived through the establishment of the "covenant of today."[60]

The "covenant of today" is made possible, both because Christ has now made atonement for the sins of the whole world and because as the risen and ascended Lord, he can now bestow the gift of the Holy Spirit in its plenitude upon those who are able to believe for themselves and through faith be born as children of God.[61]

This meant for Marbeck that he and his brotherhood had not only the authority, but also the duty, to reconstitute the Church as a gathered and disciplined community of believers only, who had voluntarily entered into the new covenant with God and pledged themselves through the power of the Holy Spirit to lead a new life for the remainder of their days.[62] Marbeck maintained that the Church had remained true to her apostolic foundations for a thousand years after the time of Christ,[63] and he held that if the custom of infant baptism had not been introduced, the Church would have retained her original purity as the community of those who were reborn through supernatural grace.[64]

This corporate nature of the Church as a regenerate, rathered, and disciplined people of the new covenant, had for Marbeck the deepest significance. The Church, as reconstituted on its apostolic foundations, was for him not only the community of the new covenant of grace. It was in its corporateness actually an extension of the incarnation, Christ's nonglorified body on earth.[65] To be received into membership in this Church was at the same time to be taken up into Christ as a member of his body. The task of the Christian as he now becomes through supernatural grace a newborn child of God is to live as Christ did while he was on earth (*Christus nach zu folgen oder gleichformich zu wandlen*).[66] The mystical union between Christ and his Church in Marbeck's thought is thus developed in terms of the Pauline metaphor of the body, rather than in terms of the bridal imagery, which is found in Hoffmann, Menno, and Dirk — and without the Celestial Flesh Christology. But the reality of that mystical union is no less intense.

Marbeck's sharp distinction between the old and the new covenants, his insistence that Abraham and the other patriarchs could not become Christians or

---

60 Marbeck, *Testamentserläuterung*, p. 134; *Vermanung*, pp. 226–28; *Verantwortung*, pp. 191–92.
61 Marbeck, *Verantwortung*, pp. 191–92, 85–86. Marbeck's argument here rests upon John 7:39, "Now this he said about the Spirit which those who believed in him were to receive; for as yet the Spirit had not been given because Jesus was not yet glorified." See also *Vermanung*, p. 219.
62 Marbeck, *Verantwortung*, pp. 85–86.
63 *Ibid.*, p. 526.
64 Marbeck, *Vermanung*, p. 221.
65 Marbeck, *Verantwortung*, p. 140. Marbeck was really aiming here at a criticism of Schwenckfeld's doctrine of the glorified Christ. He said that this doctrine turned the attention of men away from that which they *now are in Christ,* i.e., his suffering, nonglorified body, to that which they *should become* in the future life.
66 See Marbeck's *Verantwortung*, pp. 140 and 160, and *Vermanung*, p. 219. Marbeck emphasizes that the Christian is through faith born into a life of suffering from which he is freed only at death. The full significance of this aspect of Marbeck's thought is discussed under Sec. E in this chapter, "Suffering as a Mark of the True Church."

God's spiritual children before the finished work of the Man Christ,[67] seemed to Schwenckfeld the most weighty of errors.[68] Schwenckfeld's concept of the Church, as we have seen, was that of the inward, invisible, universal, and spiritual Church. He, therefore, found Marbeck's sharp distinction on the difference between the two covenants and the communities that were formed by them totally incompatible with his spiritualizing tendencies. Schwenckfeld said that the authors of the *Vermanung* by these assertions actually introduce another Christ, whom they always judge

> alone according to his physical or bodily presence. Because of this they do not wish to know anything about a church of Christ which existed also *in the Spirit* before his coming and resurrection.[69]

Schwenckfeld, like Dirk Philips, considered the Old Testament worthies, Adam, Enoch, and Noah, Christians and members of the Church which began almost as soon as the world was created.[70] Therefore, the authors of the *Vermanung*, who do not wish to admit that the holy fathers, patriarchs, and prophets were Christians or children of God and friends of God along with us or that they, too, have had forgiveness of sins, the good conscience with God and the Holy Spirit, have fallen into grievous error and that for two reasons. They know neither the *course of grace* nor the *character of faith!* [71]

The authors of the *Vermanung*, writes Schwenckfeld, are deficient in their understanding of Christian truth, because they think of the gracious activity of God as first beginning with Judaism in the covenant of circumcision, whereas the covenant of grace in actuality existed much earlier before God than the covenant of circumcision. God has from the very beginning of time practiced this grace of the new covenant, although in a hidden manner with the elect and pious fathers, so that they, too, are heirs and joint-heirs of the new covenant in Jesus Christ. The authors of the *Vermanung* show that they lack maturity, because they do not know that "true faith brings that which is in the future to the believing heart."[72]

> The believing man according to the truth of faith comes into possession of all that which he believes. Therefore, the patriarchial fathers had Christ before his incarnation as well as we. Yes, as we and all believers have benefitted in the humanity of Christ from the beginning of the world, so do we and all those benefit who now believe. For as our faith in the birth of Christ, as already occurred and everything fulfilled in him looks backward, so the faith of those who became redeemed before the birth of Christ looked forward to our Lord Jesus Christ, who is the *one* Saviour of all men, those of old and those of the present.[73] (Italics mine)

67 Marbeck, *Vermanung*, pp. 235–36.
68 Schwenckfeld, *Judicium, CS*, VIII, 199.
69 *Ibid.*, pp. 197–98.
70 *Ibid.*, p. 197. Schwenckfeld adds the phrase, *"although in a hidden manner,"* and on this point neither Dirk nor Menno would have been in agreement with him. The true Church must always be visibly manifest before and separated from the always evil world. (Italics mine)
71 *Ibid.*, pp. 198–99.
72 *Ibid.*, p. 199.
73 *Ibid.* The difference between Marbeck and Schwenckfeld on the question of the new and

Marbeck in the *Verantwortung*, as well as in the *Testamentserläuterung*, replies to Schwenckfeld's criticisms with the affirmation that the numerous passages in the Old Testament which refer to the establishment of a new covenant, such as Gen. 3:15, Num. 24:17, Deut. 30:6, Psalm 85, Isa. 45, and Jer. 31:31, are all in the future tense. "He only says, 'I *shall* set enmity between you, and not I *have* set it. He *shall* build his city, not he *has* built it. I *shall* make a new covenant, not I *have* made it.' "[74] (Italics mine)

Marbeck states that he and his brotherhood know very well that the new covenant was in the mind of God from all eternity, but that until the atonement and the ascension had actually taken place, men had still to wait for the new covenant of grace, by which the Church was established as the community of the new covenant, to be put into effect.[75] Consequently, there were no Christians before the time of Christ. Marbeck's concern is not only to show the absolute newness of the new covenant in contrast to the old, but also to safeguard the honor of Christ as the Recapitulator at the head of redeemed humanity. He expresses himself emphatically on this point as follows:

> We still today do not testify otherwise than that we, before the incarnation of Christ, regard no one as a Christian. Rather we confess the Incarnate Word as the first Christ (or Christian) of God, ... and we declare that before the incarnation of the Son of God, no Christian was in existence. He is the first [*erstling*] and the only one among all who are named or called Christians, understand among the children of men as a man. The Word became incarnate only in the fullness of time [*nach ordnung der zeit*] and according to the eternal Word, Christ is God from eternity. But before the incarnation of the Word, no one was named with Christ, nor became, or was a Christian. Rather in the Man in Christ Jesus (as in Gal. 3, the seed of Abraham, and as in Col. 1 and in Rom. 8, the beginning and firstborn from the dead brethren) is the promise fulfilled, as in Heb. 1 and Psalm 89; (Christ is) the firstborn and first Son of God. Yes, the first anointed with the spirit of sonship [*mit dem kindlichen Geist gesalbet*]. He was taken in *before* all and *for* all men. He is the first heir and *only begotten* of the *firstborn* from *among* men. All other (Christians) are only after-heirs [*nacherben*] with him and later born firstlings [*nach geborne erstling*].[76]

Now that Christ has come, the new covenant is established, for Christ has made all things new.[77] It is now mandatory that the Church be established as the regenerate gathered and disciplined community of the new covenant of grace. Marbeck rejected the idea of an invisible Church of Christ in the Spirit under the

---

old covenants really centers in the difference between the Christologies of the two men. With Marbeck the emphasis was upon Christ as incarnate and suffering, while for Schwenckfeld the main emphasis was upon the glorified and reigning Christ. The Christology of Schwenckfeld allowed him to think of the incarnation as only an interlude in the life of the preëxistent and eternal Christ, somewhat after the manner of Origen. Hence, all were Christians and members of the new covenant and members of the Church in the Spirit, who in all ages had responded to the eternal Christ, who ever draws men to himself.

74 Marbeck, *Verantwortung*, p. 328. Chapter 122 of the *Testamentserläuterung*, from which these references to Scripture are lifted, makes exactly the same emphasis.
75 *Verantwortung*, p. 328.
76 *Ibid.*, p. 311.
77 *Ibid.*, p. 318.

old covenant for two reasons. The first reason was that the believers of old (*die altglaübigen*) made use of the literal sword. To equate the community of the old covenant with the Church as the community of the new covenant of grace might lead the Church in Marbeck's own time into the danger of accepting Zwinglian, Westphalian, or Münsterite errors with regard to the literal sword.[78] But the second and by far the strongest reason why Marbeck rejected the doctrine of an invisible Church of Christ in the Spirit under the old covenant lay in his conviction that the finished work of the Man Christ had brought the *reality* which the believers of old could only hope for at some future time.

B. The Church and the Sacraments

Within the Radical Reformation where the Church itself in its corporate nature was regarded as the community of the new covenant, formed by God's regenerating grace, the sacraments of baptism and the Lord's Supper had a different significance than that found within the Magisterial Reformation. Within the latter tradition, where the forensic concept of grace under the *simul iustus et peccator* formula remained the dominant one, both baptism and the Lord's Supper were truly regarded as a sacramental *means of grace*. This was especially true within the Lutheran wing of the Magisterial Reformation.

Most of the Radical Reformers retained the use of the term, sacrament, with reference to both baptism and the Supper. But they understood by it something quite different than that which was understood by either Roman Catholic or Lutheran usage of the term. So far as the Supper was concerned, most of the Radicals, with the exception of Schwenckfeld, believed that their interpretation of the Supper was in closer agreement with Zwingli's as they understood it than to Roman Catholic or Lutheran interpretations.[79] But even Zwingli went too far for them when he defended the practice of infant baptism on the basis that it, like circumcision in the Old Testament, could be regarded as a *sign of grace*, and an external sign that the child belonged to God's people.[80]

Both Hans Denck and Hubmaier used the terms, ordinance or ceremony, with reference to baptism and the Supper.[81] Even those figures included in this study who retained the use of the term, sacrament, with reference to baptism would, with the exception of Pilgram Marbeck, have been more technically correct if they had spoken of baptism as a sign or a ceremony instead of as a sacrament. They did not think of baptism as either a means of grace or even as a sign of grace for the recipient.[82]

---

78 *Ibid.*, p. 324. See also *Testamentserläuterung*, pp. 319–20.
79 Marbeck, *Vermanung*, pp. 271–72. Marbeck lists the various interpretations of the Supper abroad in his day, by which the "learned ones had spread much strife among the common people." He says that so far as he is concerned he thinks Zwingli and Oecolampadius have come nearest to hitting the truth.
80 Menno Simons frequently objected to the statement that baptism was a sign of God's grace. Christ is our only sign of grace. What need have we of another sign? *Foundations of Christian Doctrine*, p. 124–25.
81 Hubmaier, *Vom christlichen Tauf der Gläubigen*, ca. 1525.
82 Hans Denck, *Widerruf*, *QFR*, Band XXIV, 2 Teil, 108–09.

1. The Definition and Function of Sacrament

Philip Melanchton in 1528 gave the following, not unfair, definition of what the Anabaptists understood in their use of the word, sacrament. He says:

> Sic enim scribunt nonnuli, Sacramenta esse instituta, ut per haec ostendamus gentibus, nos credere Christo, et profiteamur fidem coram hominibus, et nostro exemplo alios invitemus ad suscipiendam doctrinam Christi.[83]

Melanchton objected to this definition of the function of the sacrament, saying that it is not only a sign to distinguish Christians from heathen or a confession of faith before men which would also serve to attract them to faith. The sacrament is not only a confession of our faith before men, but also an indication of God's grace and will to us. It is not only a demonstration of our faith before men, but a reminder to us of what we have received from God.[84]

In Melanchton's faithful definition of the Anabaptist view of the function of the sacrament and in his objection to that definition is found the key to the polemic waged by both parties particularly with reference to infant baptism. The Radicals could not accept infant baptism, because they did not believe that it could bestow grace upon the recipient *ex opere operato*.

2. The Repudiation of the Practice of Infant Baptism

The reason usually advanced for the practice of infant baptism by the opposition was that it was necessary to cleanse the infant's soul from the stain of original sin.[85] This was the argument put forth by Melanchton. He reasons that all infants share in the corruption and curse of Adam's fall and that there can be no forgiveness of sins where the Word and sacrament are not present. Therefore, not to baptize infants would mean that a large portion of the human race is damned.[86]

This argument had no appeal to the Evangelical Anabaptists, who saw baptism as a confession of faith before men rather than *ex opere operato,* a means of grace from God. Infants could have no faith; therefore, infant baptism was no baptism. This was the position first expressed among the Evangelical Anabaptists of

---

83 Philip Melanchton, *Contra Anabaptistas Philippi Melanchthonius Iudicium*, 1528, CR, I, 957.

84 *Ibid.*, pp. 957–58. This work was translated into German by Justus Jonas and appeared under the title, *Underricht Philip Melanchton Wider die Lere der Wiederteuffer* (Wittenberg, 1528). A condensation of it in English translation was published by John S. Oyer under the title, "The Writings of Melanchton Against the Anabaptists," *MQR*; XXVI, No. 4 (October, 1952), 260–64. The writer is in part dependent upon Oyer's translation of the German for his English rendering of the Latin original. Melanchton used the example of Gideon and the fleece, saying that it was not only a sign to Gideon but also an indication of God's grace, and so is the sacrament to us.

85 This was uniformly true when the opposition was from the Reformed tradition. In Strasbourg infant baptism was made optional in 1524, as cited by Bender, *Conrad Grebel*, p. 127. During the formative period reformers in the Magisterial tradition seem to have developed arguments for it, because Anabaptists made it an issue.

86 Melanchton, pp. 963–64. This reference is to the Latin work in the CR, I.

Switzerland by Hubmaier in 1525.[87] These sentiments were repeated by Hans Denck in 1527[88] and by Pilgram Marbeck in 1532.[89] Menno Simons uses the same argument against infant baptism in *Christian Baptism* in 1539. To

> baptize before the thing which is represented in baptism, namely, faith is found in us . . . is as logical as to place the cart before the horse, to sow before we have plowed, to build before we have lumber at hand, or to seal a letter before it is written.[90]

Dirk Philips in 1557 stated that the proper order in baptism, according to the command of Christ, is first to teach and then to baptize. He called infant baptism "a plant not planted by God" and regarded it as something which should be rooted out of the life of the Church.[91] Melchior Hoffmann had made strenuous objections to infant baptism as early as 1530 on the basis that it was not specifically commanded in the Scriptures.[92]

It was, however, not on the basis that to baptize before faith was present in the one baptized constituted a reversal of the apostolic order that some of the Radicals found their most serious objection to the practice of infant baptism. Pilgram Marbeck, Menno Simons, and Dirk Philips all maintained that so far as original sin in children was concerned, it had been removed for all children through the universal grace of the atonement. Therefore, to practice infant baptism with the intention that through it the infant should be cleansed from original sin by means of sacramental grace was nothing short of idolatry.

Marbeck wrote in his confession of 1532 that "Christ has ascribed the Kingdom to children nakedly [*bloss*] without water or circumcision, or faith or knowledge, alone through the Word as himself."[93] One should, therefore, not seek to improve upon that which Christ has done for children by baptizing them.

> Christ has taken away the sins of the whole world through his blood; those of the ignorant through his command that little children should be allowed to come to him (Matt. 19:13-15); those of adults through faith in him.[94]

The condition of children is now even as that of Adam and Eve before the fall. They should simply be allowed to remain in that *ordnung* in which they were placed by the promise and command of Christ. Woe to him who undertakes to make them better by baptizing them.[95]

---

87 Hubmaier, *Vom christlichen Tauf der Gläubigen.*
88 Hans Denck, *Von der wahren Liebe, QFR*, Band XXIV, 2 Teil, 83. As Kiwiet points out, Denck had expressed Anabaptist ideas in relation to baptism, which in principle excluded infant baptism in his *Bekenntnis für den Rat zu Nürnberg* as early as 1525. See *QFR*, Band XXIV, 24, and Kiwiet, "The Life of Hans Denck," *MQR*, XXXI, No. 4 (October, 1957), 245, and Kiwiet, "The Theology of Hans Denck," *MQR*, XXXII, No. 1 (January, 1958), 21.
89 Marbeck, "Confession of Faith," *MQR*, XII, No. 3 (July, 1938), 183–85.
90 Menno Simons, *Christian Baptism, CWMS*, p. 259.
91 Dirk Philips, *Vander Doope, BRN*, X, 80 and 82.
92 Melchior Hoffmann, *Die Ordonnantie Godts, BRN*, V, 155. See also *SAW*, 192–93.
93 Marbeck, "Confession of Faith," *MQR*, XII, No. 3 (July, 1938), p. 185.
94 *Ibid.*
95 Marbeck, *Vermanung*, pp. 215–16.

When infant baptism is practiced with the above purpose in mind in such a manner that the people set their hope for the salvation of their children upon it (*wann die leit die seligkeyt darauff setzen*), as Marbeck said they did in his day, then it leads to idolatry.

Commenting upon the contemporary attitude toward infant baptism, Marbeck wrote:

> They talk and think as though when a child becomes or is baptized, it is then a Christian. Should it then die, it would from that hour on (from the hour the mouth opens, as one says) [the English translation hides a play on words which appears in German, i.e., *von stund an von mund auff*] go to heaven and be numbered among the choir of holy angels. But if one dies unbaptized, then this poor innocent child who knows neither good nor evil must be counted as among the unbelievers and kept in eternal darkness. That is what until now many have maintained about baptism. Is it not now a grievous idolatry that one should so practice baptism that it becomes an idol?[96]

Dirk and Menno voice almost identical objections to infant baptism as a sacramental means of grace. Menno in the *Confession of Distressed Christians* of 1552 says of infant baptism that children have the Lord's *promise* that they will be saved without baptism. Christians may rejoice in the assurance of the salvation of their children on account of that promise. Therefore, "to tie the election, grace, favor, and Kingdom of God to a few signs would be contrary to the merits, death, blood, and Word of the Lord; yes, open seduction, abomination, and idolatry."[97] Exactly the same sentiments are voiced by Menno in *Foundation of Christian Doctrine* in 1539[98] and in *Reply to False Accusations* of 1552. In the latter work he calls infant baptism the baptism of Antichrist. He notes that the Dutch Anabaptists are accused by their opponents of being "murderers of infant souls," because they do not baptize their children. But, he asks in reply, who has the greater assurance of the salvation of their children? Those who depend upon the baptism of their preachers, which is the baptism of Antichrist or those who believe the Word of the Lord that the Kingdom is *promised* them by grace. Menno answers his own question saying, "Therefore, we do not baptize them with the baptism of Antichrist. For not the *baptism of Antichrist*, but the *promise of Jesus Christ*, assures us of the salvation of our little ones if they die in infancy."[99] (Italics mine)

Dirk Philips in *Vander Doope* in 1557 wrote that it was great foolishness to baptize children in order that through this they might be kept and become saved. For children *are saved* and committed into the hand and grace of God. Therefore, to place one's hope for the salvation of the young children upon their baptism and to damn those infants who die without it

> is an open diminution and denial of the grace of God and the merits of Jezus Christ. For since the sin of Adam, yes, the sin of the whole world, has been taken away and paid for

---

96 *Ibid.*, p. 251.
97 Menno Simons, *Confession of Distressed Christians, CWMS*, p. 514.
98 Menno Simons, *Foundation of Christian Doctrine, CWMS*, p. 131.
99 Menno Simons, *Reply to False Accusations, CWMS*, p. 570.

Christ, and no sin which comes from Adam may be reckoned to children, how then may children be damned on account of Adam's sin?[100]

Clearly, the universal grace which Christ had won for children in the atonement or through his promise that the Kingdom belonged to them left no room or need for infant baptism as a sacramental means of grace.

3. The Significance of Believer's Baptism and the Lord's Supper

As we turn now to an examination of the significance of adult baptism and the Supper in Radical thought, we shall see how correct was Melanchthon's definition of the function of the sacrament as viewed by the Radical Reformers. This would be a proper definition of the significance of baptism[101] for all the figures included in this study with the exception of Marbeck and Schwenckfeld. The same is not true of Melanchthon's definition in relation to their understanding of the Supper.[102] The Celestial Flesh Christology always tended to make of the Supper something more than a simple memorial meal.

For the sake of clarity in presentation the representatives of the Radical Reformation considered in this study are separated into three distinct groups as the attempt is made to set forth briefly their views on the significance of baptism and the Supper. Denck and Hubmaier will constitute the first group; Hoffmann, Menno, and Dirk, the second group; and Marbeck and Schwenckfeld, because of the conflict and contrast between tehm, will comprise the third and last group.

As noted earlier in this chapter, both Denck and Hubmaier refer to baptism and the Supper as ceremonies or ordinances. It was Hubmaier, who baptized Denck in Augsburg while he was in flight from Zurich to Moravia, probably in May of 1526. Yet Denck's confession before the Nürnberg Council in January of 1525 contains already the definition of baptism as the covenant of a good conscience with God, based on I Pet. 3:21. This definition of baptism was later widely used by Anabaptists in both Holland and South Germany. In the *Confession* Denck specifically states that external baptism is of no value, except where it is administered to one whom the almighty Word of God has begun to cleanse from within. It is this inner baptism which is the baptism of Christ in the Spirit that establishes the covenant of the good conscience. Denck writes:

> The covenant is that he who allows himself to be baptized does it upon the death of Christ. That as he died, so also this one dies to Adam. As Christ arose, so also this one rises

---

100 Dirk Philips, *Vander Doope, BRN*, X, 91. The Radicals would not allow the *ex opere operato* difficulty, which was especially keen in connection with the practice of infant baptism, to be overcome on the basis of an *infused* or dormant faith. Hubmaier called this a *philosophy* rather than a *theology*, because he could find no basis for it in the Scriptures. Where one cannot construct theology on the basis of Scripture, he is not at liberty to suck it out of the fingers! See also Hubmaier, *Gespräch auf Meister Ulrich Zwinglis Taufbüchlein von dem Kindertauf*, 1526.
101 From this point on baptism will be used to refer to believer's baptism.
102 Supper is capitalized because it refers to the Lord's Supper.

to a new life in Christ as in Rom. 6. Where this covenant is, there the Spirit of Christ comes and kindles the fire of love which fully consumes what yet remains (of the old life or nature) and completes the work of Christ.[103]

Only where outward baptism takes place on the basis of the covenant established by the inner baptism is it a good thing. It is, therefore, not a means of grace but a sign that the covenant has been established. Furthermore, outward baptism is not necessary for salvation, but the inner baptism is.[104] In the *Widerruf* of 1528 Denck called baptism the enrolling (*einschreibung*) in the Church of believers.[105] Baptism does not *ex opere operato* confer upon the one baptized the status of a believer before God. It means only that one is recognized as a believer before the congregation insofar as it is possible to recognize this fact. The action in baptism so defined is purely human action.

Exactly the same distinction between inner and outer is made by Denck with reference to participation in the Supper. He who had placed his will in God's will through Christ, the Mediator, may eat the living invisible bread and drink the invisible wine of God, "which God has mixed from the beginning through His Son ... the Word."[106] He who eats and drinks in this manner "will become drunk and portray himself no more as himself, but will be through the love of God completely divinized [*gantz vergöttet*] and God in him will be humanized."[107]

Where one is of the disposition described above, it is a good thing to participate in the Supper, because it is then a memorial and proclamation of the Lord's death. Yet, one can live through the power of God, where His glory requires it, without this outward bread. But without the inner bread no one can live.[108] Men should, therefore, not dispute so severely with each other about external elements.[109] The Lord has not commanded them to eat bread with each other as fighting dogs *(wie zankende hund)*. The supper should rather be a memorial of Christ's suffering on our behalf and a pledge of our willingness to die for each other as he died for us.[110]

Only once does Denck suggest that under the proper circumstances the Supper may be more than a memorial meal and a pledge of mutual love among the brethren. When it is understood that eating Christ's flesh and drinking his blood *takes place spiritually, and that to eat spiritually is to know and believe Christ,*

---

103   Hans Denck, *Bekenntnis für den Rat zu Nürnberg, QFR*, Band XXIV, 2 Teil, 24.
104   *Ibid.*, p. 24. Kiwiet has apparently misunderstood this aspect of Denck's thought. He says, "The disposition of man himself gives value to the sacrament. Whoever has the willingness to die with Christ will experience the completion of his death in baptism." See "The Theology of Hans Denck," *MQR*, XXXII, No. 1 (January, 1958), 21. It is not the outer but the inner baptism that Denck refers to. The outer has no value, save as a sign, and it is not Christ's death that the believer experiences in himself, but rather Christ subduing what remains of his old nature.
105   Hans Denck, *Widerruf, QFR*, Band XXIV, 2 Teil, 109.
106   Hans Denck, *Bekenntnis für den Rat zu Nürnberg, QFR*, Band XXIV, 2 Teil, 26.
107   *Ibid.*
108   *Ibid.*
109   Hans Denck, *Widerruf, QFR*, Band XXIV, 2 Teil, 108–09.
110   Hans Denck, *Ordnung Gottes, QFR*, Band XXIV, 2 Teil, 101. An emphasis similar to this is made in *Von der wahren Liebe*, pp. 81–82.

then Christ's body will quicken our souls, and his blood which is the wine of God's love will make us glad and joyful. We will then become completely one with Christ. He will remain in us and we in him, "even as food and drink to a certain extent [*etlichermass*] unite itself with human nature."[111]

Yet Denck has said just prior to this that the believer is free of all external things. However, according to the measure of his ability the believer exercises care that the glory of God is not diminished in his freedom nor the love of the neighbor frivolously despised.[112]

> He who is zealous in his practice of the ceremonies [*wer sich in den ceremonien hart bemiet*], yet does not gain much. For even though one should lose them all, he yet would suffer no harm himself. And certainly it is better to be without them than to abuse them.[113]

It is clear then that for Denck the Supper was not a means of grace in the sense that it either contained the *real* presence of Christ or *actually* became his blood and body.

Hubmaier's position on the significance of baptism is very similar to that of Denck, although the strand of medieval mysticism, so important in the formation of Denck's thought, is not present in Hubmaier. No external thing can cleanse the heart. Only faith can, and faith comes through preaching. The purpose of preaching is, therefore, to awaken faith in God, our heavenly Father, as One Who is gracious and merciful, Who carries us and cares for us as a man cares for his child or a hen for her brood of chicks.[114] Such heartfelt trust in God through Jesus Christ, because of the goodwill which God, the Father, has toward His beloved (*allerliebsten*) Son, is the true faith (*recht glaub*). In this faith we should cry out, plead with, and call to God (*schreyen, bitten, und ruffen*), that He for the sake of His Son will be gracious to us.[115]

Hubmaier's order of salvation is as follows. First, one must be led through the Word of God to a knowledge of his sins, and he must confess that he is a sinner. Second, one must be taught again by the Word of God that he should cry to God, the Father, for the forgiveness of his sins for Christ's sake. Third, where one now does this in faith and does not doubt, God cleanses his heart in faith and trust and forgives him all his sins. After one experiences this grace and goodness, he gives himself to God and pledges himself inwardly in his heart to lead a new life after the rule of Christ.[116]

Only at this point does water baptism become meaningful. It is thus neither a means of grace nor an aid to faith, but simply a testimony to faith. This is made very clear in Hubmaier's *Eine Form zu taufen in Wasser die im Glauben Unterrichteten*, written at Nikolsburg in 1527. The *Form* is a confession of faith in the Holy Spirit, the holy Christian Church, which has the key to the forsaking (*ablas-*

---

111 Hans Denck, *Widerruf*, QFR, Band XXIV, 2 Teil, 108–09.
112 *Ibid.*
113 *Ibid.*
114 Hubmaier, *Vom christlichen Tauf der Gläubigen*, 1525.
115 *Ibid.*
116 *Ibid.*

sung) of sin, the resurrection of the flesh, and eternal life. It contains a pledge that the one who has made the confession will renounce the world and the devil and in the strength of Christ seek to lead a new life. It contains a pledge that in the event of future sin, one would obediently accept brotherly discipline from the congregation.[117] In the *Form* Hubmaier like Denck calls baptism an *einschreibung* in the Christian Church.

Baptism so defined is not a sacrament or a means of grace. It is a sign of one's own faith, a testimony of that faith before the congregation, and a fitting manner in which to become a member of the Church of the reborn; nothing more, and nothing less.

Hubmaier's view of the Supper is not any more sacramental than his view of baptism. He expressed these views in two brief works. The first of these, *Ein einfältiger Unterricht auf die Worte: das ist mein Leib, in dem Nachtmahl Christi*, appeared in 1526, and the second in 1527 under the simple title, *Eine Form des Nachtmahles Christi*. In the first work Hubmaier discusses what the Supper *is*, while the latter is an order of service for the *conduct* of the Supper within the worship of the congregation.

Hubmaier stresses the *memorial* aspect of the Supper. The breaking, distribution, and eating of the bread is not participation in the body of Christ. Christ is bodily in heaven at the right hand of the Father.[118] The bread and wine are the body and blood of Christ in memorial only, and not otherwise. Hubmaier's words are, *"in der gehaltenen gedechtnuss und nit anders."*[119]

Hubmaier regards any doctrine of the *real presence* within the elements of bread and wine as idolatry with which the triune God is thrust from His throne.[120] In the form for the observance of the Supper he says that it is properly observed by a gathering of the faithful, who meet in faith and love,[121] at a specified time and place. Each individual should examine *himself* before participation, not the elements of bread and wine.[122] The Supper is a remembrance of Christ's bitter martyr death and a pledge by those who participate in it that they are prepared to die for each other, even as Christ died for them. So defined, the Supper is not a *means of* grace, but rather a *sign of grace* already received.

As Balthasar Hubmaier carried the practice of adult baptism from Switzerland to South Germany, so Melchior Hoffmann carried it from Strasbourg to Emden

---

117 Hubmaier, *Eine Form zu taufen in Wasser die im Glauben Unterrichteten*. Hubmaier is aware that baptism so interpreted may lead some to say, "What need have I of baptism? I already have the Holy Spirit." He finds support for it on the basis that it was the command of Christ. "He who sees the command of Christ before his eyes does not dispute further." Only where water and a baptizer are not available may baprism be omitted. See also Hubmaier, *Vom christlichen Tauf der Gläubigen*.
118 Hubmaier, *Ein einfältiger Unterricht auf die Worte: das ist mein Leib, in dem Nachtmahl Christ*, Nikolsburg, 1526.
119 *Ibid.*
120 *Ibid.*
121 Hubmaier, *Eine Form des Nachtmahles Christi*, Nikolsburg, 1527.
122 *Ibid.* Hubmaier's polemic in his treatise on the Supper is directed against both Luther and Zwingli. He had read Luther's treatment of the sacrament written in 1519. His encounters with Zwingli were personal.

and Holland.[123] Hoffmann's views on baptism and the Supper are expressed in *Die Ordonnantie Godts* of 1530. The medieval mysticism which was very important in the formation of Hoffmann's thought comes to the fore in the bridal imagery which Hoffmann uses to illustrate his concepts of both baptism and the Supper.

Baptism is the sign of the betrothal. Even as Christ was betrothed to his Father in baptism, so the believer is betrothed to Christ in his own baptism. As Christ gave his will completely into the hands of his Father in baptism, so the believer in baptism gives his will completely into the hands of Christ.[124] Hoffmann never calls baptism the means by which the covenant of betrothal is established. It is only those who have through the urging of the Gospel surrendered themselves to the Lord who should be baptized publicly "through that true sign of the covenant, the water bath and baptism."[125] That Hoffmann did not think of baptism as a means of sacramental grace is made clear by the fact that baptism was for him the initiation into a wilderness experience, which was fraught with danger, temptation, and the threat of destruction.[126]

As baptism is the sign of the covenant of betrothal, so the Supper is both the marriage and the marriage feast. The bread and wine of the Supper are the ring which Christ, the heavenly bridegroom, offers to his bride, the believer, who in baptism has pledged her absolute obedience to Christ. Just as a bridegroom is not physically in the engagement ring which he gives his bride, so Christ does not corporally exist in the bread of the Supper, nor does the wine of the Supper become his physical blood.[127] The supper is thus not a sacramental means of grace in either a Roman Catholic or Lutheran sense.[128] Yet, at the same time it would be incorrect to say that the Supper was for Hoffmann *only* the memorial of Christ's suffering and death. The Supper is also the symbol of the closest possible union with Christ. In a mystical way the Bride physically receives and eats the noble Bridegroom with his blood in such a way that the outpouring of his blood is one with hers.[129] The disciples who were simple fisherfolk well understood that the Christ, who sat with them at the table, was not *corporally present in* the bread and wine. What they did understand

> that *through* the bread and belief in the Word they should receive that body which sat by them there, that same body should be their own which would be burned at the cross.

---

123 *ME*, II, 781. Christian Neff, author of the article on Hoffmann, states Hoffmann can be considered the founder of the Anabaptist congregation in Emden, which is still in existence.
124 Melchior Hoffmann, *Die Ordonnantie Godts*, *BRN*, V, 152. See also *SAW*, pp. 189–90.
125 *SAW*, p. 187. Also *BRN*, V, 150.
126 *SAW*, pp. 189–90. Also *BRN*, V, 153. For a full discussion of the wilderness motif in Hoffmann's thought on baptism see the Introduction by Williams in *SAW*, pp. 182–83, and the footnotes on pp. 188–89.
127 *SAW*, pp. 193–94. Also *BRN*, V, 157–58.
128 The polemic in Hoffmann's view of the *real presence* in the Supper is directed against Luther, even though he did use Luther's *Von dem Misbrauch der Messe*, in support of his own views, which were declared heretical by the Lutheran clergy in the Disputation at Flensburg, and Hoffmann was ordered to leave his hometown within two days and Danish territory within three additional days. See *ME*, II, 780. See also Leendertz, pp. 119–35.
129 *SAW*, p. 194. Also *BRN*, V, 158.

And (they believed) that theirs also was the physical blood which should be poured out from the cross. [130] (Italics mine)

Thus, in the close union of the believer as the Bride of Christ with Christ as the Bridegroom, which is symbolized by the Supper, but not affected through it, the collective Church herself becomes the Bride and Body of Christ. His *real presence* is in the believers, and their sufferings become an extension of his own passion.

The views of Menno Simons and Dirk Philips on baptism are similar enough that they may be treated together. It is fair to say in the beginning that neither of them thought of baptism as in any sense a sacramental act in which divine as well as human action is involved. Menno in the *Foundation of Christian Doctrine* in 1539 calls baptism the covenant of the good conscience with God. He is careful to observe that on the basis of I Pet. 1:21 it is not the outer baptism of water that saves but the inner baptism of regeneration and faith which both come from the Word of God.[131] Outward baptism follows the inner as a *sign of obedience*, which comes from faith. It is not the means by which faith is awakened or regeneration is effected.[132] Menno found himself unable to accept the definition of baptism as a *sign of grace*, which was the definition proposed by Zwingli and later used by Reformed ministers with whom Menno had personal contact. This definition of baptism was developed as support for the practice of infant baptism, and it rested largely on the assumption that baptism in the New Testament was the equivalent of circumcision in the Old.

Menno rejected both this definition of baptism and the argument which supported it as being exegetically unsound. The Christian believer stood in a new and different situation from that in which the ancient patriarchs were involved. Since Christ had not yet come in their time, he was prefigured to them in signs "by coats of skin to Adam and Eve, by the rainbow to Noah, by circumcision to Abraham."[133] By these signs, said Menno, the ancients were assured of the divine covenant. "But we are assured by God of His divine grace and eternal peace by this one sign which is Jesus Christ."[134] The fathers received assurance and comfort by means of signs that the promise would be true and sure. We testify in baptism that we believe the Word of the Lord, that we repent of our former manner of life, and that we believe in the forgiveness of sins through Jesus Christ, in whom all figurative signs have come to an end.[135] Baptism is not a *sign of grace* but a *sign*

---

130 *SAW*, p. 195. Williams in n. 28, p. 195, points out that the word which he has translated as "burned" in the passage cited above appears in the original Dutch as "*gebraden*," which means roasted. He asks, "Has Hoffmann allowed the common image of the heretic's pyre to replace that of the cross. Or is he thinking of martyrdom as the consummation of the imitation of Christ, whereby one becomes the roasted paschal Lamb?" The answer is found, I think, in this quasi-physical mystical union of Christ and the believer. Through this the sufferings of the believer actually become the sufferings of his Lord, and he completes in his body what yet remains of the suffering of Christ. Col. 1:24. Whether the pain inflicted upon the believer is that of martyrdom or a lesser one is, therefore, immaterial. *BRN*, V, 158.
131 Menno Simons, *Foundation of Christian Doctrine*, CWMS, p. 124.
132 *Ibid.*, p. 125.
133 *Ibid.*
134 *Ibid.*
135 *Ibid.*

of obedience, "which proceeds from faith as proof *before God and His Church* that they firmly believe in the remission of their sins through Jesus Christ.[136] (Italics mine)

Although baptism itself is neither a *means of grace* nor a *sign of grace* in Menno's thought and has nothing to do with establishing the precious covenant of grace, he does not regard it as, therefore, unimportant. He who despises the ceremonies commanded by God and regards their performance as useless and trivial excludes himself from the covenant by disobedience.[137]

Dirk Philips, like Menno, stressed an inner and outer baptism, in which the outer water baptism plays only the minor role of a testimony to the inner baptism of the Holy Spirit.[138] Baptism is to be administered to one who has been instructed in the faith, has remorse for his sins, believes the Gospel, confesses his faith, and desires to be baptized.[139] Baptism shall be performed by one who is a minister and servant of the Lord upon one who *willingly* offers and gives himself to God and to the service of righteousness, yes, to the servanthood (*knechtshaft*) of God in fellowship with Christ and all the saints.[140] The action in baptism is again human action, although Dirk does show concern that it be performed by a properly ordained minister.

Dirk does speak of baptism as the water bath of regeneration, based upon the Eph. 5:26–27 passage,[141] and he states that he does not think it incorrect to apply this to water baptism, though there are some of his contemporaries, apparently Anabaptists, who think that this passage applies only to the baptism of the Spirit. But Dirk reasons that the Ephesians passage may be fittingly applied to water baptism. The reason is that regeneration is nothing other than that which God works in man through faith in Jesus Christ, when he renews the divine image

---

136 Menno Simons, *Christian Baptism, CWMS*, p. 244.

137 *Ibid.*, p. 262. For an extended and excellent discussion of the significance of baptism in Menno's thought and the difficulty he fell into by placing so much stress on obedience see Vincent G. Harding, "Menno Simons and the Role of Baptism in the Christian Life," *MQR*, XXXIII, No. 4 (October, 1959), pp. 323–34.

The full exploration of the significance of baptism for Menno is beyond the scope of this study, since we are here concerned only with the question of whether or not baptism was a means of grace. Harding is absolutely correct when he says, "Baptism brings nothing to the believer except an opportunity for him to act, for him to testify, for him to show his obedience to God. It brings opportunity, no more."

Menno wrote often on the question of baptism in the course of controversy and in the appeals for toleration for his brotherhood. *Confession of Distressed Christians*, 1552, *Reply to False Accusations,* 1552, *A Pathetic Supplication to All Magistrates*, 1552, *Brief Defense to all Theologians*, 1552, and *Reply to Gellius Faber*, 1554, all contain sections on baptism and infant baptism. But when the question is asked whether Menno ever saw baptism as having any sacramental significance the answer is no.

138 Dirk Philips, *Vander Doope, BRN*, X, 69.

139 *Ibid.*, pp. 69–70.

140 *Ibid.*

141 *Ibid.*, p. 76. The Ephesians passage reads, "Husbands, love your wives, as Christ loved the church and gave himself up for her, that he might consecrate her, having cleansed her by the washing of water with the Word, that the church might be presented before him in splendor, without spot or wrinkle or any such thing, that she might be holy and without blemish."

in him and makes him through the power of the Holy Spirit participate in the divine nature.[142] Dirk says that the newborn children are not washed with the power of the elements of natural water, but alone through the power of the blood and the Spirit of Jesus Christ, with which the consciences of believing Christians are baptized and cleansed.[143] Yet water baptism may be called a *sacramental sign*, a testimony to the baptism of the Spirit. For as the blood which flowed from Christ's riven side[144] bears testimony to his true humanity, and it is that with which he has sprinkled his Church and cleansed her from all sin, so that she is without spot or wrinkle, so baptism is the sacramental sign of the water of the Spirit, which Christ has poured out upon the Church.[145]

When Dirk speaks of baptism as the covenant of the good conscience with God, he means, as does Menno, that God first binds Himself to us by the grace which He has shown us in Christ, and that we then bind ourselves to God in the pledge that we will no longer live in sin, but uprightly as those who have waked from sleep and raised from the dead.[146] The action in baptism thus remains on the human side, but it is action in response to God's approach.

The views of Menno and Dirk on the Supper are also similar. Both men resisted as the grossest blasphemy any doctrine of the corporeal presence within the material elements of the Supper itself. Menno developed his views of the Supper in opposition to both the Roman Catholic doctrine of transubstantiation and the Lutheran doctrine of consubstantiation. Menno wrote:

> Some of the learned ones call us profaners of the sacraments because we do not believe that the bread and wine of their Supper is the actual real flesh and blood of the Lord; or as some have it, because we do not believe that we through the wine and bread actually partake of the actual flesh and blood of the Lord.[147]

Menno had absolutely no confidence in frequent participation in the material elements of the Supper as a possible means of grace. He felt that leaders of the Magisterial Reformation, who urged this, grossly misled their people.

> Therefore they console themselves and think that if they partake of it, they are the people of the Lord. Oh, no, the ceremony makes no Christian, for so long as they do not become converted and do not become new men born of God, of spiritual mind, all baptizing and partaking of the Lord's Supper is meaningless, even if it were administered by Peter of Paul.[148]

This was consistent with the position which Menno expressed as early as 1539 in

---

142 *Ibid.*, p. 77. See also John 1:12–13.
143 *Ibid.* See also I Pet. 1:21.
144 *Ibid.*, pp. 77–78. See also John 19:34 and John 4:2–4.
145 *Ibid.*, p. 78.
146 *Ibid.*, p. 80. The Scriptural passages which Dirk uses here are I Pet. 1:21, I Cor. 15:3, and Eph. 5:14. See also Menno Simons, *Foundation of Christian Doctrine, CWMS*, p. 125.
147 Menno Simons, *Reply to False Accusations, CWMS*, p. 571.
148 Menno Simons, *Confession of Distressed Christians, CWMS*, p. 516.

the *Foundation of Christian Doctrine*. Dirk wrote *Van dat Auontmael* in 1557, in which he took a similar position.[149]

Both Menno and Dirk, as opposed to Luther, appealed to the sixth chapter of John as a basis for the correct or spiritual interpretation of the Supper. Their interpretation of the Supper hinged in part, like that of Calvin, on the ubiquity question. Menno says that because Christ has ascended to heaven he cannot be masticated or confined in an alimentary tract;[150] Dirk states that he is not bodily in the sacrament and that he is not touched or handled there.[151] Yet, for Menno and Dirk alike, the Supper is something more than a memorial meal. It is, of course, a memorial of Christ's suffering and death, but, spiritually understood on the basis of John 6, it is the communion of the Living Bread from heaven. To eat Christ's flesh and to drink his blood is to believe that he is God's Son and that he died for our sins.[152] The sacrament must be received in faith, for one does not participate in the Supper through the outward sign alone. Judas was present at the supper and received the elements of bread and wine but did not participate in the Supper.[153]

Dirk, using the analogy of the last will and testament, says that as the maker of a will is not present in the will, though his power is, so Christ with his divine power is present in the covenant of the sacramental Supper, while he remains bodily in heaven, and with his spirit he quickens the hearts of the believing ones.[154]

The close relationship between the Christology and the soteriology and their view of the spiritual eating of the Supper is equally close. It is here that the new creature in Christ, which is the ontological result of grace in the believer, is fed and nourished. This is very clearly expressed in the following excerpts from the writings of Menno and Dirk. Menno writes:

> But where the Lord's church, the dear disciples of Christ, have met in Christ's name to partake of the Holy Supper in true faith, love, and obedience, there the outward perishable man eats and drinks perishable bread and wine, and the inner imperishable man of the heart eats in a spiritual sense the imperishable body and blood of Christ which cannot be eaten nor digested, as was said. Like is benefited by like. This is incontrovertible. The visible man is nourished with visible food, and the invisible man is fed with invisible "bread," as we may plainly learn from the words of the Lord in John 6.

> All then who are in Christ and with believing, penitent hearts trust in the pure sacrifice of the body and blood of Christ confess that it is the only cleansing and atonement for their sins, the only and eternal means of grace. These really eat the flesh, and really drink the true blood of Christ, not with their mouths, but believingly in the spirit, as was said before.[155]

---

149 *BRN*, X, 112.
150 Menno Simons, *Foundation of Christian Doctrine*, *CWMS*, p. 153.
151 Dirk Philips, *Van dat Auontmael*, *BRN*, X, 119.
152 Menno Simons, *Foundation of Christian Doctrine*, *CWMS*, p. 153.
153 *Ibid.*, p. 144. Also, Dirk Philips, *Van dat Auontmael*, *BRN*, X, 112, 113–16.
154 Dirk Philips, *Van dat Auontmael*, *BRN*, X, 127–28.
155 Menno Simons, *Foundation of Christian Doctrine*, *CWMS*, pp. 153–54.

Dirk also similarly says:

> Therefore, whosoever believes in the Lord Jesus Christ, the Son of the living God, who was crucified and died for us, and trusts in Him, receives Jesus Christ, the Word of the Father, is fed with the heavenly manna; yea, he eats the flesh and drinks the blood of Jesus Christ, but spiritually with the mouth of the soul, and not literally with the natural mouth. For spiritual food (that is the flesh and blood of Christ) must be spiritually received.[156]

According to the view of Menno and Dirk, it would be only those who are born out of God who possess the invisible man of the heart, the new creature in Christ, and it is only this that is nourished in the spiritual eating of the Supper. In this spiritual eating, however, the process of incarnation is again reversed, and man takes on the divine nature.

Dirk reflects the influence of a well known passage from the *Didache*, as he writes:

> For just as out of many grains thrown together and ground up the bread is made, and the bodies of many grains become the body of one loaf, in which every single grain loses its own body and form, and the same with the grapes, which in the transformation of their form become the body of a common drink, so also all Christians must be unified with Christ and with each other. In the first place with Christ, whom they receive through faith and are nourished [*gespijst*] with him. But this is certainly not a greater [mystery] than that in the least [of things] the one who is nourished, and the nourishment cannot be separated from each other, since the nourishment goes into and is transformed into the nature and being of him who is nourished. Thus, also true Christians are by faith in Jesus Christ completely united and incorporated in and with him; yea, changed and transformed, so as to be like him in character and nature.[157]

One cannot say, therefore, that Menno and Dirk regarded the Supper as a means of grace in either the Roman Catholic or Lutheran usage of that term. They did not think that it could bestow grace either *ex opere operato*, or that one who did not participate in the Supper in faith, nevertheless, partook of the body and blood of Christ. The Supper was only a means of grace to one who was already *in* Christ.

Dirk speaks of the Supper as a sacramental sign and is very careful to point out that the sign must be used in such a way that it points beyond itself to Christ, who is the true reality.[158] With their interpretation of the spiritual eating of the Supper, Menno and Dirk found the contemporary debates about the nature of the corporeal presence within the material bread and wine of the Supper both tedious and beside the point. Menno said "the learned ones" dispute much about the sign, but the thing signified they forget.[159] Yet, despite their impatience with the disputes about signs, Menno and Dirk did not push their spiritualizing tendencies so far that they were ready to discard all external signs. Probably the strongest

---

156 Dirk Philips, *Van dat Auontmael, BRN*, X, 114.
157 *Ibid.*, pp. 122–23.
158 *Ibid.*, pp. 101–02.
159 Menno Simons, *Foundation of Christian Doctrine, CWMS*, pp. 142–43. In some respects the thought of Menno and Dirk on the question of the sacramental character of the Supper approaches the thought of Calvin. See *Institutes*, IV, Chapter 17, and *Calvini Opera*, VII, col. 77, *CR*, XXXV.

reason for this was that they looked upon the observance of the Supper as one of the specific commands of Christ. And obedience to this command, as in the case of baptism, was a sign of faith.

The question of the sacramental character and value of baptism and the Supper for Pilgram Marbeck and Caspar Schwenckfeld is best answered through a study of the controversy between the two men as a result of Schwenckfeld's *Judicium* of Marbeck's *Vermanung*. Both works appeared in 1542, the latter evidently in late summer, the former in December of the same year.[160] In order to understand the aversion of Schwenckfeld to Marbeck's statement in the *Vermanung*, that where faith is present in the one baptized, he received forgiveness of sins in baptism,[161] it is necessary to be aware of Schwenckfeld's definition of what a sacrament is and of how grace is *related to* or rather *distinct from* the sacraments.

Schwenckfeld defined a sacrament in classical Augustinian terms as "the outward and visible sign of an inward and spiritual grace."[162] His Spiritualist orientation coupled with the mystic's desire for the soul's immediate contact with the divine source of grace in the glorified Christ caused him to think in terms of an absolute separation between the *signum* and the *signato*. Schenckfeld exegetes Augustine's definition of a sacrament by saying that a sign is that which when seen in its own form brings to our awareness or memory something else.

> As when I see human footprints in the snow or a smoke ascending or a crown of thorns, I do not think only of that which appears before my eyes but rather of that which it implies and to which my thoughts finally turn. Also, and far more so, an entire sacrament then consists of the visible sign and the invisible power of spiritual graces, of bodily elements and earthly services, and heavenly treasures.
> Yes, of that which the mind comprehends and of what is understood through a believing heart. And the two may not be intermingled, but each according to their nature and character must be as distinct from each other as are heaven and earth.[163]

The distance between grace and the sacraments is, therefore, as great as that between *signum* and *signato*. In Schwenckfeld's view the sacraments, whether it be baptism or the Supper, cannot be a means of grace in the sense that the grace of God in Christ comes to us *through* the sacraments or is bestowed *by* them,[164] for Christ is the only Mediator and the *source* of grace. The *course* of grace does not flow in a *mediated* manner from Christ *through* the sacraments but is the *immediate* activity of the Holy Spirit, sent by authorization of the glorified Christ into the heart of man.[165]

---

160 For an introduction to the controversy see *ME*, III and IV, 494–501 and 1121–23. For an extended and thorough discussion of the controversy and the issues involved in it see "Pilgram Marbeck und Seine Auseinandersetzung mit Caspar Schwenckfeld" by Torsten Bergsten, published in *Kyrkohistorisk Arsskrift* (Uppsala, 1957–58).
161 Marbeck, *Vermanung*, pp. 213–16; *Verantwortung*, pp. 101–02
162 Schwenckfeld, *Judicium, CS*, VIII, 180. The reference to Augustine listed by the editors of the *Corpus* is found in P. J. Migne's critical edition of *Augustini Opera Omnia* in *Patrologiae Cursus Completus*... Series Latina, *Traditio Catholica* (Paris: Vrayet, Pres La Barriere D'Enfer, 1865) XXXIII, col. 401, and XL, col. 344.
163 Schwenckfeld, *Judicium, CS*, VIII, 179–80.
164 Schwenckfeld, *Der XXVI sendbrieff an Alle Christliche guthertzige Menschen von der Gnaden Gottes...*, *CS*, III, 86–98.
165 *Ibid*.

This was the position which Schwenckfeld held on the sacraments as a means of grace as early as 1528. Although he developed these views primarily with reference to the Supper in the controversy with Marbeck, he applied them with equal vigor to baptism. It appeared to him that Marbeck's statement, "where faith is present in the one baptized, forgiveness of sins is received in baptism," confused the *signum* with *signato* and the creaturely element of water with *divine* grace.[166] Baptism, in Schwenckfeld's view of the function of a sacrament and of the *immediate* rather than the *mediated* course of grace, could bring nothing to the recipient. It might be regarded as a sign of repentance, but it could not bring forgiveness of sins.[167] Though one were to be baptized by the father of all the Anabaptists himself, he would not be baptized before God unless reborn through the power of the Holy Spirit, which alone is the baptism of Christ and makes one righteous before God.[168]

Marbeck's view of the significance of both baptism and the Supper is found in his decision to use the term, sacrament, even though he felt that it was unscriptural and freighted with much antichristian meaning, especially with reference to the Supper. For this he blamed Lutherans as well as Catholics. He complains that the "learned ones" have been much exercised in his time over the meaning of the words, "this is my body," but have been unable to come to any agreement. In the course of their dispute these "learned ones" have stirred up strife, division, doubt, and misunderstanding among the people.[169] Marbeck shows that he is familiar with Lutheran, Catholic, and Zwinglian views of the Supper and states his preference for the latter view.[170] Yet he did use the term, sacrament, and his concept of baptism is something more than a public confession of one's faith before men, and his concept of the Supper, something more than a memorial meal. Both are for Marbeck a *means of grace* though in a restricted rather than in an *ex opere operato* or an objectively efficacious manner.

In his own definition of baptism in the *Vermanung* and in his reply to Schwenckfeld's criticism of that definition, Marbeck used the term, *"mitzeugniss,"*[171] here translated a cowitness. Because of the new situation in which the believer stands on account of the finished work of Christ, it is not sufficient to call baptism a sign of repentance, as Schwenckfeld wishes to do. This would push the time of Christ back into the time of John, the baptist, and confuse the new covenant with the old.[172] Christian baptism can, of course, not be properly administered in the absence of faith. This means that the Word must first be preached through which faith is created. But where grace through faith is present, baptism is more than a sign of repentance. It is the apostolic baptism of forgiveness of sins which was promised from heaven.[173]

---

166 Schwenckfeld, *Judicium, CS*, VIII, 213–14.
167 *Ibid.*, p. 182.
168 *Ibid.*, p. 214.
169 Marbeck, *Vermanung*, p. 253.
170 *Ibid.*, pp. 270–71.
171 Marbeck, *Vermanung*, pp. 208–09.
172 Marbeck, *Verantwortung*, p. 112.
173 *Ibid.*, p. 83.

Baptism thus becomes baptism only in the presence of faith and the Word. Marbeck insists that he means by the *true* Christian baptism both the outward baptism by water and the accompanying inner baptism of the Spirit. He knows very well that water remains water, and it does not follow that one who is externally baptized with water is also baptized before God, but the latter does not take place without the first. Within these carefully defined limits baptism was for Marbeck a *means* of grace.[174]

If Schwenckfeld's absolute separation between *signum* and *signato*, and his concept of the *immediate* rather than the *mediated* course of grace is kept in mind, the reason for his objection to Marbeck's definition of the Supper as found in the *Vermanung* becomes clear. Marbeck had defined the Supper as a gathering of believers who assemble in faith and love at a common meal in memory of Christ as he commanded.[175] Yet Christ is not present in the sacrament. Paul told people to prove themselves, not bread and wine.[176] Where those who participate in this Supper are from the heart disposed toward their brethren as Christ was toward them, and not only toward their brethren but also toward their friends and enemies, there the breaking of the bread and the drinking of the cup is a true communion of the body and of the blood of Christ.[177]

It was the latter part of this definition that Schwenckfeld objected to. He felt that Marbeck had confounded Lutheran and Zwinglian errors and that the end result was worse than either error alone.[178] Schwenckfeld's doctrine of the

---

174 *Ibid.*, p. 75. Marbeck thus shows the influence of his brief association with the Lutheran wing of the Reformation. The outlines of the Augsburg Confession that the true Church is present where the Word is rightly preached and the sacraments rightly administered are clearly present, though applied in Marbeck's own way.
175 Marbeck, *Vermanung*, p. 254.
176 *Ibid.*
177 *Ibid.*, pp. 259–67 and 268.
178 Schwenckfeld, *Judicium, CS*, VIII, 180. The reason for Schwenckfeld's reaction to Marbeck's formulation is clearly seen in the following quotation from Schwenckfeld's *Ein Christlicher Sendbrieff Vom span und rechten Mittel zwischen der Luthrischen und Zwinglischen opinion im Artickel des Herrn Nachtmals....*:

"The sum of it is this, that the Zwinglians as well as the Lutherans do not correctly understand the words of Christ, 'This is my body.' And yet, as has previously been said, a correct understanding of the words is the entire basis for the spiritual eating of the Lord's Supper. For the Lutheran interpretation makes of the words of Christ an addition [zusatz], where they in this passage in which Christ says, 'This is my body,' interpret this to mean the bread, which they also do in the definition of the Gospel, where Paul says in Rom. 1:16 that the Gospel is the power of God unto salvation to all that believe. The Lutherans place the emphasis upon the words of the mouth and say the spoken Gospel is the power. Both positions give rise to great errors and introduce a grievous idolatry. That is, they take the visible sacramental bread for Christ, our Lord and God, *signum pro signato*, the picture for the truth and the outward word which is preached for God's saving power, yes, and the creature for the Creator.

"The Zwinglian concept makes the literal word of the Lord, 'This is my body,' into a *mere sign*. [*Italics mine*] Zwingli and also Oecolampadius want to make out of the *est* a sign or a figure, though the Lord Jesus had only spoken of the sign, in which case the food of the body of Christ would then be excluded from the Lord's Supper, and the words of Christ would not remain spirit and life, which is against the meaning [*sinn*] of the Lord. These words, as they have now been interpreted by both Zwinglian and Lutheran parties, are turned away from the humanity of the glorified Christ, which now stands before God in eternity and is yet the food of our souls unto eternal life,[179] was really at the heart of his objection to Marbeck's statement that given the right attitude on the part of the communicants, participation in the Supper is a true communion of the body and blood of Christ. The Supper must be spiritually eaten. Christ and the creature must not be confused. Schwenckfeld had said as early as 1528 that the sacraments have their office and power, which is to *signify* and *indicate*, but to *bring* and *distribute* the grace of God belongs alone to Christ and not to the sacraments.[180] The value of the Supper lay for Schwenckfeld in the fact that through it the new man in Christ is nourished. John 6 is the Scriptural basis for Schwenckfeld's interpretation of the spiritual eating of the Supper, as it was also for Menno Simons and Dirk Philips. Eating and drinking of the Supper takes place inwardly and in the spirit of faith. Where it takes place in this manner

> we have communion with God ... [for] in this Supper our dear Lord Jezus Christ feeds us, gives us to drink, refreshes the believing soul with his holy body, flesh, and blood... [which has] become a food and drink for the satiation of the soul and for the receiving of the divine life, as the Lord Christ has taught of eating and drinking such food. John 6. Where among other things he says, "The bread which I shall give for the life of the world is my flesh."[181]

Only Christ is the bread of God, and he must not be confused with the sacramental bread. It is only through the spiritual eating and drinking, not the sacramental eating, that one receives the bread of God that is food for the divine life received in regeneration, and only the regenerate can participate in the spiritual eating.[182] Schwenckfeld saw Marbeck's definition of the Supper as one that robbed Christ of his glory as the *only source* of grace.

Marbeck rejected this criticism of the Supper on the same basis that he rejected the criticism of his view of baptism. He knows very well that bread and wine remain bread and wine. They cannot satisfy the soul. Yet where the Lord's Supper is participated in by believing men who have assembled in faith and in love, in memory of Christ, Christ is really present, though not in the bread and wine of the Supper. These are a cowitness *(mitzeugness)* of Christ's presence in the hearts

---

divine truth, which is Christ, to the picture, from that which is signified to the sign, from the inner to the external, and from God to the creature which is an entirely misconstrued thing.

"One cannot rightly observe the Lord's Supper where these words are not correctly understood, for the reason that the body and blood of Christ is received out of this word as food for the soul."

179 Schwenckfeld, *Ein Christlicher Sendbrieff vom span und rechten Mittel zwischen der Luthrischen und Zwinglischen opinion im Artickel des Herrn Nachtmals...*, CS, XIV, 112.
180 Schwenckfeld, *Der XXVI Sendbrieff an Alle Christliche guthertzige Menschen von der Gnaden Gottes...*, CS, III, 83–98.
181 Schwenckfeld, *Der VI Sendbrieffe an vorgenanten Herrn Johan Kneller... Mit anhangender Rechenschafft oder Bekantnus vom Nachtmal und vom Brote des Herren, CS*, VIII, 242.
182 *Ibid.* For an English translation of Schwenckfeld's views on the Supper see *SAW*, Sel. VIII.

of the believers.[183] This is the natural sense in which the Supper may not be improperly called a *sacrament*, even though the word is not in Scripture.[184] In this sense the Supper is a *means* of grace. It does not *ex opere operator* bestow grace, nor is it a means of grace to awaken or strengthen faith in those who are weak in faith. The Supper does heighten the sense of the presence of Christ within the gathered congregation, which is itself the nonglorified body of Christ on earth.[185]

C. The Place of the Ban

All of the Evangelical Anabaptists within the Radical Reformation stressed the *voluntary* character of membership within the *gathered* or *true Church*. William Keeney has pointed out that both

> Calvinists and Lutherans tended to look upon the Church [*Kerk*] as an institution divinely ordained to make available to man tne means of grace. Thus they wanted to included the whole society within the Church, so that all men might have access to this means of grace... Anabaptists generally conceived of the Church [*Gemeente*] as a fellowship of holy

---

183 Marbeck, *Verantwortung*, pp. 90–94.
184 Marbeck, *Vermanung*, p. 254.
185 Marbeck, *Verantwortung*, p. 140. It is noticeable that in Schwenckfeld's doctrine of the spiritual eating of the Supper he is in some respects much closer to the Dutch Anabaptists, Menno Simons and Dirk Philips, than they are to their South German cousin, Pilgram Marbeck. Menno, Dirk, and Schwenckfeld all held to the Celestial Flesh Christology. All of them found support for the spiritual eating of the Supper in John 6:33–64, and especially did they find support for this view in John 6:62–63, which reads as follows: "Then what if you were to see the Son of Man ascending where he was before? It is the spirit that gives life, the flesh is of no avail; the words that I have spoken to you are spirit and life."
In addition to the two factors mentioned above which Menno, Dirk, and Schwenckfeld held in common was the mutual reliance of all three upon Augustine as the authority for their interpretation of John 6. Both Menno and Schwenckfeld appeal directly to Augustine's *Tracts on St. John: Credere enim in eum, hoc est manducare panem vivum. Qui credit, manducat: invisibiliter saginatur, quia invisibiliter renascitur. Infans intus est, novus intus est: ubi novellatur, iti satiatur. In Augustini Opera Omnia*, ed. J. P. Migne, in *Patrologiae Cursus Completus* (Paris: Vrayet, Pres La Barriere D'Enfer, 1865), XXXV, col. 1607. Menno's *Foundation of Christian Doctrine*, CWMS, p. 155, and Dirk's *Van dat Auontmael*, BRN, X, 111–34, contain no direct reference to Augustine, but his influence upon Dirk's thought seems obvious. Schwenckfeld's dependence upon Augustine has already been noted.
Schwenckfeld is also closer to Menno in the role which he is willing to ascribe to baptism than he is to Marbeck. Menno says that baptism may not be a sign of grace, for Christ only can be that. Dirk and Marbeck are more nearly in agreement on the sacramental character of baptism. Dirk uses the same passage that Marbeck does, Eph. 5:26, to call water baptism a witness to the inner baptism of the Spirit.
However, on the question of the suspension of either baptism or the Supper, Dirk and Menno would have agreed with Marbeck. Marbeck found in Schwenckfeld one of erring spirits who did not know that because we are creatures we have need of creaturely things. One of Dirk's last works was a criticism of Sebastian Franck for having advocated a position similar to Schwenckfeld's "still stand" on the Supper in a letter to John Campanus. See Dirk Philips, *Verantwoordinghe ende Refutation op twee Sendtbrieven Sebastiani Franck*, BRN, X, pp. 483–505. This was not a direct reply to Franck, who died in 1543, while Dirk's work was written about 1566.

beings. The visible church included the believers who *were gathered because they had already received grace and were partakers of the divine nature.*[186] (Italics mine)

Where the visible Church was itself the community of grace and the body of Christ, a way had to be found to maintain the purity of the Church. The way was provided in carefully worked out steps of discipline and the ban. The ban resulted in the expulsion from the community of those members who refused to accept its discipline and who erred in *doctrine* or *life*.

In the main, two Biblical images were employed by the Radicals to illustrate the need for discipline and the ban to keep the Church pure. One was that of the Church, as the Bride of Christ, without spot or wrinkle, based upon Eph. 5:27 and Rev. 21:2. The other was the image of Israel as the *holy community* separated from the evil world. Favorite Biblical passages cited in connection with the latter image were Josh. 7:25–26, which relates the stoning of Achan because of his theft of the forbidden spoils of battle, and Num. 12:9–16, which speaks of Miriam's exclusion from the camp of Israel during the time that she was smitten with leprosy as a result of her criticism of Moses' choice of a Cushite woman as wife. I Pet. 1:13–16 and I Pet. 2:9–10 were also applied to the visible Church and used as texts which proved the necessity of the use of discipline and of the ban in keeping the Church pure.[187]

The purpose of discipline within the Church so conceived was to deal with those members of the community who did not manifest the fruits of grace in their lives. Since God has opened up new possibilities for those who are regenerate, care must be exercised that grace does not degenerate into cheap grace. Hubmaier expresses this in the title of his work on the ban which appeared in 1527. Hubmaier says that where the ban is not properly used according to the orderly and earnest command of Christ, nothing but sin and shame and blasphemy rules within the Church.[188]

The ban is to be used only after attempts at discipline based upon the formula found in Matt. 18:15–18 have failed.[189] After all these attempts at discipline fail, the ban is to be used. Hubmaier calls it an open separation and exclusion *(ausschliessung)* of one out of the Church *(gemainschaft)* of Christ because of a gross *(ergerlichen)* sin, which the one placed under the ban will not abandon.[190] Hubmaier's argument has particular cogency here, because it rests upon the new grace that is available to men in Christ and enables them to master their passions. The reasons which Hubmaier lists for the use of the ban upon one who will not

---

186 Keeney, "The Development of Dutch Anabaptist Thought and Practice from 1539–1564," p. 256.
187 Dirk Philips, *Vanden Ban, BRN*, X, 256.
188 Hubmaier, *Vom christlichen Bann.*
189 The text in the R. S. V. reads as follows:
"If your brother sins against you, go and tell him his fault, between you and him alone. If he listens to you, you have gained your brother. But if he does not listen, take one or two others along with you, that every word may be confirmed by the evidence of two or three witnesses. If he refuses to listen to them, tell it to the church; and if he refuses to listen even to the church, let him be to you as a Gentile and a tax collector."
190 Hubmaier, *Vom christlichen Bann.*

yield to discipline in the steps outlined above are four in number:

1. Such a person should be banned so that the whole Church will not be put to shame by one member.
2. In order that new members who are weak may not be given a bad example.
3. So that by the open punishment of the erring member before the whole congregation others may be frightened to fear evil.
4. The Church is the Bride of Christ, and as such she must keep herself pure.[191]

In a fifth point Hubmaier deals with the question of the attitude of the members of the Church toward a person who has been placed under the ban. His counsel is that members of the Church should have nothing to do with such persons. They should neither eat nor drink with them, so that the ban may do its work.[192] Hans Denck also wrote briefly on the ban, but did not expand on the manner in which it ought to be applied. He saw the ban as the final and remorseful action which might be necessitated by divine love in the event that earnest rebuke failed.[193] Men must always exercise care and wisdom that they do not place the love of man above the love of God.[194] This in certain instances involved the necessity to rebuke an offending member. To refuse rebuke when this is needed is not to love a man according to God's love and truth but in fact to hate him.[195] "Yet for the sake of divine love one may not hate [a person] beyond the extent that he earnestly rebukes him, and where he does not hear it with heartfelt remorse, shun him."[196]

Denck called this "the separation of the children of God from the evil world," and the ban or exclusion *(ausschliessung)* of the false brethren, "which must take place exclusively because of true love."[197]

In naming the ban as the only legitimate means which the children of God may use to separate themselves from the evil world, Denck touched upon a theme that was emphasized also by Menno and Dirk. Under the old covenant of law Achan and his household had been stoned to death. Under the new covenant of grace the death penalty was out of place.[198] The ban did not involve the loss of life or the use of violence.

The procedure which Menno and Dirk advocated for the use of discipline and the ban was essentially the same as that of Hubmaier. The ban was for Menno the means which God had appointed for the brother or sister "whom we cannot convert by gentle services."[199] The hope that Menno held was that by such means one who had erred in doctrine or in life could be "shamed into repentance and

---

191 *Ibid.*
192 *Ibid.*
193 Hans Denck, *Von der wahren Liebe, QFR*, Band XXIV, 2 Teil. 82–83.
194 *Ibid.*
195 *Ibid.*
196 *Ibid.*
197 *Ibid.*
198 Menno Simons, *A Clear Account of Excommunication, CWMS*, pp. 471–72. See also Dirk Philips, *Vande Gemeynte Godts, BRN*, X, 406. Dirk says that what is done beyond the ban either to bring one to faith or to expel one from the congregation is neither Christian nor evangelical nor apostolic.
199 Menno Simons, *A Kindly Admonition on Church Discipline, CWMS*, p. 413.

made to acknowledge to what he has come and from what he has fallen."[200] Menno was aware that some of his critics within the Magisterial Reformation regarded the ban as practiced by the Dutch Anabaptists a weapon of hatred. The other reformers, Calvin and Luther, also wrote on the ban, but their interpretation of it generally involved only exclusion from the sacrament of the Supper.[201] The Dutch Anabaptists, because of their concept of the Church and its close association with the Celestial Flesh Christology, felt that excommunication and the ban involved not only exclusion from the Supper but also the social shunning of the excommunicated.[202]

Menno was aware that the ban could become a weapon of personal vengeance. He urged discretion, gentleness, and prudence in its use.[203] Yet he, as well as Dirk, thought that those who could not be otherwise won would have to be sorrowfully expelled from the Church for the reason that a little leaven leavens the whole lump[204] and because the unfruitful branches not pruned away will injure the good and fruitful branches.[205] Both Menno and Dirk felt that the ban was necessary in order to maintain the reputation of the Church before the world. It is generally conceded that one reason for the severity with which the ban was enforced by the Dutch Anabaptists was their desire to disassociate themselves entirely from the ill-fated revolutionary episode at Münster in 1534. Menno himself stated that this was the case,[206] and Mennonite historians have also noted it.[207] But even aside from the Münsterite episode, Menno and Dirk had precedence for the strict interpretation of the ban in their forerunner, Melchior Hoffmann.

200 *Ibid.*
201 Luther wrote *A Treatise Concerning the Ban* in 1520, and the ban is also mentioned in *An Open Letter to the Christian Nobility*, written in the same year. In these writings Luther's statements on the ban are not too different from those of the Anabaptists. It should be used neither for vengeance nor profit but only for the correction of one's neighbor. The ban should not involve the death penalty. See *Works of Martin Luther*, trans. W. A. Lambert (Philadelphia: A. J. Holman Co. and General Council Publication Board, 1916), II, 39. Luther restricted the ban to exclusion from the Supper and said that its purpose was not, as some think, "to deliver a soul to Satan and deprive it of intercession and all good works of the Church." P. 53. In the *Open Letter to the Christian Nobility*, Sec. 17, Luther states that the ban should not be used except where the Scriptures prescribe its use "against those who do not hold the true faith, or who live in open sin." Luther expresses his regret that things are now the other way around, and that the ban is used mostly to defame and plunder other people. See *Three Treatises by Martin Luther* (Philadelphia: The Muhlenberg Press, 1947), p. 72.

Calvin also wrote on the ban and gave the same three reasons for its practice that were commonly found among the Anabaptists. Yet in spite of the similarities between Calvin and the Anabaptists on this question, and even the possibility of mutual influence, Calvin understood the ban primarily as exclusion from the Lord's Supper. Calvin had great confidence in the redemptive power of the Church. He defended his policy of allowing men of doubtful character to remain within the Church, "because it is certain that the word and sacraments cannot be unattended with some good effects." *Institutes*, IV, Chap. 1, Sec. 9, Vol. 2, 282.
202 Menno Simons, *Instruction on Excommunication, CWMS*, p. 968.
203 *Ibid.*, p. 974.
204 Menno Simons, *A Clear Account of Excommunication, CWMS*, p. 471.
205 Dirk Philips, *Vande Gemeynte Godts, BRN*, X, 399.
206 Menno Simons, *Reply to Gellius Faber, CWMS*, p. 730.
207 John C. Wenger, *Glimpses of Mennonite History*, (Scottdale: Mennonite Publishing House, 1946), p. 75.

Hoffmann stressed the voluntary manner in which the Church, as the bride, and Christ, as the bridegroom, enter into the nuptial relationship with each other. The relationship which is voluntarily established can be dissolved if the bride fails to remain faithful. As a bride who becomes an adultress is divorced by her husband, so the heavenly bridegroom, through his apostolic emissaries (the ministers) would let an unfaithful bride (an individual member of the Church) be thrown out of his congregation and house. He would divorce her from his fellowship and take from her the bread and wine, and thus indicate that the vow had been broken and that she no longer had any portion of him.[208] Hoffmann held that the practice in regard to the ban, since apostolic times, had been to eject from Jesus Christ those who persisted in living according to the will of Satan after three warnings. By implication a person under the ban was to be spurned, even as a bridegroom would divorce and spurn his wayward bride.[209]

In the controversy between Marbeck and Schwenckfeld the question of the ban was a marginal issue. Yet the fact that it became an issue at all shows that Marbeck thought the ban necessary in order to maintain the purity of Christ's nonglorified body on earth. In the *Judicium* Schwenckfeld had protested Marbeck's declaration that those who did not confess the outward doctrines of baptism and the Supper as Christ had taught them were erring spirits.[210] Schwenckfeld asks that Marbeck and his brotherhood should not act so hastily, "for across the brook from you there may also be people who are Christians whom you have never learned to know."[211]

Marbeck replied in the *Verantwortung* that he did not presume to pass judgment upon those outside the community of the new covenant. The Church does not deal with the whole world but only with those who have voluntarily entered the covenant relationship.[212] In the use of the ban within the Church itself Marbeck felt that the congregation should not outrun the Holy Spirit. Only "when the Holy Spirit punishes a sin which was committed, to Him alone it pertains first to punish before any external punishment of His saints."[213] If, however, the Holy Spirit has revealed a sin, then the saints must cotestify with the Spirit that sins may not be tolerated on the body of Christ, and they must be separated from the body.

---

208 *SAW*, p. 197. Also *BRN*, V, 159.
209 *SAW*, p. 196. Also *BRN*, V, 159. The reference to wine and bread is, of course, exclusion from the Supper, while the reference to spurning means shunning the one who has been banned by the other members of the congregation.
210 Schwenckfeld, *Judicium, CS*, VIII, 186.
211 *Ibid.*
212 Marbeck, *Verantwortung*, pp. 85–86.
213 "Two Letters by Pilgram Marbeck," trans. William Klassen, *MQR*, XXXII, No 3 (July, 1958), 195. Of the two letters mentioned above one is titled, "On the Inner Church," and the other, "Concerning the Humanity of Christ." The two letters, according to Torsten Bergsten, were evidently written by Marbeck in Augsburg about 1545 and addressed to an Anabaptist congregation in Moravia with which he had connections. The letters are found in the *Kunstbuch*, discovered in Berne in 1955 and described and explained in the *Archiv für Reformationsgeschichte*, 1956, pp. 212–41. See page 192 of the above mentioned *MQR* for fuller details.

Marbeck also makes a distinction between *secret* and *open* sins. Where the Holy Spirit punishes the former inwardly "through grace unto grace with the comfort of forgiveness, no creature in heaven or upon earth may inflict punishment upon him." But where the Holy Spirit has convicted of sin, and a man refuses to confess before God or man, even though the sin is openly known and seen on him, such a man, if he refuses admonition and punishment, belongs to the world.[214]

Marbeck saw two extremes at work in the Church of his time on the question of the ban. On the one hand there were those who in their eagerness to apply the ban outran the Holy Spirit.[215] On the other hand, there were those who completely despised and wished "to discontinue admonition, prayer, ban, punishment, teaching, baptism, Lord's Supper, and the forgiveness of sins in the fellowship of the saints."[216] It was Marbeck's conviction that in order to maintain the purity of the Church as the body of Christ, the ban was a necessity, but he felt that its application should be neither too severe nor too lax.

Behind this concept of the Church as a gathered and disciplined community lay the conviction that the believer who had experienced the grace of God in regeneration was a new creature in Christ. Through the *participation in the divine nature, or the presence of the Holy Spirit in His plenitude, or the rebirth of the fallen soul*, the believer received the power to live the new life in Christ. Where evidence of the new life was not objectively present, the Radicals felt that the claim to the experience of grace was nullified by performance. Where discipline was not exercised the Radicals felt that the preaching of salvation by grace alone as it was understood in its forensic aspects by both Lutheran and Reformed traditions led to "cheap grace" and produced only "mouth Christians."[217]

D. Vocation outside the Community of Grace

It was Luther, who first expressed the great Protestant principle of the universal priesthood of all believers in the famous treatise concerning the Baylonian captivity of the Church. Luther went so far as to dissuade anyone from entering the priesthood or a religious order unless forearmed with the knowledge that in the sight of God the work of a priest or a monk was no better than that of a "rustic toiling in the field or a woman going about her household tasks."[218] In general, the Anabaptists followed Luther at this point, yet with some modifications. The last of the eighteen points which Hubmaier drew up for debate at Waldshut upon his return from Zurich in 1524 condemns idleness and states that

---

214 *Ibid.*, p. 195.
215 *Ibid.*, p. 196.
216 *Ibid.* Marbeck may well have had in mind here not only Schwenckfeld's attitude toward an organized church, but also the more severe attitude of the Dutch Anabaptists where the ban involved not only exclusion from the Lord's Supper but also the social shunning of the banned. This was rejected by the Swiss Brethren Anabaptists at a conference in Strasbourg in August, 1555, as well as the Celestial Flesh Christology. See John Horsch, "Strasburg, a Swiss Brethren Center," *MQR*, XIII, No. 1 (January, 1939).
217 Hubmaier, *Von der Freiheit des Willens.*
218 Luther, *A Prelude on the Babylonian Captivity of the Church*, printed in *Three Treatises by Martin Luther* (Philadelphia: The Muhlenberg Press, 1947), p. 192.

he who does not earn his bread by the sweat of his brow is not worthy of the food that he eats.[219] This was perhaps intended as a thrust at the mendicant monastic orders of which late medieval Europe was full, Luther himself having belonged to one of them during his days as a monk.

The emphasis upon the open character and the visible fruits of Christian faith and life in the Radical Reformation, as opposed to an emphasis upon its sometimes more hidden character within the Magisterial group, led the Radicals to a renunciation of the world which in some respects resembled the strictness of the monastic orders. Robert Friedmann has emphasized the fact that "Anabaptism almost converged toward monasticism, yet in contrast to it stays in the world, carrying on a normal life with family and profession.[220] The Radicals had learned their lesson from Luther at this point, and, like him, they eliminated the distinction between the sacred and the secular on the question of vocation.

To work with one's hands is both an honor and an obligation. Menno Simons regarded laziness a sufficient reason for excommunication from the community of the new covenant. A member of the community had a double obligation to work when he could. One side of that obligation was to provide for his own needs, so that he would not live as a parasite off the efforts of the other members of the community. The other side of the obligation to work was found in the duty of mutual helpfulness to the brethren in need.[221] The writer found no attempt in any of the primary sources used to describe the kind of vocation in which the members of the "holy community" may most fittingly engage.

In a work on the nurture of children, written in 1557, Menno expresses the opinion that children should be taught the art of spinning and other handcrafts "suitable, useful, and proper to their years and persons."[222] Menno also felt that in order that they might be prepared to lead a useful life, children of both sexes should be taught to read and write, but beyond this he makes no suggestions.

There is no doublt that some sense of vocation in daily life outside the holy community did exist among the Radicals, although it does not become particularly vocal. The fact that laziness was considered an offense serious enough to merit the ban is at least an indication that they considered work honorable. During the long centuries of persecution the Anabaptists developed a reputation as industrious people and were often sought by independent dukes as desirable settlers for their lands.[223]

219 Hubmaier, *Schluzzreden die Balthazar Fridberger dem J. Eckio die meysterlich zu examinieren fütbotten hat.* See Vedder, p. 71, for English translation.
220 Robert Friedmann, "Anabaptism and Protestantism," *MQR*, XXIV, No 2 (January, 1950), 20.
221 Menno Simons, *Instruction on Excommunication, CWMS*, p. 968.
222 Menno Simons, *The Nurture of Children, CWMS*, pp. 951–52.
223 Bender, "Anabaptism in Germany," *ME*, II, 490–91. The most scholarly work so far done on the vocations in which Anabaptist were generally engaged is that of Paul Peachey, *Die Soziale Herkunft der Schweizerischen Taüfer, 1525–1540* (Zürich, 1953). Peachey has shown that the majority of the Swiss Anabaptists of the period who came from groups of citizens and craftsmen were weavers, shoemakers, tailors, hatters, goldsmiths, etc. For an English directory of the Swiss Anabaptists from 1525 to 1540, which includes both names and trades see Paul Peachey, "Social Background and Social Philosophy of the Swiss Anabaptists, 1525–1540," *MQR*, XXVIII, No. 2 (April, 1954), 123–27.

Anabaptist leaders universally objected to the fact that ministers received their support from the civil authority. This was the complaint of Pilgram Marbeck against Martin Bucer in 1531. Marbeck rebuked Bucer and the other Strasbourg Reformers because they accepted support from the civil authority and did not preach under the cross and suffering.[224] Menno Simons makes disparaging references to the ministers of the Magisterial Reformation, who live a life of ease on fat stipends from the government, while he must live in poverty as a hunted exile.[225]

Such references have at times been used as proof texts to show that Menno believed in a nonsalaried ministry in which every minister, after the manner of Paul, had his own trade by which he supported himself.[226] The fact is, however, that Menno both asked for support from the brotherhood which looked to him for leadership and specifically stated why he needed such support.[227] What Menno, like Marbeck, objected to was that the ministers in Magisterial churches sought support from the civil government..

One must remember that most of the later leaders within the Radical Reformation were not professionally trained theologians but lay people, who already had their own trade or profession before they became involved in the movement. Most of them continued in the vocation in which they were trained before their conversion to Anabaptist or Radical ideas.[228] After the Anabaptists were outlawed by imperial decree, the movement had to go underground in order to survive.[229] Continued work at the vocation in which they were trained became for the leaders a practical necessity.

E. Suffering as a Mark of the True Church

The view of the Church as the community of the new covenant of grace, made up of those who through the new birth shared in the divine nature and who were gathered and disciplined and separated from the evil world, left little room within the Radical Reformation for a doctrine of the invisible Church. Separation from the evil world in itself demanded that the Church become visible before the world. The insistence that the true Church must be visible before the evil world

---

224 Rörich, p. 54.
225 Menno Simons, *Reply to Gellius Faber*, CWMS, p. 674.
226 Acts 18:1–4.
227 Menno Simons, *Personal Note to Rein Edes and the Brethren in Waterhorne*, ca. 1558, CWMS, p. 1056.
228 For example, of the representatives of the Radical Reformation included in this study three had trades or professions at which they continued to work after joining the Anabaptist movement. Hans Denck was a linguist of some note; Melchior Hoffmann, a furrier; and Pilgram Marbeck, a civil engineer. The Evangelical Spiritualist, Caspar Schwenckfeld, was a nobleman, whose income from the ancestral estate continued to support him during his life of exile. Only Menno, Dirk, and Hubmaier appear to have had neither trade nor profession nor independent income.
229 The edict of the Diet of Speyer, which outlawed the Anabaptists throughout the empire, was issued April 22, 1529. For details see G. Franz, *Wiedertauferakten, 1527–1626, Urkundliche Quellen zur Hessizchen Reformationsgeschichte*, IV, 1951. See also Karl Schornbaum, *Quellen zur Geschichte der Wiedertäufer*, II, Sec. 1 (Leipzig: M. Heinsius Nachfolger, 1934). See also *ME*, II, 446–53.

appears early in the thought of both Dutch and South German Anabaptist leaders. It is found in Menno Simons' *Foundation of Christian Doctrine* in 1539, in Marbeck's *Verantwortung* of 1544, and in Dirk Philips' *Verantwoordinghe ende Refutation op twee Sendtbrieven Sebastiani Franck*, ca. 1558. This aspect is perhaps less emphasized in the thought of Hans Denck, because he was at heart the Contemplative Anabaptist. Yet, as he advocated the use of the ban as a means of separation from the evil world, it is not absent from his thought. Hubmaier, too, makes less of this aspect of Anabaptist thought insofar as he could see a legitimate Christian use of the sword,[230] and, therefore, his Church was not so sharply set over against the *always* evil world. Yet, because he also advocated the use of the ban and a disciplined congregation, he would also have found the doctrine of an invisible Church as advocated by Sebastian Franck and Caspar Schwenckfeld incompatible.

Menno in the 1539 work urges Christians to set their light on a candlestick, to build their city on a high mountain, to live without reproach, and to behave as Christians in all things.[231] Members of the Church are asked to prove themselves as those who are born out of God, by the fact that they neither accept false doctrine nor return evil for evil.[232]

Menno's polemic was not directed so much against a doctrine of an invisible Church in the Spirit as was that of Marbeck and also that of Dirk in reply to Sebastian Franck, as it was against the contention of the Magisterial Reformers that the Anabaptists were schismatics who introduced division among God's people by withdrawing from the established Church. All of the Evangelical Anabaptists answered this charge, of course, by the reply that the Church had become apostate, and this required that the true Church separate herself from an apostate church as well as from an evil world. This is evident in Menno's *Reply to Gellius Faber* of 1554. Gellius calls the Anabaptist practice of constituting themselves a church a shameful disgrace which is contrary to the example of the prophets and of Christ.[233] Menno retorts that both Old and New Testaments indicate that the Church must be a people separate from the world and that this condition has not obtained in the contemporary situation for many years. The Anabaptists are compelled by the Spirit and Word of God to gather a penitent congregation out of all impure sects to the praise of Jesus Christ and to the service and love of the neighbor.[234] The implication of this is that the Anabaptist could not take comfort, as the Magisterial Reformers did, in the thought that hidden underneath the *imperfections* of the visible institutionalized Church was after all the invisible Church of which all the elect who were known only to God were members. That Marbeck, no less than Dirk, would have supported Menno in this position is seen in the program which each of them followed.

The demand that the true Church must be visible before the world and separated from the apostate church as well involved also the conviction that the true

---

230 See Chapter VI on the ethics of grace for a full treatment of this point.
231 Menno Simons, *Foundation of Christian Doctrine, CWMS*, p. 224.
232 *Ibid.*
233 Menno Simons, *Reply to Gellius Faber, CWMS*, p. 679.
234 *Ibid.*

Church will be a suffering church. Pilgram Marbeck held that Caspar Schwenckfeld with his doctrine of an invisible Church in the Spirit sought to escape the persecution of the world.[235] Dirk Philips' criticism of Sebastian Franck's doctrine of an invisible Church of the Spirit scattered among many people is almost identical.[236] Marbeck felt that Schwenckfeld's *still stand* on the Supper and his attempt to get Marbeck to take the same position in regard to baptism was a denial of Christian responsibility before the world and before fellow Christians.[237] The Christian must expect to bear the cross.[238] The Church in the world must be a *suffering* rather than a *ruling* Church.[239]

In the *Reply to Gellius Faber* of 1554 Menno listed suffering as the fifth and sixth signs of the true Church. The true Church will confidently confess Christ's name, will, and Word in the face of all cruelty, tyranny, tumult, fire, and sword. Where the Church seeks to escape persecution by acting as the magistrate wishes, she is a hypocrite, and those who "are enlightened by the Word and taught by the Spirit may well judge what kind of Church that is."[240] The *pressing cross of Christ*, which is borne for the sake of his testimony, is a sure sign of the true Church which is seen not only in the testimony of Scripture but also in the example of Christ, the apostles, prophets, and "the first unfalsified Church."[241]

Dirk Philips also taught that the true Church must be a suffering Church. The seventh ordinance of the true Church is that all Christians must suffer and be persecuted as Christ has promised them (John 16:33),[242] but the true Church in turn may persecute no one because of his faith.[243] The congregation that is formed by grace may neither rule nor be ruled by violence.[244]

Although the Evangelical Anabaptists in particular, with the exception of Hubmaier, looked upon suffering as a sure sign of the true Church, they did not seek suffering for the sake of suffering. Both Marbeck and Menno made appeals to the magistracy for toleration. Marbeck upon his own expulsion from the city of Strasbourg in December of 1531 asked the authorities to deal more gently with the Anabaptists who had fled to the city for refuge and had no other place in the

---

235 Marbeck, *Verantwortung*, pp. 73–132 and 160.
236 Dirk Philips, *Verantwoordinghe ende Refutation op twee Sendtbrieven Sebastiani Franck, BRN*, X, 502–03.
237 Marbeck, *Verantwortung*, p. 125.
238 *Ibid.*, p. 160. The criticism here is directed at Schwenckfeld's doctrine of the glorified Christ. Marbeck says that Schwenckfeld teaches only the inner and glorified and unsuffering Christ and not the sorrowing one on earth. "Yes, only the word of his glory and splendor, and not of his cross and sorrow." Such preaching does not hurt the flesh. It makes *lustige* Christians and tickles the flesh in honor. "If now Schwenckfeld says he still has cross enough, even though he does not keep the command of Christ in regard to outward baptism as well as other things, the answer is that no one can give true testimony to the cross of Christ apart from abiding in his word and sayings [reden]."
239 Wenger, "Pilgram Marbeck, Tyrolese Engineer and Anabaptist Elder," *Church History*, IX (March, 1940), p. 35.
240 Menno Simons, *Reply to Gellius Faber, CWMS*, p. 741.
241 *Ibid.*, pp. 741–42.
242 Dirk Philips, *V-nde Gemeynte Godts, BRN*, X, 404.
243 *Ibid.*, p. 405.
244 *Ibid.*, pp. 405–06.

world where they might live in freedom of conscience. He reminded the civil authority that the city had thus far been spared the shedding of blood on account of faith, and he looked upon this as no small favor (*Gnad*) from God.[245]

Menno made various appeals for toleration for the Dutch Anabaptists. The earliest appears in the *Foundation of Christian Doctrine* of 1539 and was addressed to magistrates, common people, and sects.[246] *Confession of Distressed Christians* and *A Pathetic Supplication to All Magistrates*, both written in 1552, are renewed appeals for toleration. *The Cross of the Saints*, written in 1554, had as its central purpose the encouragement of those who had to undergo persecution and face possible martyrdom.

Yet, while the Evangelical Anabaptists of the Radical Reformation made appeals for religious toleration, they gave at the same time a positive interpretation to such suffering as they had to endure. Christ had predicted that his saints would suffer. And though they are so severely dealt with by the world that

> their lives may appear to the foolish world to be nothing but frenzy, and their end without honor; yet we know that they are the people and children of the Lord, the apple of His eye, and that their blood and death are dear to Him.[247]

Not only did the experience of suffering for the faith hold the prospect of eternal reward,[248] but through suffering the kingdom of heaven was extended, and the Word of God was made known, and weak brethren were strengthened by examples of courage.[249] Last but not least, Christians because of the mystical union with Christ could, if they had to suffer in any case, complete in their own suffering what remained of the suffering of Christ. Menno in the *Epistle to Martin Micron* of 1556 appeals to him for tolerant treatment of himself and his brethren, but ends the appeal by asking, "But what will help? The innocent, defenseless Lamb must be hated and murdered in His members."[250] Pilgram Marbeck, although he understood the mystical union in terms of the Pauline metaphor of the body rather than the bridal imagery as already noted, gave the same interpretation to suffering. He writes:

> Pray God the Father through Christ that we all may fulfill and complete (the suffering of Christ which is left over in His body), each according to the manner of love unto and through death as faithful fellow-witnesses of the tribulation of Christ; that we also suffer one for another, as Christ has suffered for us unto the end.[251]

The thought is based upon Col. 1:24, where Paul states that in his sufferings he completes what is lacking in Christ's afflictions for the sake of his body, the

---

245 *Rörich*, pp. 57–58.
246 Menno Simons, *Foundation of Christian Doctrine*, CWMS, p. 190, n. 44.
247 Menno Simons, *The Cross of the Saints*, ca. 1554, CWMS, p. 593.
248 *Ibid.*, p. 620. Also Dirk Philips, *Vande Gemeynte Godts*, BRN, X, 407. Dirk rested his case on I Pet. 4:14, II Tim. 2:12, and Rom. 8:17.
249 Menno Simons, *The Cross of the Saints*, CWMS, p. 620.
250 Menno Simons, *Epistle to Martin Micron*, 1556, CWMS, p. 926. Similar passages appear in *The Cross of the Saints*, pp. 587 and 597.
251 Bergsten, "Two Letters by Pilgram Marbeck," trans. William Klassen, *MQR*, XXXII, No. 3 (July, 1958), p. 196.

Church. Marbeck interprets the passage in such a way that the suffering of the members of the Church for each other completes what remains of the affliction of Christ, for the Church corporately is Christ's nonglorified body, and to be received into membership in the Church, through the narrow door of believer's baptism,[252] is at the same time to be taken up into Christ.[253]

There was present within the Radical Reformation, as a result of prolonged persecution, on the one hand, and the refusal of the Radicals to resort to violence to defend themselves or advance the faith by force of arms, on the other, a rather well developed theology of martyrdom.[254]

---

252 Marbeck, *Vermanung*, p. 229.
253 Marbeck, *Verantwortung*, p. 140.
254 For the two best and most extended treatments of the martyr motif in Radical Reformation thought so far written see Ethelbert Stauffer, "The Anabaptist Theology of Martyrdom," trans. by Robert Friedmann, *MQR*, XIX, No. 3 (July, 1945), 179–214, and A. Orley Swartzentruber, "The Piety and Theology of the Anabaptist Martyrs in Van Braght's *Martyrs' Mirror*, I and II," *MQR*, XXVIII, No. 1 and 2 (January and April, 1954), pp. 5–26 and 128–42, respectively.

CHAPTER V

THE HERMENEUTICS OF GRACE

A. *The Rupture of an Ancient Synthesis*

In the centuries prior to the Reformation both the distribution of grace through the sacraments and the interpretation of the Bible as *one* source of divine revelation were under the control and authority of the Church. The second source of divine revelation which prior to the Reformation was regarded as equally authoritative with the Bible was the tradition of the Church Fathers.

The Church as a visible institution was thus, while not the *immediate* source of grace, yet divinely appointed to *mediate* the grace of God in Christ through the sacraments. The same Church which could through the administration of the sacraments either grant or withhold the flow of divine grace had also canonized the holy Scriptures. It was, therefore, not strange that this Church should claim the sole right to interpret correctly those Scriptures which had been canonized under her authority. In this way the Church controlled not only the flow of grace through the sacraments but also the divine revelation found within the Scriptures.

The coming of the Reformation disrupted not only the flow of grace through the sacraments, which were reduced in number from seven to two by both wings of the Reformation movement, but it disrupted also the Church's right to be the sole interpreter of Scripture. The latter derived from an ancient synthesis which had endured without serious challenge since the close of the fourth century. Within this synthesis the authority of Scripture as divine revelation was seen as derived from the authority of the Church.[1]

During the Reformation and afterward the authority of the Bible was pitted against the authority of the Church by both groups of Reformers. Luther's "*sola Scriptura*" and Menno Simons' "*according to the Scriptures*" were the standards used by Magisterial and Radical Reformers alike to reform the Church and purge her life from those abuses which had crept in because of the neglect of the Bible.

Yet, as every exegete of holy Scripture knows, it is not enough to enunciate the principle, *sola Scriptura*, once the sole right of the correct interpretation of Scripture by an authoritarian and institutionalized Church has been denied. The moment this is done the individual interpreter is driven to search for some hermeneutical method of his own which will enable him to discover some thread of unity in what is otherwise a bewildering variety of material. It was in the course of their quest for such a method that the Radical Reformers developed what can in some respects best be described as the hermeneutics of grace.

---

[1] George H. Tavard in "Holy Church or Holy Writ — A Dilemma of the 14th Century," *Church History*, XXIII, Vol. 3 (July, 1954), 195–206, has shown that this synthesis was already theoretically questioned as early as the fourteenth century. But until the eve of the Reformation the question remained, except for a few scattered advocates of reform like Wycliffe and Huss, largely an academic one. First published in 1954, this essay has now been enlarged into a book by Father Tavard, and in its enlarged form it covers also the Reformation era. The book appeared in 1959 under the title, *Holy Writ or Holy Church; the Crisis of the Protestant Reformation* (London: Burns and Oates, 1959).

1. The Three Main Hermeneutical Groups

The hermeneutical methods developed by the representatives selected for this study, although they differ widely, fall into three rather broad but fairly distinct groups. In the first group are found men like Hans Denck and Caspar Schwenckfeld, who believed that divine revelation, like divine grace, could not be mediated to the human soul by anything that was external. The Bible as a book belonged to the category of external things; hence it could not be considered by either Denck or Schwenckfeld as the Word of God. These men developed what is known in Radical Reformation thought as the hermeneutics of the inner and outer Word, in which they made a sharp distinction between Christ as the *Eternal Word of God* and the Bible as a witness to God's revelation of Himself in Christ.[2] Fundamental to this view of the Bible in relation to Christ was the conviction that what is witness to revelation cannot be the same thing as revelation itself. Therefore, to equate the Bible with Christ as the Word of God was to rob Christ of his glory as the *only* Word of God.

Melchior Hoffmann may be considered as a representative of a second hermeneutical group within the Radical Reformation, which placed great emphasis upon the distinction between letter and spirit. Only the exegete who could rightly distinguish between the two could hope to arrive at the true meaning of Scripture. When the terms, inner and outer Word, were used with reference to this method, the dead letter of Scripture was the outer Word under which the kernel of external truth lay hidden in the inner Word. Spiritualists of various shades had great fondness for this hermeneutical method,[3] but it was also employed to some extent by the Evangelical Anabaptists.

---

2 This was in basic disagreement with Calvin, who identified the Word of God very closely with the written Scriptures. See *Institutes*, Book III, Vol. II, Chap. 17, Sec. 2, p. 55, where Calvin implies that all Scripture is inspired by the Holy Spirit and that the Holy Spirit would not be inconsistent with Himself.

Luther's attitude toward the Bible was both more flexible and more complex. He could call the Scriptures the crib in which Christ lies, state that the Gospel was more than the records of the Synoptics and John, since it embraced the incarnation and all that it meant, and declare the epistle of James a "right strawy epistle." Yet when it suited his purpose in polemics against Rome or against those who differed with him on the interpretation of the words, "This is my body," Luther could identify the Word of God with the Scriptures. For a statement of Luther's which seems to identify the Word of God with Scripture see the Latin text of the *Commentary on Galatians, Werke WA*, Vol. 40, Sec. I, 589, which reads as follows:

Ideo nostra theologia est certa, qui ponit nos extra nos: non debeo niti in conscientia mea, sensuali persona, opere, sed in promissione divina, veritate, quae, non potest fallere. Hoc papa nescit, ideo disi: nemo sicit, etiam iusti.

3 See Alfred Hegler, *Geist und Schrift bei Sebastian Franck, Eine Studie zur Geschichte des Spiritualismus in der Reformationzeit* (Freiburg, 1892) for a complete discussion of this method and of Sebastian Franck as one who employed it. See also Sebastian Franck's *Paradoxa*, Eingeleitet von W. Lehman, Herausgegeben von Heinrich Zeigler (Jena: Eugen Diederichs, 1909) for illustrations of the application of this method.

The distinction between *letter* and *spirit* was, of course, neither the invention nor the discovery of the Radical Reformers of the sixteenth century. The problem is as old as the Church itself and has roots in the antiquity of the pre-Christian world. For a discussion of this

The third distinct hermeneutical group within the Radical Reformation developed the hermeneutics of the new and old covenants. Pilgram Marbeck, Dirk Philips, and Menno Simons belonged to this group. They did not hesitate to call the entire Bible, both Old and New Testaments, the Word of God, but they did find between the two Testaments two different levels of revelation. Within the framework of the two covenant concepts the Old Testament was always made subordinate to the New.[4] This was achieved by means of variant hermeneutical methods, but regardless of the particular method by which such subordination was achieved, behind every method lay the fundamental presupposition that in Christ a new grace had come and a new revelation had been given which made everything before Christ look pale by comparison. Hence, the Old Testament was regarded as the *covenant of promise* while the New Testament was designated as the *covenant of fulfillment.*

2. The Influence of the Mystics

Those who developed the hermeneutics of the inner and outer Word in either of the two forms mentioned above were strongly influenced by the Christian mystics who produced not only the *Theologia Germanica* and the various editions of the *Imitatio Christ* but also a "great collection of mystical literature of a semifictitious sort produced anonymously by the Rhine groups of the Friends of God."[5] It is a known fact that Hans Denck was familiar with the *Theologia Germanica* and evidently carried a copy of it on his person as he fled from city to city, seeking refuge and finding none.[6] Rembert says that by the second half of the fifteenth century mysticism had already laid down the fundamental proposition that the essence of religion was not to be found in any outward observance "but in love to God and neighbor and in the purification of the heart."[7]

Among the mystics this distrust of all outward observances and of all things external included also to some extent the Bible. One of the most striking examples of this is found in a little tract published by Schwenckfeld in September of 1552. The editors of the *Corpus Schwenckfeldianorum* believe that the mystic, Johannes Tauler, who made preaching tours into the Rhineland, where he came into contact with the Friends of God, is the original author of the tract which was first published in Augsburg in 1508 and republished by Schwenckfeld

---

problem from Homer through the first and second centuries of the Christian era to the time of the Alexandrian Allegorists, Clement and Origen, see Robert M. Grant, *The Letter and the Spirit* (New York: The Macmillan Company, 1957).

4 This again was not the mind of either Luther or Calvin on this question, who closely equated the two Testaments. See especially Luther's *Lectures on the Psalms* and his *Commentary on Genesis, Werke, WA*, 40, 2, and 42–44, respectively, and Calvin's *Institutes*, II, Chap. X, "The Similarity of the Old and New Testaments."

5 Rufus M. Jones, *New Studies in Mystical Religion* (New York: The Macmillan Company, 1927), p. 162.

6 See Fellmann, pp. 18–19.

7 Karl Rembert, *Die Wiedertaüfer im Herzogtum Julich*, Studien zur Geschichte der Reformation, besonders am niederheim (Berlin: R. Gaertners Verlags buch handlung, 1899), pp. 10–11.

in 1552 under the title, *Ehn tröstliche Christenliche underweisung unnd verstand des eusserlichen und innerlichen worts Gottes.*[8]

Schwenckfeld reprints the tract with evident approval and without significant editorial alteration. The following excerpt from the tract illustrates the difficulty which those within the Radical Reformation, most influenced by the Christian mysticism of the preceding century, felt with the Bible as the source of revelation when they believed that Christ spoke directly to the soul.

> The holy, divine prophetic and evangelical Scriptures are true and loving words of God..., but they are not the Spirit which makes alive nor the living Word upon which souls are fed. Rather Christ alone is the living Word, in which all salvation is found... The divine, holy Scripture is not our Head, but it does point us to Him, who is our Head... For though the divine Scriptures come from God through the prophets and apostles, they are nevertheless not the Spirit which makes alive nor the living Word of God on which the soul is fed and receives the life whereof Christ spoke in Luke 11:28.[9]

It was with presuppositions similar to those in the reference cited above that Hans Denck developed his own doctrine of the inner and outer Word. The first item in Denck's confession to the city council at Nürnberg deals with the question of the relationship of the Bible to saving faith — Can faith be based upon the Bible? Denck is aware that this is what his contemporaries say must be the source and ground of faith, but he sees two difficulties with the proposition. The first difficulty is with himself as interpreter; the second, with the Scriptures themselves. Denck writes:

> Because there is such a darkness within me, it is impossible that I could on every occasion interpret the Scripture. Therefore, if I do not understand it, how shall I create faith out of it?[10]

Denck regards the Scriptures

> as a lantern that shines in the darkness, but which cannot (because they are written with human hands, spoken by human mouths, and heard with human ears) entirely remove that darkness.[11]

The difficulty which Denck finds within himself as an interpreter of Scripture is overcome through the revelatory work of the Holy Spirit. Man, however, cannot command or control this. He can only wait for it. He

> who does not want to wait for the revelation from God, but usurps for himself the work which belongs to the Holy Spirit of God, he makes for himself out of the secret of God contained in the Scriptures [*in der schrift verfasset*] an ugly abomination... and draws the grace of our God to the gall of bitterness as shown in the epistles of Jude and II Peter.[12]

8 *CS*, XIV, 351–57.
9 *Ibid.*, pp. 352–53.
10 Hans Denck, *Bekenntnis für den Rat zu Nürnberg, QFR*, Band XXIV, 2 Teil, 22.
11 *Ibid.*, p. 21.
12 *Ibid.*, p. 22.

But how does one know whether or not the Holy Spirit is at work as interpreter, so that he does not undertake to do for himself what only the Holy Spirit illuminating him can do correctly? Denck found the solution in a collection of eighty Scripture passages arranged in forty pairs of apparently contradictory sayings. He called these *paradoxes* or *Gegenschriften*. A few selections from the paradoxes at this point will sufficiently illustrate their character.

> The First
> For who has known the mind of the Lord? Rom. 11:34a.
> For he has made known to us in all wisdom and insight the mystery of his will. Eph. 1:9a.
>
> The Third
> Because God made not death; neither delighted he when the living perish. Wisd. 1:13.
> Fire, and hail, and famine, and death, all these are created for vengeance. Sir. 39:29a.
>
> The Sixth
> For the gifts and the call of God are irrevocable. Rom. 11:29.
> I repent that I have made Saul king. I Sam. 15:11a.
>
> The Seventh
> ... for I am not come to judge the world but to save the world. John 12:47b.
> Jesus said, For judgment I came into this world. John 9:39b.
>
> The Fourteenth
> And he said, Go into all the world and preach the gospel to the whole creation. Mark 16:15.
> Do not give dogs what is holy; and do not throw your pearls before swine. Matt. 9:6a.[13]

The *paradoxes* or *Gegenschriften* appeared in 1526 under the title, *Wer die Wahrheit wahrlich lieb hat*, and were probably arranged during Denck's sojourn at Augsburg and almost certainly before his arrival in Strasbourg in November of the same year. In the preface to the paradoxes is found the significance which Denck attached to them. He laments that both previously and in his own time so many different sects have arisen because of different interpretations of the same passage of Scripture. This, says Denck, would never have happened if people had respect for the one teacher (*leermayster*) of the Scriptures, the Holy Spirit.[14] To those who have not the Spirit, the Scriptures appear to be contradictory in many places, but those who have the Spirit will know that two contradictory Scriptures are both true.

> But one is enclosed within the other as the lesser in the greater, time within eternity, and place within infinity. He who allows the contradictions to remain and cannot harmonize them, this one lacks the ground of truth.[15]

---

13 Hans Denck, *Wer die Wahrheit wahrlich lieb hat*, 1526, *QFR*, Band XXIV, 2 Teil, 68–70. The English translations of Old and New Testament passages are from the R. S. V. Those from the *Apocrypha* are from the Revised Version of 1894, Thomas Nelson and Sons, New York.
14 *Ibid.*, p. 68.
15 *Ibid.*

The difficulty which Denck felt with the Bible as divine revelation, modified by the fact that though inspired by the Holy Spirit the inspiration was yet humanly received, was solved by his own peculiar doctrine of the inner Word. The inner Word was for Denck neither the kernel of eternal truth hidden underneath the husk of the dead letter, as it was for Sebastian Franck,[16] nor the occasional flash of immediate divine revelation, as it was for Thomas Müntzer.[17] Nor was the inner Word for Denck the "spark of divinity," which is part of human nature itself, as in Meister Eckhart.[18] Denck did not actually use the term, "inner Word," but spoke of "that which dwells within us but is not of us."[19] Denck meant by this expression the preincarnate Christ or *Logos*, "who dwells within all men and preaches to each one in particular in the measure that he listens to it."[20]

The Bible cannot give one what this inner Word or *Logos* can for the reason that "where God is not, to that place He may never be brought by anything that is creaturely."[21]

> The Kingdom of God is within you, says the Truth. Whoever looks toward and awaits it from outside himself, to him it will not come. He who in truth seeks God already has Him. For without God man may neither seek for God nor find Him.[22]

Thus it is not the Bible, as the outer Word, which can bring to man the saving knowledge of God. It is rather the inner Word, which drives men to read the Bible in search of testimony to that which the inner Word itself speaks directly to the soul. Therefore Denck can say:

> Insofar as I out of my own ability interpret the Scriptures, I understand nothing. Insofar, however, as that which is within me drives me, to that extent I understand it, but not through merit.

---

16 See Hegler.

17 *Thomas Müntzer, Sein Leben und Seine Schriften*, Herausgegeben und eingeleitet von Otto S. Brandt (Jenna: Eugen Diederichs Verlag, 1933), pp. 126–31.

Jan J. Kiwiet in "The Theology of Hans Denck," *MQR*, XXXII, No. 1 (January, 1958), pp. 5–6, points out that when Denck speaks of the Word of God, he does not mean the "living voice of God," as did Thomas Müntzer, and that, therefore, it is a mistake to use the expression, "inner Word," with reference to either Müntzer or Denck. He says, "Whereas the living voice of God was a special religious experience to Thomas Müntzer, the Word of God in the heart of men was for Denck a continuing reality for sinner as well as believer. It is the divine imperative in man or "*der anknüpfungspunkt*," as Brunner calls it.

This distinction of the difference between Müntzer and Denck is important and, I think, essentially correct. But it is important to point out that Denck did not think of the "*anknüpfungspunkt*" as a part of human nature as such. It was rather a share in the reasonable being of the divine eternal *Logos*, which God graciously granted to all men.

18 See Otto Piper, "Mysticism and the Christian Experience," *Theology Today*, X, No. 2 (July, 1953), 163. Piper shows that Eckhart far transcended the Augustinian idea that the *imago* of the Trinity is found in the human soul, and that he postulated the essential oneness of the spark of the soul with the Godhead. This then was a mysticism very different from that of Denck.

19 Hans Denck, *Bekenntnis für den Rat zu Nürnberg*, QFR, Band XXIV, 2 Teil, 21.

20 *Ibid.*, pp. 33–34.

21 *Ibid.*

22 *Ibid.*

> By nature I can never believe the Scriptures. But that within me which is not mine, say I, but that which drives me without my will or consent [*zuthun*], this drives me to read the Scriptures for the sake of testimony.
>
> Therefore, I read the Scriptures and find in part evidences here which mightily bear testimony to that within me which drives me. This is Christ, to whom the Scriptures give testimony, that he is the Son of the Most High.[23]

Denck refers to the Bible as a letter which men have received from God. He warns that men must now exercise care in order that they will not come to love the letter more than they love Him, who sent it.[24] He also emphasizes the fact that one trusts this letter as the outer Word, because the knowledge of God has already been received through the activity of Christ, the inner Word. It is through the activity of the inner Word that the prophecy of Jer. 31:33 is fulfilled. Once this has taken place men will no more say, "Know the Lord," for the knowledge of God received through the inner Word is the highest and best knowledge.[25]

Yet he who has this knowledge does not despise testimony to it from any source, however humble. This is the highest honor which Denck is able to give to the Bible. It belongs to the order of creaturely things, and one cannot regard the Scriptures more highly than to acknowledge that it is they which teach a man that he should love God from the heart.

> He who knows the Scriptures and is cold in divine love, let him see that he does not make an idol out of the Scriptures, which all scribes do who are not taught for the kingdom of God.[26]

The fear that Denck expressed in the event that the Bible should be given a value which exceeded its proper office as a witness to the inner Word was the fear of bibliolatry. His aim was to guard against this by never allowing the Bible anything more than this secondary role in the experience of divine revelation. Denck expresses this in imaginary dialogue with his reader as follows:

> You may say, He who does not know God, is it wrong that he should regard the Scriptures highly, so that through them he may come to the knowledge of God?
>
> Answer: If someone should send you a letter, and in it promise you great good, and you did not know him, however pious and rich he might or might not be, then it would be foolishness to depend upon the letter. But [even] if he is already as the letter indicates, you may not bank or depend upon it, until you in part experience whether he is like this or not. If you find that he is so rich and pious, then you say, "Ah, dear lord, let me be your servant. I do not inquire about your letter, for I desire no other reward than that I should be your servant and that you should be my lord.[27]

At the same time Denck could warn his readers not to neglect the Bible. Al-

---

23 *Ibid.*, pp. 21–22.
24 Hans Denck, *Vom Gesetz Gottes, QFR*, Band XXIV, 2 Teil, 60–61.
25 *Ibid.*, p. 60.
26 *Ibid.*, pp. 60–61.
27 *Ibid.*

though he found it impossible to grant the Bible its normative place in the life of the Church as the Word of God, he valued the Scriptures above all human treasures.[28]

In Caspar Schwenckfeld we find the doctrine of the inner and outer Word developed in a different form than that which was seen in the thought of Hans Denck. Whereas in the thought of Hans Denck the inner Word dwelt within all men, in believer and sinner alike, and was in this sense a share in the reasonable being of the *Logos* which had become incarnate in Jesus, for Schwenckfeld the inner Word was something which only the regenerate man could experience. Kiwiet is, I think, wrong, therefore, when he says that Schwenckfeld meant by the Spirit of God the divine element in man.[29] Schwenckfeld was always extremely careful to distinguish between the divine and the creaturely. It was only in the experience of regeneration which was wrought in the heart of the believer through the direct activity of the Holy Spirit that one passed from the level of a creature of God to the level of a child of God. The regenerate man does participate in the divine nature, but this is the result of his supernatural regeneration rather than his natural generation. It is, therefore, a mistake to speak of a divine element within human nature as such for Schwenckfeld. He saw human nature as totally corrupt because of the fall and original sin. Hence, the hope for salvation lay not within the divine element in man but within the regenerating power of the Holy Spirit in the heart of the elect believing man.[30]

It was only this man, in Schwenckfeld's thought, who had the inner Word. He developed his doctrine of the inner Word in reaction against Luther's doctrine of Word and Sacrament. Schwenckfeld felt that Luther identified the Word of God too closely with the written word of Scripture and the spoken word of the minister. Schwenckfeld wrote extensively about this issue, and much that he wrote was written in the context of the controversy between Schwenckfeld and Luther and between Schwenckfeld and Luther's followers. In the controversy between Schwenckfeld and Pilgram Marbeck on the same question Schwenckfeld simply restates the position he had already developed in the controversy with Luther as early as 1530.[31]

Where Luther and the Lutherans, as well as Pilgram Marbeck and the Anabaptists, spoke of the Bible as the Word of God, Schwenckfeld felt con-

28 Hans Denck, *Widerruf, QFR*, Band XXIV, 2 Teil, 106.
29 Jan J. Kiwiet, "The Theology of Hans Denck," *MQR*, XXXII, No.,1 (January, 1958), 7.
30 See Chapter III above.
31 The earliest criticism of Luther's doctrine of the Word of God is found in Schwenckfeld's *Judicium ober die Augspurgische Confession*, ca. 1530, *CS*, III, 862–940. That Christ is the only Word of God appears already in Schwenckfeld's criticism of Augsburg's position on Word and Sacrament. In addition to this early criticism of Lutheran views of the Bible as the Word of God, Schwenckfeld wrote *Judicium auff Doctor Martin Luther's schrieben vom Worte Gottes und der heiligen Schrifft*, 1550, *CS*, XII, 59–67. The following years he wrote *Von der hailigen Schrifft, irem Innhatt, Ampt, rechten Nutz, Brauch und Missbrauch*, *CS*, XII, 419–541, which was both a criticism of Luther and an attempt to give the Bible a positive value. In 1553 Schwenckfeld wrote two works which dealt with his view of Scripture. One is a criticism of a book by Matthias Flacius Illyricus, *CS*, XIII, 365–508, which had been directed against Schwenckfeld's views, and the second, a brief reply to the same work, *Von der h. Schrifft: Der Wittenbergischen und Leipzischen Theologen Judicium*, *CS*, XIII, 509–20.

strained to make a sharp distinction between the Bible and Christ. Christ only was the eternal Word of God, and the Bible, a *witness* to Christ.

Like Denck, Schwenckfeld had been influenced by the type of Christian mysticism found in the *Theologia Germanica* and among the Rhine groups of the Friends of God. In his earlier criticisms of Luther's view of the Bible as the Word of God, Schwenckfeld did not develop anything that differed at any essential point from the tract by Tauler, which he republished in 1555. It seems likely, therefore, that this tract was in Schwenckfeld's hands for some time before he published it, and that it played a decisive role in shaping his own view of the Bible as a *witness to* rather than a *source of* divine revelation.

This republished tract of 1555 values "the holy divine, prophetic and evangelical Scriptures as true and loving words of God, because beyond doubt they come to us from God."[32] But the author of the tract then goes on to say that "Christ alone is the living Word in whom all salvation is found,"[33] and that

> while holy Scripture is the standard by which every *other* writing shall be measured and judged, ... Christ alone is the living Word by whom alone *all our lives*, our deeds, and our misdeeds shall be judged.[34]

It is Christ, as the living Word in whom men must believe, and Christ, not the Bible, in whom men must seek their salvation. The conclusion of this unknown author is that if he were to build his hope for the saving knowledge of God upon the Scriptures, as some men say he should, then he would no longer have Christ, but the Scriptures in themselves would be his redeemer.[35] Such a view of Scripture would honor Scripture too highly, and this is clearly against Scripture, "which shows us, as Paul says, 'that the letter kills but the Spirit makes alive'."[36]

Compared with the views expressed above, those of Schwenckfeld are strikingly similar. He, too, believed that the holy, divine Scriptures, both Old and New Testaments, are a worthy precious treasure and a *testimony* to our Christian faith.[37]

The word, *witness* or *testimony*, is of fundamental importance for an understanding of Schwenckfeld's attitude toward the Bible and his approach to an hermeneutical method. The crux of the whole matter for Schwenckfeld centers in the question of whether or not the Bible as inspired Scripture is equal to the revelation of God in Christ. Can the Scriptures convey the saving knowledge of the grace of God in Christ, who alone is the source of grace? Can divine revelation be contained in or confined to the Bible? Schwenckfeld's answer is an emphatic *no*. The Bible is both useful and necessary for Christians, but it cannot "be

---

32 *Ehn tröstliche Christenliche underweisung unnd verstand des eusserlichen und innerlichen worts Gottes, CS*, XIV, 352.
33 *Ibid.*, p. 353. It is quite certain, I think, that Schwenckfeld did not understand Luther's view of Scripture becoming the Word through the activity of the Spirit at the moment of encounter.
34 *Ibid.*
35 *Ibid.*
36 *Ibid.*
37 Schwenckfeld, *Von der hailigen Schrifft, irem Innhalt, Ampt, rechten Nutz, Brauch und Missbrauch, CS*, XII, 424.

properly handled without the Master through whom it was wirtten, that is, without the Holy Spirit."[38]

Knowledge of Hebrew and Greek is no substitute for the aid of the Spirit in the interpretation of Scriptures. Without the aid of the Spirit in the interpretation of the Scriptures men will make of them a hindrance and a destructive thing. Those who would *use* rather than *abuse* the Bible must first bring to the Bible a believing heart and seek nothing but Christ in it.[39]

The danger that besets those who come to the Bible without the believing godly heart, which is the result of the work of the Holy Spirit, is twofold. Such men either read into the Scriptures their own understanding and so create misunderstanding, or else they cannot penetrate beyond the dead letter and then "along with the Jews they must hear from the Master, Christ, 'You err because you know not the Scriptures, neither the power of God'."[40]

Schwenckfeld, however, goes much further than to warn of the possible abuse or misinterpretation of Scripture when that interpretation is undertaken by human wisdom, unaided by the Holy Spirit, who is the gift of grace from the reigning Christ in glory. It is not simply that men unaided by the Spirit misinterpret the message of Scripture, but rather that they cannot interpret it properly at all. Only those who turn to Christ before coming to the Scriptures can have the veil removed which hangs over their hearts, so that they cannot understand them. II Cor. 3:14–17.[41]

If one finds the Scriptures forbidding and difficult, then it is a sure sign that such an one has not yet turned to the Lord with his whole heart and that he does not yet have the Spirit from the Lord, which is a spirit of wisdom and understanding. This veil, which prevents man in his own wisdom from understanding the Scriptures correctly, can only be removed by a genuine conversion to Christ, which then brings with it the gift of the Holy Spirit.[42] Thus, it is only the new man in Christ who has the inner Word.

In a moving beautiful passage Schwenckfeld compares the unveiling and unlocking of the Scriptures by the inner Word with the experience of the two disciples on the Emmaus road:

> I say that it is our Lord Jesus Christ, who opens up the Scriptures, that locked book, which no one can read without him, who also kindles our hearts, so that we read and hear the Scriptures with joy and love. This happened to the two disciples as they journeyed to Emmaus when the Lord appeared to them on the way and opened up to them the Scriptures, so that they afterwards said, "Dit not our hearts burn within us, while he spoke with us and opened up to us the Scriptures.[43]

One who comes to the outer Word of the written Scriptures without the inner Word of the Spirit will not be able to create out of the dead letter either the Spirit

---

38 *Ibid.*
39 *Ibid.*, p. 425. Schwenckfeld here makes a distinction between *"Gott gelehret"* and *"Schrifft gelehret,"* which is a common distinction used by all shades of Spiritualists.
40 *Ibid.*
41 *Ibid.*, pp. 427–28.
42 *Ibid.*, p. 428.
43 *Ibid.*

or divine wisdom, nor from the picture lay hold on eternal *reality* and *truth*. "No one on earth can bring heaven down, except through faith in Jesus Christ, to whom the Scriptures point.[44]

Despite the fact that Schwenckfeld saw the Bible only as a *witness* to the saving faith of the knowledge of God, and not as the *source of that faith*, he none the less found four areas of life wherein the Bible may render valuable service to those who have already become believers. These areas are:

1. That a man may learn from the Bible how he should conduct himself toward every man in a pure and holy manner through the examples of Christ, patriarchs, prophets, and all the friends of God.

2. That through the Bible the disobedient, erring, and seditious may be disciplined and condemned, for in it the divine truth of God's wrath and judgment is set forth.

3. That by the *witness* of the Scriptures to the grace of God we may improve what is right and correct what is in error. The Bible is particularly valuable when the Church wishes to reform, for it tells us how things were when the Church was first born.

4. Through the Bible Christians may be disciplined and learn how to lead their lives according to the will of Christ and his righteousness which is from the heart.[45]

Along with these four positive values of the Bible Schwenckfeld is concerned with two specific abuses which can only be avoided when the right hermeneutical method is employed. The first of these is that men often use the Bible to find support for their own views, while no attempt is made to lead a godly life. Such people, when rebuked, hunt for texts which excuse their godless lives and cover over and quiet the bad conscience. The second abuse is more subtle than the first, because it has a splendid appearance. It seeks either to equate the Scriptures with Christ, the living Word, which is what Schwenckfeld accused Luther of doing, or it confounds and intermingles the two, which was Schwenckfeld's accusation against Marbeck.[46]

Schwenckfeld believes that the time has come when this abuse of the Bible must be opposed. He writes:

> With this the first Word of God, Jesus Christ, is not revered. He is thrust out of his place and his office is darkened. In the same manner, the true worth of Holy Scripture (which God in this time has shown as being to strive against Antichrist and a preparation for Christ) is for the most part destoyed. I say that in this sense man makes an idol out of the outer words and gives them forth as the selfsame powerful Word of God.[47]

Thus it can be said that for both Denck and Schwenckfeld the concept of the inner Word reduced the normative value of the Bible for faith to a considerable extent. The Bible is useful as a witness to faith, or in the nurture of a faith already

---

44 *Ibid.*, p. 431.
45 *Ibid.*, pp. 433–34.
46 *Ibid.*, pp. 485–88. See also Schwenckfeld's *Judicium* of Marbeck's *Vermanung* in *CS*, VIII, 196, in which he says that Marbeck speaks as though there were two Words of God.
47 *CS*, XII, 488.

formed, but it is no longer divine revelation in the sense that from it one may receive the saving knowledge of God. Neither Denck nor Schwenckfeld disparaged the Bible when used within the limits and interpreted by the hermeneutics which they prescribed. Both of them feared that going beyond those limits or working without these hermeneutics would lead to bibliolatry.

3. The Inner and Outer Word as the Distinction between Letter and Spirit

Melchior Hoffmann is the one representative of the Radical Reformation of those considered in this study who most thoroughly applied the above distinction in his hermeneutical method. Unfortunately works by Hoffmann, in which his hermeneutical method is most clearly discernible, are not presently available in this country in their entirety. Yet, from the *Bijlagen* in the work on Hoffmann by Leendertz[48] and from the reaction of Dirk Philips to Hoffmann's allegorical interpretation of the tabernacle, it is possible to draw a fairly accurate picture of Hoffmann's hermeneutics. His importance in this chapter of this study is that he provides the transition from the hermeneutics of the inner and outer Word to the hermeneutics of the new and old covenants among the Dutch Anabaptists. The excerpt from the *Bijlage* printed by Leendertz is taken from Hoffmann's treatise on the tabernacle, which was written in 1533[49] immediately after his imprisonment. The excerpt reads as follows, and it shows in seminal form the structure of Hoffmann's hermeneutical method:

> So now this candlestick will be interpreted through the Holy Spirit of God Himself. Rev. 1. That it has seven branches signifies seven congregations and points toward seven people of the Spirit which shall be in the New Testament, while, of course, they shall be known and named by the Lord as one church and one body. Yet the one body and courtyard, while it is divided into seven (parts) and even into eight, is yet undivided in unity as one hereafter shall see and hear.
>
> Therefore, one must note in the first place that the tabernacle of Moses and the secret of the courtyard signify the time of the Old Testament and the Letter, and the holy place, the time of the Sabbath of the New Testament or the acceptable year and the time of grace. By the Holy of Holies heaven itself is signified.[50]

The remainder of Hoffmann's work on the tabernacle is not available in this country, but its main outlines are fairly clear from the objections to it which Dirk Philips makes in his own interpretation of the spiritual significance of structure of the tabernacle. It is known from Dirk's objections to Hoffmann's interpretation that Hoffmann had allegorized the structure of the tabernacle so that its various divisions represented two distinct grades of Christians. Those placed within the courtyard and the holy place by Hoffmann were designated by him as children of Esau, or children of strife or fleshly and once-born children of God, while the Holy of Holies symbolized the spiritual and twice-born children of God.[51]

48 See Leendertz, p. 374. Kawerau, pp. 32–45, also gives an excellent analysis of Hoffmann's hermeneutical method upon which this section of this thesis must heavily rely.
49 For the full title of this work see p. 56 above.
50 Leendertz, p. 374.
51 Dirk Philips, *Wtlegginghe des Tabernakels ofte der Hutten Moysi, BRN*, X, 290.

Hoffmann applied this method of allegory in a most thoroughgoing manner to both Old and New Testaments. Overtones of the influence of Joachim of Floris upon him have already been noted. Hoffmann did not follow Joachim in detail, but like Joachim he divided history into three ages with the "age of the Spirit" being the final one. This was basic to Hoffmann's hermeneutical method, for the "age of the Spirit" was identical in his thought with the "time of grace." During this age, consequently, Scripture could be properly interpreted only by one who had the Spirit.

Christians must, therefore, be aware that the Scriptures are of a twofold nature, composed of both flesh and spirit. To understand the Scriptures only according to the flesh or letter is to understand them by the light of the moon. So understood, they are only a precious promise of things to come. But to understand the Scriptures according to the Spirit is to understand them in the light of the sun. Here promise is replaced by fulfillment, and shadow, by reality.[52] Since the "time of grace" and the "age of the Spirit" are identical, man unaided by the Spirit can achieve only false interpretations of Scripture. If one does not wish to master the Scriptures, but is willing to be mastered by them, then one "must be taught by God or Christ concerning their meaning. Hoffmann presses this so far that the 'key of David' becomes necessary fror the interpreter. The interpreter receives the key from Christ."[53] Hoffmann explains the significance which the "key of David" had for him through his interpretation of Rev. 3:7. Christ received the power and key of David from the Father. With this power and key he unlocks for his own through the Spirit the door of grace, which is Christ himself. He opens up to us through the Holy Spirit the mysteries of God, which are within himself. No one can close this door of knowledge against one to whom Christ has opened it, and no one on earth can open it for any one from whom Christ withdraws his spirit.[54]

Not only must the Scriptures be interpreted by the Spirit during the "age of the Spirit" and the "time of grace," but he who would understand the Spirit's interpretation must be aware that the Scriptures have cloven hoofs; that Scripture is made up of thesis and antithesis. The two claws can be harmonized with each other, but such harmonization will require much meditation upon the exact meaning of each word under the probing of the Spirit. One should not resist the Spirit, but should allow Him to move where He will.[55] Rightly understood, with their two claws harmonized with each other, the Scriptures are for Hoffmann the Bread of Life. Understood in their prophetic and allegorical sense, they are the source of the highest good and an overflow of God's mercy and grace. But misinterpreted, the Scriptures are poison, which men use to their harm and make fools of themselves.[56]

---

52 Kawerau, pp. 35–36. See also *BRN*, V, 167–68.
53 Kawerau, p. 38.
54 *Ibid.*, p. 39.
55 *Ibid.* See also *SAW*, pp. 129–30, for a discussion of Hoffmann's view on the cloven hoof of Scripture.
56 Kawerau, pp. 40–45.

B. The Importance of the Epistle to the Hebrews

1. Dirk Philips: The "Time of Law" and the "Time of Grace"

Throughout this study the problem of the logical versus the chronological method in the presentation of the material has frequently asserted itself. Chronologically Pilgram Marbeck's hermeneutics should follow those of Melchior Hoffmann. Logically, however, because the hermeneutics of Dirk Philips were developed in opposition to those of Hoffmann, on the one hand, and to those of Bernhard Rotmann, on the other, it seems best to present the three men who developed the hermeneutics of the old and new covenants in the following order: Dirk Philips, Menno Simons, and then Pilgram Marbeck.

Philips wrote two works which deal primarily with the problem of a satisfactory hermeneutical method. The first of these, *Wtlegginghe des Tabernakels ofte der Hutten Moysi*, was written to refute Melchior Hoffmann, and its exact date is unknown. The second was written to refute Bernhard Rotmann and appeared and appeared under the title, *Vande geestelijcke Restitution*, in 1559.

In his repudiation of Hoffmann's allegorical interpretation of the tabernacle Philips relies heavily on the epistle to the Hebrews, particularly chapters eight and nine. He finds here the Scriptural support for the position he wishes to take against Hoffmann. Aware that his use of allegory in the interpretation of Scripture goes somewhat beyond that of the author of Hebrews, Dirk defends his method by saying "the present need and the misunderstanding of several brothers rouse us and compel us to explain the matter more fully."[57] Dirk's position is that the courtyard of the tabernacle has no allegorical significance, since it contained no furnishings and no sacrifices were conducted within it. The Holy Place represents the "time of law" as a shadow of the good things that were to come in Christ. The Holy of Holies represents the "time of the Gospel" as the eternal reality, which has indeed come in Christ.[58]

> The Law and Gospel are one Word and one truth of God, but they are also divided. The Law has the shadows of those things which are to come. The Gospel is the reality of these things themselves.[59]

The true interpreter of the tabernacle must build upon the apostolic foundation laid down in the epistle to the Hebrews, for it was given by the Holy Spirit.[60] He who does this will discover that the tabernacle with its two divisions, each having its own vessels and its own sacrifices, represent the two dispensations of Law and Gospel. The Old Testament is the Law and the "time of law." The New Testament is the Gospel and the "time of grace." Yet the two Testaments are not two truths, but "one and the same truth in the Spirit. For as there is not more than one God, so also there is not more than one truth, for God Himself is truth."[61]

---

57 Dirk Philips, *Wtlegginghe des Tabernakels ofte der Hutten Moysi*, BRN, X, 284.
58 *Ibid.*, p. 290.
59 *Ibid.*, p. 285.
60 *Ibid.*, p. 284.
61 *Ibid.*, p. 285.

The Law, however, must be understood according to its spirit, meaning, and intention, rather than according to the letter.

> The Law has many types and ceremonies which all have end in Christ, but the Gospel has the firmly established truth which will abide forever. The Law [when understood literally] is the letter which kills, but the Gospel is the Spirit which makes alive.[62]

It is only the literal meaning of the Law which comes to an end in Christ. Thus the literal command for circumcision of the flesh comes to an end, but the command to circumcise the heart spiritually remains.[63] The end result of this method, says Dirk, is that when the Law or the Old Testament is properly interpreted

> the truth of the New Testament is established through this on a more unshakeable foundation, for the shadows and sayings of the Law are to be harmonized with the evangelical truth of the Gospel.[64]

Dirk finds support for his view of the transient nature of the Law, when interpreted according to its *literal* meaning, by comparing the Law with the daily service of sacrifice in the first tent of the tabernacle. The daily sacrifice symbolizes the imperfect nature of the Law, which could, in the language of Hebrews, serve only as the preparation for a better hope.[65]

The *yearly* sacrifice offered annually by the highpriest in the Holy of Holies represents the sacrifice made by the perfect highpriest, Jesus Christ. He offered himself in a sacrifice that reconciles us to God and need never be repeated, because it is sufficient for the sins of the whole world.[66] For Dirk the incarnation and the atonement are the events which establish the "great divide" between the Old and New Testaments. The true interpreter must, therefore, develop a hermeneutic which is conscious of the division between the two Testaments and can yet discover their underlying unity by spiritually interpreting the Old Testament and making it always subordinate to the New.[67]

He who would interpret the tabernacle correctly then must remember that the priests represent Moses and the Law or the "*time of the Old Testament*," while the highpriest represents Christ and the New Testament or the Gospel and the "*time of grace*." During the latter period God writes His law upon the hearts of Christians through the Holy Spirit, rather than with His finger upon tablets of stone, as He did during the "time of law."[68]

In his later work of 1559, which he titled *Vande geestelijcke Restitution*, Dirk applied the hermeneutical method which he developed in his refutation of Hoffmann's errors to the whole of the Old Testament in refuting those of Bernhard Rotmann. Rotmann's *Restitution* appeared in 1534, and in it he defended the

---

62 *Ibid.*
63 *Ibid.*
64 *Ibid.*
65 Heb. 7 and 8.
66 Dirk Philips, *Wtlegginghe des Tabernakels ofte der Hutten Moysi*, BRN, X, 286.
67 *Ibid.*, pp. 286–87.
68 *Ibid.*, p. 289.

practices of the revolutionary Anabaptists at Münster. Dirk did not write a direct reply to Rotmann, who had died in 1535 probably during the seige of the city, but he does complain that Rotmann's errors cause trouble in the brotherhood, and he regards them as the source of much mischief.[69]

Rotmann's *Restitution* is divided into seventeen chapters. The third chapter deals with the distinction between the Old and New Testaments. In the opening sentence of the foreword to the work Rotmann expresses his concern for the "undivided holy Scriptures which one calls the Bible."[70] In the opening sentence of the third chapter he expresses his concern that the Old Testament tends now to be neglected and despised.[71] Rotmann argues that the Old Testament should not be interpreted *only* figuratively. The foundation (*grund*) of the New Testament is to be found in the Old. As there is but one God, so both Testaments witness to one truth.[72] Thus, in principle Rotmann subordinated the New Testament to the Old.[73] Dirk felt that the process should be reversed. In the preface to his *Vande geestelijcke Restitution* he wrote that he had undertaken

> through the grace of God to deal briefly with everything that has happened from the beginning to show that all this is in Christ, and his kingdom has been spiritually repeated [*wedergebracht*] in order to instruct the simple a little, so that they will not allow themselves to be deceived by the false prophets, who make fragrant their deceitful doctrines with the old stuff [*wesen*] of the letter and with shadows and figures. For everything which they cannot support (or prove) with the New Testament, that they wish to show with the Old Testament and the letter of the prophets.[74]

Dirk wished to emphasize that all he and his followers sought or expected was a spiritual restitution of the kingdom in contrast to the literal one, which Rotmann and others had sought at Münster.

The contention of Dirk was that the entire history of Israel was a foreshadowing of the life of Christ. Everything that happened in Israel's history, therefore, is spiritually reënacted in Christ's life. As this hermeneutical principle is applied in practice to the whole of Israel's history beginning with Abraham, the spiritual Abraham is God, the Father. The two wives of Abraham become the two Testaments, the first of which was barren until the time of the promise. Hagar represents the Jewish people and the Levitical priesthood with its imperfect ceremonies and sacrifices, which can justify no one or make him perfect. Isaac represents Jesus Christ, his supernatural birth and his work as the recapitulator of a new humanity.[75]

The history of Isaac spiritually reinterpreted means that

---

69 Dirk Philips, *Vande geestelijcke Restitution, BRN*, X, 341.
70 Bernhard Rotmann, *Restitution rechter und gesunder christlicher Lehre* (Münster, 1534), reprinted as No. 77 and 78, *Neudrucke deutscher Litteraturwerke* (Halle a.S.: Max Niemeyer, 1888), p. 18.
71 *Ibid.*, p. 21.
72 *Ibid.*, pp. 25–26.
73 It was this principle which gave rise to the practice of polygamy at Münster as well as the sanction of the use of the literal sword. See pp. 75–89 for Rotmann's arguments in favor of polygamy and pp. 92–113 for his description of the glory of Christ's kingdom upon earth.
74 Dirk Philips, *Vande geestelijcke Restitution, BRN*, X, 341.
75 *Ibid.*, p. 348.

> Jesus Christ is the true Isaac, who has opened up again the stopped up fountains of Holy Scripture and has brought the darkened Word of God again to the light of day. He has allowed the pure clear Gospel to be preached everywhere through his servants, the apostles. But the uncircumcised Philistines, the scribes and Pharisees, the uncircumcised at heart, the Antichrist and the false teachers, set themselves against it and strive with the ministers [*dienaers*] on account of the fountains of living water, which they hold and reckon as their own. For they alone went to be interpreters of Scripture and say stoutly, "Our tongue shall take the upper hand. To us alone belongs the right to speak. Who is our master?" Therefore, there is and remains strife between the servants of Jesus Christ and the false teachers, who are true Philistines, enemies of the Gospel and of the spiritual Israel.[76]

The hermeneutical principle here illustrated in Dirk's interpretation of the spiritual significance of Isaac is then applied to Jacob, Joseph, Samson, David, and to all the leading figures of the Old Testament. The ladder in Jacob's dream is a type of Jesus Christ, who is the only way to the Father.[77] Joseph, in his sale into slavery in Egypt, is a type of Christ in the humility of the incarnation. His elevation to a position of power, second only to that of the king, foreshadows Christ's exaltation at the right hand of God in eternal glory.[78] Samson in his exploits of great strength, as he carries the gates of the city of Gaza to the top of the hill that is before Hebron, is a type of Christ, the true spiritual Nazarene, who on his cross carried the sins of the whole world.[79] In his death the literal Samson destroyed more of his enemies than he had during his life, and in his death Christ, the spiritual Samson, overcame the devil and vanquished death, for his death is the death of death.[80]

At the end of *Vande geestelijcke Restitution*, after he has demonstrated his hermeneutical principle by applying it to the whole of the Old Testament, Dirk writes:

> In summary, the whole *Restitution* must be understood according to this rule and be changed out of the letter into the Spirit. And thereby the ground of our most holy Christian faith will become very firmly established, as we openly see and understand that all which we believe and confess is first portrayed by God with many beautiful figures, and afterward by the eternal Truth itself, that is through Jesus, is made clear, testified to, and established.[81]

Thus Dirk subordinates the Old Testament to the New by allegorizing the former, while the latter is taken quite literally with the exception of sections that are obviously eschatological. While some of Dirk's allegory tends to rob the Old Testament of any religious significance for its own history, he did seek to control

---

76 *Ibid.*, p. 351. Dirk's spiritual interpretation of Isaac is based upon the incident recorded in Gen. 26:17–22. Dirk applies his hermeneutical principle in two directions; backward to the time of Isaac, and forward to the time of his own contemporary situation. The false teachers who now muddy the fountains of living water given in the Scriptures by God, the heavenly Father, and by the spiritual Abraham are obviously the ministers of the Magisterial Reformation, who think that they alone can interpret Scripture properly.
77 *Ibid.*, p. 352.
78 *Ibid.*, p. 353.
79 *Ibid.*, pp. 361–62. The Scriptural reference is to Judg. 16:1–3.
80 *Ibid.*, p. 362.
81 *Ibid.*, p. 375.

it by that history. Whereas Dirk regarded Melchior Hoffmann's method of allegory as completely arbitrary, he strove for a method that was guided on one side by actual events within Old Testament history, and on the other, by Christian unity.[82] Granted the historical situation of the trouble which Rotmann's *Restitution* caused within the Dutch Anabaptist brotherhood with its emphasis upon the literal restitution of Christ's kingdom upon this earth and its advocacy of the use of the literal sword to establish that kingdom, Dirk's hermeneutical method was an effective protest.[83] In the absence of the context of the historical situation in which it arose the method becomes questionable.

2. Menno Simons and the Hermeneutics of the Old and New Covenants

The hermeneutical method of Menno Simons is similar to that of Dirk, though neither so neatly defined nor so clearly outlined. Menno himself does not seem to be always aware that he works with a precise hermeneutical rule. Nevertheless, Menno's approach to the Scriptures is a Christo-centric one.[84] He works out a fairly consistent method of subordinating the Old Testament to the New.

Menno regards both Testaments as the Word of God. He hopes

> no one of rational mind will be so foolish a man as to deny that the whole Scriptures, both the Old and New Testament, were written for our instruction, admonition, and correction, and that they are the true scepter and rule by which the Lord's kingdom, house, church, and congregation must be governed.[85]

Yet, although Menno accepts both Old and New Testaments as the Word of God, he early lays down the fundamental proposition that Scripture must be interpreted in such a way that the *figure* of the Old Testament, when applied to the truth of the New, will reflect the reality; the image, the being, and the letter, the Spirit.[86] Thus the guiding principle of Menno is clear. Reality and truth are found in the New Testament. And here it is not alone Christ's words that give one guidance in the interpretation of Scripture, but his life as well. The public utterances of Christ are more to be trusted as norms by which the Church should regulate her liturgy than doubtful and obscure passages of Scripture, which may teach the exact opposite from that which Christ taught in public.[87]

---

82 Dirk Philips, *Wtlegginghe des Tabernakels ofte der Hutten Moysi*, BRN, X, 290–91. Dirk objects to Hoffmann's method of allegorical interpretation, saying that it is contrary to Scripture in every way. Esau is not a type of Christ but of Jews and Israelites. Christians are not two people, but *one body*, in Christ.

83 Rotmann, pp. 92–106.

84 See Krahn, pp. 107–10.

85 Menno Simons, *Foundations of Christian Doctrine, CWMS*, pp. 159–60.

86 Menno Simons, *Blasphemy of John of Leiden, CWMS*, p. 42. Menno's thrust is against John of Leiden's claim that he was the spiritual King David, who should bring joy to all the earth by the establishment of the city of Münster as the new Jerusalem. Menno maintains that David is a figure of Christ.

87 Menno Simons, *Foundations of Christian Doctrine, CWMS*, p. 186. Menno's criticism is aimed at the contemporary Roman Catholic Church and those practices within it, which he regards as contrary to the plain word of Scripture.

Menno, however, does not always subordinate the Old Testament to the New by a spiritual or allegorical interpretation of the former. When contradictions between the two Testaments arose in terms of the ethical conduct enjoined by each, Menno did not hesitate to state that what was valid for Jews under the old covenant was not valid for Christians under the new.

Both the swearing of oaths and the bearing of arms were supported by the Magisterial Reformers on the basis of Old Testament texts. Menno stated that it is "plain that it was allowed to the Jews under the Law to swear sincerely, but that to us Christians it is forbidden."[88] The dispensation of the Law, which allowed swearing, was an *imperfect* dispensation.[89] Those who now say, in spite of Christ's plain words, that we may nevertheless swear when the love, profit, and need of our neighbor require it, flatly contradict Christ, who is the eternal wisdom and truth of God.[90]

> It is very plain that according to the New Testament no love of neighbors nor father, mother, wife, or child, nor peril of life may bend or break the Word of the Lord. Matt. 10:37; Mark 8:38.[91]

It is clear from the above that Menno means by the Word of the Lord, not the Bible in its entirety, but the spoken word of Jesus Christ as recorded in the New Testament. Where Old and New Testaments give conflicting advice on matters of conduct, the New Testament is superior to the Old, because it is closer to the mind and spirit of Christ.

Menno took the same position in regard to the Christian's participation in warfare. Speaking of the magistrates who persecuted the Anabaptists, often at the instigation of theologians from the Magisterial Reformation, who drew their Scriptural support for such action from the Old Testament, Menno wrote:

> I am well aware that these tyrants who boast themselves to be Christians justify and make good their abominable warring, their sedition and bloodshed, with a reference to Moses, Joshua, etc. But they do not reflect that Moses and his successors have served their day with their sword of iron, and that Christ has now given us a new commandment and has girded us with another sword ... Nor do they reflect that that selfsame cross, the sword, which they wield contrary to the evangelical Scriptures, is used by them to stab their own brethren; namely, those who are of the same faith, who have received the same baptism, and who eat the same bread with them, and who therefore are the members of one and the same body. Alas, what a strange, bloody stir the Lutherans have made for several years in order to introduce or substantiate their doctrine, I will leave to them to reflect upon.[92]

Again the Old Testament is made subordinate to the New, not by allegorizing the former, but by placing the authority of Christ's word and example above that of Moses and Joshua. William Keeney has shown that Menno, consistent with his

---

88 Menno Simons, *Confession of Distressed Christians, CWMS*, p. 520.
89 *Ibid.*, p. 518.
90 *Ibid.*, p. 520.
91 *Ibid.*
92 Menno Simons, *The Cross of the Saints, CWMS*, p. 603.

Christo-centric approach to the Scriptures, had a hierarchy of values in which the New Testament was cited three and one-half times as often as the Old and that forty percent of his New Testament citations are from the Gospels.[93] Menno felt that from the New Testament, and particularly from the Gospels, it was possible to discover the *intention* of Christ by paying close attention to the words of Christ. It is possible to miss his intent by confusing his metaphors, as John of Leiden did, in his interpretation of the parable of the tares.[94] Once the intention of Jesus Christ has been discovered, one may then proceed to interpret the entire Bible from that stance. Menno writes:

> All Scripture both of the Old and New Testament rightly explained according to the intent of Christ Jesus and His holy apostles is profitable for doctrines, for reproof, for correction, for instruction in righteousness. II Tim. 3:16. But whatever is taught contrary to the Spirit and doctrine of Jesus is accursed of God. Gal. 1.[95]

Menno found further support for his Christo-centric hermeneutical principle by dividing humanity into two kingdoms, the kingdom of Christ and the kingdom of Antichrist. Within the former kingdom the prince is Jesus Christ, and his kingdom is a kingdom of peace. Christ's messengers are messengers of peace; his word, a word of peace; and his children, the seed of peace.[96] In the kingdom of Antichrist, however, everything is the reverse of peace. The prince of this kingdom is the prince of darkness. His kingdom is one of tumult, raging, murder, and blood. Menno concludes his description of the two princes and their two kingdoms with the following words:

> Kind reader, earnestly reflect upon this our brief delineation of the two princes and their kingdoms, and by the grace of God, it will give you no mean insight into the Scriptures.[97]

Menno's attitude toward the whole Bible is well summed up as follows:

> All the Scriptures, both the Old and the New Testaments, on every hand, point us to Christ Jesus that we are to follow Him. Whosoever does not hear Him, it will be required of him. Therefore take heed. As I have said before, although all the pious from the beginning were one congregation, church, or body, yet at different periods they have had different doctrines, ordinances, and worship. Moses gave the Law and Israel had to obey it until Christ, who was promised, appeared. To His Spirit, Word, and ordinances we are now directed.[98]

Menno's position is clear. What was valid for Israel under the Law is not valid for Christians, who are under grace. The Old Testament must now yield to the New, and the Law must give way to the Gospel. Menno's manner of subordinating the Old Testament to the New is thus more satisfactory than that of Dirk. The

---

93 Keeney, "The Development of Dutch Anabaptist Thought and Practice from 1539–1564," p. 47. See also the footnotes on the same page.
94 Menno Simons, *Blasphemy of John of Leiden, CWMS*, p. 48.
95 Menno Simons, *Why I Do Not Cease Teaching and Writing*, 1539, *CWMS*, p. 312.
96 Menno Simons, *Reply to False Accusations, CWMS*, p. 554.
97 *Ibid.*, p. 557.
98 Menno Simons, *Reply to Gellius Faber, CWMS*, p. 749.

subordination is achieved without denying that the Old Testament has a religious significance of its own.

3. Pilgram Marbeck: The "Covenat of Yesterday" and the "Covenant of Today"

The hermeneutics of Pilgram Marbeck, like his anthropology, was developed in the course of the controversy with Caspar Schwenckfeld over his *Judicium* of Marbeck's *Vermanung*. Both the abovementioned works appeared in 1542. The first part of Marbeck's *Verantwortung* appeared in 1544; the second, not until several years later. The second part of the *Verantwortung* draws heavily upon material found within Marbeck's *Testamentserläuterung*, which was not completed until around 1550.

Schwenckfeld, distressed by Marbeck's assertion that the patriarchs who lived before Christ had died in hope without receiving either forgiveness of sins or eternal life,[99] had replied that Abraham was a Christian before he became a Jew.[100] Schwenckfeld's doctrine of the invisible Church of the Spirit did not permit him to restrict Christian revelation to the New Testament as Marbeck wished to do.

Both in the *Verantwortung* and in the *Testamentserläuterung*, Marbeck aims to reply to Schwenckfeld's contention that there is no distinction between the Testaments, as well as to his doctrine of the inner and outer Word. What Marbeck seeks to do is, first, to establish a broader theological base for the sharp distinction between the Old Testament as a "covenant of promise" and the New Testament as a "covenant of fulfillment"; and second, to define more accurately what he meant by referring to the Scriptures as the Word of God. Because of this Schwenckfeld had accused him of speaking as though there were two Words of God. In the development of Marbeck's theological position in the first part, chapters ten and eleven of the epistle to Hebrews played a decisive role.[101]

Marbeck in the introduction of the *Testamentserläuterung*, 1544–1550, wrote that the purpose of the work was "to settle the strife in the church because of difference of opinion over the question of the difference between the Old and New Testaments."[102] Whether the strife in Marbeck's brotherhood over differences of opinion in regard to the nature of the two Testaments arose *wholly* as a result of Schwenckfeld's *Judicium*, which circulated among Marbeck's followers, or *partly* because of difference with the Strasbourg Reformers, Capito and Bucer, on this same issue is not entirely clear. What is abundantly clear from the latter part of the *Verantwortung* is that Marbeck blamed Schwenckfeld for the controversy. He also reminded Schwenckfeld that at an earlier time he had held a position on the relationship between the two Testaments which was very similar to that of the Anabaptists.[103]

---

99 Pilgram Marbeck, *Vermanung*, pp. 227–28.
100 Schwenckfeld, *Judicium, CS*, VIII, 200.
101 See especially Heb. 11:39 and Marbeck's *Vermanung*, p. 235.
102 Marbeck, *Testamentserläuterung*, Introd., p. 3. See also *Verantwortung*, p. 581.
103 Schwenckfeld had written in 1531 a treatise on the difference between the Old and New

For Marbeck the difference between the Old and New Testaments is as sharp as the difference between the "grace of yesterday" and the "grace of today." The center of history is the incarnation and the atonement. One cannot make this retroactive to the time of the patriarchs, as Schwenckfeld wishes to do, without invalidating the central significance of Christ's work as Redeemer. To erase the time line between the Testaments is thus to deny the uniqueness of Christ as the only Saviour from sin.

In order to present his case for this point of view the more forcefully, Marbeck in the *Testamentserläuterung* systematically arranges the contents of the entire Bible under the categories of *"yesterday"* and *"today"*. The format of a typical page from the *Testamentserläuterung* would look as follows: *Gnad Gestern, Gnad Heut, Gestern Verheyssen.* Marbeck's method is then to assemble under each category a series of Scripture passages together with partial quotations which in his judgment both support and describe the categories under which he assembles them. When, for example, the passages of Scripture which Marbeck assembles under the category of *"yesterday"* in relation to the question of *Obrigkeit* (Marbeck's spelling was *Oberkeit*) are analyzed, nearly all are taken from the Old Testament.[104] They emphasize the temporal character of the *Oberkeit* of *"yesterday,"* its authority over men, and its power to shed blood.[105] Under the caption, *"Oberkeit Gewalt und... Macht Heut,"* Marbeck assembles a series of passages that are with one exception taken from the New Testament, with far the largest number coming from the Gospels.[106] These passages reflect the spiritual authority of Christ in his Church during the period of history known as "today."

The relationship of the Old Testament to the New is, therefore, the same as that between shadow and light, or figure and reality.[107] The Old Testament is alone a testament of the promise of the new reality (*wesens*), which has come in Jesus Christ.[108] Marbeck is fond of the distinction between the figurative and the *wesentlich* as applied to the two Testaments. The Old Testament is always the figurative and belongs almost in its entirety under the category of "yesterday." The New Testament, on the other hand, belongs almost in its entirety under the category of "today." In the New Testament that which was only figuratively portrayed in the Old has actually (*wesentlich*) come into existence.[109]

Marbeck's subordination of the Old Testament to the New is thus so thorough that it leads him into a New Testament monism so far as his doctrine of the

---

Testaments, in which he took essentially the same position which he now criticised in Marbeck. It appeared under the title, *Underschaid Des Alten und Newen Testaments der Figur und waarhait*, and is printed in *CS*, IV, 414–43. See also the definitive article on Caspar von Schwenckfeld in English by William Klassen in *ME*, IV, col. A, 1123.

104 The one exception is Luke 23:7, where Pilate sends Jesus to Herod for judgment.
105 Marbeck, *Testamentserläuterung*, pp. 322–23.
106 *Ibid.*, pp. 325–26. The one exception here is Rom. 13, which Marbeck said applied to the worldly and heathen *Obrigkeit*, which was in the world in Paul's day, and still is, as an instrument of God's wrath.
107 Marbeck, *Vermanung*, pp. 332–33
108 *Ibid.*, pp. 227–28.
109 Marbeck, *Testamentserläuterung*, chapter 19. See also *Verantwortung*, p. 401.

Church and his ethics are concerned.[110] Marbeck found support for this not only in chapters ten and eleven of Hebrews but also in the Sermon on the Mount, where Christ sets his word over against that of Moses. As John C. Wenger has pointed out, this emphasis upon the difference between the Testaments, which was made by Marbeck as well as by Menno Simons and Dirk Philips, may have been the source of the Covenant theology as developed by Zwingli and his followers. By this term, however, they meant to emphasize the similarity of the two Testaments, which is the very opposite of what the Anabaptists sought to do.[111] The relationship between the hermeneutics of grace and the ethics of grace within the Radical Reformation is thus very close, as will be shown in Chapter VI.[112]

As for Schwenckfeld's accusation that the Taufbrüder handle the Scriptures in such a manner that they equate the Bible as the Word of God with Christ, who alone should be so honored, Marbeck replied:

> We do not call ink and paper or what is creaturely and corruptible in Holy Scripture or the spoken word of man the Word of God, Spirit, and Life. But we mean the inwardly contained intention and meaning of the written and spoken word.[113]

The efficacy of Scripture depends altogether on the presence of faith in him who reads the Scripture or hears preaching.[114] Faith is believing that the Scriptures are true, because they were written by the Holy Spirit through the hands of the apostles and prophets, even as the scribe of Jeremiah rewrote the scroll, and Moses, the Ten Commandments. For that reason one calls them the Word of God,[115] and the Scriptures are rather to be trusted than human reason.[116]

---

110 John C. Wenger in "The Life and Work of Pilgram Marpeck," *MQR*, XII, No. 3 (July, 1938), 162, has also noted the effect of this New Testament monism upon the ethics of Marbeck.
111 John C. Wenger, "The Theology of Pilgram Marpeck," *MQR*, XII, No. 4 (October, 1938), pp. 207–10. See also "Bibel," pp. 216–17, and "Bergpredigt," p. 165, in *Mennoitisches Lexikon*, I, herausgegeben von Christian Hege und Christian Neff, im Selbstverlag der Herausgeber Frankfurt am Main und Weierhof (pfalz, 1913). Also Gottlob Schrenk, *Gottesreich und Bund im älteren Protestantismus, Vornemlich bei Johannes Coccijus* (Gütersloh, Germany, 1928), pp. 36–50. The thesis of Schrenk is that the Covenant or Federal theology, as developed by Coccijus, had its origin in Zwingli's strife with the Swiss Brethren at Zurich. He holds that Bullinger and Calvin borrowed from Zwingli at this point.
112 Balthasar Hubmaier is an exception to this general statement. Therefore, his hermeneutics are not considered in this study. Hubmaier gives a good example of his hermeneutical method in his *Vom Schwert* of 1527. He maintains that Christians are wrong in applying John 18:36, "My kingdom is not of this world," to themselves. Christians are sinful and of this world. The text applies only to Christ, who alone was born and remained sinless. Moreover, in a sinful world the *Oberkeit*, is obliged to use the sword in defense of the fatherless, widows, and pious and just men. Hubmaier uses Old Testament texts and the Old Testament examples of Moses, Joshua, and Abraham to support his arguments for the use of the sword from Scripture. This shows that Hubmaier worked with a completely different hermeneutical principle from that of the other evangelical Anabaptists considered in this study. (From the microfilm of Hubmaier's Complete Works)
113 Marbeck, *Verantwortung*, pp. 521–22.
114 *Ibid.*
115 *Ibid.*, p. 521.
116 *Ibid.*, p. 133.

In the presence of faith defined as both belief and trust the Bible becomes more than a book of paper and ink. It is the Word of God, for its words are bearers of meaning and revelation. Marbeck writes:

> Schwenckfeld should know that the invisible content, meaning [*synn*] and intention [*verstand*] of the holy Scriptures, and the outwardly preached word in sound and voice [*im laut und stymn*] is the word to which the Scriptures ascribe (as will follow hereafter) honor and glory as God's natural Almighty Word, which is Spirit and Life, yes, God Himself. And it is not the visible corruptible book of paper and ink. Yes, it is even the eternal living and essential [*wesentlich*] Word of God, to which the Scriptures and the outwardly preached word not alone point or bear witness, as Schwenckfeld says; but it is ... through its invisible spiritual meaning and intention, in itself from God, going forth as Spirit and Life, yes, God, Jesus Christ, and the Holy Spirit in the heart through faith. And because Christ is also in us, so it is even the Word to which Scripture gives so much glory and power, that Word through which all things were made. John 1. Col. 1. And so since it is also in addition in the external (as in Scripture and in preaching) a co-voice of their inner meaning and intention, there are in summary not two, nor two kinds of words, but only a single undivided Word of God.[117]

Marbeck's meaning, though rather awkwardly expressed, is clear enough. The inner meaning of Scripture not only points to Christ, but when faith is present it brings Christ into the heart. One may, therefore, speak of the Bible as the Word of God without dishonoring Christ. This is especially true with respect to the spoken words of Christ and the apostles, whose words as now recorded in Scripture are Spirit of Life. Who would have thought, asks Marbeck, that such a learned man as Schwenckfeld would have wavered so much or written so erroneously about the Word of God?[118] The Holy Spirit does not only speak inwardly in the heart as Schwenckfeld imagines, but also inspires one to express in words what is inwardly experienced. This again is the case with the words of Christ and the apostles, and Schwenckfeld, with his doctrine of the inner and outer Word, alters the Scriptures unworthily.[119] Yet, even though the Holy Scriptures have been written by the Holy Spirit, apart from faith, those who have the Bible have the Word of God only in books.[120]

For Marbeck the Bible is the inspired Word of God, but his theory of inspiration is not mechanical. His view of the necessity of faith and of the aid of the Holy Spirit,[121] as the prerequisites for the proper interpretation of Scripture, guard him from the danger of bibliolatry. The Bible as the Word of God has not displaced Christ as the Word.

---

117 *Ibid.*, p. 518.
118 *Ibid.*, p. 519.
119 *Ibid.*, pp. 519–20.
120 *Ibid.*, pp. 521–22.
121 *Ibid.*, p. 525.

CHAPTER VI

ANABAPTIST OR RADICAL ETHICS AND THE WORKS OF GRACE

*A. The Role of the Holy Spirit in the
Development of a Rigorous Ethic*

The ethics of grace within the Radical Reformation reflect strongly the influence of the *Imitatio Christi*. Yet, although there is much emphasis upon discipleship in conformity with the example of Christ, the Radicals do not imagine that the possibility of following this example lies within the range of the natural man's ability. Only the man who is "born out of God," and by reason of his regeneration shares in the divine nature through the indwelling presence and power of the Holy Spirit, possesses this ability. The Holy Spirit is seen both as *enabling grace* and *motivating power* within the new life of the Christian man.

Hans Denck maintained that while temptations to sin remain within the new man, temptation is never so great but what it may be overcome in the strength of the Spirit. So far as the new man is concerned, he knows that "there is much in him which transgresses all God's law and design again and again."[1] According to the flesh, therefore, the new man weeps and complains because he would rather be freed from the struggle, even though he is not overcome by it, "for he who is his Lord overcomes within him."[2] Yet, "in the Spirit" the new man rejoices, because, like Paul, he knows that he will triumph no matter how long the struggle must continue.[3] The new man, however, can claim no merit for the triumphant life, "for all glory belongs to God through whose grace a way is given which was previously impossible for the whole world."[4]

In Balthasar Hubmaier's thought, as previously noted, the Holy Spirit plays a very important role in the conversion experience of his tripartite man. It is only with the aid of the Holy Spirit that the unfallen spirit of man can control the always worthless flesh and make it, contrary to its nature, go even into the fire.[5] The significance which Hubmaier gave to the Holy Spirit in the victorious life of the Christian man also comes to the fore in the confessional formula which he developed and used at Nicolsburg. Candidates for baptism confessed, first of all, faith in the Holy Spirit and promised in the strength of Christ to renounce the devil and all his works.[6]

Melchior Hoffmann held that the Christian puts on Christ in baptism in such a way that he is in Christ and Christ in him. Such a man can no longer be made guilty by the law, because he now lives according to the Spirit rather than according to the flesh.[7] The newly baptized Christian, like Christ after his baptism, is driven by the

---

1 Denck, *Vom Gesetz Gottes, QFR*, Band XXIV, 2 Teil, 55.
2 *Ibid.*
3 *Ibid.*, pp. 57–58.
4 *Ibid.*, p. 58.
5 Hubmaier, *Von der Freiheit des Willens.*
6 Hubmaier, *Eine Form zu taufen in Wasser die im Glauben Unterrichteten.*
7 *SAW*, p. 188. See also *BRN*, V, 152.

Holy Spirit into a spiritual wilderness for a time of testing. Yet by the Spirit's aid the newborn Christian can come through the temptation experience to a victorious end.[8] It is the Holy Spirit that drives Christians to bring forth the fruit of the Spirit. It is through the Spirit's aid that the possibility of falling again into sin, which is ever present, throughout life, is none the less greatly reduced.[9]

Menno Simons saw the work of the Holy Spirit as the divine power which prevented a wound inflicted upon Christians by surprise from becoming fatal. Christians who were "born out of God" had what Menno called "the anointing of God."[10] This was a term used by both Menno and Dirk to designate the presence of the Holy Spirit in the life of the believer. There are many passages in the writings of both Menno and Dirk where they do not distinguish sharply between the Holy Spirit and the indwelling Christ. There is one passage in Dirk's *Vande geestelijcke Restitution*, where the two are regarded as identical.[11] A similar identification of the Holy Spirit with the indwelling Christ appears to be present in the passage from Menno cited above. Christians have not only the Holy Spirit but also the true Samaritan and physician with them, who is able to bind up and heal their wounds and has compassion on their frailty.[12]

Whether it is the Holy Spirit or the indwelling Christ who acts through the Spirit, enabling Christians to resist sin and fight against it, it is because of a power not their own that "they are not so wholly overcome that they cast aside their weapons and surrender, to become servants of sin again and to be ruled by it."[13]

The Holy Spirit, as the gift of God's grace, thus enables the converted and regenerate man to resist sin and to overcome it. Though momentary lapses are not denied, through the aid of the Spirit these can be prevented from becoming permanent or fatal. Even as Christians are caused to triumph in the new life through the presence and power of the Holy Spirit, so preachers and teachers who are sent of God and born of God so that they are of a godly nature are driven by the Spirit to rebuke the flesh with the gospel of grace.[14]

Pilgram Marbeck's concept of the role of the Holy Spirit in shaping the conduct of the Christian man cannot be better stated than he himself states it:

> We maintain that this is a true Christian faith through which the Holy Spirit and the love of God comes into the hearts and is active in them; mighty and active in all outward obedience and requested works. And that alone through such faith (Gal. 3) is one God's child and free from the law and servitude. Where the Spirit and the power of God dwells and has his drive [*trib*] and activity, here is freedom, and such children are free, as the Lord says in Matt. 17:26. One comes to this liberty through abiding in the word of Christ. John 8. Yes, through the law of the Spirit, whereby one is set free from the law of sin and death (Rom. 8) and not free from the law of Christ, as obedient to those things which he has taught and commanded us to do ... .[15]

8 *SAW*, p. 190. See also *BRN*, V, 153.
9 *SAW*, pp. 199–201. See also *BRN*, V, 165.
10 Menno Simons, *The Spiritual Resurrection*, 1536, *CWMS*, p. 57.
11 Dirk Philips, *Vande geestelijcke Restitution*, 1536, *BRN*, X.
12 Menno Simons, *The Spiritual Resurrection*, *CWMS*, p. 57.
13 *Ibid.*
14 Menno Simons, *Confession of Distressed Christians*, *CWMS*, p. 511.
15 Marbeck, *Verantwortung*, p. 153. The polemic is directed against Schwenckfeld, who was

Marbeck thus sees the Christian life as a life of discipleship in obedience to the commands of Christ. Such obedience, however, is not possible for the natural man. It is possible only for one who through faith is born a child of God and who is aided in his desire to follow the commands of Christ by the Holy Spirit.

For the Evangelical Spiritualist, Caspar Schwenckfeld, the work of the Holy Spirit is more directly connected with the work of the reigning and glorified Christ. Schwenckfeld's mystical orientation with the mystic's desire for the soul's immediate contact with God also affected his concept of the work of the Holy Spirit. But for Schwenckfeld, too, the Holy Spirit is the gift of God's grace, which slowly but surely fashions the new man in Christ. The new life is possible because the "birth out of God" has taken place and because the Holy Spirit makes the believer a participant in the divine nature.[16]

Present throughout the Radical Reformation, as noted in Chapter IV, was the dualism between the holy Church and the evil world. This dualism was less severe in the thought of Hubmaier and Schwenckfeld than in that of the other representatives of this wing of the Reformation considered in this study. But wherever it did appear, this Radical dualism had a profound effect upon the ethics of grace developed within the Radical Reformation. As God, who calls men who are sinners sinners into fellowship with Himself through the new birth, is holy, so those whom He calls are to become holy as well. Through the gift of the Holy Spirit God graciously supplies to the believer the means toward the goal which He has set for those who would live in fellowship with Him. "Ye shall be holy, for I am holy."[17] How the Radicals sought to maintain the tension which must always exist between the Church as the regenerate gathered people of God and the ungathered and unregenerate world is the problem which the remainder of this chapter will seek to answer.

B. *The Ethics of Grace in Relation to the State*

1. *The Legitimate Place and Function of the State*

The guiding principle of the ethics of grace among the Evangelical Anabaptists of both Holland and South Germany is well stated by Menno Simons, when he says that what he teaches is "the true love and fear of God, the true love of our neighbor – *to aid and assist all men and to injure none* . . ."[18] The ethics of grace thus embraces love to God and neighbor with the latter strongly influenced by the *imitatio Christi* pattern. As Christ injured none and aided all, so Christians as his disciples were to conform their own conduct to that of their Lord.

This, for most of the Evangelical Anabaptists, meant that they were automatic-

---

claiming in Marbeck's mind "a liberty in Christ," which he had no right to claim. Schwenckfeld's "still stand" on the Supper and his minimizing of the importance of baptism were regarded by Marbeck as a violation of the specific commands of Christ.
16 Schwenckfeld, *Von der Sünd und Gnad. Adam und Christo, CS*, VI, 598–649.
17 See I Pet. 1:14–16.
18 Menno Simons, *Why I Do Not Cease Teaching and Writing, CWMS*, pp. 304–05 (Italics mine.)

ally excluded from any participation in the conduct of government. To be a magistrate who used force or imposed the death sentence upon another human being involved the Christian disciple in an impossible compromise. In this study Balthasar Hubmaier and Caspar Schwenckfeld, the Evangelical Spiritualist, appear as exceptions to this general rule. For the sake of clarity in the presentation of the material in this chapter, the thought of the seven representatives of the Radical Reformation whose writings are considered as the basis for this study will be considered chronologically rather than logically. At the same time an attempt will be made to present a synthetic overall view of the ethics of grace at points where the Radicals differed with the Magisterial Reformers.

Despite the widely held conviction among the Evangelical Anabaptists that a Christian could not serve as a magistrate without compromising his discipleship, they nevertheless found a legitimate place for the state. They saw the state primarily as an instrument of the *wrath of God*, by means of which justice was maintained and established among the unregenerate, who were not within the Church as the holy community of the gathered and regenerate people of the "new covenant." The state, no less than the Church, was ordained of God, but they saw the state also as a means to provide for the common good of all.

As early as 1527 Hans Denck wrote that a Christian cannot be in a position of authority (*Obrigkeit*). His reason for this position is that "it is not allowed to any Christian who would glory in his Lord to proceed with force [*faren mit gewalt*]"[19] At the same time Denck can also say that from the point of view of the evil world force is not wrong, "for it serves the wrath of God."[20] Love, however, teaches all her children something better, "namely, that they should serve God and His grace. For it is the nature of love that it does not wish to be hurtful to anyone, but rather serve everyone for his own improvement insofar as this is possible."[21]

In July of the same year in which Denck wrote the work mentioned above Hubmaier wrote his *Vom Schwert*. Although he does not share the pacifist views of the other Evangelical Anabaptists, he does stress the role of the *Obrigkeit* in the maintenance of justice. The *Obrigkeit* is called of God to use the sword in the defense of the fatherless, widows, and pious and just men.[22] Hubmaier also raises,

---

19 Hans Denck, *Von der wahren Liebe, QFR*, Band XXIV, 2 Teil, 84.
20 *Ibid.*, p. 85.
21 *Ibid.*
22 Hubmaier, *Vom Schwert*. For an English translation of this work in its entirety see Henry C. Vedder, *Balthasar Hubmaier, the Leader of the Anabaptists* (New York: Putnam's Sons; London: The Knickerbocker Press, 1905), pp. 279–310. For an excellent summary see Johann Loserth, *Doctor Balthasar Hubmaier and die Anfange der Wiedertaufe in Mähren* (Brunn, 1893), pp. 166–70.

Hubmaier's *Vom Schwert* is, for the most part, a commentary on fifteen passages of Scripture, which his opponents used as proof texts for their position that a Christian may not serve as a magistrate or soldier. The first two of these texts are John 18:36 and Matt. 26:53–54. Commenting on the first passage, Hubmaier says that Christians are wrong in applying "My kingdom is not of this world," to themselves. Christians are sinful, and they are of this world. The text applies only to Christ, who alone was sinless. Of the Matthew text Hubmaier observes that Christ did not tell Peter to remove his sword but to put it in its place. The place of the sword is at the side of the magistrate who is ordained of God to use it. If he

in an indirect way, the question as to how far the *imitatio Christi* pattern should be regarded as obligatory for Christians, who after all have not Christ's office as Redeemer. Christ did not judge or punish men for the reason that he came to save them; hence, the incarnation. This does not mean, according to Hubmaier, that no Christian may ever serve as a magistrate nor wield the sword under any circumstances. Rather, one who is appointed of God to serve as a magistrate is then required to use the sword to punish the wicked for the good of the pious and innocent.[23]

Hubmaier was anxious to refute the slander which his enemies spread against him, that he was a revolutionary who could find no basis in Scripture for the *Obrigkeit*. He maintained that he, more than any other minister within a twenty-mile radius, had sought to show the Scriptural foundation for governmental authority. While Hubmaier admitted that he had criticised magistrates who ruled tyrannically, he denied that he had advocated revolution. Where changes for the better could not be brought about without revolt, he urged that the common citizen should rather submit to tyranny and injustice.[24] Thus the conflict between Hubmaier and the other Evangelical Anabaptists was not over the question of whether or not the state had a rightful place within the divine order. It was over the question of whether or not the Christian as a disciple can participate in the administration of justice which is the state's sphere of operation.

Caspar Schwenckfeld's view of the divinely ordained place and function of the state is strangely similar to that of Hubmaier. The earliest date upon which Schwenckfeld is known to have expressed his mind on this point is January of 1532. The occasion for a statement from Schwenckfeld on this subject was a letter from Baron Leonhard von Liechtenstein of Nicolsburg to Wolfgang Capito in Strasbourg. Von Liechtenstein had given his blessing and protection to Hubmaier and his Anabaptist followers until the mandates of Ferdinand forced him to allow the seizure of Hubmaier in August of 1527. On March 10 of the following year Hubmaier died a martyr's death at the stake in Vienna.[25] His removal from the scene in the barony of the Von Liechtensteins left the way open for further disturbances from men of lesser ability and training than Hubmaier possessed. One of these men was Oswald Glaid, who had served as a minister in the Lutheran congregation at Nicolsburg until the arrival of Hans Hut. After Hut's arrival Glaid accepted his chiliastic ideas as well as his view that a Christian might

---

takes the life of a criminal or a turbulent man in the course of his administration of justice, he may do so as a Christian. The remaining texts upon which the commentary, *Vom Schwert*, is based are:

Luke 9:54–55; Luke 12:13–14; Matt. 5:40; I Cor. 6:7–8; Matt. 18:15–17; Matt. 5:38–39; Eph. 6:14–17; II Cor. 10:4–5; Matt. 5:43–48; Matt. 5:21; Luke 22:25–26; Rom. 12:19; Eph. 1:4–5; Col. 1:2.

23 Hubmaier, *Vom Schwert*. For the English translation see Vedder, p. 283.
24 Hubmaier, *Ibid.*, Also Vedder, p. 304. Hubmaier was wanted by the Austrian authorities because of his previous activity at Waldshut. He was accused by them of having aided and abetted the Peasants' War by writing the famous *Twelve Articles*. See Loserth, pp. 94–106. Loserth shows that this charge is completely unfounded.
25 *ME*, II, 833.

not serve as a magistrate. After Hubmaier's death Glaid went to Silesia and there wrote a book on the Sabbath, in which he claimed that the observance of the seventh day was obligatory upon all Christians.

A copy of this book found its way to the barony of von Liechtenstein and caused further disturbances among his subjects. He now sent a copy of the book, together with a letter, to Capito and requested an opinion from him. At the time of the arrival of this letter from von Liechtenstein, Schwenckfeld was a guest in the home of Capito. Capito was already overburdened with work, and he knew that Schwenckfeld had become personally acquainted with Glaid before beginning his voluntary exile from Silesia. Schwenckfeld was also familiar with the sabbatic movement, and, therefore, Capito turned von Liechtenstein's letter over to him with the request that he write the reply.[26]

Glaid's book is no longer extant, but from Schwenckfeld's reply it is evident that he, like William Miller, maintained that the command to observe the Sabbath had never been abrogated. Glaid apparently argued that if Christians are not obligated to observe the Sabbath, then they are under no obligation to observe the remainder of the Ten Commandments either. Christians may then lie and steal, commit murder, adultery, and fornication, and go unpunished.[27] Schwenckfeld replies in the form of a question: "For what purpose then does the *Oberkeit* exist?[28] The heathen, he says, who do not have Moses, have the whole content of law written on their hearts by nature. One cannot say, therefore, that failure to observe the Sabbath of necessity leads to lawlessness in every other area of life. The *order* of the magistrate is, therefore, not molested if one ceases to observe the Mosaic Sabbath and observes it as it is observed within Christendom.[29] It has a base within the law of nature as well as within the law of Moses. The magistrate does not bear the sword in vain. "It is God's servant of wrath to punish him who does evil."[30] Throughout the world, within or without Christendom, Schwenckfeld saw the *Obrigkeit* as established by God to maintain justice in a fallen world. Like Hubmaier, Schwenckfeld felt it possible for a Christian to serve in the office of magistrate without involving himself in an impossible compromise between the demands of office, on the one hand, and those of discipleship, on the other. Indeed, he said, a Christian should know best of all how to serve as a magistrate or how and when to use the sword.[31]

Melchior Hoffmann, like Hubmaier, appeared in the popular image of the sixteenth century as a revolutionary spirit. This was due to the fact that his chiliastic ideas were appropriated by the revolutionary Anabaptists of Münster. Yet the aspect of Hoffmann's thought appropriated by the Münsterites and used by them in support of their revolutionary program was only one side of his versatile mind, and not the most important side at that.

26 The material on the incidents which led Schwenckfeld to express his views on the rightful place of the state is selected from the Introduction to *Vom Christlichen Sabbath und underscheid dess alten und newen Testaments*, 1532, CS, IV, 449–51.
27 *Ibid.*, p. 480.
28 *Ibid.*
29 *Ibid.*
30 Schwenckfeld, *Judicium, CS*, VIII, 196–97.
31 *Ibid.*

The earliest known writing of Hoffmann is a letter which he appended to one written on his behalf by Luther and Bugenhagen to the Christians in Livland. Written in June of 1525, this letter had the lengthy title, *Jhesus. Der Christlichen gemenn zu Derpten ynn Liefflandt wunschet Melcher Hoffman Gnad und fride, sterckung des glaubens von Gott dem vater und dem hern Jhesu Christo. Amen.*[32] In this letter Hoffmann earnestly admonishes the Christians in Livland to strive for peace and harmony and to avoid becoming entangled in the *"auff ruhr,"* which *"yetzt vorhanden ist."*[33] The *"auff ruhr"* is obviously a reference to the Peasants' War. Hoffmann advises his former congregation that it is much better to suffer injustice (*unrecht*) than to become involved in this tumult. He considers the fanatical spirits (*Schwärm Geister*) a visitation of the wrath of God,[34] and warns that he who fights with the sword will also be judged by it.[35] One in whom Christ has enkindled faith will do injury to no one, and because he will not seek to return evil for evil, he knows that vengeance belongs to God.[36]

, For a Christian looks alone to God, and has given himself entirely into His hands to let Him do with him as He will, and he is mindful of the example [*ebenbildts*] of his Saviour, Jesus Christ.[37]

In Hoffmann's commentary on Romans, which appeared in print early in 1533,[38] the emphasis upon strict obedience to the established *Obrigkeit* appears even more strongly. Hoffmann now "rejects the bearing of arms, and definitely demands unconditional obedience to the government for God's sake."[39] Again the familiar pattern of the ethics of grace in relation to the state comes to the fore. Christians, because they must ever strive to follow the example of Christ, may not serve in *Obrigkeit*, and yet the *Obrigkeit*, too, is ordained of God.

The earliest known expression of Pilgram Marbeck's attitude toward the state was made at the time of his expulsion from the city of Strasbourg in December of 1531. Marbeck notified the city council that he would leave the city as they had requested, because he had always been obedient to the *Obrigkeit*.[40] In the *Vermanung* of 1542 Marbeck wrote that inasmuch as the Kingdom of Christ is not of this world, it is not fitting for a Christian to be a magistrate or a worldly prince or

32 *D. Martin Luther's Werke, WA*, 18, 426.
33 *Ibid.*, p. 427.
34 *Ibid.*, p. 428. This early letter of Hoffmann, as well as the later commentary on Romans, shows that Hoffmann is done an injustice by those who cast him solely in the spirit of a revolutionary.
35 *Ibid.*, p. 429.
36 *Ibid.*
37 *Ibid.*
38 *ME*, II, 782. This commentary was evidently written while Hoffmann was at Leeuwarden in the Netherlands under the title, *Die eedele hoghe enn trostlike sendebrief, den die heylige Apostel Paulus to den Romeren gescreuen heeft, verclaret enn gans ulitich mit ernste van woort to woorde utgelecht Tot eener costoliker nutticheyt enn troost allen godtvruchtigen lief hebebbers er eewighen onentiliken waerheyt.*
39 *Ibid.* Unfortunately this excerpt from the commentary on Romans is the only section which deals with Hoffmann's ethics now available in this country. The excerpts from the commentary which appear in *BRN*, V, deal with Hoffmann's Christology.
40 Rörich, p. 56.

to exercise authority over city, land, or people.[41] Schwenckfeld in the *Judicium* of the same year interprets Marbeck as saying that "no true Christian may possess city, land, or people, or rule with force [*gewalt*] as earthly rulers do. For such things belong to earthly lordship but not at all to true Christians."[42] In the *Verantwortung* of 1544 Marbeck restates his position and complains that Schwenckfeld interpreted his words, so that he makes Marbeck appear as one who doubts that the *Obrigkeit* is from God.[43] Marbeck states that what he protests against is not the *Obrigkeit*, when it remains within the limits and carries out the functions for which it was ordained of God. Marbeck declares that "the abuse and disorder among men, brought about by rulers and subjects alike," had neither caused him to err nor doubt

> that the worldly power has the sword in the worldly situation ..., and authority from God to use it, since it was ordained of Him. Which ordinance we not only do not question. Much more, we pray God for it and also render it praise and honor and glory.[44]

The worldly power is here as an instrument of God's wrath[45] to maintain justice among fallen men, and it has also the positive duty of caring for the widow and the orphan.[46]

Yet, although Marbeck honors the *Obrigkeit* as ordained of God and prays for it, he sees insolubable difficulties for a Christian as a "*gelassner mensch*" in the office of magistrate. If such a man should assume this office and rule in the world without violence, how long would he remain a ruler of the world? If, in the discharge of the duties of his office, the Christian magistrate would have to employ violence, how long would his conscience allow him to remain as a ruler of the world? Marbeck then asks:

> If such a man did not obey his conscience, would he not forsake his God, yea, the Lord Jesus Christ and Christian patience, warfare, and judgment [*ritterschaft*]? Would he not because of this receive harm in his soul or in his Christian profession? Because no man can serve two masters, the king or the emperor in worldly authority, and Christ in the spiritual or heavenly kingdom, according to the word of Christ in Matthew 6.[47]

Thus, while Marbeck sees a legitimate place for the state, so long as it operates within that sphere for which it was ordained of God, he also sees irreconcilable difficulties for a Christian who assumes the duties of state. If a Christian rules in

---

41 Marbeck, *Vermanung*, pp. 217–18.
42 *CS*, VIII, 196–97.
43 Marbeck, *Verantwortung*, pp. 303–04.
44 *Ibid.*, p. 304.
45 Marbeck, *Testamentserläuterung*, pp. 325–26.
46 Marbeck, *Verantwortung*, p. 304.
47 *Ibid.* Schwenckfeld in his criticism of Marbeck had used the example of the Italian centurion, Cornelius, as an example of one who became a Christian and yet remained in the service of the *Obrigkeit*. To this Marbeck replies: "So far as the centurion Cornelius is concerned, he was a centurion before Christ made the Gospel known to him, and before he became a Christian and received the Holy Spirit. He did not first become a centurion after he had become a Christian. And who knows how long the Holy Spirit and his conscience, after he became a Christian, allowed Cornelius to continue in the office of centurion?"

the state as a Christian, the worldly power will soon renounce him. If he does not rule as a Christian, he forsakes God and Christ and does harm to his own soul. Therefore, the only way out of the dilemma for the Christian who wishes to live by the ethic of grace is to retire from any active participation in the affairs of the *Obrigkeit*. The insistence that the Christian life must manifest itself in the fruits of Christlikeness prevented Marbeck, as well as other leaders within the Radical Reformation, from seeking a way out of the dilemma by making the distinction between *person* and *office*, as Luther and Calvin did. The distinction which the Radicals made was rather between the way of Christ and the way of the world. The tension between Christ and culture was never relaxed.[48]

In the thought of Menno Simons and Dirk Philips there is found an even more positive attitude toward the legitimate place and function of the state than that which has been seen in Pilgram Marbeck. Menno says that emperors and magistrates alike are called of God to punish and chastise evil doers in the fear of God and in fairness and Christian discretion.[49] It is the maintenance of justice that falls within the sphere of jurisdiction within which the magistrate is divinely ordained to function. He is to deal with "manifest criminals." Under this classification Menno lists thieves, murderers, Sodomites, adulterers, seducers, sorcerers, violent highwaymen, robbers, etc.[50] Menno says:

> Your task is to do justice between a man and his neighbor, to deliver the oppressed out of the hand of the oppressor; also to restrain by reasonable means, that is, without tyranny and bloodshed, manifest deceivers who so miserably lead poor helpless souls by hundreds of thousands into destruction.[51]

Menno looked upon the office of magistrate as one that was "both responsible and dangerous"[52] and yet as one that could be conducted "according to the will of God."[53] It was not the *Obrigkeit* as such to which either Menno or Dirk objected, but the abuse which places the word of the magistrate above the Word of God. Menno complains that when he seeks to find a magistrate who fears God, performs his office *properly*, and uses his sword *correctly*, he generally finds nothing except a Lucifer, an Antiocus, or a Nero, who places himself in Christ's stead, so that his edict must be respected as above the Word of God.[54] Menno cites Ex. 18:21, Deut. 1:16–17, II Chron. 19:6–7, and Rom. 13:3–4 as Scriptural sources from which magistrates may learn how their office ought to be conducted.[55] Having cited these sources, Menno then proceeds to state what they mean.

---

48 The statement of Kiwiet that Marbeck had a more positive attitude toward culture than that which generally prevailed among Anabaptists would thus appear to be erroneous.
49 Menno Simons, *Foundation of Christian Doctrine, CWMS*, p. 193.
50 *Ibid.*
51 *Ibid.*
52 *Ibid.*, p. 197.
53 Menno Simons, *Why I Do Not Cease Teaching and Writing, CWMS*, pp. 298–99.
54 *Ibid.*
55 Menno Simons, *Reply to False Accusations, CWMS*, pp. 550–51.

> You may understand from these Scriptures that you are called of God and ordained to your offices to punish the transgressors and protect the good; to judge rightly between a man and his fellows; to do justice to widows and orphans, to the poor despised stranger and pilgrim; to protect them against violence and tyranny; to rule cities and countries justly and by a good policy not contrary to God's Word, in peace and quiet, unto the benefit and profit of the common people ...[56]

Menno avows that it will never be found true that the Dutch Anabaptists are disobedient to the magistracy "in things to which they have been ordained of God."[57] These things include, according to Menno, the maintenance of dikes, roads, waterways, the collection of taxes, tribute, etc.[58] These are items necessary to the common good of any society. The ethic of grace summed up in the words "to aid and assist all men and to injure none" showed clearly where Christian responsibility lay in matters that pertained to public welfare.

Dirk Philips strikes a similar note for the Dutch Anabaptists as he writes:

> We desire to live our lives in quietness, *obedient* to the authorities in all things not against God, and insofar as possible to live at peace with all men.[59]

Dirk echoes the sentiments of the entire Radical Reformation, the revolutionary Anabaptists of Münster excepted, when he says that the *Oberkeit* has received.

> the sword from God ... not to judge in spiritual matters ... but to maintain the subjects in good government (police) and peace, to protect the pious and to punish the evil.[60]

In summary it may be said that all of the representatives of the Radical Reformation here considered had a positive attitude toward the state, so long as it limited its activity to that sphere for which it was divinely ordained. They differed on the question of whether or not a Christian may serve as a magistrate, Hubmaier and Schwenckfeld saying, "Yes," Denck and Marbeck, "No." Menno and Dirk are not as clear on this point as Marbeck. Menno especially gives the impression that a magistrate may learn from Scripture how to conduct his office as a Christian.[61] But there was agreement by all that the state should not rule by force in matters of faith.

2. The Limits of the State's Sphere of Activity Defined by the Ethic of Grace

The ethic of grace, as shaped by the *imitatio Christi* pattern, precluded the use of violence for the purpose of spreading the Christian faith or defending it against heretics. A statement from Menno Simons' *Foundation of Christian Doctrine* in

56 *Ibid.*
57 Menno Simons, *The Cross of the Saints, CWMS*, p. 604.
58 *Ibid.*
59 Dirk Philips, *Vander Doope, BRN*, X, 111.
60 Dirk Philips, *Vande Gemeynte Godts, BRN*, X, 406. See *SAW*, p. 253, for the English translation.
61 Menno Simons, *Foundation of Christian Doctrine, CWMS*, p. 204.

1539 again reflects fairly the attitude of the whole Radical Reformation on this point. Menno appeals to the magistrates to "let the almighty king, Christ Jesus, be sovereign over men's souls; even as he was appointed by his Father."[62] The magistrate may rule in all temporal affairs, but he shall

> not usurp the judgment and kingdom of Christ, for He alone is the ruler of the conscience, and besides Him there is none other. Let Him be your emperor in this matter and His holy Word your edict, and you will soon have enough of storming and slaying.[63]

Hans Denck, Balthasar Hubmaier, Pilgram Marbeck, and Caspar Schwenckfeld would have no quarrel with such a position. Hubmaier, even though he did think it possible for a Christian to be a magistrate, did not want the magistrate to deal with matters of faith. Where discipline was required, the Church had recourse to the ban and excommunication.[64] While Schwenckfeld, too, felt that it was possible for a Christian to be a magistrate or carry the sword, he did not want the magistrate to meddle in matters of faith. Commenting on Oswald Glaid's contention that the magistrate should enforce Sabbath observance, Schwenckfeld said:

> The Lord forgive him and all other such fellows who would sic the magistrate into dealing with matters of faith. Their sins are so severe they do not know what else they do.[65]

When Pilgram Marbeck left Strasbourg at the request of the city council in December of 1531, because he recognized the legitimate place of government, he also stated that if the Holy Spirit should ever lead him to return, he would do so without hesitation.[66] Marbeck thus also enunciated the principle "that Christ only is Lord of the conscience." Although Menno and Dirk are the more articulate in giving expression to this principle, it was adhered to throughout the Radical Reformation.

Both Menno and Dirk appeal to the parable of the tares (Matt. 13:24–33) as a basis for religious toleration and nonviolence. God Himself will judge heretics and false prophets at the time of the eschaton. The Church in the meantime may rid herself of their harmful influence through the exercise of the ban.[67] The command of God to Moses to kill the false prophets was an Old Testament command. In the

---

62 *Ibid.*, p. 120.
63 *Ibid.*, p. 204. The plea which Menno makes is that magistrates should cease persecuting the Anabaptists as heretics because of the imperial edicts against them. He warns that magistrates who extend no mercy to these oppressed people will receive none from God on the Judgment Day. Menno contends that even the *reasonable law of nature* teaches one to be more kind than are the magistrates, who carry out these unreasonable imperial edicts, p. 117.
64 Hubmaier, *Vom Schwert.* See Vedder, p. 288, for the English translation.
65 Schwenckfeld, *Vom Christlichen Sabbath und underscheid dess alten und newen Testaments, CS,* IV, 485.
66 See William Klassen, *op. cit.*, pp. 27–28.
67 Dirk Philips, *Vande Gemeynte Godts, BRN,* X, 406. Menno Simons, *Brief Defense to All Theologians, CWMS,* p. 537. See also Roland H. Bainton, "The Parable of the Tares as the Proof Text for Religious Liberty to the End of the Sixteenth Century," *Church History,* I, No. 2 (June, 1952), 67–89, for similar interpretation of this parable.

New Testament we have another command which enjoins Christians to beware of the false prophet and to shun him but not to kill him.[68] Dirk writes:

> The congregation of the Lord may neither exercise dominion over the consciences of men with the outward sword, nor seek by violence to force unbelievers to believe, nor kill the false prophets with sword and fire.[69]

Menno voices almost identical sentiments as he writes:

> Where do the holy Scriptures teach that in Christ's kingdom and church we shall proceed with the magistrate, with the sword, and with physical force and tyranny over a man's conscience and faith, things subject to the judgment of God alone?[70]

As God uses constraint rather than compulsion in bringing men into the relationship of saving faith in Christ, the messengers of the gospel of grace must do likewise. The only means of propagating the Gospel that are in harmony with Christ's word and example are the methods of peaceful persuasion through preaching, teaching, and writing. The Radicals considered force in matters of faith equally wrong, whether engaged in by the Church or by the state, acting on behalf of the Church. Indeed, so far as the persecutions of the Anabaptists and the various edicts against them were concerned, they often felt that the ministers and theologians of the Magisterial Reformation were responsible for provoking them.[71] The reply often given, that it was the state as the civil arm of society that carried out these penalties and not the Church, had little appeal to the Anabaptists.

It is noteworthy that the Radicals differed markedly at this point from both Luther and Calvin. Although Luther appears to have been doubtful whether the death penalty should be inflicted upon heretics in his earlier years, Melanchton favored the death penalty for Anabaptists from the beginning.[72] The later Luther was more like the early Melanchton, and Calvin's responsibility for the death of Michael Servetus at the stake cannot be denied.[73] Within the Radical Reformation where the ethic of grace, informed by Christ's word and example, defined that area which the state, though divinely ordained may yet not invade as man's

---

68 *BRN*, X, 406. Also *CWMS*, p. 537.
69 *BRN*, X, 406.
70 *CWMS*, p. 537. In his *Reply to Gellius Faber*, p. 779, Menno makes a statement much in the same vein: "I would say further, If the magistracy rightly understood Christ and His kingdom, they would in my opinion rather choose death than to meddle with their worldly power and sword in spiritual matters which are reserved not to the judgment of man but to the judgment of the great and Almighty God alone. But they are taught by those who have the care of their souls that they may proscribe, imprison, torture, and slay those who are not obedient to their doctrine, as may, alas, be seen in many different cities and countries."
71 It is a matter of historical record that the Anabaptists were correct in this judgment. See G. Franz, *Wiedertaüferakten, 1527–1626, Urkündliche Quellen zur Hessizchen Reformationsgeschichte*, IV, (1951).
72 John Oyer, "The Writings of Luther Against the Anabaptists," *MQR*, XXVII, No. 2 (April, 1953), 110. Also Oyer, *"The Writings of Melanchton Against the Anabaptists," MQR*, XXVI, No. 4 (October, 1952), 264–65.
73 Roland H. Bainton, *Hunted Heretic: the Life and Death of Michael Servetus, 1511–1533* (Boston: Beacon Press, 1953).

conscience of which Christ only is Lord, such a tragedy would have been averted. Within this frame of reference, of the state as divinely ordained, yet strictly limited in its activity to "temporal affairs," the Radicals found the vantage point from which they could be critical of the state, while yet within a measure obedient to it. That such a vantage point is a necessity in every age to prevent the state from becoming demonic is demonstrated by the emergence of the super state in the contemporary situation.

C. The Ethics of Grace and the Refusal to Take the Oath

The attitude toward the swearing of the oath was not uniform throughout the Radical Reformation. Among the representatives considered in this study, Hans Denck, Menno Simons, and Dirk Philips write specifically against the swearing of the oath: Denck, in 1526; Menno, in 1552 and 1556; and Dirk, in 1654. Marbeck, though he does not express himself on the issue, would, it seems fair to say, have opposed it in principle.[74] Denck in his final work modified his position on the oath,[75] while Dirk makes the refusal to take the oath one of the seven signs of the true Church.[76] Hoffmann's attitude toward the oath is uncertain, while Hubmaier and Schwenckfeld experienced no difficulty with it. Where objections to the swearing of the oath do appear, they are again based upon the words and example of Christ.

It was on the basis that Jesus has transcended Moses, Daniel, and all patriarchs that Hans Denck first objected to the oath.[77] In his so-called *Retraction* (*Widerruf*), published posthumously by Oecclampadius, Denck still appeals to the words of Christ, "Swear not at all," and considers them a warning to those who think that what man promises cannot fail.[78] So long as one now swears only to that which it is his duty to do in any case and which he may do with a good conscience, Denck thinks that swearing may be permissible.[79] What one can speak with truth, that he may also bear testimony to with an oath. Denck reasons that Christ did not intend to prohibit the serious oath, through which the one swearing expresses a desire that is in harmony with the mind and spirit of Christ, but only the lighthearted oaths that are sworn daily without thinking.[80]

In the work of 1552, as well as that of 1556, Menno bases his reason for the rejection of the oath upon the word and example of Christ. The refusal to take the oath was one thing that constantly brought the Anabaptists into conflict with Catholics, as well as with Lutheran and Reformed groups, throughout Germany and the Netherlands. This refusal was one of the things that made them targets for

---

74 Marbeck, *Vermanung*, p. 251. Marbeck objects that those who baptize their infants, saying that it may not do any good, but it can do no harm either, forget that they use God's name in vain. It is, of course, an argument from silence, but it seems reasonable to suppose that Marbeck would have rejected the oath on the same basis.
75 Hans Denck, *Widerruf, QFR*, Band XXIV, 2 Teil, 110.
76 Dirk Philips, *Vande Gemeynte Godts, BRN*, X, 404.
77 Hans Denck, *Von der wahren Liebe, QFR*, Band XXIV, 2 Teil, pp. 78–79.
78 Hans Denck, *Widerruf, QFR*, Band XXIV, 2 Teil, 110.
79 *Ibid.*
80 *Ibid.*

persecution. In the *Confession of Distressed Christians*, 1552, Menno sets forth very carefully the Scriptural basis upon which the Dutch Anabaptists reject the oath.

Menno finds three reasons why Christians should not swear. The first reason is that in the Old Testament itself the manner of swearing was not uniformly the same. There was a difference between the manner in which the patriarchs swore before the law and the manner in which the Israelites swore under the Law. Before the Law a man might swear in regard to such a matter as finding a wife for his master's son by placing his hand upon his thigh, as in Gen. 24:3. The second reason is that Israel under Law was permitted to swear *only* in matters of life and death, as in Ex. 22:11. But the third and most important reason is

> that Christ Jesus does not in the New Testament point His disciples to the Law in regard to the matter of swearing – the *dispensation of imperfectness* which allowed swearing, but He points us now from the Law to yea and nay, as to the dispensation of perfectness, saying, ... Matt. 5:33–37.[81] (Italics mine)

At the close of this Scriptural quotation Menno says, "Here you have Christ's own doctrine and ordinance concerning swearing."[82]

Once again the hermeneutics of grace, whereby the Old Testament is made completely subordinate to the New, is seen to have its effect upon the ethics of grace. The work of 1556 is in part a defense of Menno's hermeneutical method as well as a restatement of his ethical position in regard to the oath. He had been engaged, reluctantly, in a private disputation with Martin Micron, a minister in the Reformed Church, over this and other issues. The work of 1556 was a reply to what Menno considered Martin's slanderous attack upon him in making public the disputation, misinterpreting Menno, and at the same time, revealing his hiding place. Micron attacked Menno for the way in which he arrived at his position in regard to the oath by subordinating the Old Testament to the New. Menno retorts that Micron would do well to reflect soberly on what he writes concerning the oath, lest he be found to contradict Christ, the Son of God, and his holy apostle, James. Christ and James (Jas. 5:12) both say, "Swear not at all," but Micron says that one may swear to the truth. "And thus the eternal Wisdom Himself and His holy witness James, alas, must be your pupils and flunkies."[83]

The ethics of grace, when the magistracy insisted upon the oath, left the Christian disciple no alternative except to disobey and thereby incur the disfavor of the magistrate. It would be better to disobey the magistrate than to displease one's Lord.[84] The ethic of grace is one that requires an obedience "even unto death." It cannot seek refuge from this radical obedience in a compromise that is nonetheless a responsible response to an existential situation.[85]

81 Menno Simons, *Confession of Distressed Christians*, pp. 518–19.
82 *Ibid.*, p. 519. Menno in 1552 did appear to allow the oath in "spiritual matters." But close examination of the text seems to indicate that he meant by this little more than an affirmation that a given statement was true.
83 Menno Simons, *Epistle to Martin Micron, CWMS*, p. 924.
84 Menno Simons, *Confession of Distressed Christians, CWMS*, p. 519.
85 Calvin and the Magisterial Reformers generally supported the swearing of the oath on the basis of Old Testament practices. See the *Institutes*, II. viii. 22–27, especially 26.

D. The Irreconcilable Conflict between the Duties of the Soldier and the Conduct of the Disciple

While the position of the Radicals on the question of whether or not a Christian may be a magistrate varied from the unconditional affirmative in Hubmaier and Schwenckfeld to the unconditional negative in Marbeck, with the rather ambiguous position of Menno between the two extremes, the picture is less complex in regard to the question of war. Hubmaier and Schwenckfeld see no irreconcilable conflict between the duties of the soldier and the call of the disciple to conform his own life to the example set by his Lord. Denck, Marbeck, Menno, Dirk, and Hoffmann are in essential agreement that he who is a soldier cannot be a disciple.

Denck wrote in 1526 that he who serves as a soldier thrusts himself from the Rock that is Christ.[86] For those who sought to defend the work of the soldier on the basis that he sometimes took life in order to protect the innocent, and who based their argument upon the example of Moses and the word of John, the Baptist, Denck had a typical Anabaptist answer. Christ has transcended both Moses and John, the Baptist. Moses sought to drive out evil with evil and to protect the pious with power, but this occurred under the Law.[87] God now wishes to beget out of the old coarse Israel, a new Israel, which is now bidden to live by the law of perfect love. Christ has brought to an end the Law and the prophets which lasted until the time of John.[88] He who would now live by this perfect law of love may lose his own life for the sake of another, but he may not take the life of another.[89] While John, the Baptist, proclaimed the wrath of God to all who did not abide under the words of the Law in order that they might repent, Christ proclaimed grace and freely promised men much "through which they could without doubt live according to the good pleasure of God."[90]

Denck was well aware that this doctrine of the renunciation of all violence on the part of the Christian would seem foolishness to the evil world. He writes:

> And even though the whole world does not wish to endure this doctrine, or is able to in the attitude which it takes, therefore, this is a comfort to all the children of God that their Father is stronger and mightier than the whole world, together with its leader, the devil. Yes, he is also so faithful that he will not allow anyone to be brought to shame of all those who depend upon him. Woe to him who spares the truth because of offence and yet wants to be right. For this is the devil's love with which he blinds his children, and desires [to blind] the children of God, so that they fear more to act against man than against God.[91]

It is the man who fears to take this nonviolent position because of the offence which it may bring in the world, that will, in Denck's words, thrust himself from the Rock that is Christ. While Denck modified his position on the oath in the *Widerruf*, he did not renounce his nonviolent attitude toward war.

---

86 Hans Denck, *Von der wahren Liebe, QFR*, Band XXIV, 2 Teil, 86.
87 *Ibid.*, pp. 78–79.
88 *Ibid.*, pp. 85–86.
89 *Ibid.*, p. 76.
90 *Ibid.*, p. 85.
91 *Ibid.*, pp. 85–86.

Pilgram Marbeck, Menno Simons, and Dirk Philips all make <u>a distinction between what Menno called "the sword of justice," on the one hand, and the "sword of war," on the other.</u> The former, used in police action in order to maintain justice, had God's approval. The latter is violence employed for the purpose of conquest, and in this the Christian who lives by the *imitatio Christi* ethic may not have any part.

It was the difference between the state, acting to maintain justice within its own borders or seeking to extend itself by means or armed conquest, that Marbeck sought to emphasize in his reply to Schwenckfeld's criticism of his view that a Christian could not serve as a magistrate.[92] Marbeck protests that what he really said was that "no genuine Christian may *take* possession of either city, land, or people as earthly rulers do *with force.*"[93] (Italics mine) Marbeck laments that both Papists and Evangelicals (as they call themselves) do resort to force and boast of what they have gained by conquest.[94] This Marbeck calls an "appearance of faith" (*schein*) rather than a true faith which can only lead to tragedies similar to the Peasants' War.[95] While the state as the arbiter of justice has a place within the divinely ordered scheme of society, the state engaged in the conquest of another state through force of arms has not.

The Christian who lives according to the words and example of Christ cannot, therefore, participate in such conquest. Marbeck says that Christians may learn from the following passages of Scripture whether or not the use of the fleshly Mosaic sword of iron has today ceased in Christ.[96] The passages which he cites are Ps. 46:9, Isa. 2:4, Mic. 4:3, Isa. 65:25, Hos. 2:18, Zech. 9:9–10, and Jn. 18:36.[97] The force of these passages taken together, contends Marbeck, is that it is no longer proper for those who are "in Christ" and "in his Church" (the two were, as has been previously noted, synonomous in Marbeck's thought) to use the Mosaic sword.[98] One may learn, says Marbeck, from Luke 12:51–53, Rom. 6:13, II Cor. 10:4, and Heb. 4:12 that the "sword of today," which has been given to Christians who live under the "grace of today," is a *spiritual* rather than a *literal* sword.[99]

Menno's position in regard to a Christian's participation in warfare for the sake of conquest is similar. It was one that Menno held consistently from 1536 to 1556. The Revolutionary Anabaptists of Münster supported their rebellion on the basis of Old Testament texts and examples. They were the instruments of God to punish wicked Babylon (Rome).[100]

Menno replies that the Biblical Babylon had indeed been destroyed by a foreign foe at the command of God. He is convinced that the Roman Babylon will not escape a like visitation of divine wrath, but also is convinced that this should not

---

92 Pilgram Marbeck, *Vermanung*, pp. 217–18.
93 Marbeck, *Verantwortung*, pp. 303–04.
94 *Ibid.*
95 *Ibid.*
96 Marbeck, *Testamentserläuterung*, pp. 320–21.
97 *Ibid.*
98 *Ibid.*
99 Marbeck, *Testamentserläuterung*, p. 321.
100 Menno Simons, *Blasphemy of John of Leiden, CWMS*, p. 46.

be administered through the hands of Christians. The Biblical Babylon was destroyed by a heathen land. But "not by Christians is the Babylonian harlot to be destroyed, and Christians should not exterminate."[101]

While Menno saw the office of magistrate as one that was both difficult and dangerous, he does not unequivocally say that a Christian may not be a magistrate and wield the civil sword.[102] At least he infers that Christians may give their consent to the use of the literal sword by the magistrate "when it must be used."[103] But from the very beginning of the Anabaptist phase of his life to its close Menno saw a totally irreconcilable conflict between the duties and activities of a soldier and the mind and spirit of a disciple of Christ. Only Antichrist, said Menno, rules by force and sword. "Christ rules by patience with his word and spirit. He has no other sword or saber."[104]

As Christ does, so also must those who would be his disciples conform their own conduct to the example set by their Lord. Menno wrote:

> Our weapons are not weapons with which cities and countries may be destroyed, walls and gates broken down, and human blood shed in torrents like water. But they are weapons with which the spiritual kingdom of the devil is destroyed and the wicked principle in man's soul is broken down, flinty hearts broken, hearts that have never been sprinkled with the heavenly dew of the Holy Word. We have and know no other weapons besides this, the Lord knows, even if we should be torn into a thousand pieces, and if as many false witnesses rose up against us as there are spears of grass in the fields, and grains of sand upon the seashore.
>
> Once more, Christ is our fortress; patience our weapon of defense; the Word of God our sword; and our victory a courageous, firm unfeigned faith in Jesus Christ. And iron and metal spears and swords we leave to those who, alas, regard human blood and swine's blood about alike.[105]

At the same time that Christians are *forbidden* by Christ's word and example to use the sword in conquest, they are bidden by the same word and example to assist their brethren in an evangelical manner with money, food, and clothing at the risk of their own lives. While it was permissible to the people of God under the Old Testament to fight and do battle with swords, in the New Testament it is not so. The Christian who by grace participates in the divine nature, and is by reason of that participation a member of the community of the new covenant of grace, may not take the life of another in warfare, but he has a duty to share his goods for the welfare of his brethren in distress.

One of the most strongly worded passages in Menno's writings on this point is found in his reply to the accusation that the Dutch Anabaptists practiced the "community of goods." Menno replies that the ties which bind their community

---

101 *Ibid.*, pp. 46–47.
102 The one possible exception to this is where Menno questions whether the death penalty should ever be inflicted, even upon "manifest criminals." See *Epistle to Martin Micron, CWMS*, pp. 920–21.
103 Menno Simons, *Brief and Clear Confession*, 1544, *CWMS*, pp. 423–24. See also *The True Christian Faith*, where Menno says "the civil sword we leave to those to whom it is committed." *CWMS*, pp. 347–48.
104 Menno Simons, *Foundation of Christian Doctrine, CWMS*, p. 190.
105 *Ibid.*, p. 198.

together are spiritual rather than economic. Yet these spiritual ties have economic consequences. Menno compares the different members of the Church of Christ to the various members of the human body. It is not customary, he observes, that an intelligent person cares for one part of his body and leaves the other part destitute and naked.[106] It should be the same for all those who are members of Christ's Church and body, because

> all those who are born of God, who are gifted with the Spirit of the Lord, who are, according to the Scriptures, called into one body and love in Christ Jesus, are prepared by such love to serve their neighbors, not only with money and goods, but also after the example of their Lord and Head, Jesus Christ, in an evangelical manner, with life and blood.[107]

Menno goes on to say that it is the community of mutual helpfulness to brethren and strangers in distress that he teaches, but not the community of mutual property ownership as some falsely charge.[108] This community of mutual helpfulness, says Menno, the Dutch Anabaptists have practiced for seventeen years. He thanks God that though much of their property has been taken from them, and is still daily taken, and though many parents have been martyred and economic conditions are hard, none of those who have joined the Anabaptists or their orphaned children have been forced to beg.[109]

Not only has the Christian, who is "born out of God" and with his brethren shares through grace in the divine nature, the duty to share money and goods with them, but also he has the duty to risk his life on their behalf. Menno uses the Biblical example of Abraham, who risked his own life and that of his servants to rescue Lot, his kinsman, according to the flesh, from the four kings. Gen. 14:1–20. Abraham, however, risked his life to assist Lot with the literal sword. He is thus an example to all his spiritual children (Christians)

> that they should so love their brethren who are with them, born of the incorruptible seed of the holy divine Word, that they will not only assist them with money and goods, but also in an evangelical manner, risk and give their lives for them in time of need. I say, in an evangelical manner, for to aid with the sword is forbidden to all true Christians. In the New Testament all true believers should suffer patiently and not fight and do battle with swords and muskets.[110]

Risking one's life in an evangelical manner according to the New Testament means providing food and shelter for those who have been dispossessed "and driven forth for the sake of the Word," even when one knows beforehand that to be apprehended by the authorities will mean the death penalty. "This example we have in Christ, who for our sakes did not spare Himself, but willingly yielded His life that we through Him might live."[111]

---

106 Menno Simons, *Reply to False Accusations, CWMS*, p. 558.
107 *Ibid.*
108 *Ibid.*
109 *Ibid.*, pp. 558–59.
110 Menno Simons, *The True Christian Faith, CWMS*, pp. 347–48.
111 *Ibid.* Menno's reference to the possibility of the death penalty for giving shelter to a

The effect of the hermeneutics of grace upon the ethics of grace is again plainly seen. So also is the effect of the *imitatio Christi* upon the conduct of the Christian disciple, as well as the mystical union of the believer with Christ. The ethic of grace had for Menno both positive and negative connotations. Its negative aspects were, in the main, the result of the attempt to relate the faith and conduct of the Christian disciple to that level of life which obtained in the unregenerate world which was outside the community of the new covenant of grace. Its positive aspects were mostly concerned with defining the duty of mutual helpfulness within the brotherhood.

Dirk Philips does not discuss the issue of Christian participation in warfare for the purpose of territorial conquest as fully as do Marbeck and Menno. It is characteristic of Dirk that he gives a thorough treatment of one aspect of Christian doctrine, and then turns his attention to other matters. Yet Dirk says enough on this point that one may fairly say that here, too, he and Menno were in fundamental agreement. Dirk enjoins Christians to pray for the authorities,[112] and to be obedient to them in those things for which they have been ordained of God.[113] Yet, he also says that Christians may not employ carnal weapons.[114] In his discussion of the signs of the "true Church" Dirk called this nonviolent way of life "the heavenly philosophy"[115] which the Church had received from her Lord, and by which she was to live on earth. Though persecuted for their faith, Christians must persecute no one in return but patiently endure suffering.[116]

Thus, the ethic of grace involved the Christian disciple in the duty of mutual helpfulness toward the members of the brotherhood. It was a duty that required obedience "even unto death," according to the word and example of Christ. It required also willing obedience to the authorities in those things for which they were ordained of God. When those authorities exceeded those limits and sought to use force in matters of faith, or when they waged war for the purpose of conquest, the Christian disciple who lived by the ethic of grace had but one alternative; passive resistance to the state's illegitimate encroachment upon the domain of Christ and the patient endurance of affliction.

Certainly this complete rejection of the Christian's participation in warfare rested in part upon the rejection of the idea that the Church as the *Corpus Christi* was coterminous with society as the *Corpus Christianum*. Luther and Calvin did not really reject this idea, and, therefore, it was easier for them to find justification for the Christian's participation in a just war undertaken by the *Obrigkeit* as the civil arm of the divinely ordered society. The fact that they made a distinction

---

brother in distress was no idle remark. After the Anabaptists were outlawed by imperial decree in 1528, giving shelter to them was a crime punishable by death. One Anabaptist in Germany paid with his life because he had given shelter to Menno himself. See *A Brief Biography of Menno Simons, CWMS*, p. 21.
112 Dirk Philips, *Een Lieffelijcke Vermaninge, BRN*, X, 444.
113 Philips, *Vande Gemeynte Godts, BRN*, X, 406.
114 Philips, *Vande geestelijcke Restitution, BRN*, X, 360.
115 Philips, *Vande Gemeynte Godts, BRN*, X, 404.
116 *Ibid.*, p. 405.

between person and office, which the Anabaptists, because of the closeness of the believer with Christ through the mystical union, could not make, also helped them to overcome the tensions which for the Anabaptists were simply irreconcilable.[117]

---

117 Hugh Thompson Kerr, "Whether Soldiers, Too, Can Be Saved," *A Compend of Luther's Theology* (Philadelphia: The Westminster Press, 1943), p. 200. See also Calvin's *Institutes*, IV. xx. 782–85.

CHAPTER VII

SUMMARY AND EVALUATION

*A. A Synoptic View of the Concept of Grace
in the Radical Reformation*

Viewed synoptically and according to the chronological age of man from the cradle to the grave, grace in Radical Reformation thought is, indeed, a complex and many-sided concept. With regard to infants or young children and their freedom from the stain and guilt of original sin, grace was largely soteriologically based upon what might well be called a forensic view of the atonement. The grace won by Christ for infants and children through the atonement was believed to be universally efficacious, so that no child of believer or unbeliever was damned because of Adam's sin. What remained of original sin in the infant or the child was, for Christ's sake, not imputed as sin until the child reached the age of responsibility. Texts which were frequently quoted in support of this forensic and universal view of grace by the Anabaptists, in both South Germany and in the Netherlands, included such widely divergent passages as Gen. 22:18 and John 1:29b.[1]

While the base of this universal grace was largely soteriological, it was also, to a limited extent, anthropological. Both in South Germany and in the Netherlands Anabaptist leaders maintained that Christ would not have set little children before men as an example which they should follow, if he had not seen something innately good in them. In the thought of Pilgram Marbeck the anthropological and the soteriological graces are both available to children until they reach the age of responsibility. Through the universal grace which Christ has won for children through his forensic atonement they are again in the state of innocence, which Adam and Eve enjoyed before the fall. At the same time, because they were potentially in Adam, both when he sinned and when he received the promise of redemption, children have inherited not only original sin but also the *lux naturalis* as the opposite and positive side of original sin. As the child grows to maturity, the innocence won by Christ through the atonement dies off, and he must come to Christ through his own faith, while the *lux naturalis* remains throughout life and is the necessary precondition to lead men to faith in Christ. The Scriptural support for grace, as viewed from its anthropological side, was found by Marbeck in Rom. 1 and 2 and in Eccl. 13. The significance of this dual aspect of the concept of grace is that it includes a doctrine of creation as well as a doctrine of redemption.[2]

---

1 Gen. 22:18 – "and by your descendants shall all the nations of the earth bless themselves, because you have obeyed my voice."
  John 1:29 – "Behold, the Lamb of God, who takes away the sin of the world!"
2 For the significance of a doctrine of creation see the article on "Creation" by Fred Denbeaux in *A Handbook of Christian Theology* (New York: Meridian Books, Inc., 1958), pp. 65–67. Denbeaux says in part: "The historical task of the Reformation was to direct attention not to the creation but to the Creator, not to the order of the world but to the

The theological significance of Christ as the second Adam was taken with utmost seriousness by such men as Melchior Hoffmann, Dirk Philips, and Menno Simons. This again led, particularly in the case of Hoffmann, to a doctrine of universal grace, which was soteriologically oriented and not limited to infants and children only. Hoffmann argued that as the transgression of the first Adam had plunged mankind into universal bondage to Satan, so the obedience and death of Christ as the second Adam had brought about a partial universal liberation. Man's will, which was through the transgression of the first Adam placed into universal bondage, is now liberated through the atonement of Christ as the second Adam. Because of the atonement, and only because of it, the power of making a real decision is again placed within the capacity of otherwise still fallen man. Thus, the universal grace purchased through the atonement brings about a partial restoration of man's original humanity.

Finally, grace was, as we have seen, inseparably linked with the concept of salvation as the divinization of man. Through grace as God's act of regeneration man is actually made a participant in the divine nature itself. On this level, grace is the active agent in a gradual process of divinization which begins when the divine image is recreated in the believer through the work of the Holy Spirit. The recreated divine image is "the new creature in Christ," and this is nourished through an inner and spiritual eating of the Lord's Supper, which is in a restricted sense a means of grace. Because the believer must also carry throughout this life the burden of the sinful nature, which he has received from the first Adam, participation in the divine nature does not mean the possibility of a sinless life in the present world. Yet, the presence of grace in the believer's life, as it actualizes his participation in the divine nature, means that the believer now has the possibility of striving against sin and, in a measure, of overcoming it. The process of divinization is not completed until the believer reaches his eternal destiny as a theanthropic individual.

B. The Strength of the Radical or Anabaptist Concept of Grace

1. The Ontological Base for the Christian Life and the Constant Source of Renewal for the Church

The "new creature in Christ," which was wrought within the regenerate man

---

faithfulness of Him who had redeemed it. A high price was paid for this victory. Although new vigor was given to the doctrine of redemption, the idea of creation was all but lost . . . It cannot be said that Protestantism has a clear doctrine of creation. As yet there is no Protestant equivalent of natural law. There is, however, movement in that direction. Protestantism has emerged from a weary Scholasticism into a world which receives God, into a world which has been marked by God as eternally His own. To understand those markings without forsaking its doctrine of redemption is surely the next task of Protestant theology."

Perhaps there is in the *lux naturalis*, which Marbeck borrowed from Hubmaier, via Leonhard Schiemer, at least a rudimentary doctrine of creation with which present-day Protestantism could well begin to build its own.

through the Holy Spirit's renewal of the divine image, and thus made the believer a participant in the divine nature, was the ontological result of grace within Radical Reformation thought. This emphasis upon grace as the act of God, which brought about not only a change in status before God through forensic justification but an actual metaphysical change within man's nature, was what lay at the heart of the Radical's insistence that the experience of grace can and must be made manifest in the new life of the Christian. It is grace so understood that enables the regenerate man to act in accordance with the divine commands. One does not obey the divine command in order to win divine favor. Indeed, the unregenerate man who has not experienced grace on its highest or supernatural level finds it impossible to obey the divine command. The Radicals thus looked upon such obedience merely as the *fruit of grace*. It was never the *means* by which such grace was won.

On the personal level the demand that faith must be active in love arose out of this concept of grace. Positively, the believer gave evidence that he had experienced grace as the spiritual reality of the "new creature in Christ" through the concern which he manifested for the material and spiritual welfare of his brethren who with him had been "born out of God." Negatively, the believer gave evidence of his experience of grace by refusing to resort to violence and warfare. The Radicals saw that unless the experience of grace brought about some fruits that were objectively verifiable by others, the fact that one was or claimed to be a Christian made little practical difference within the present world. Admittedly, the emphasis upon good works as the evidence or the fruit of grace has its dangers. It can lead to an overly moralistic emphasis in theology. On the other hand, the lack of sufficient emphasis in this direction is equally dangerous. Luther himself admitted his frank disappointment with the moral fruits of his Reformation to Schwenckfeld. The Radical Reformers thus attacked the Magisterial Reformers at a point where they, by their own admission, felt that they were vulnerable.[3]

The Radicals saw very clearly that this metaphysical change within his nature is not something that fallen man can bring about by the sheer force of his own will. They also realized that this new reality is not created by the institutionalized Church, nor distributed by the Church, in a mechanical way through the sacraments. Where the change in man's nature occurs through the renewal of the divine image and the creation of the "new creature in Christ," it is the result of the direct activity of God in Christ through the Holy Spirit. This means that religion can never become only ceremonial, institutional, or static. It is living and dynamic, and the individual experience of regeneration which is mediated through the Church as the gathered and regenerate people of the "new covenant of grace" becomes at the same time a source of restitution for the Church in every generation.

---

3 Schwenckfeld, *Der IIII. Sendbrieff an den Edlen und Ehrentuesten Friedereich von Walden, CS,* II, 281f.

2. The Principle of Voluntarism as Rooted in the Radical Concept of Grace

So many recent studies in the Radical Reformation have dealt with the contribution which the Anabaptists as a whole have made in applying this ontological principle on the corporate level to the doctrine of the Church, that, as William Keeney says, "it scarcely needs further elucidation."[4] Yet, to the best of my knowledge no one has yet pointed out that the principle of voluntarism, which in consequence led to the separation of Church and state, had its roots in the concept of grace which prevailed within the Radical Reformation. But this was, I think, the case. In one form or another, as this study has revealed, all of the Radicals rejected the doctrines of double predestination and the bondage of the will, which prevailed within the Magisterial Reformation.

The rejection of these doctrines by the Radicals was based upon their conviction that some vestiage of the divine image remained in fallen man, which left within his power the possibility of a real decision when confronted with the claims of Christ. Sometimes, as in the case of Melchior Hoffmann, this possibility of choice was in itself a partial liberation from the universal bondage, into which mankind had been cast by the disobedience of the first Adam through the atonement of Christ as the second Adam. This universal liberation of mankind, hitherto in bondage to Satan, was in itself a form of grace. With others, such as Denck, Hubmaier, and Marbeck, the possibility of real decision lay either in the inner Word, which was present in all men as the principle of God's imminence in the world, or in a doctrine of natural law, which was regarded as a first grace, or in the unfallen spirit of man, which though a prisoner between the soul and the flesh, could still cry out for new grace, even though the grace of the original condition had been lost. Common to all, however, was the conviction that God does not bring people into His service by means of compulsion. Christ desires the Church as a bride that comes voluntarily. Since God compels no one to believe, the Church may not do so either. The only methods that are in harmony with spreading the gospel of grace are the methods of peaceful persuasion. He who cannot be persuaded by preaching, teaching, or writing must simply be regarded as one who belongs to the world rather than to the Church.

Thus, it is, I think, clear that the principle of voluntarism and its corollary, the separation of Church and state, both had their roots, if not within the concept of grace in the Radical Reformation, then in the close relationship of that concept to the Radical doctrine of the freedom of the will.

Considered seditious in the time of the sixteenth century, these principles have today been accepted in America as fundamental to our religious liberty. As mediated to America, however, the principle of religious liberty has come in secularized form through the influence of John Locke's *Letters of Toleration*. In the concept of grace within the Radical Reformation the principle of voluntarism is seen in its unsecularized theological form. Whether or not the Radicals assumed too sharp a dichotomy between the Church and the state is a question that will be

---

4 William Keeney, "The Development of Dutch Anabaptist Thought and Practice from 1539–1564," p. 317.

further discussed.⁵ Suffice it to say here that their insight into the necessity of a basic conflict between the methods of the state and those of the Church has been a major positive contribution to the American scene.

3. The Abiding Values of the Hermeneutics of Grace

That the various representatives of the Radical Reformation were not fighting straw men, as they struggled to develop their hermeneutical methods, is evidenced by the fact that the same problems they faced still confront the Biblical interpreter today. The common consensus among the best Biblical scholars of our time is that the Bible is the record of testimony to the "mighty acts of God," beginning in the call of Abraham and culminating in the mightier acts of incarnation and resurrection. The contention of those who developed the hermeneutics of the inner and outer Word, that one should have faith in Christ, whom the Bible witnesses to rather than in the Bible itself, is thus not very far removed from the presentday neo-orthodox scholar who says essentially the same thing.⁶

Again, if the incarnation is viewed seriously as an invasion of our history from beyond history, then some sort of distinction between the Old and New Testaments and their value for Christian faith and doctrine seems to me not only valid but necessary. The incarnation viewed in this perspective links continuity in the "covenant community" of Israel with radical discontinuity in the Church of Christ as the community of the new covenant of grace. The Old Testament is the "covenant of promise," and the New Testament is the "covenant of fulfillment." This necessitates some form of typological or allegorical interpretation of the Old Testament, if it is to be retained in the canon of sacred and inspired Christian Scripture. It is, indeed, impossible to resolve some of the paradoxes of the Bible at all, unless certain parts of the Old Testament are either allegorized or seen as the earlier stages in a progressive revelation that reached its culmination and fulfillment in the incarnation, which now provides the standard by which all earlier revelations are weighed, measured, judged, and corrected.

Admittedly, the Radicals sometimes carried their typology and their allegory too far as they interpreted the Old Testament. But insofar as this enabled them to make a legitimate distinction between the Old and the New, it had important and legitimate consequences for their doctrine of the Church and for their view of Christian ethics.

---

5 See p. 179 below.
6 See the article on "The Bible," by Bernhard W. Anderson in *A Handbook of Christian Theology*, p. 37, where Anderson says: "To speak of having 'faith in the Bible' is a violation of the Protestant principle, according to which all historical forms stand under the judgment of God. Admittedly, Protestant biblicism has sometimes lapsed into bibliolatry – the veneration of the Bible as a perfect, infallible, divine book. To the discerning Protestant, however, this idolatry defies the prophetic message of the Bible itself, just as much as the absolutizing of the Church, the State, or Reason. The Bible is holy because it bears witness to Jesus Christ, who alone is Lord."

C. Weaknesses Inherent in the Radical Concept of Grace

1. The Tendency to Classify Sins into Major and Minor Categories

Within the Evangelical Anabaptist wing of the Radical Reformation, particularly on its Dutch side, there was a strong tendency to classify sins into major and minor categories with the so-called "sins of the flesh" regarded as the more serious. Such sins were so seriously regarded, because they were actually looked upon as a relapse into the old and sinful nature of the old Adam on the part of the Christian, who had been by grace transplanted into the new and good nature of Christ, the new Adam. This tendency to look upon the sins of the flesh as the more serious led to a consequent obscuration of the equal seriousness of the sins of the disposition. A member of the Church who became involved in some aberration in sexual behaviour was at once subject to discipline and the ban. One who harbored a censorious spirit was less easily singled out; yet his sin might in the long run prove the more harmful. Behind this tendency to classify sins in this manner there lies, of course, the substructure of Scholastic theology, which made the distinction between mortal and venial sins.

2. The Concept of Grace as Related to the Celestial Flesh Christology and Its Consequent Effect upon the Created Order and the Doctrine of the Atonement

The Celestial Flesh Christology was at least instrumental in leading the Dutch Anabaptists to an almost Gnostic dualism between the holy Church and the evil world. One cannot make the dogmatic statement that this was true throughout the Radical Reformation. Schwenckfeld held a doctrine of the Celestial Flesh Christology without the radical dualism between holy Church and evil world, but he could ease the tension through his doctrine of the invisible Church in the Spirit. The same dualism between Church and world was present in Marbeck, and he did not have the Celestial Flesh Christology. However, in Marbeck's thought becoming a member of the Church meant at the same time becoming a member of the Body of Christ. Within the Church the Holy Spirit was present in His fullness, while outside the Church those who had not been reborn by supernatural grace belonged still to the world.

The statement that the Celestial Flesh Christology alone led to a negative view of the created order must be made with some caution, and it must be limited in its application to the Dutch side of the Radical Reformation. Within these limits, however, such a statement is true. Hoffmann, Menno, and Dirk all visualized the Christian life as a pilgrimage out of the Egypt of this world to the promised land of the new heaven and the new earth. The only place where the redemptive activity of God was thought to be at work was within the encampment of the holy Church. The wilderness outside the camp was still the possession and domain of the devil. The concept of grace as related to the Celestial Flesh Christology was not without its effect upon this dualistic view of the human situation within the present world.

The same is true of the Dutch Anabaptists in the manner in which they related the Celestial Flesh Christology to their theory of the atonement. In their theory the Celestial Flesh Christology was necessary, so that the *pure humanity* of Christ might be offered in his death as an adequate payment for sin. Otherwise, they reasoned he would have to die for his own sin and not for grace. In effect, this reduced original sin to original debt and led to an interpretation of grace which was highly legalistic in character. The South German Anabaptists, as has been noted in Chapter I, were less legalistic than their Dutch brethren. The absence of the Celestial Flesh Christology among them, which was essentially docetic in character, accounts in part for this fact.

3. The Limits Placed upon the Acceptance of Social Responsibility by the Ethics of Grace

That the Anabaptists as a whole made an important contribution to the post-Reformation development by the application of the ontological results of grace to their doctrine of the Church has already been noted. It was through this that they discovered the principle of voluntarism and the necessary dichotomy between Church and state. This was on the positive side of the contribution of their concept of grace. Negatively, however, this led to serious limitations in regard to their acceptance of social responsibility. Hubmaier and Schwenckfeld are exceptions to this general rule. But on the whole it can be said that the Anabaptists accepted the order of the state as divinely ordained to maintain justice among men. Some of their representatives even said that the state was as necessary within this life as daily bread itself.[7] Yet, when it came to the administration of justice, the Anabaptists felt that they themselves could not take part in it. The question of social responsibility is a knotty one for the disciple who seeks to live by the *imitatio Christi* ethic. Yet one must ask whether the disciple who admits the need for the state has any right to unload the whole burden of social responsibility upon the shoulders of others.

It is at this point that the Magisterial Reformers were on the most solid ground when they accused the Radicals of being "work's righteousness people." There was within their concept of Christian ethics no room for the administration of justice as a service of love to the neighbor,[8] nor was there any point at which they would have admonished the disciple to have the courage to incur guilt[9] for the sake of others in the administration of justice.

---

7 Hans J. Hillerbrand, "An Early Anabaptist Treatise on the Christian and the State," *MQR*, XXXII, No. 1 (January, 1958), 28–33.
8 Kerr, "Secular Authority: To What Extent It Should Be Obeyed," *A Compend of Luther's Theology*, pp. 220–21.
9 Dietrich Bonhoeffer, *Ethics*, ed. Eberhard Bethge (London: S. C. M. Press, 1955), pp. 208–09.

BIBLIOGRAPHY

The Ausbund. Oldest hymnbook of the Swiss Brethren and quoted by the opponents of the Swiss Brethren at the Frankental colloquium. Earliest edition, 1564.

Bergsten, Torsten. "Two Letters by Pilgram Marpeck." Translated by William Klassen. *Mennonite Quarterly Review*, XXXII, No. 3 (July, 1958), 192–210.

Bibliotheca Reformatoria Neerlandica. Edited by Samuel Cramer and Fredrik Pijper. The Hague: Martinus Nijhoff, 1903–14. Vols. V, VII, and X.

Bucer, Martin. *Getrewe Warnung der Prediger des Evangelii zu Strassburg über die Artickel, so Jakob Kautz, Prediger zu Wormbs, kürtzlich hat lassen ausgohn, die frucht der schrifft und Gottes worts, den kinder Tauff, und erlösung unsers herren Jesu Christi, sambt anderm, darin sich Hans Dencken, und anderer widertäuffer schwere yrrtumb erregen, betreffend. Beweren die geyster, ob sie aus Got sind, dann es sind vil falscher propheten inn die welt ausgangen. I. Johan. IV.* Strasbourg, 1527. Photostat copy in the Mennonite Historical Library, Goshen, Indiana.

Corpus Schwenckfeldianorum. Vols. II, III, IV, VI, VIII, XII, XIII, and XIV. Edited by Chester David Hartranft, et al. Leipzig: Breitkopf and Härtel, 1911, 1913, 1914, 1922, 1927, 1932, 1935, and 1936.

Denck, Hans. *Bekenntnis für den Rat zu Nürnberg. 1525.* In *Hans Denck Schriften.*
- *Ordnung Gottes.* [1527]. In *Hans Denck Schriften.*
- *Vom Gesetz Gottes.* [1526]. In *Hans Denck Schriften.*
- *Von der wahren Liebe. 1527.* In *Hans Denck Schriften.*
- *Was geredt sei, dass die Schrift sagt. 1526.* In *Hans Denck Schriften.*
- *Wer die Wahrheit wahrlich lieb hat.* [1526]. In *Hans Denck Schriften.*
- *Widerruf.* [1528]. In *Hans Denck Schriften.*

Fellmann, Walter (ed.). *Hans Denck Schriften.* 2. Teil, Religiöse Schriften. Quellen und Forschungen zur Reformationsgeschichte, Band XXIV. Gutersloh: C. Bertelsmann Verlag, 1956.

Franz, G. *Wiedertaüferakten, 1527–1626. Urkündliche Quellen zur Hessizchen Reformationsgeschichte*, IV, 1951.

Handelinge van der disputacie in Synodo te Straesburch teghen Melchior Hoffman door die predicanten derseluer stadt. 1533. In *Bibliotheca Reformatoria Neerlandica*, Vol. V.

Hoffmann, Melchior. *Die Ordonnantie Godts.* Anno. 1530. 1611 in *Bibliotheca Reformatoria Neerlandica*, Vol. V.
- *Die... sendebrief to den Romeren... verclaert.* 1533. In *Bibliotheca Reformatoria Neerlandica*, Vol. V.
- *Verclaringe van den geuangenen ende vrien wil.* Ca. 1532. In *Bibliotheca Reformatoria Neerlandica*, Vol. V.

Hubmaier, Balthasar. *Achtzehen schluszrede so betreffende ein gantz Christlich leben.* (N. p., 1524). Microfilm copy of the complete works of Hubmaier in Andover-Harvard Library, Harvard Divinity School.
- *Das andere Buchlein von der Freiwilligkeit des Menschen.* (Nikolsburg, 1527). Microfilm copy in Andover-Harvard Library, Harvard Divinity School.
- *Ein einfältiger Unterricht auf die Worte: das ist mein Leib, in dem Nachtmahl Christi.* (Nikolsburg, 1526). Microfilm copy in Andover-Harvard Library, Harvard Divinity School.
- *Eine Form des Nachtmahles Christi.* Nikolsburg, 1527). Microfilm copy in Andover-Harvard Library, Harvard Divinity School.
- *Eine Form zu taufen in Wasser die im Glauben Unterrichteten.* (Nikolsburg, 1527). Microfilm copy in Andover-Harvard Library, Harvard Divinity School.
- *Gespräch auf Meister Ulrich Zwinglis Taufbuchlein von dem Kindertauf.* (1526). Microfilm copy in Andover-Harvard Library, Harvard Divinity School.
- *Schluszreden die Balthazar Fridberger dem J. Eckio die meysterlich zu examinieren fütbotten hat.* (N. p., n. d.). Microfilm copy in Andover-Harvard Library, Harvard Divinity School.
- *Vom christlichen Bann.* (Nikolsburg, 1527). Microfilm copy in Andover-Harvard Library, Harvard Divinity School.

- *Vom christlichen Tauf der Gläubigen.* (N. p., ca. 1525). Microfilm copy in Andover-Harvard Library, Harvard Divinity School.
- *Vom Schwert.* (1527). Microfilm copy in Andover-Harvard Library, Harvard Divinity School.
- *Von der Freiheit des Willens.* (Nikolsburg, 1527). Microfilm copy in Andover-Harvard Library, Harvard Divinity School.

Marbeck, Pilgram. "Confession of Faith." Edited by John C. Wenger. *Mennonite Quarterly Review*, XII, No. 3 (July, 1938), 167–202.
- *Testamentserläuterung.* (Augsburg: ca. 1544–1550). Microfilm in Andover-Harvard Library, Harvard Divinity School.
- *Verantwortung.* Vienna and Leipzig: Johann Loserth, 1929.
- *Vermanung* in *Gedenkschrift zum 400 Jährigen Jubiliäum der Mennoniten oder Taufgesinnten, 1529–1925.* Herausgegeben Christian L. Neff. Ludwegshafen: Konferenz der Süddeutsche Mennoniten E. V., 1925.

Philips, Dirk. *Bekentenisse onses gheloofs.* In *Bibliotheca Reformatoria Neerlandica*, Vol. X.
- *Bekentenisse vander scheppinge, verlossinge, ende salichmakinghe.* In *Bibliotheca Reformatoria Neerlandica*, Vol. X.
- *Drie grondighe Vermaningen ofte Sentbrieuen aen de Gemeynte Godts.* In *Bibliotheca Reformatoria Neerlandica*, Vol. X.
- *Een Apologia, ofte verantwoordinghe.* In *Bibliotheca Reformatoria Neerlandica*, Vol. X.
- *Een Lieffelijcke Vermaninge.* In *Bibliotheca Reformatoria Neerlandica*, Vol. X.
- *Van dat Auontmael.* In *Bibliotheca Reformatoria Neerlandica*, Vol. X.
- *Van der Menschwerdinghe ons Heeren Jesu Christi.* In *Bibliotheca Reformatoria Neerlandica*, Vol. X.
- *Van der Sendinghe der Predicanten oft Leeraers.* In *Bibliotheca Reformatoria Neerlandica*, Vol. X.
- *Van der wedergeboorte ende nieuwe Creatuere.* In *Bibliotheca Reformatoria Neerlandica*, Vol. X.
- *Vande geestelijcke Restitution.* In *Bibliotheca Reformatoria Neerlandica*, Vol. X.
- *Vande Gemeynte Godts.* In *Bibliotheca Reformatoria Neerlandica*, Vol. X.
- *Vande rechte kennisse Jesu Christi.* In *Bibliotheca Reformatoria Neerlandica*, Vol. X.
- *Vanden Ban.* In *Bibliotheca Reformatoria Neerlandica*, Vol. X.
- *Vander Doope.* In *Bibliotheca Reformatoria Neerlandica*, Vol. X.
- *Verantwoordinghe ende Refutation op twee Sendtbrieven Sebastiani Franck.* In *Bibliotheca Reformatoria Neerlandica*, Vol. X.
- *Wtlegginghe des Tabernakels ofte der Hutten Moysi.* In *Bibliotheca Reformatoria Neerlandica*, Vol. X.

Protocol dat is de Gansche Handelinghe des Gespreche to Franckenthal inder Tuerhorstelicher, met dien welche men Wederdoopers noemt, den 28 May begonnen, ende den 19 June deses Jares 1571 Voleyndicht. Dortrecht, 1571.

Rotmann, Bernhard. *Restitution rechter und gesunder christlicher Lehre.* (Münster, 1534). Reprinted as No. 77 and 78, *Neudrucke deutscher Litteraturwerke.* Halle a.S.: Max Niemeyer, 1888.

Schiemer, Leonhard. "Von Drierlei Gnad," in *Glaubenszeugnisse ober deutscher Taufgesinnter.* Edited by Lydia Müller. *Quellen und Forschungen zur Reformationsgeschichte*, Band XX. Leipzig: M. Heinsius Nachfolger, 1938.

Schwenckfeld, Caspar. *Der IIII. Sendbrieff an den Edlen und Ehrentuesten Friedereich von Walden.* 1525. In *Corpus Schwenckfeldianorum*, Vol. II.
- *Der XXVI Sendbrieff an Alle Christliche guthertzige Menschen von der Gnaden Gottes...* 1528. In *Corpus Schwenckfeldianorum*, Vol. III.
- *Judicium ober die Augspurgische Confession.* Ca. 1530. In *Corpus Schwenckfeldianorum*, Vol. III.
- *Underschaid des Alten und Neuen Testaments der Figur und Waarhait.* 1531. In *Corpus Schwenckfeldianorum*, Vol. IV.
- *Vom Christlichen Sabbath und underscheid dess alten und newen Testaments.* 1532. In *Corpus Schwenckfeldianorum*, Vol. IV.

- *Von der Sünd und Gnad. Adam und Christo.* 1539. In *Corpus Schwenckfeldianorum*, Vol. VI.
- *Der VI Sendbrieffe an vorgenanten Herrn Johan Kneller... Mit anhangender Rechenschafft oder Bekantnus vom Nachtmal und vom Brote des Herren.* 1542. In *Corpus Schwenckfeldianorum*, Vol. VIII.
- *Judicium.* 1542. In *Corpus Schwenckfeldianorum*, Vol. VIII.
- *Judicium auff Doctor Martin Luther's schrieben vom Worte Gottes und der heiligen Schrifft.* 1550. In *Corpus Schwenckfeldianorum*, Vol. XII.
- *Klari zeugnuss auss den Büchern dess Neuen Testaments von der göttlichen herrligkait der Menschhait Christi in der Glorien.* Ca. 1541. In *Corpus Schwenckfeldianorum*, Vol. XII.
- *Von der hailigen Schrifft, irem Innhalt, Ampt, rechten Nutz, Brauch und Missbrauch.* 1551. In *Corpus Schwenckfeldianorum*, Vol. XII.
- *Criticisms of Matthias Flacius Illyricus' Book.* 1553. In *Corpus Schwenckfeldianorum*, Vol. XIII.
- *Von der h. Schrifft: Der Wittenbergischen und Leipzischen Theologen Judicium.* Ca. 1553. In *Corpus Schwenckfeldianorum*, Vol. XIII.
- *Ein Christlicher Sendbrieff vom span und rechten Mittel zwischen der Luthrischen und Zwinglischen opinion im Artickel des Herrn Nachtmals...* 1554. In *Corpus Schwenckfeldianorum*, Vol. XIV.
- *Ehn tröstliche Christenliche underweisung unnd verstand des eusserlichen und innerlichen worts Gottes.* 1555. In *Corpus Schwenckfeldianorum*, Vol. XIV.

Simons, Menno. *The Complete Writings of Menno Simons, c. 1496–1561.* Translated from the Dutch by Leonard Verduin and edited by John C. Wenger, with a biography by Harold S. Bender. Scottdale: Mennonite Publishing House, 1956.
Blasphemy of John of Leiden, 1535.
Brief and Clear Confession, 1544.
Brief Defense to All Theologians, 1552.
Christian Baptism, 1539.
A Clear Account of Excommunication, 1550.
Confession of the Distressed Christians, 1552.
The Cross of the Saints, ca. 1554.
Epistle to Martin Micron, 1556.
Foundation of Christian Doctrine, 1539.
The Incarnation of Our Lord, 1554.
Instruction on Excommunication, 1558.
A Kindly Admonition on Church Discipline, 1541.
Meditation on the Twenty-fifth Psalm, ca. 1537.
The New Birth, ca. 1537.
The Nurture of Children, ca. 1557.
A Pathetic Supplication to All Magistrates, 1552.
Personal Note to Rein Edes and the Brethren..., ca. 1558.
Reply to False Accusations, 1552.
Reply to Gellius Faber, 1554.
The Spiritual Resurrection, ca. 1536.
The True Christian Faith, ca. 1541.
Why I Do Not Cease Teaching and Writing, 1539. In *The Complete Writings of Menno Simons.*
- *Dat Fundament der Christelycker Leere.* 1539. In *Opera Omnia Theologica.*
- *Een Fundament en Klare aenwysinge van de salighmakende Leere Jesu Christi.* 1562. In *Opera Omnia Theologica.*
- *Een gantsch duidlyk ende bescheyden Antwoordt... op Martini Microns...* 1556. In *Opera Omnia Theologica.*
- *Een klare Beantwoordinge over een Schrift Gellii Fabri.* 1554. Reprinted as *Sommarie ofte By-een-vergaderinge van sommige schriftelijke bekentenissen des geloofs; mitsgaders eenige waerachtige verantwoordingen, op sommige Schriften van Gellio Fabro en Joanne a Lasco.* N. d. In *Opera Omnia Theologica.*

- *Een klare onwederspreekelyke Bekentenisse en Aenwysinge... dat de geheele Christus Jesus, Godt en Mensche, Mensche en Godt, Gods eengeboren en Eerstgeboren eygen sone is... Met een grondelijke Confutation, Beantwoordinge en Oplossinge der voornaemster Tegenspreuken van Johanne a Lasco.* 1554. In *Opera Omnia Theologica.*
- *Opera Omnia Theologica.* Edited by Hendrick Jansz Herrison. Amsterdam: Joannes van Veen, 1681.

Spiritual and Anabaptist Writers. Vol. XXV of *The Library of Christian Classics.* Edited by George H. Williams. Philadelphia: The Westminster Press, 1957.

OTHER LITERATURE

Anderson, Bernhard W. *A Handbook of Christian Theology.* "The Bible." New York: Meridian Books, Inc., 1958.

The Apocrypha. Revised version of 1894. New York: Thomas Nelson & Sons.

Augustini Opera Omnia. Edited by J. P. Migne, in *Patrologiae Cursus Completus... Series Latina. Traditio Catholica.* 40 vols. Tomus Sextus. Paris: Vrayet, Pres La Barriere D'Enfer, 1865. Vols. XXXIII, XXXV and XL.

Bainton, Roland H. *Hunted Heretic: the Life and Death of Michael Servetus, 1511–1533.* Boston: Beacon Press, 1953.

- "The Parable of the Tares as the Proof Text for Religious Liberty to the End of the Sixteenth Century." *Church History,* I, No. 2 (June, 1932), pp. 67–89.

Barth, Karl. *Natural Theology: Comprising "Nature and Grace" by Emil Brunner and the Reply "No" by Barth.* Translated by Peter Fraenkie. London: Geoffrey Bles, 1946.

Baum, Johann Wilhelm. *Capito und Butzer, Strassburgs Reformatoren.* Elberfeld: R. L. Friderichs, 1860.

Beachy, Alvin J. "The Inner and Outer Word." A study of the hermeneutical principles employed by selected representatives of the Radical Reformation. Unpublished paper in Church History 233 for George H. Williams, June 5, 1957. Copy on deposit in Andover-Harvard Theological Library, Harvard Divinity School.

Bender, Harold S. "Anabaptism in Germany." The *Mennonite Encyclopedia,* II, 486–91.

- *Conrad Grebel, c. 1498–1526, the Founder of the Swiss Brethren.* Goshen, Indiana: The Mennonite Historical Society, 1950.

Bergsten, Torsten. "Pilgram Marbeck und Seine Auseinandersetzung mit Caspar Schwenckfeld." *Kyrkohistorisk Arsskrift.* Uppsala: Utgiven av Svenska Kyrkohistoriska Foreningen, 1957.

The Holy Bible. Revised Standard Version. New York: Thomas Nelson & Sons, 1952.

Biblia Sacra. Romae, Tornaci, Parissis: Desclee et Socii, 1947.

Bonhoeffer, Dietrich. *Ethics.* Edited by Eberhard Bethge. London: S. C. M. Press, 1955.

Brown, Harold O. J. "Joachim of Floris and the Third Age in History." Unpublished S. T. M. thesis, Harvard Divinity School, 1959.

Bullinger, Heinrich. *Von dem unverschampten fräfel, ergerlichem Verwyrren, und unwarhafften leern, der selbsgesanden Widertouffern.* Book I. Zurich: Christoffel Froschauer, 1531.

Calvin, John. *Brieve Instruction Pour Armer tous bons fidels contre les Erreurs de la secte des Anabaptisten.* Geneve, 1544. In *Corpus Reformatorum,* XXXV.

- *Institutes of the Christian Religion.* 2 vols. Translated by John Allen. 7th American edition. Philadelphia: Presbyterian Board of Christian Education, n. d.

Calvini Opera. Vol. VII in *Corpus Reformatorum,* XXXV. Brunswick: C. A. Schwetschke & Sons, 1868.

Cornelius, C. A. *Geschichte des Münsterischen Aufruhrs.* 2 vols. Leipzig: T. O. Wiegel, 1855–60.

Corpus Reformatorum. Vols. I and XXXV. Edidit Carolus Gottlieb Bretschneider. Halis Saxonum: C. A. Schwetschke et Filium, 1834 and 1868.

Denbeaux, Fred. *A Handbook of Christian Theology.* "Creation." New York: Meridian Books, Inc., 1958.

Franck, Sebastian. *Paradoxa*. Eingeleitet von W. Lehman. Herausgegeben von Heinrich Zeigler. Jena: Eugen Diederichs, 1909.
Friedmann, Robert. "Anabaptism and Protestantism." *Mennonite Quarterly Review*, XXIV, No. 1 (January, 1950), pp. 12–24.
— "The Doctrine of Original Sin as Held by the Anabaptists of the Sixteenth Century." *Mennonite Quarterly Review*, XXXIII, No. 3 (July, 1959), 206–14.
Garrett, James Leo. "The Nature of the Church According to the Radical Continental Reformation." *Mennonite Quarterly Review*, XXXII, No. 2 (April, 1958), 111–27.
Grant, Robert M. *The Letter and the Spirit*. New York: The MacMillan Company, 1957.
Harding, Vincent G. "Menno Simons and the Role of Baptism in the Christian Life." *Mennonite Quarterly Review*, XXXIII, No. 4 (October, 1959), 323–34.
Harnack, Adolf. *Outlines of the History of Dogma*. Translated by Edwin Knox Mitchell with an introduction by Philip Rieff. Boston: Beacon Press, 1957.
Hegler, Alfred. *Geist und Schrift bei Sebastian Franck, Eine Studie zur Geschichte des Spiritualismus in der Reformationzeit*. Freiburg, 1892.
Hillerbrand, Hans J. "The Anabaptist View of the State." *Mennonite Quarterly Review*, XXXII, No. 2 (April, 1958), 83–110.
— "An Early Anabaptist Treatise on the Christian and the State." *Mennonite Quarterly Review*, XXXII, No. 1 (January, 1958), 28–33.
Hoekstra, Syste. *Beginselen en Leer der Oude Doopsgezinden...* Amsterdam: P. N. van Kampen, 1863.
Horsch, John. "Strasburg, a Swiss Brethren Center." *Mennonite Quarterly Review*, XIII, No. 1 (January, 1939).
Introduction to St. Thomas Aquinas. Edited, with an introduction, by Anton C. Pegis. New York: Random House, 1948.
Joachim, Abbot of Floris. *Exposito in Apocalypsim*.
Venice: F. Bindonus and M. Pasimus, 1527.
Jones, Rufus M. *New Studies in Mystical Religion*.
New York: The Macmillan Company, 1927.
Kawerau, Peter. *Melchior Hoffmann als Religiöser Denker*.
Haarlem: De Erven F. Bohn N.V., 1954.
Keeney, William. "An Analysis of Calvin's Treatment of the Anabaptists in the *Institutes*." Unpublished paper written for Ford Lewis Battles, Hartford Theological Seminary, 1958.
— "The Development of Dutch Anabaptist Thought and Practice from 1539–1564." Unpublished Ph. D. thesis, Hartford Theological Seminary, May, 1959.
— "Dirk Philips' Life." *Mennonite Quarterly Review*, XXXII, No. 3 (July, 1958), 171–91.
— "The Writings of Dirk Philips." *Mennonite Quarterly Review*, XXXII, No. 4 (October, 1958), 298–306.
Kerr, Hugh Thompson. *A Compend of Luther's Theology*. Philadelphia: The Westminster Press, 1943.
Kiwiet, Jan J. "The Life of Hans Denck." *Mennonite Quarterly Review*, XXXI, No. 4 (October, 1957), 227–59.
— "The Theology of Hans Denck." *Mennonite Quarterly Review*, XXXII, No. 1 (January, 1958), 3–27.
Klassen, William. "Caspar von Schwenckfeld." *The Mennonite Encyclopedia*, IV, 1120–24.
Koehler, Walther. *Dogmengeschichte als Geschichte des Christlichen Selbstbewusstseins des Zeitalter der Reformation*. Zurich: Max Niehans Verlag A.C., 1951.
Krahn, Cornelius. *Menno Simons (1496–1561)*. Karlsruhe i.B.: Heinrich Schneider, 1936.
Leendertz, W. I. *Melchior Hofmann*. Haarlem, 1883. Microfilm copy, 4282C-48, in Widener Library, Harvard University.
Linden, Friedrich Otto zur. *Melchior Hoffmann ein Prophet der Wiedertaüfer*. Haarlem: De Erven F. Bohn, 1885.
Littell, Franklin H. *The Anabaptist View of the Church*. An Introduction to sectarian Protestantism. 2d ed. revised.
American Society of Church History, 1958.

Loserth, Johann. *Doctor Balthasar Hubmaier und die Anfänge der Wiedertaufe in Mähren.* Brunn: Rudolph M. Rohrer, 1893.
Löwith, Karl. *Meaning in History, the Theological Implications of the Philosophy of History.* Chicago: University of Chicago Press, 1949.
Luther, Martin. *The Bondage of the Will.* A new translation of *De Servo Arbitrio* (1525) by J. I. Packer and O. R. Johnston. London: James Clarke & Co., 1957.
- *A Commentary on St. Paul's Epistle to the Galatians.* Based on lectures delivered at the University of Wittenberg in 1531. Revised and completed translation based on Middleton edition of the English version of 1575. London: James Clarke & Co., 1956.
- *D. Martin Luther's Werke.* Kritische Gesamtausgabe. 17, and 40–44. Weimar: Herman Böhlaus Nochfolger, 1883–1932.
  Auff den andern Sontag hynn der fasten Evangelion, 17.
  Commentary on Galatians, 40, 1.
  Commentary on Genesis, 42–44.
  Lectures on the Psalms, 40, 2.
- *Three Treatises by Martin Luther.* Philadelphia: The Muhlenberg Press, 1947.
- *Vorlesung über den Römerbrief, 1515–1516.* Vol. II. München: Chr. Kaiser Verlag, 1957.
- *Works of Martin Luther.* Translated by W. A. Lambert. Vol. II. Philadelphia: A. J. Holman Co. and General Council Publication Board, 1916.
- *Works of Martin Luther.* 6 vols. Vol. III. Philadelphia: The United Lutheran Publication House, 1915–32.
Melanchton, Philip. *Contra Anabaptistas Philippi Melanchthonis Iudicium, 1528. Corpus Reformatorum*, I.
The Mennonite Encyclopedia. 4 vols. Edited by H. S. Bender, C. Henry Smith, et al. Scottdale: Mennonite Publishing House, 1956–59.
Mennonitisches Lexikon. Vol. I. Edited by Christian Hege and Christian Neff. Frankfurt am Main: Published by the editors, 1913.
Müntzer, Thomas. *Sein Leben und Seine Schriften.* Herausgegeben und eingeleitet von Otto S. Brandt. Jenna: Eugen Diederichs Verlag, 1933.
Neff, Christian. "Melchior Hoffmann." *The Mennonite Encyclopedia*, II, 778–85.
Niebuhr, H. Richard. *Christ and Culture.* New York: Harper and Bros., 1951.
Nygren, Anders. *Eros und Agape.* Gestaltwandlungen der christlichen Liebe. Erster und zweiter Teile. Gütersloh: T. Bertelsmann, 1930.
Oyer, John. "The Writings of Luther Against the Anabaptists." The *Mennonite Quarterly Review*, XXVII, No. 2 (April, 1953), 100–10.
- "The Writings of Melanchton Against the Anabaptists." *Mennonite Quarterly Review*, XXVI, No. 4 (October, 1952), 259–79.
Peachey, Paul. *Die Soziale Herkunft der Schweizerischen Täufer, 1525–1540.* Zürich, 1953.
- "Social Background and Social Philosophy of the Swiss Anabaptists, 1525–1540." *Mennonite Quarterly Review*, XXVIII, No. 2 (April, 1954), 102–27.
Pestalozzi, Carl (ed.). *Heinrich Bullinger, Leben und Ausgewahelte Schriften.* Elberfeld, 1858.
Piper, Otto. "Mysticism and the Christian Experience." *Theology Today*, X, No. 2 (July, 1953), 156–69.
Quiring, Horst. "The Anthropology of Pilgram Marbeck." *Mennonite Quarterly Review*, IX, No. 4 (October, 1935), 155–64.
Rembert, Karl. *Die Wiedertäufer im Herzogtum Julich.* Studien zur Geschichte der Reformation, besonders am niederheim. Berlin: R. Gaertners Verlags, 1899.
Rörich, T.W. "Strassburgische Widertaüfer." *Zeitschrieft für Historische Theologie.* Edited by C. W. Riedner. Gotha: Frider Andr. Porthes, 1860.
Sachsse, Carl. *D. Balthasar Hubmaier als Theologe, Neue Studien zur Geschichte der Theologie und der Kirche.* Edited by N. Bonwetsch and R. Seeberg. Berlin: Trowitzsch & Sohn, 1914. Vol. XX.
Schornbaum, Karl. *Quellen zur Geschichte der Wiedertaüfer.* Vol. II. Leipzig: M. Heinsius Nachfolger, 1934.
Schrenk, Gottlob. *Gottesreich und Bund im alteren Protestantismus, Vornemlich bei Johannes Coccijus.* Gütersloh, 1928.

Seeberg, Reinhold. *Textbook of the History of Doctrines.* 2 vols. Translated by Charles E. Hay. Grand Rapids, Michigan: Baker Book House, 1958.
- *Die Theologie des Johannes Duns Scotus.* Leipzig: Dieterich'sche Verlags-Buchhandlung Theodor Weicher, 1900.

Smits, Luchesius. *Saint Augustin Dans L'oeuvre de Jean Calvin.* Vol. I. Assen: Van Gorcum & Comp. N.V.-G. A. Hak & H. J. Prakke, 1957.

Spykman, Gordon J. *Attrition and Contrition at the Council of Trent.* Kampen: J. H. Kok, N.V., 1955.

Stauffer, Ethelbert. "The Anabaptist Theology of Martyrdom." Translated by Robert Friedmann. *Mennonite Quarterly Review*, XIX, No. 3 (July, 1945), 179–214.

Swartzentruber, A. Orley. "The Piety and Theology of the Anabaptist Martyrs in Van Braght's *Martyrs' Mirror*, I and II." *Mennonite Quarterly Review*, XXVIII, Nos. 1 and 2 (January and April, 1954), 5–26 and 128–42, respectively.

Tavard, George H. "Holy Church or Holy Writ – A Dilemma of the 14th Century." *Church History*, XXIII, Vol. 3 (July, 1954), 195–206.
- *Holy Writ or Holy Church: the Crisis of the Protestant Reformation.* London: Burns and Oates, 1959.

Troeltsch, Ernst. *The Social Teachings of the Christian Churches.* 2 vols. Translated by Olive Wyon. New York: The Macmillan Company, 1931.

Vedder, Henry C. *Balthasar Hubmaier, the Leader of the Anabaptists.* New York: G. P. Putnam's Sons, 1905.

Wenger, John C. *Glimpses of Mennonite History.* Scottdale: Mennonite Publishing House, 1946.
- "The Life and Work of Pilgram Marpeck." *Mennonite Quarterly Review*, XII, No. 3 (July, 1938), 137–66.
- "Pilgram Marpeck, Tyrolese Engineer and Anabaptist Elder." *Church History*, IX, Vol. 2 (March, 1940).
- "The Theology of Pilgram Marpeck." *Mennonite Quarterly Review*, XII, No. 4 (October, 1938), 205–56.

Wray, Frank J. "The Anabaptist Doctrine of the Restitution of the Church." *Mennonite Quarterly Review*, XXVIII, No. 3 (July, 1954), 186–96.

APPENDIX

I. ANABAPTISM: THE RADICALIZATION OF PROTESTANTISM OR THE SURVIVAL OF MEDIEVAL MYSTICISM?

A. Introduction

The purpose of this particular Appendix is to bring up to date the previous chapters of a work written at an earlier time. This means that later publications, which have come into existence since the earlier chapters were written and whose major findings have important contributions to make to the work as a whole, must be carefully taken into account if the Appendix is to have any real value.

The weight of the combined evidence of two books by Steven E. Ozment and two articles by George H. Williams, published respectively in *The Mennonite Quarterly Review* and in *Review and Expositor*, plus one article by Hans J. Hillerbrand published in *Church History*, is such that scholarly integrity demands that the title for this section be cast as an interrogative one. The need to reply to James M. Stayer's *Anabaptists and the Sword*, which was published in 1972, has made it necessary to include a brief discussion of the Swiss Brethren at the conclusion of the Appendix. They were not a part of the original study.

In Ozment's first book, *Homo Spiritualis*, he engages, as the full title of the work would indicate, in a comparison of the anthropologies of two medieval mystics, Johannes Tauler and Jean Gerson. This comparison eventually comes to be a contrast between the anthropologies of these two mystics and that of Martin Luther from 1509–1516. An effort is made to set each man's anthropology in the context of his theology.

The thesis which Ozment develops in this first book is that both Tauler and Gerson, albeit in different ways, held to the conviction common to mystical theology that there is in man

> an organ or receptor for the divine,[1] an inalienable and irrepressible "spark of the will and reason" (*synteresis voluntatis et rationis*) or "ground of the soul" (*Seelengrund*) – an indestructible orientation to God, which one can speak of simply as the direction of the heart or the testimony of conscience.[2]

Furthermore, the nature of this anthropological resource endowed with soteriological possibilities is such that the initiative in salvation belongs to human rather than to divine action. The mysticism of both Tauler and Gerson makes the prior activity of a soteriologically endowed anthropology the "indispensable condition for the divine presence."[3]

---

[1] George H. Williams, "German Mysticism in the Polarization of Ethical Behavior in Luther and the Anabaptists," *MQR*, XLVIII, No. 3 (July, 1974), Preface, 276.
[2] Steven E. Ozment, *Mysticism and Dissent: Religious Ideology and Social Protest in the Sixteenth Century* (New Haven: Yale University Press, 1973), p. 3.
[3] Steven E. Ozment, *Homo Spiritualis: A Comparative Study of the Anthropology of Johannes Tauler, Jean Gerson and Martin Luther (1509–16) in the Context of Their Theological Thought* (Leiden: E. J. Brill, 1969), p. 32.

Ozment also presents significant evidence from Luther's own writings, especially the *Dictata on the Psalms* and the *Commentary on Romans*, which shows Luther's eventual rejection of both Tauler's *gemuete* or *Seelengrund* and Gerson's *synteresis*. The soteriological activity attributed by these medieval mystics to these human faculties are by Luther transferred to the activity of the Holy Spirit. It is He who performs the harsh and alien work of God in persons in contrast to God's proper work by interpreting and communicating to God the "unutterable groanings" which persons are incapable of communicating.[4] On the basis of this evidence, Ozment maintains that far from being Luther's first teachers in the *sola gratia*, Tauler and Gerson were, in fact, his earliest major conscious opponents.[5]

In the second book, *Mysticism and Dissent*, Ozment traces some of the tension between the Magisterial and Radical Reformers to the fact that the latter retained the mystical emphasis upon an anthropology endowed with soteriological resources, which Luther vigorously rejected. Ozment supports this view by pointing out that the mystical tract, *Theologia Deutsch*, was abandoned by Luther soon after 1518, but among the Anabaptists it went through six different editions after Hans Denck had written his *Etliche Hauptreden* for the Worms edition of 1528.[6]

Williams supports the view of Ozment that the Anabaptists followed the mystics of the preceding centuries rather than Luther in the development of their anthropology. They continued to emphasize "a human faculty or region of man's being that was never implicated in the fall and was hence susceptible of cultivation of the devout life in preparation for grace."[7]

Although Hans Hillerbrand in his "Anabaptism and the Reformation: Another Look" does not specifically relate Anabaptism to medieval mysticism as such, he, nevertheless, questions the validity of Harold S. Bender's view that Anabaptism with its emphasis on discipleship presupposed the Reformation doctrine of justification by faith alone. Instead of seeing this emphasis as simply the "proper and practical extension" of the central Reformation doctrine, Hillerbrand raises the question whether "the very concept of discipleship does not embody certain synergistic presuppositions."[8] Then Hillerbrand makes the statement that while it is true that the Anabaptist person cannot earn grace, "he can voluntarily respond and by living in obedient discipleship pull the lever which extracts such grace."[9]

It is the combined weight of the evidence which these various authors bring that compels the question, "Was Anabaptism the radicalization of Protestantism or the survival of medieval mysticism?"

---

4 *Ibid.*, pp. 187–88. Also see Williams, *op. cit.*, pp. 282–83.
5 Ozment, *Homo Spiritualis*, p. 2.
6 Ozment, *Mysticism and Dissent*, pp. 19 and 25. It should be pointed out that in addition to this "human receptor for the divine" which Ozment calls "the subjective pole of mystical theology" mysticism found another resource in the "*potentia Dei absoluta*" or the objective pole. Most simply stated, this involved the concept of the "sovereign freedom of God to operate beyond what he himself has established as normative." P. 2.
7 Williams, *op. cit.*, p. 293.
8 Hans J. Hillerbrand, "Anabaptism and the Reformation: Another Look," *Church History*, XXIX, No. 4 (December, 1960), 415.
9 *Ibid.*

Before this question can be satisfactorily answered, the evidence which these authors marshall in support of their views must be more fully presented. Our method will be to present first a comparison of the anthropologies of Tauler and Gerson in the context of their mystical theology and Luther's eventual repudiation of their insistence upon the presence of an indestructible human receptor for the divine within all persons. When the theological or the anthropological distance which Luther placed between himself and these medieval mystics becomes clear, it will also become possible to determine whether it is true that Anabaptism was, as Ozment and Williams explicitly maintain, more mystical than Protestant. It will also be possible to determine whether Hillerbrand is correct in his view that Anabaptism, through its emphasis on discipleship, is disqualified to share in the inheritance of the truly Protestant saints. Or was it the particular manner in which the Anabaptists either consciously or unconsciously appropriated the mystical heritage that in the end was the decisive factor in making Anabaptism neither Catholic nor Protestant?[10]

B. An Analysis of the Mystical Anthropology of Johannes Tauler

Tauler's mysticism has as its ultimate goal the return of the soul to its precreated nature in God. To facilitate this return Tauler makes a careful distinction, according to Ozment, between the *gemuete* and the *grunt (Grund)* of the soul which must not be lost sight of if one wishes to understand the radical nature of Tauler's *Seelengrund* doctrine. This *Grund* is "the firmly established dwelling place in the soul, where God is present, and from which he neither can nor desires to separate himself."[11]

The *gemuete* on the other hand is human nature in all of its rational and volitional powers.[12] Though the *gemuete* is created rather than precreated nature as the *Seelengrund*, it, nevertheless, stands for the highest *powers* of the soul. The *Grund* by contrast is the deepest or most secret *place* in the soul, the area that has not been vitiated by original sin.[13]

Between the *Seelengrund* and the *gemuete* there "is interaction and intercourse," as it were, "between the uncreated and created 'grounds'."[14]

Because of God's "prior commitment to the ground of man's soul,"[15] and an inclination of the soul toward its origin in God, even though one may be unaware of it, the ground of the soul serves as the historical meeting place between a person and God. Historical communion between God and the soul assists the soul in progress toward the goal of ultimate union with God on the level of being or uncreated nature. Since

---

10 The question is an indirect reference to Walter Klaassen's *Anabaptism: Neither Catholic Nor Protestant* (Waterloo, Ontario: Conrad Press, 1973).
11 Ozment, *Homo Spiritualis*, p. 22.
12 *Ibid.*, p. 19.
13 *Ibid.*, p. 22.
14 *Ibid.*, p. 25.
15 *Ibid.*

> the ground of the soul is an inalienable residence of God in human being [or nature], it gives man a natural, creational claim to salvation, which places God historically in man's debt.[16]

The above is an attempt to summarize what Ozment describes as a "natural covenant" in Tauler's theology, which makes a distinction between the "order of creation" and the "order of being."

One might suppose that within the context of this natural covenant, which places God historically in humanity's debt in Tauler's theology, the salvation of mankind would, therefore, be automatically assured. The situation, however, is more serious and complex than the natural covenant would imply, for created nature, or the *gemuete*, has become a knave through the fall. It is not that nature or creation itself was bad, "a Thomistic thrust against Manichaeism,"[17] but that nature has turned away from its ground in God to itself. In this self-invertedness

> man loves himself (his createdness) more than God, God's angels and all that God has ever made... Here a poisoning occurs and penetrates to the very ground of the soul, where it establishes a false ground in the spirit and in nature, a ground which becomes manifest when one thinks that he is completely God and that all he does is his own.[18]

The only cure for this sickness, or poisoning brought on by this self-inversion in self-love, is the resolute and sustained practice of *gelassenheit* or *abgescheidenheit*. Tauler's goal in salvation is ultimate union with God. But this goal can never be reached as long as a person has any inclination toward self-will or attachment to nature.

> The less nature and its joy live, the more God and His will live; the more one wishes to live in the Spirit, so much more must he teach natural things to die. He who would follow Christ must give nature its "walking papers."[19]

God wills to fill all things in heaven and on earth, but He cannot or will not come to the soul that is filled with self-will and self-love. Human preparatory activity is, therefore,

> an indispensable condition for divine presence. When the Holy Spirit finds that man has done his part, *then* He comes with His light, and pours in the supernatural virtues of faith, hope and love with His grace. Without the achievement of a separation from all that is not God (*abgescheidenheit*) and a pure disposition to God in mind and will, the Holy Spirit and His gifts are not received.[20]

Ozment maintains that this and several other statements of Tauler, which stress the necessity of *prior human activity* in *gelassenheit* as the condition for the presence and activity of the Divine,

16 *Ibid.*
17 *Ibid.*, p. 27.
18 *Ibid.*
19 *Ibid.*, pp. 28–29.
20 *Ibid.*, p. 32.

go so far as to place the acquisition of God's saving presence in the context of a good business deal. It is a "fair bargain" (*ein gelich kouf*): we draw the lower powers into and subordinate them to the higher powers of the soul, and God draws us into His highest and ultimate powers. "So much of our own, so much then of His own: it is a fair bargain."[21]

It is exactly this "fair bargain" policy which disqualifies Tauler, in Ozment's opinion, from serving as one of Luther's teachers in the *sola gratia*. For despite all that Tauler may say to the contrary elsewhere, the successful operation of this policy rests ultimately on human capacity to prepare the ground for the divine presence.

C. An Analysis of the Mystical Anthropology of Jean Gerson

The goal of Jean Gerson's theology, in comparison with that of Johannes Tauler, is far less radical. Gerson's aim was to find a more effective way to the knowledge of God in this life rather than the return of the soul to its precreated nature in God. Though Gerson's goal was less radical, his anthropology was no less complex.

In Gerson's time, if one may judge from his vigorous defense of mystical theology, there was some criticism that it was too subjective and thus lacking in the ability to lead to a true knowledge of God. The criticism evidently came from persons who were learned in or favorable to systematic or speculative theology rather than mystical theology. Gerson maintained to the contrary "the experiential knowledge of those who are learned in the subject of mystical theology" is just as valid as that learned through "a trusting acceptance of the authority"[22] of the learned doctors of the church.

> For just as symbolic and systematic or speculative theology draws upon natural analogies and extrinsic effects and data . . ., so the doctrines of mystical theology are drawn from internal experiences in the hearts of the devout.[23]

As Ozment indicates, Gerson also rejects the *via negativa* of Dionysius, the Areopagite, to the extent that this would imply that mystical theology can make no valid claim to the positive knowledge of God.

> . . . if philosophy is defined as all knowledge proceeding from experience, then mystical theology will be 'philosophy,' and all who are experienced therein, even though to the technically skilled they may appear to be ignorant, are not to be denied the title, 'philosophers.'[24]

Gerson's purpose, however, is not merely to argue for the equality of mystical with speculative theology but for the *superiority* of the former over the latter. The reason for this lies in what could well be called Gerson's elaborate "anatomy of the soul." The full details of this anatomy are of no immediate interest to this

21 *Ibid.*
22 *Ibid.*, p. 50.
23 *Ibid.*
24 *Ibid.*, p. 51.

study. It is sufficient to state that the anatomy divides the soul into the *affective* and *intellective* powers. On both sides the powers are arranged in an hierarchial order in such a manner that the arrangement provides for reciprocal action between the powers.

This reciprocal action between the powers of the soul is important in Gerson's "order of salvation." Like that of Tauler, it involves the soul and God in a natural 'covenant.' Unlike Tauler, however, Gerson does not base this natural 'covenant' upon God's dwelling place in the "precreated ground of the soul," which is identical with the divine nature itself. For Gerson the relationship between God and the soul is rather to be explained as follows: "Man was in and with God as an idea is in and with the mind of an artist, i.e., not in essential unity, but in ideational participation."[25]

Although, in Gerson's thought, the soul is not identical with the divine nature, it, nevertheless, bears even in its created state (*esse realis*) certain traces of its precreated state (*esse idealis*). Because the soul only is "made capable of communion with God and is a participant in God through intelligence and reason, it is to the soul only that the power to return to God, 'through knowledge and love,' is granted."[26]

In spite of the consequences of sin, "the ontological structure and goal of the soul remain so firmly established for Gerson that he can argue for the 'necessity' of a future resurrection":

> As theological divines and learned metaphysicians have taught, the face of the soul is situated on the horizon of two worlds, so that through it all things are borne back to God by its knowing and using what has gone forth from Him when He created. Hence, Aristotle in Book I of the *Politics* and the Platonists said that all things are made for the sake of man and man for the sake of God. And, therefore, the necessity of a future resurrection (*necessitas resurrectionis futurae*) is concluded. Otherwise a naturally established end would be in vain ...[27]

The above should not be interpreted to mean that Gerson denies the effects of original sin upon the soul. It is rather to be understood in the light of his anatomy of the soul where the powers of the soul are divided into the *intellective* and the *affective*. The affective powers of the soul are seen as much less severely vitiated by sin than the intellective ones. The effects of sin upon the latter are regarded by Gerson as severe.

> Before the fall of Adam ... the eye of contemplation, with its undistracted view from the top of the mountain of God, was most lively, pure and efficacious in its operation. Now, however, *post peccatum Adae*, it is practically totally extinct, just as the rational eye is almost totally blind, and the sensitive eye almost totally corrupt.[28]

The *affective* powers of the soul have, by comparison with the havoc wrought upon the *intellective* ones, escaped virtually unscathed. To be sure, there is

25 *Ibid.*, pp. 56–57.
26 *Ibid.*, pp. 56–57.
27 *Ibid.*, p. 57.
28 *Ibid.*, p. 69.

danger, at least theoretically, since the powers interact, that the corruption of the *intellective* powers may spread to the *affective* ones. But Gerson chose to emphasize the opposite and positive side of the coin.

> This reciprocity implies that the greater purity and *soteriological* possibilities of the affective powers will not be without significance for the reformation and salutary fulfillment of the intellective powers.[29]

It is then in the affective powers of the soul that Gerson finds that purer anthropological base, which both provides the way to a fuller knowledge of God in this life and assures the return of the soul to God through the fulfillment of the natural 'covenant.' Yet it would not be incorrect to say that while the fulfillment of this natural 'covenant,' which assures a future resurrection, is seen as a divine necessity, the fulfillment of the covenant and the renewal of the intellective powers must, nevertheless, make prior human activity a possibility.

> The greater purity of the affective powers *post peccatum Adae*, which grants them soteriological resources for the *regressus ad deum in via* – although not in disunion with sacramental mediation – entitles them to be the locus of mystical theology.[30]

The affective powers in their greater purity and in the reciprocal action between the power assist in the "historical approximation of Adamic manhood" at the peak of the mystical experience.[31]

D. An Analysis of Luther's Rejection of the Mystical Anthropology

The sharp contrast between the anthropologies of Tauler and Gerson and that of Luther, which was only briefly alluded to earlier, can now be presented in greater detail.

First, Luther refuses to divide the soul into its higher and lower parts but speaks rather of the soul as being the whole person. "The whole soul is in every part. Therefore, when the soul employs one member the whole is in that member; indeed, all powers cooperate in what the soul is busy doing."[32]

Second, although Luther, as Ozment states, can shower a multitude of dignifying titles upon the soul, and even declare that it is by nature immortal, since it was created *ex nihilo* by God, side by side with these titles of honor appear certain limiting qualifications. Ozment lists these qualifications in the following order:

1. To the celestial nature of the soul Luther joins "the imperative, *debere*. The soul ought to seek heavenly goods; the interior man ought to be spiritual through faith. That the soul is 'heavenly' and 'spiritual' is not a conclusion deduced automatically from its intrinsic nature."[33]

29 *Ibid.*, p. 71.
30 *Ibid.*
31 *Ibid.*, p. 82.
32 *Ibid.*, p. 93.
33 *Ibid.*, p. 96.

2. Luther does not find the dignity of the soul residing in its own immortal quality alone, but in the promise of God to dwell there. "The sanctuary of God is nothing else than the soul spiritually turned to God. Since the soul is the seat of wisdom and in the middle of the people (i.e. in their hearts), He promises to dwell there."[34]

3. The last of the qualifying or limiting statements with reference to the soul's dignity involves that of a tendency toward annihilation (*nihileitas*), which runs through all creaturely existence. This tendency is not overcome through the soul's innate immortality but "through 'faith in Christ.' The soul is a womb in which the words of God are conceived, but 'through faith.' And Christ sits in the souls of the faithful, but 'upon faith.' "[35]

The third and last major point to be noted in Luther's anthropology, in contrast to that of Tauler and Gerson, is that the soul, along with heart, spirit, and mind, is not only a subject worthy of dignifying titles, but also one of the

> places where the enemies of God are at home. Not only are good things in the soul, but also sins, miseries and evils. Pride appears in the spirit, in the heart and in the mind. Flesh and its understanding are not only the enemies of the interior man, but "members of his very household!" Conscience is a "basket of sins," a "bed of suffering" – "suffering from its sins." And it is in the heart and conscience that righteousness and truth find, engage and accuse iniquity and impiety.[36]

As a result of all these qualifications which accompany Luther's dignifying titles for the soul, it is obvious that the preparatory functions of Tauler's *gemuete* and Gerson's *synteresis* have, in effect, been denied. It is not that Luther has denied their universal presence or their capacity to create a legal righteousness between persons. But neither *gemuete* nor *synteresis* are any longer seen as anthropological resources endowed with the soteriological possibilities of creating a righteousness that can endure before God. For this a special divine activity is now required.[37]

Much in Ozment's presentation of Luther's position versus Tauler and Gerson cannot be dealt with here. A fair assessment of the basic difference between them, however, would note the following. The initial and preparatory soteriological functions which were assigned to the *gemuete* by Tauler and by Gerson to the *synteresis*, were by Luther attributed to the work of the Holy Spirit. It is through the Spirit's activity that we learn to put our trust and our hope "on the promises of God that are outside of us."

In support of this conclusion we quote, as Ozment does, Luther's interlinear gloss on Romans 8:26–27.

> *In a like way the Holy Spirit helps* [by] making us petition and groan deeply *our infirmity* ... our impotence and impossibility. *For what* as regards the object of our prayer *we should pray for* as regards the affect or manner in which our petition is made *we do not know* ... But *the* Holy *Spirit asks* makes us ask *for us with unutterable groanings* which can be expressed in words by no man; nor is anyone able to sense them except God – this

---

34 *Ibid.*, p. 97.
35 *Ibid.*, pp. 97–98.
36 *Ibid.*, pp. 99–100.
37 *Ibid.*, p. 151.

is not the same for everyone. But God alone *who searches the hearts* [of men], the innermost place, which is closer to us than we to ourselves *knows* acknowledges, senses and approves *what the* Holy *Spirit desires*, and to Him these groanings are not incommunicable. Therefore, I say the Spirit knows *because He asks* makes us ask *for the saints in accordance with God* i.e. for those things which are pleasing to God according to the will of God.[38]

Luther's distance from the medieval mystics, Tauler and Gerson, has now been firmly established. His *"homo spiritualis nititur fide"* is a judgment upon and a rejection of the anthropologies of both. What remains now to be explored further before the question raised in the title of this section can be answered is the relationship of Anabaptism to Luther and to medieval mysticism. Did Anabaptism, as Harold S. Bender maintained, presuppose the reformation doctrine of justification by faith alone to such a degree that its "motif of discipleship . . . is merely its proper and practical extension,"[39] or did Anabaptism retain so much more of the medieval mysticism repudiated by Luther that in the final analysis he emerges as the true radical of the era, so far as the repudiation of the mystical anthropology is concerned?[40]

E. Luther's Initial Approval and Eventual Rejection of the *Theologia Deutsch*

Luther's high praise for the mystical tract known as *Theologia Deutsch* is so well known that it needs no documentation here. What does appear strange, in view of Luther's distance from the medieval mysticism of Tauler and Gerson, so clearly established by 1516, is that he should have lent his support to the mysticism of *Theologia Deutsch.* Yet Luther wrote approving prefaces to both the 1516 and 1518 editions of this mystical tract. One should note, however, that although the *Commentary on Romans* reveals a definite break with the theology of Rome well before the fateful event of October 31, 1517, Luther himself did not seem immediately aware of the theological gulf that now separated him from the official theology of the Roman See. It apparently took Tetzel's crass peddling of indulgences to jolt Luther into conscious awareness of the vast difference between his own theological outlook and that of Rome, although the difference was there well before the posting of the ninety-five theses. It may well be that this mystical tract used by Anabaptists and other sixteenth-century dissenters, long after Luther had abandoned it, served as the catalyst that brought him to a sharper awareness of the distance that now separated him from the mystical heritage.

The foregoing should not be interpreted to mean that nothing in the *Theologia Deutsch* would have touched a responsive chord in the young Luther's heart. Ozment finds at least five separate motifs in the tract to which Luther's "own theological predilections in the formative years between 1513–1517"[41] would have been receptive. These can be summarized as follows: (1) The emphasis on the

---

38 *Ibid.*, pp. 187–88.
39 Hillerbrand, *op. cit.*, p. 415.
40 Williams, *op. cit.*, pp. 303–304.
41 Ozment, *Mysticism and Dissent*, p. 21.

"bitterness" of the true Christian life because of the aversion to suffering of both selfish human nature and reason; (2) The criticism of "spiritual pride" which affirms independence from both Scripture and doctrine; (3) The description of "the perfect man" as one freed both from the fear of hell and the desire for selfish reward; (4) The effort to bring the whole person into the religious life through an emphasis upon the importance of both faith and knowledge; (5) The various motifs which describe "the perfect man" as groaning under the persistence of sin, willing to suffer damnation if it be God's will, and trying always to suppress selfishness by "the hard way of the cross."[42]

One reason then why Luther was willing to write an approving preface to the 1516 edition of the *Theologia Deutsch* was simply because, as Ozment states, he found much in it with which he was in basic agreement. He also maintains, however, that a comparison of the two prefaces which Luther wrote for the 1516 and 1518 editions of this late medieval mystical tract will show the former as being almost perfunctory in contrast to the latter. A primary reason for the difference in tone in the prefaces to the 1516 and 1518 editions, in Ozment's opinion, is that in the latter Luther is using the *Theologia Deutsch* to defend himself against charges of innovation in the light of all that had taken place since October 31, 1517. Luther writes:

> I now for the first time became aware of the fact that a few of us highly educated Wittenberg theologians speak disgracefully, as though we want to undertake new things, as though there had been no people previously or elsewhere [who had undertaken these things]. Indeed, there have been others...
> Let anyone who wishes read this little book, and then let him say whether theology is original with us or ancient, for this book is not new.[43]

Other motifs in the *Theologia Deutsch*, however, were not congenial to the Martin Luther of 1518 or later. Ozment notes these as "the mystical anthropology" with its soteriological resources, the rejection of which by Luther has already been noted; "speculation on man's union with God"; and closely connected with the mystical anthropology, "the call for man to do the best that is in him if he hopes to achieve union with God."[44] Ozment observes that seen from the standpoint of Luther's lectures on the Psalms, 1513–1516, even the subtle mystical form of passive resignation (*gelassenheit*) is "a doing which is a 'doing nothing' – this is still allied to that semi-Pelagian *facere quod in se est*"[45] which Luther overcame in those lectures.

Ozment summarizes Luther's changing attitude toward the three major presuppositions of mystical theology in these words:

> In summary, we could say that, of the three areas of mystical theology – (1) ontology and anthropology, (2) the steps of salvation, and (3) the union with God – Luther is

---

42 *Ibid.*, p. 22.
43 *Ibid.*, p. 20.
44 *Ibid.*, p. 24.
45 *Ibid.*

interested primarily in what the *German Theology* has to say about the second and he shies away from the conclusions drawn in the first and third areas.[46]

After 1518 Luther manifested no interest in writing further prefaces or publishing new editions of the *Theologia Deutsch*. Williams sees Luther's pilgrimage from the initial acceptance of mysticism to its eventual rejection as involving the following stages:

1. A greater distinction or distance between justification and sanctification than that which had obtained within Roman Catholicism with its sacramental system *prior* to the Reformation or within Anabaptism minus the sacramental system *after* the Reformation. The Anabaptists, as Williams states, "did not understand or accept Luther's ever clearer disavowal of any realm or part or organ or substance or faculty in man capable of preparing the soul for salvation."[47]

2. A distinction between God's alien work, *opus alienum*, and God's proper work, *opus suum*. The former, seemingly harsh and destructive, can also be described as God's invisible or unrecognizable work. Human foolishness (*insapientia*) cannot recognize the harsh work as the work of God. Luther did not shrink from calling this first work of God the "*Kakangelion*," the bad news, "in contrast to the Good News of redemption from man's inveterate preoccupation with self."[48]

3. A metamorphosis of the technical terminology of mysticism involving such terms as purgation, illumination, ecstatic and essential union, as

> Luther's matured formulation of the spiritual experience of the righteousness of God in Christ as wholly unmerited gift in faith... [led to the] existential acceptance of man's helplessness and salvation... Even the sighs of the believer aware of his sin and finitude are inspired by the interceding Holy Spirit (Romans 8:26);...[49]

Despite the fact that Ozment and Williams both see Luther as initially indebted to the mystical emphasis on *gelassenheit* for his freedom from the tyranny of the late medieval Roman Catholic merit system,[50] the mature Luther retained virtually nothing from this heritage except the mystical concept of vocation in the world which was turned by his emphasis on forensic justification in a socially conservative direction.[51]

F. The Continued Use of the Mystical Tradition by Anabaptists and Other Dissenters

While Luther tended more and more to repudiate the mystical anthropology,

---

46 *Ibid.*
47 Williams, *op. cit.*, p. 279.
48 *Ibid.*, pp. 282–84.
49 *Ibid.*, pp. 287–88. It should be pointed out that this attempt to identify or delineate certain stages in Luther's removal from the mystical heritage is that of the author rather than that of Williams.
50 Ozment, *Homo Spiritualis*, pp. 214–15 and Williams, *op. cit.*, p. 286.
51 Williams, *op. cit.*, p. 303.

the reverse was true among the Anabaptists and other dissenters.[52] They not only continued to use the mystical tradition embedded in the *Theologia Deutsch*, but they also proceeded to enlarge and revise it. Ozment sees a basic unity among the sixteenth-century dissenters arising from their common use of the mystical heritage. He regards this unity as more impressive than any variety implied by various exercises in typology. In this judgment Williams, who had earlier developed a typology of the Radical Reformation in *Spiritual and Anabaptist Writers*, now concurs.[53]

The most obvious place to begin the discussion of the impact of mysticism upon Anabaptist theology through its continuous use of the *Theologia Deutsch* is a consideration of the alterations made in the 1528 Worms edition as compared with the 1518 Wittenberg edition.

According to Ozment's analysis, these additions and alterations are five in number and can be described as follows:

1. The elimination of Luther's preface to the 1518 edition in preference for one written by Peter Schoeffer, friend of and publisher for Ludwig Haetzer and Hans Denck. In this preface the reader is assured that all previously coarse and incomprehensible passages in the book are now fully understandable.

2. The elimination of honorific titles such as "Meister" and "Sanctus." This can be regarded as more nearly in keeping with the biblicistic attitude of the Anabaptists, following the admonition of Matt. 28:8–10. It may, however, be more significant as an effort to undercut academic or ecclesiastical establishments that sought to buttress their authority by an appeal to the tradition of certain masters or saints.

3. A significant change in the second chapter where the Wittenberg edition reads: "Scripture, faith, and truth say..."; amended in the Worms edition to read: "Truth, faith, and Scripture say..." The change, as Ozment notes, would be in keeping with the insistence of many dissenters (Hans Denck included) "that Scripture is a 'witness' to and not the truth itself."[54]

4. The alteration of the prayer in the Wittenberg edition so that the Worms edition by contrast has a definitely theocentric and even antitrinitarian thrust.

5. The addition of Hans Denck's *Etliche Hauptreden*.[55]

The last addition is no doubt the most important so far as the continued use of the *Theologia Deutsch* by the Anabaptists was concerned. This addition not only placed the stamp of Anabaptist ownership upon a previously existing mystical

---

52 Ozment, *Mysticism and Dissent*, p. 25. The full text reads in part: "The mystical way to salvation will certainly be embraced, but it is the presuppositions of mystical anthropology and reflection on man's union with God in this life that will be of primary interest to those who dissent from the gospel according to Rome, Wittenberg, Zurich, and Geneva."

53 *Ibid.*, p. x of Introduction; Williams, *op. cit.*, p. 303.

54 Ozment, *Mysticism and Dissent*, p. 27. For a full discussion of the implications of this statement for the hermeneutics of Hans Denck see Ch. V, pp. 132–36 above.

55 *Ibid.*, pp. 27–28. Also see Ch. IV, pp. 90–99, 113–17, and Ch. V, pp. 149–52, above, as well as Ozment's *Mysticism and Dissent*, pp. 133–36. These texts will show that Marbeck used the mystical heritage not radically to dehistoricize and deinstitutionalize the Truth, as Ozment says, but to stress the absolute newness in which the believer stood because of the Christ event.

tract, but also legitimatized its continued use by Pilgram Marbeck and the Marbeck circle. Marbeck, as we have indicated, used the mysticism of the *Theologia Deutsch* in a rather different manner from that of Hans Denck because of his controversy with the Evangelical Spiritualist, Caspar Schwenckfeld.[56]

G. Hans Denck and Taulerian Mysticism

The essence of Denck's mystical position is contained in the *Hauptreden*. Although his position is not identical with that of Johannes Tauler, since he gives a larger, though some would hold still minimal, place to the incarnate Christ, and though there is nothing in his anthropology that equals Tauler's "*gleich Kauf*" or fair bargain policy, Denck stands nearer to Tauler in his mystical position than any other Anabaptist.

As already indicated, the essence of Denck's mysticism is found within the *Hauptreden*, and Ozment has presented us with an analysis of these, which is both lucid and thorough. We shall rely heavily upon that analysis in order to present a brief summary of Denck's mystical theology.

According to Denck, God is One and the source of all unity. He is unalterably opposed to the disunity which comes from willing anything that is contrary to God's will. Persons in their fallen state, however, know and experience disunity, while salvation is unity with God. Denck accepts the axiom of medieval thought "that like can be known only by like." It must follow, therefore, that persons who were created and endowed with the creaturely freedom which enables them to remain free in God, or to turn from God and oppose the One who created them, are at the same time endowed with "a 'seed' or 'image' of God indestructibly present within every man . . . which craves freedom incessantly."[57]

However, in Denck's thought the "seed" or "image" or "Word" within is not only "an omnipresent anthropological structure," such as Tauler's *Seelengrund* which makes possible the return of the soul to God, because God has chosen never to be separated from it. Denck can also speak of "a particular historical example of perfect return to God . . . (Jesus Christ of Nazareth)."[58] He is the truest example of perfect freedom and perfect union with God because his will was his own yet remained one with the will of God.

Persons who have the "Word" within and the example of the historical "Word" without are now in a position to exercise the divine gift of freedom. Unless they do so, it will be lost. Exhorts Denck, "He who chooses to do it can do it; let him who doubts it only try it."[59]

The way of return, however, involves the strenuous practice of *gelassenheit*, resignation, abandonment of the love of the creaturely. "He who does his best in obedience to the seed of God within and in imitation of the life of Jesus without

---

56 See Ch. V, pp. 149–52. above.
57 Ozment, *Mysticism and Dissent*, p. 30.
58 *Ibid.*
59 *Ibid.*, p. 31.

may achieve self-surrender which is 'Christ' and thereby claim that power which is of the Father."[60]

Denck's practice of *gelassenheit* is not human preparatory activity as a condition for the divine presence on exactly the same basis as in Tauler. In Denck's thought the "seed" or "image" is already universally present in every human being. Nevertheless, the cultivation and practice of *gelassenheit* as advocated by Denck would from Luther's point of view amount to "a doing which is doing nothing."

Denck secures the subjective pole of his mystical theology by the emphasis on the word "within." But he also secures the objective pole by placing the *Hauptreden* as a whole under the authority of the Holy Spirit. He thus places them beyond the pale of criticism from the "most eminent of historical authorities,"[61] by placing them under the *potentia Dei absoluta*. Thus, clad in the full armor of the mystical theology, Denck was prepared to do battle on four fronts with the Lutheran solae: *sola scriptura, solus Christus incarnatus, sola fides ex auditu verbi, and sola gratia.*[62]

We shall have occasion to return to a further consideration of the *potentia Dei absoluta* as it relates to several important Anabaptist practices at a later time. At this point we turn our attention to a second way in which the mystical anthropology affected the Anabaptist way of salvation.

H. Gersonian Mysticism in the Tripartite Anthropology of Balthasar Hubmaier and Modifications thereof within Anabaptism

The tripartite anthropology of Balthasar Hubmaier has been known in the world of Anabaptist scholarship for such a long period of time and expounded by so many different sources that further elaboration thereof is unnecessary here.[63]

---

60 *Ibid.*, The material in this summary, even where not quoted directly, is dependent upon Ozment's presentation, pp. 29–31.
61 *Ibid.*, p. 32.
62 *Ibid.*, pp. 125–26. The full text from which these references are drawn reads as follows: "While in Augsburg, Denck wrote his two major indictments of Luther's view of human destiny: *What Scripture Means When it Says that God is the Cause of Good and Evil* and *On the Law of God: How the Law is Abolished and Yet Still Must be Fulfilled.* Together these treatises form a frontal assault on the three Lutheran solae: *sola scriptura* as authoritative revelation; *solus Christus incarnatus* as the agent of salvation; and *sola fides ex auditu verbi* as the narrow gate to Christian life."

I would include in this an attack on the *sola gratia*, since Denck's treatise on the Law was a protest against Luther's forensic justification, which Denck understood as a new form of indulgence. It should also be pointed out that Ozment and Williams differ on the significance which they see Denck attaching to the incarnate Christ. Ozment states that Denck's aim is nothing less than "to dehistoricize and deinstitutionalize 'Truth' absolutely." Williams, on the other hand, states that if Denck appears to minimize the incarnate Christ, it is only in order to maximize "the Lamb slain from the foundation of the world ..." See Williams, *op. cit.*, p. 296.

For a full discussion of the issues in Denck's conflict with Lutheran theology and clergy, see Ch. III, pp. 71–72, above. Since the impact of mysticism upon Denck's theology is covered in some detail in Ch. II, pp. 47–50, it will not be further discussed here.
63 See *SAW*, pp. 112–35. Also see Ch. II, pp. 50–53, above.

What had not been known, prior to the publication of the two books by Ozment and the article by Williams which is in some respects a response to Ozment's work, is the extent to which this anthropology had roots in the medieval mystical tradition. Indeed, several scholars, the writer included, were under the impression that this anthropology was original with Hubmaier and that it emerged in the context of his controversary with the Lutheran doctrines of predestination and bondage of the will.[64]

The parallels between the mystical anthropology, endowed with soteriological resources, and the anthropology of Balthasar Hubmaier have now been firmly established. The mystics and Hubmaier presupposed the existence of some region or faculty in human nature that had escaped the ruinous consequences of the fall. The relationship between these two anthropologies is so close that the attempt to deny the influence of the first upon the second would be vain as well as foolish. Williams has even suggested that Hubmaier's trichotomic anthropology, as Friedmann called it, may have been indirectly inspired by one of Johannes Tauler's mystical sermons.[65] Although Hubmaier appeals more directly to the Latin Vulgate text of I Thess. 5:23, the parallel between the Tauler sermon and the Hubmaierian anthropology is, indeed, striking as the quotation from Vetter's edition of Tauler's sermon, 348.22ff, will indicate:

> Although he is one man, man exists as if he were three men. The first is the outward, animal, sensing man; the second, the rational man with his rational powers; and the third is the *gemuete*, the highest part of the soul. [And as there are various kinds of men in man] so there are various kinds of will in man, each according to its own manner.[66]

Despite the rather obvious affinity of Hubmaier's anthropology with the tripartite model found in Tauler's sermon, I have chosen to label the traces of mysticism which appear in Hubmaier's anthropology as Gersonian rather than Taulerian. The reasons for doing this are simply that what remains of mysticism in the thought of Hubmaier is more closely related to the thought of Gerson than to that of Tauler. Like Gerson, Hubmaier speaks of the lost powers of the soul. Like Gerson, he seeks only the recovery of the ideal of Adamic manhood. Neither Gerson nor Hubmaier were interested as Tauler was in the mystical absorption of the soul into God, where the distinction between the divine and the human is lost and "in this abyss the spirit loses itself and knows neither God nor itself, neither like nor unlike."[67] While Hubmaier's quest cannot be regarded as identical with that of Gerson's, namely, a "more effective way to knowledge of God in this

---

64 See Robert Friedmann, *The Theology of Anabaptism* (Scottdale, PA: Herald Press, 1973), pp. 91–98. Friedmann discusses Hubmaier's trichotomic anthropology, as found in his very profound tract, *Von der Freiheit des Willens*, at some length. But he seems totally unaware that the views expressed by Pilgram Marbeck and Leonhard Schiemer were modifications of Hubmaier or that Hubmaier himself had been influenced, whether consciously or unconsciously, by the mystical tradition.
65 Williams, *op. cit.*, p. 273.
66 Ozment, *Homo Spiritualis*, p. 15. The English translation of Tauler's sermon is that of Ozment. For the original German see p. 15, n. 3.
67 *Ibid.*, p. 38.

life,"⁶⁸ it is not totally dissimilar either, for Hubmaier's quest involved a way to recover the lost capacity of the fallen will of the soul to distinguish between good and evil.

The anthropologies of Pilgram Marbeck, Leonhard Schiemer, and Leopold Scharnschlager can well be considered variations of the same trichotomic scheme found in Hubmaier. His anthropology may justifiably be regarded as the normative model for an understanding of the effects of the mystical anthropology upon the Anabaptist way of salvation, especially in South Germany.⁶⁹ In Holland the Celestial Flesh Christology and the bridal imagery of the mystics played an equally important role.

I. The Anabaptists as Heirs of Late Medieval Mysticism

According to Williams, the fact that the Anabaptists "safeguarded a faculty or region of man's being that was never implicated in the fall"⁷⁰ was decisive in separating them theologically from Luther. It altered their concept of salvation from that of Luther, who totally repudiated this anthropological faculty in three significant areas.

The first of these was the manner in which the Anabaptists again conjoined justification and sanctification, whereas Luther, as Hans Hillerbrand has so forcefully stated, had completely separated them. He did so when he "began with the *agnitio peccati*, the recognition of one's utter sinfulness as the will of God, and held that justification takes place *propter Christum per fidem* – the sinner is justified solely through trust in Christ's perfect obedience."⁷¹

In Anabaptism, however, justification and sanctification are again conjoined, much as they were within Roman Catholicism, though without the added burden from the Anabaptist point of view of the whole sacramental system.

The manner in which the Anabaptists again conjoined justification and sanctification involved not only their retention of the mystical anthropology but also the saving work of Christ as Second Adam for all infants and imbeciles. This was an emphasis they picked up from their continued use of *Theologia Deutsch*. Concerning the effect of this added mystical strand in the soteriology of the Anabaptists Williams says,

> The Anabaptist *became* heterodox and schismatically sectarian when he agreed *mutatis mutandis* with *Theologia Deutsch* that the definitive atonement of Christ on Calvary had in some way affected all mankind. Said the Anonymous Mystic:
> Wherefore God took human nature, or manhood, upon himself and was made man,

---

68 *Ibid.*, p. 83.
69 The two exceptions to the above statement are the mysticism of Hans Denck, which has already been noted, and the centrality which many Anabaptists gave to the universally saving work of Christ as the Second Adam with respect to infants, young children, and imbeciles, that will be briefly alluded to in this section. A discussion of the wider redemptive work of Christ as the Second Adam, i.e., for those who are neither children nor infants nor imbeciles, will take place in the next section of the appendix. For a discussion of these same themes see Ch. II and Ch. IV, above.
70 Williams, *MQR*, XLVIII, No. 3 (July, 1974), *op. cit.*, 293.
71 Hillerbrand, *op. cit.*, p. 406.

and man was made God (*vergottet*). Thus was the amendment [for the first man's sin] brought to pass.[72]

Ultimately the manner in which the Anabaptists used this second strand from the mystical theology was dependent upon the presence of the first, namely, an anthropology endowed with soteriological resources. Within Roman Catholicism, where mysticism was an underground current rather than an open revolt, the guilt of original sin was washed away through the sacrament of infant baptism. The Anonymous Mystic, however, insisted that the *viator*, baptized in infancy, had still in his mature years to purge himself of his "I" and "Me" and "Mine," before he could personally appropriate the benefits of this universal atonement. Without such personal appropriation the universal atonement was of no avail.[73] What made such appropriation possible from the mystical and Anabaptist point of view was the anthropological capacity to make justification manifest by willing one thing, God's will. The Anabaptist differed from the mystic only in that the guilt of original sin was washed away without the aid of infant baptism, and the further purging of what remained of sinful inclinations was postponed until the time of the confessional baptism of the mature believer.[74]

The second area of difference between the Lutheran and Anabaptist way of salvation lay in the oft repeated accusation of the latter that neither Luther nor the Lutherans were sufficiently concerned about good works and the visible fruit of justification. As Hans Hillerbrand points out, the Anabaptists misunderstood both Luther and the Lutheran Confessions, since Luther as well as the Lutheran Confessions emphasize that justification must lead to good works. These, however, cannot be the cause of justification. The reason for this is twofold.

First, within the framework of Lutheran theology Christian existence remains throughout life an existence within the tension of *simul justus et peccator*. Second, and perhaps the more important reason, however, is that on the surface the good works of the Christian did not materially differ from those of the good pagan. Hans Hillerbrand in the following quotation vividly describes the difference between the Anabaptist demand for some outward manifestation of justification and the Lutheran insistence that the deepest motives of the Christian life always remain hidden:

> For Luther . . . such external acts were *res inferiora* whose outward observance or nonobservance did not make a Christian. Reading the lengthy descriptions of the characteristics of the Christian life in Anabaptist writings one is impressed not only by the high ethical vigor, but also by the fact that most of the points covered were, for Luther, either part of general morality with no specific Christian quality or altogether unessential. To note just one example: Peter Riedemann's *Rechenschafft* writes at great length about such matters as "the making of clothes," "greeting," "the giving of the hand and embracing," "celebrating," "traders," "innkeepers," "standing drinks," and "coming together." Luther, on the contrary, felt that "the church is hidden, the saints are hidden" and held that even the heathen could lead an outwardly moral life when he expressed the hope that most people "were good pious heathen who kept the natural law." In a

---

72 Williams, *op. cit.*, p. 294.
73 *Ibid.*, p. 293.
74 *Ibid.*, p. 299.

penetrating analysis W. V. Loewenich has shown how Luther's understanding of God as *deus absconditus* and of faith as *argumentum rerum non apparentium* led to the postulate of the "hiddenness" of the Christian life, which, unlike differences of sex or race, cannot be perceived empirically. Here the difference between the Reformer and the Anabaptists emerges most clearly.[75]

More than anything else, this difference is due to the fact that the Anabaptists retained the mystical anthropology endowed with its inalienable soteriological resources, while Luther repudiated these in their entirety.

The third area of difference between Lutheran and Anabaptist ways of salvation is closely related to the second, though dependent on still a third strand which the Anabaptists borrowed from the treasury of mystical theology in *Theologia Deutsch* and then wove into the fabric of their own theological thought. This is the definition of sin as disobedience rather than lack of faith. The Anabaptist leader most deeply affected by the Anonymous Theologian's definition of sin was Pilgram Marbeck. Williams has collected into one single quotation all the various passages cited by Marbeck in the second part of his *Antwort*, which give support to this definition of sin. In this concentrated form, states Williams, the passage is extensive enough to reveal "what the Anonymous Theologian himself intended and then secondly to see how the Anabaptist leader used the chapter and related material in his theology of sanctification and communal righteousness."[76]

What the Anonymous Theologian intended, and how the Anabaptist leader used this and other related materials, had, in the opinion of Williams, a remarkable similarity. Marbeck had earlier embraced the mystic's view of Christ as the Second Adam, who through "his selfless, prayerful obedience in the Garden of Gethsemane" had made an universal atonement for all infants and imbeciles throughout the world. This not only opened the way for Marbeck to reunite justification and sanctification in the formulation of his own theological position; it also led inevitably to his definition of sin as disobedience.

Justification and sanctification were reunited for all those who upon reaching the age or mental level of moral discrimination were faced with

> the strenuous task of purging themselves of the residual impulse from original sin and also of all supervening personal sinfulness by the imitation of the divine Exemplar. Thus for Marpeck mystical conformity to the divine will and progressive sanctification and

---

75 Hillerbrand, *op. cit.*, pp. 414–15.
76 Williams, *op. cit.*, p. 298. The full text of the quotation, pp. 297–98, referred to above follows:

All who follow Adam in pride, in lust of the flesh, and in disobedience, are dead in soul and never will be made alive but in Christ, that is, in obedience. And for this cause so long as a man is Adam or his child, he is without God ... He who is in disobedience is in sin, and sin can never be atoned for or amended but by returning to God. This comes about in humble obedience. For so long as a man continues in disobedience, his sins can never be forgiven him; let him do what he will, it avails him nothing Yea, let us ponder on this: that disobedience is itself sin. But when a man returns into obedience, all is amended and atoned for and forgiven, and not else ... If the Devil himself would come into true obedience, he would become an angel again, and all his sin and wickedness would be amended and atoned for (*gebuesst*) and fully forgiven ...

lifelong suffering on one level of experience or another were both the consequence and the confirmation of the mystery of the divine justification.[77]

As Williams notes, the particular way in which Marbeck made use of these mystical strands in the formulation of his own theological position is related to the fact that he struggled against the Spiritualizer, Caspar Schwenckfeld, on the one hand, and the *solafideist* Luther on the other. Even so, Marbeck felt that he had gone beyond the Anonymous Theologian only as he located "the movement of doing penance" and the resolution to conform "to the will of the Second Adam" in the confessional baptism received in the years of discretion.[78]

To the extent that Marbeck went beyond his early teachers, he did so, as Williams indicates,

> only to return to what he supposed was the sole usage of the primitive Church:
> ... according to the common evangelical [Lutheran] teaching, the promise and the work of Christ really do not affect the sinner, for they do not reach him in his heart, through faith unto forgiveness and through the Holy Spirit unto the expulsion and mortification of sins and unto the resurrection and the revivification from death in and through Christ and unto the second or new birth. And therefore, [we say in contrast that] whoever did not sin like Adam [through wilful disobedience: an imbecile or an infant, for example] will not be condemned like Adam and [by the same measure, that] whatever sinner does not do penance [for personal sins in confessional baptism] and does not *suffer with Christ* will not benefit from Christ's righteousness and merit and will not co-rule with him in blessedness.[79]

In light of the above quotation from Marbeck's *Antwort*, it would be correct to say that blessedness was for him as for the Anonymous Mystic, "the consummation of the process of a double action: the departure of self and the entry of the divine."[80]

The concluding observation of Williams on the above quotation from the *Antwort* is entirely correct. Williams writes,

> Thus in contrast to Luther, sin for Marpeck is essentially not lack of faith but lack of obedience. Discipleship, imitation of Christ, suffering with Christ, obedience to his eschatological and exacting ethical code, while one separates from the world and all its works, are Marpeck's unequivocal ethical inference from the willing of one thing in *Theologia Deutsch*.[81]

At last we have reached a point in the presentation of our evidence where adequate preparation has been made to answer the question raised in the beginning of this section. Was Anabaptism, with its emphasis on discipleship as Bender maintained, simply the "proper and practical extension"[82] of the Reformation doctrine of justification by faith alone, and thus the radicalization of the original

---

77 *Ibid.*, p. 299.
78 *Ibid.*
79 *Ibid.*
80 *Ibid.*, p. 294.
81 *Ibid.*, p. 299.
82 Hillerbrand, *op. cit.*, p. 415.

Protestant vision? Or was it the survival or revival of late medieval Christian mysticism, stripped now of all the encumbrances of the sacramental system of Roman Catholicism through its reliance on the *potentia Dei absoluta* of the mystical way? Or as a third option, was it a serious attempt to return to faithfulness to the New Testament, minus the conscious awareness that the presuppositions of mysticism provided the lens through which this document was read?

The accumulated evidence compels us to decide in favor of the latter option. Hans Hillerbrand is undoubtedly correct in his view that a prerequisite for developing or maintaining the Protestant doctrine of justification by faith alone is an anthropology centered in the bondage of the will and the complete repudiation of any soteriological resources within human nature itself.[83] The retention of just such an anthropological faculty was, as we have seen, very much a part of Anabaptist theology. And at least a part of the reason for the Anabaptist emphasis on discipleship was that they retained the mystical anthropology endowed with soteriological resources which Luther so thoroughly repudiated.[84]

Therefore, when the question, "Who was the true radical of the sixteenth-century Reformation?", is raised with respect to anthropology, the surprising answer is Luther![85] Not only has George H. Williams noted this, but also the Roman Catholic theologian, Rosemary Radford Ruether. In her book, *The Radical Kingdom*, she notes that for Luther and Reformation theology, in general, man is viewed from his fallen historical nature and seen as such a wretched creature that

---

83 *Ibid.*, p. 406.
84 Williams, *op. cit.*, pp. 303–304.
85 David C. Steinmetz has come to the same conclusion in a comparison of the differences between Luther and Hubmaier on justification. However, he attributes this difference to nominalist motifs in Hubmaier's theology rather than to the influence of mysticism. The title of his article, "Scholasticism and Radical Reform: Nominalist Motifs in the Theology of Balthasar Hubmaier," would indicate this. See *MQR*, XLV, No. 2 (April, 1971).

Steinmetz traces these nominalist motifs in Hubmaier's thought to the nominalist doctrine of God and the sharp distinction which the nominalists made between the *absolute* and *ordained* powers of God. Steinmetz maintains that the nominalist doctrine of God as Creator and Lord, as well as the nominalist doctrine of God as Redeemer, can only be understood on the basis of the interaction of these two powers. (pp. 125–27)

Although the nominalists' doctrine of God as Creator and Lord is fascinating, it is their doctrine of redemption that had its impact on the theology of Hubmaier. Like the nominalists, Hubmaier rejects predestination and affirms the freedom of the will. Hubmaier tried, as did the nominalists, to preserve a place for the prevenience of God's grace in the order of salvation. God has the initiative in that He has provided a structure within which salvation is possible and endowed humanity with a nature that is redeemable in the thought of both Hubmaier and the nominalist. Yet it is also true in the thought of both that the salvation or damnation of a particular individual is due to human response or the lack of it. (pp. 125–31) Hubmaier picks up the nominalist doctrine of the two powers in relation to the hidden and revealed will of God. (p 131) See Ch. II above for a fuller discussion.

In the end, whether we attribute the difference between Luther and Hubmaier on justification to nominalist motifs in the theology of the latter or to the influence of mysticism, the practical outcome is the same. Steinmetz sees Hubmaier's view of baptism and the voluntary church as representing "a break with the past and the anticipation of new currents which gained significance after his death." (p. 137) When it comes to the issue of grace and free will, Steinmetz sees Hubmaier as more dependent on "conservative theological

God's grace must come upon him as an alien garment. The Anabaptists, on the other hand, viewed man

> not from his fallen, historical nature, but from his original, created nature. Hence the radicals insisted that man has a natural capacity for God. As God's creation, man has a natural affinity for his Creator. Although he has fallen into sin, he has by no means lost this affinity, which still remains his "true nature." Consequently when God's grace descends on man, it is not as a garment of alien righteousness clothing a wretched being; rather, it speaks to the depths of man's proper self as like to like.[86]

Although Ruether does not trace the indebtedness of the Anabaptists to the mystics of the preceding centuries in detail, as do Ozment and Williams, she, nevertheless, notes that they "are more the heirs of late medieval mysticism and pietism" than of "the nominalist Augustinianism of the Reformers."[87]

Rollin S. Armour and Walter Klaassen have recently maintained that Anabaptism was neither Catholic nor Protestant.[88] Neither one of these two authors, however, has noted how deeply the Anabaptists were indebted to late medieval mysticism.[89] Therein lies the reason that Anabaptism will not fit neatly into either a Catholic or a Protestant pigeonhole. The fact that the Anabaptists had drunk so deeply from these wells and continued to draw nourishment from them after Luther had abandoned them as "broken cisterns,"[90] while the Catholics in their counter-Reformation reaffirmed the centrality of the sacramental system along with papal infallibility, thus denying the validity of the *potentia Dei absoluta*, caused the Anabaptists to be misfits in either camp.

---

insights from the late Middle Ages," specifically those that come from "late medieval nominalism and from Old Franciscan theology." (p. 137) These are set over against the radically Augustinian theological insights of Luther with the result that "when the subject is justification, then it is Martin Luther and not Balthasar Hubmaier who is the flaming radical." (p. 137) Although Steinmetz has here attributed Hubmaier's more conservative stance on justification to the influence of nominalism on his theology rather than that of mysticism, he, nevertheless, finds support for his view in Ozment's *Homo Spiritualis*. In a footnote to the above he writes the following: "S. E. Ozment has argued, with convincing documentation, that *synderesis* operates for the young Luther *coram hominibus* and not *coram deo*, i.e., as an ethical but not as soteriological resource. Luther locates all soteriological resources outside man. (Ozment, *Homo Spiritualis*, 214–16) For Hubmaier, however, the will of the spirit or the *synderesis voluntatis* is an anthropological resource within the order of salvation." (p. 137)

86 Rosemary Radford Ruether, *The Radical Kingdom: The Western Experience of Messianic Hope* (New York: Harper & Row, 1970), p. 23.
87 *Ibid.*, p. 22.
88 See Rollin Stely Armour, *Anabaptist Baptism* (Scottdale, PA: Herald Press, 1966), pp. 136–37. Also see Walter Klaassen, *op. cit.*
89 This is an oblique reference to the fact that Armour in his *Anabaptist Baptism* does trace the influence of the mystics, Thomas Müntzer and Hans Denck, upon the baptismal theology of Hans Hut.
90 An indirect reference to Jeremiah 2:13b.

II. ANABAPTIST MODIFICATIONS OF THE MYSTICAL HERITAGE

A. The Sources of the Anabaptist Concept of Christ as the Second Adam and the Impact of this Concept upon Their Theology

While the Anabaptists did not repudiate the heritage from late medieval mysticism as Luther had done, neither did it pass through the crucible of their largely lay theological minds in unmodified form. It should be noted, of course, that Felix Mantz, Balthasar Hubmaier, Conrad Grebel, and Hans Denck were all university-trained persons. Though their early martyr deaths robbed the Anabaptist movement of their continuing leadership, their theological contributions to the movement were not insignificant. One of the sources of modification for the mystical anthropology which the Anabaptists inherited from the preceding centuries was the great significance they attached to the work of Christ as the Second Adam and Recapitulator of a new humanity, somewhat after the manner of Irenaeus. This aspect of their thought is discussed above in Chapter IV, pages 100-103, in regard to their theological basis for the repudiation of infant baptism, and also in Chapter II, pages 35-56. In this latter section not only is their repudiation of infant baptism discussed but also the universal restoration of a genuine freedom of the will for the mature person.

At the time these earlier chapters were written, however, the author was not able to identify with any degree of certainty the source or sources of the view that the obedience of Christ as the Second Adam had universally undone much of the mischief wrought by the disobedience of the first Adam, though several possible sources were suggested.[1]

The mysticism of *Theologia Deutsch* has now been identified as one of the sources of the Anabaptist interpretation of Christ as Second Adam.[2] What was peculiarly Anabaptist in this interpretation was the conviction that the obedience of the Second Adam had, to a large extent, overcome the disastrous consequences of the disobedience of the first Adam. As a result of the obedience of Christ as Second Adam, the eternal salvation of all infants and imbeciles was assured. This view made infant baptism as a means of washing away the guilt of original sin not only unnecessary but even idolatrous. Williams has now identified additional sources for this motif in Anabaptist theology and has shown more clearly than the author was earlier able to do the uniqueness of the manner in which the Anabaptists applied the soteriological implications of Christ as the Second Adam to infants as well as to mature persons.

The analysis of Williams' presentation will show that this view, condemned as heretical by the Lutherans and denied as the official teaching of the church by the Roman Catholics, had widespread popular support among the common people,

---

1 See n. 2, p. 42 and pp. 53-56, above.
2 See pp. 204-205, above.

and was embraced by the Anabaptists as a major emphasis in their theology of redemption.[3]

Williams shows first how inextricably the Anabaptist practice of believer's baptism was bound up with their concept of Christ as the Second Adam and the Inaugurator of a new and universal kingdom, in which all ties to presently existing kingdoms would be dissolved. In order to do this, however, Williams also calls our attention to the fact that the continuation of the practice of pedobaptism was a problem throughout the Magisterial Reformation. The problem arose from the fact that "the proclamation of salvation by faith alone"[4] should theoretically have led to the abandonment of infant baptism and the inauguration of believer's baptism. But in this area theory and practice were not brought together for two reasons. First, the Reformers were not prepared to break "completely with ... tradition and postbiblical creed so long as these were not in patent contradiction to faith and the Scripture."[5] Second, in the nature of the situation in which the Reformers found themselves, infant baptism became "the most important link in and symbol of the continuity of the Church they were vigorously reforming but which they had no intention of dismantling or replacing."[6]

The Anabaptists, on the other hand, had no desire to continue the Constantinian synthesis of Church and State, since this was one of the surest marks of the "fall" of the Church. In their return to believer's baptism and in the martyr theology which they developed in support of this practice, "the threefold baptism in water, in the Spirit, and in *blood*," the ideal of

> the pre-Constantinian Church .. was never forgotten ... Baptism was never understood as an escape from the world but as the beginning of the confirmation of one's election as a subject of the imminent Kingdom which would bring the present aeon to an end.[7]

The Anabaptist movement was outlawed by imperial decree in 1529. With the publication of this decree believer's baptism became a crime punishable by death. When the Anabaptists, nevertheless, submitted to it, they were doing much more than flouting an existing civil law. Rather, as Williams says,

> by perpetrating the capital offense of submitting to believers' baptism, the Anabaptists signalized as by an oath their induction as subjects of a Kingdom yet to be established or vindicated. Yet like the early Christians, they recognized the divine authority of the magistrates even when they suffered at their hands. They did not hold the state to be demonic. They were even willing to grant it the authority of the covenantal state of old Israel. But *they* belonged to the universal Kingdom of Christ.[8]

This vivid sense of belonging to a coming universal Kingdom, even while continuing to love in the midst of an old order that was already dying, was again

---

3 See George H. Williams, "Sectarian Ecumenicity: Reflections on a Little Noticed Aspect of the Radical Reformation," *Review and Expositor*, LXIV, No. 2 (Spring, 1967), 141–60.
4 *Ibid.*, p. 142.
5 *Ibid.*
6 *Ibid.*
7 *Ibid.*, p. 145.
8 *Ibid.*, p. 146.

related to the presupposition of the solidarity of the human race in Adam and the provisional atonement of Christ as the Second Adam. During the classical patristic period Christ's death was viewed as the ransom to the devil. During the medieval period, under the influence of Anselm of Canterbury's *Cur Deus Homo*, the death of Christ was seen as "the sufficient sacrifice to satisfy the divine Majesty in his righteous governance of sinful mankind."[9]

The Anabaptists continued the same basic presuppositions as to the solidarity of the human race in Adam and its provisional redemption in Christ as Second Adam, but, as Williams says, with

> an extraordinary shift in the inherited structure of theology which subjected the received theories of the atonement to revision. The bulk of the radicals, without in most cases expressly denying original sin, disposed of it in their working theologies by postulating the potential salvation of all mankind by virtue of Christ's sacrifice in taking away the sins of the whole world and this without a child's knowing it or of a pagan's ever having heard about it.[10]

The medieval antecedents for such a view in *Theologia Deutsch* have already been discussed. Several more are in the article now under discussion but are not directly related to this study.[11] What is of interest is the fact that the origin of the Anabaptist view of the universality of Christ's work as Second Adam has now been more precisely located in what Williams calls "Magisterial Protestant analogues."[12]

We shall discuss first the analogue from Protestant Zurich. This appears in connection with Ulrich Zwingli's treatise on original sin in a document titled *De peccato originali.* In this document Zwingli set forth the certainty that " 'original sin cannot condemn infants of Christians' and that quite possibly 'the infants of the Gentiles' are likewise saved 'by the benefit of Christ,' also without baptism."[13]

Williams sees Zwingli's tract as the possible source of a similar conviction among the Swiss Brethren. He points out that when Zwingli under pressure from the Anabaptist separatist movement appealed to Heinrich Bullinger's view that pedobaptism under the new covenant was but the continuation of circumcision under the old, the Anabaptists nearly won the debate. The radicals struck back with an argument they had first learned from Zwingli when he was still their chief mentor. Not only were they rejecting the Zurich *Corpus Christianum*, of which pedobaptism remained the most important symbol, since it was at one and the same time a civic and an ecclesiastical rite. They were now accepting as

---

9 *Ibid.*
10 *Ibid.*
11 *Ibid.*, pp. 144–45.
12 *Ibid.*, p. 147. These analogues come indirectly from Lutheran Wittenberg and from Reformed Zurich. Though Williams discusses them in that order, we shall reverse the order in our presentation and discussion. The reason for this is that the analogue which comes indirectly from Wittenberg appears to us to have had the most far-reaching effect upon the Anabaptists in the way they reworked the inherited structure of the theology of the atonement.
13 *Ibid.*, p. 151.

undoubtedly true that Christ had effectually redeemed his elect without the sacramental infusion of grace in each individual recipient of the benefit of his work on Calvary. Following the surmise of Zwingli but without his stark predestinarianism, the Swiss Brethren asserted that the work of Christ as Second Adam, in taking from mankind the burden of the first Adam's guilt, was indeed applicable to the whole human race without the ceremony of infant baptism. Thus Christ as Restorer had made possible for all men everywhere the recovery and implementation of a free will which Adam lost in Paradise through voluntary disobedience. They maintained further that it was thus that God had truly fulfilled his promise to Abraham that in his seed all the nations of the earth would be blessed.[14]

The second analogue from the Magisterial Reformation, which serves as another possible source for the way in which the Anabaptists reworked the inherited theology of the atonement, arises out of a dispute between Lutherans and Roman Catholics at the time the Augsburg Confession was formulated in 1530. Spokesmen for the Lutheran party were the Lutheran pastor, Urbanus Rhegius, and the Lutheran theologian, Philip Melanchton. In the second part of this confession, states Williams, "the Evangelicals, cataloguing their grievances against the old Church for malpractice and faulty doctrine, asserted in connection with the Mass":

> There was added an opinion which increased private Masses infinitely: to wit, that Christ by his passion did satisfy for original sin, and appointed the Mass, whereby an oblation should be made for daily sins, both mortal and venial.[15]

While the Lutherans felt it necessary not only to repudiate the above view, but also "its corollary that 'the Mass is a work that taketh away the sins of the quick and the dead *ex opere operato*,' the Augsburg Evangelicals declared that 'the passion of Christ was an oblation and satisfaction, not only for original sin, but also for all other sins,' citing Hebrews 10:10, 14."[16]

Williams states that the Catholic theologians for their part were not only indignant at the accusation that this false teaching of the double sacrifice was the official teaching of the Roman Catholic Church, but also were at a loss to know the source of the Lutheran impressions that such was the case. Melanchton, after having read the *Confutatio* of the Catholics, obliged by citing the precise source of

---

14 *Ibid.*, p. 152. Whether or not Williams is correct in his opinion that Zwingli was the first teacher of the Swiss Brethren in the view set forth above, a very similar view is expressed by Conrad Grebel in his *Programmatic Letters of 1524*. Commenting to Thomas Müntzer on the fate of unbaptized children, Grebel wrote as follows: "On the basis of the following Scriptures we hold that all children who have not yet come to the discernment of the knowledge of good and evil, and who have not yet eaten of the tree of knowledge, are certainly saved through the suffering of Christ: Genesis 8, Deuteronomy 1, 30, 31, I Corinthians 14, Wisdom 12, I Peter 2, Romans 1, 2, 7, 10, Matthew 18, 19, Mark 9, 10. Christ is the New Adam who has restored their ruined life, for they would have been subject to death and damnation only if Christ had not died. Also, they have not yet grown up to the infirmity of our broken nature – unless indeed we could be shown that Christ did not suffer for the children!" See *Conrad Grebel's Programmatic Letters of 1524*. Transcribed and translated by John C. Wenger. (Scottdale, PA: Herald Press, 1970), p. 31.
15 *Ibid.*, p. 147.
16 *Ibid.*

"what Catholic 'opinion' the Evangelicals had in mind,"[17] as he revised his *Apologia Confessionis* of 1531.

The source was a spurious work of thirty-two chapters titled, *De venerabili sacramento altaris*, which appeared printed among the works of Thomas Aquinas, though it was not from his pen. The offending passage in which the double sacrifice is, indeed, suggested reads as follows:

> Ut sicut corpus Domini semel oblatum est in cruce pro debito originali, sic offeratur jugiter pro nostris quotidianis delectis in altari, et habeat in hoc Ecclesia munus ad placandum sibi Deum super omnia legis sacramenta vel sacrificia pretiosum et acceptum.[18]

It is the opinion of Williams that it was probably Urbanus Rhegius who called the attention of Melanchton to this passage. It was Rhegius who recalled in his *Materia cogitandi de Missae negocio*, published in Augsburg in 1528, that seventeen years earlier he had heard the double sacrifice view expounded as he studied under John Eck. And it was also Rhegius, as Williams notes, who in 1527 at the "Martyrs' Synod" in Augsburg had "argued against the claim of Hans Denck and Balthasar Hubmaier that freedom from sin was a possibility for Christians because of Christ's work."[19]

As we have already indicated, this view of the double sacrifice – the sacrifice of Christ on Calvary, making satisfaction for original sin, and the sacrifice of the Mass for daily sins – was condemned as heretical by Augsburg and denied as the official teaching by Rome. Rome further refined her denial that the double sacrifice was the official teaching of the Church in the refinement that the *Confutatio* was subjected to in Session XXII of the Council of Trent. Despite this condemnation by Protestants and the denial by Catholics, the view of the double sacrifice lived on in popular Catholic opinion. This "widespread popular Catholic assumption," says Williams, was taken over in due course by the Anabaptists,

> namely, that Christ took away the guilt of original sin from all mankind on Calvary but left even for the would-be saints the necessity of programmatic self-discipline and penitential austerity as the commuted and temporal form of the original eternal punishment.[20]

While the Lutherans regarded this teaching as negating the once-for-all character of the sacrifice on Calvary, and the Catholics felt that the Lutherans had perhaps even willfully misconstrued their teaching on original sin and the Eucharist, the Anabaptists, as Williams says,

> took over in a positive sense this popular (though now assailed and denied) assumption about Christ's work, holding that Christ has indeed accomplished – and without any sacramental mediation like pedobaptism – the restoration of all mankind to its prelapsarian state. Without denying the universal proclivity to sin despite Christ's work, the Anabaptists now assigned to confessional baptism the role which was hitherto supposed to be discharged by penance and the "Catholic" Mass, while in still Catholic categories they

---

17 *Ibid.*
18 *Ibid.*, p. 148. N. 10 on the same page cites extensive sources of the above quotation.
19 *Ibid.*
20 *Ibid.*, p. 150.

found sanction for strenuous post-penitential (post-baptismal) efforts to live, as behoved the redeemed saints, in suffering and austerity and self-discipline.[21]

How positive the sense in which the Anabaptists took over this assailed and denied though still popular assumption, as they subjected the received theories of the atonement to revision, will be best expressed in the words of Williams himself.

> The Anabaptists, without being fully conscious of all the moral, theological, and ecumenical implications of their daring and hazardous innovation, reaffirmed in a new idiom the covenantal headship of Christ (*capitanus, Hauptmann*) in the redemptive history of mankind; and, while maintaining the essential unity of mankind in the first and Second Adam, they reasserted the moral accountability of man everywhere and the freedom of his will to choose on some momentous day whom to serve in perfect freedom. By thus accenting the potential solidarity of mankind in the Second Adam, the Anabaptists had won essential ground for a more universal view of human history, a more responsible view of Christendom's stewardship of the Gospel, and possibly a more realistic view of man and of men, of sin and accountability, than the more broadly humanistic Zwingli and the more class-bound Luther. Confident that Christ, by his self-sacrificial and paradigmatic obedience and righteousness, had given fallen mankind a fresh start, the Anabaptists would appropriate with uncommon courage, energy, vision, and a sense of unencumbered spiritual mobility the command of Jesus in Mark 16:16f.: "Go into all the world and preach the gospel to the whole creation. He who believes and is baptized will be saved."[22]

The point of this entire discussion on the solidarity of the human race in Christ as the Second Adam is the far-reaching implication it has for modifications in that

21 *Ibid.*
22 *Ibid.*, p. 153. Williams cites Melchior Hoffmann as the Anabaptist leader who gave the fullest articulation to this "universalizing thrust in Anabaptism," as does this author above in Chap. II, pp. 53–56. In support of this conclusion Williams quotes the same Passage from Hoffmann's *On the Will in Bondage and Free*, as quoted above in Chap. II, p. 54. In order, however, that the reader may have the benefit of Williams' introductory comments, plus his translation of the same passage without the annoyance of having to turn back to an earlier chapter, both are given here in their entirety:
"Sometime Lutheran lay evangelist, forerunner of both the Münsterites and the Mennonites, Hofmann broke away from Luther's conception of the bondage of the will of fallen man and perceived the universal implication of the mighty act of God in Christ on Calvary. In his *On the Will in Bondage and Free* (c. 1531) Hoffmann explained the basis of his moral confidence and his ascription of moral accountability to every conscience. He interpreted the children of Israel in bondage to Pharaoh as paradigmatic of all mankind.
Only the liberating act of God made it possible for Israelites to depart from bondage in Egypt and in the wilderness of Sinai freely to choose to be loyal (or disloyal) to the covenant. By hermeneutical analogy Hofmann held that God's liberating act on Calvary was valid for the whole human race (not only for the elect), whether peoples in lands remote from Christendom (or even at its center) knew this to be true or not! They had long since been freed from bondage to the Pharaoh of world and self by the once-for-all act of redemptively obedient *justitia* of the Second Adam:
'God says to his Son: I will give to thee the heathen for an inheritance and the ends of the world for a possession... For, it is not a part of mankind that was given to Christ as Redeemer, as some suppose, but rather *all people* were given to him by his Father, *both the heathen and the Jews*, as God said elsewhere to the holy patriarch Abraham... He made man from the beginning, that is, he has "born" him again from out of the first death of Adam through his Word, Christ Jesus, unto life so that (John 8:36) man has become now a truly free creature.' " (See *BRN*, V, 188, 194 for original).

anthropology, which the Anabaptists had received from the Christian mystics of the earlier centuries. With the mystics, as we have seen in both Tauler and Gerson, the emphasis was upon an anthropological resource with soteriological possibilities, prior activity of which was the necessary precondition for the divine presence.

Whether or not the Anabaptists themselves were consciously aware of the implications of the universally liberating act of Christ as Second Adam for modifications in their mystical anthropology may be open to question. At least the most conscious thrust of this particular motif in Anabaptist theology, whether developed in Switzerland, South Germany, or Holland, was against the Magisterial position of predestination and bondage of the will. Yet the implications for rather major modifications within the mystical anthropology are certainly present in the Anabaptist view of Christ's universally redemptive act as Second Adam, whether the Anabaptists themselves were consciously aware of it or not.

These modifications would involve a minimizing of the importance of a region or faculty in human nature that was never implicated in the fall. The prior activity of this anthropological resource endowed with soteriological possibilities as the necessary precondition for the divine presence is, in large measure, shifted to the restorative power of Christ as the Second Adam. It is because of his cosmic renewal of the whole race that human beings once more have true freedom of the will rather than *alone* because of some region or faculty in human nature that was never implicated in the fall.

A further modification deriving from Christ's role as the Second Adam would be the elimination of a natural 'covenant' which played so large a role in the mystical theologies of Johannes Tauler and Jean Gerson. Nothing in Anabaptist theology even remotely resembles Tauler's natural 'covenant' which places God historically in humanity's debt. Nor is there a parallel in Anabaptist theology to Gerson's view of the necessity of a future resurrection.

The natural 'covenant' of mystical theology is thus replaced in Anabaptist theology with the supernatural cosmic renewal of Christ as the Second Adam. In this, God rather than humanity has the initiative. The cosmic renewal is seen as the fulfillment of a divine promise.

B. The Difference between Mystical and Anabaptist Anthropology: A Question of the Difference between Before and After

Anabaptists did, as Armour, Ozment, and Williams have each indicated, have an anthropology which led to the view that it was possible and even necessary for persons to prepare for grace *de congruo*. Only Ozment and Williams indicate, however, that this was due to the influence of the mystics upon the Anabaptists. Their work is thorough and they have presented their viewpoints convincingly. Nevertheless, the mystics and the Anabaptists differed vastly on where they placed the greatest emphasis.[23] With the mystics and their elaborate anatomies of

---

23 See Armour, *op. cit.*, pp. 34, 136; Ozment, *Mysticism and Dissent*, p. 3; Williams, *MQR*, XLVIII (July, 1974), 278.

the soul, almost the full weight of their emphasis fell upon the *prior* human activity which is the condition for the divine presence. The soteriological resource resident within the depths of human nature must first prepare the ground for the divine presence. "When the Holy Spirit finds that man has done his part, *then* He comes..."[24]

Among the Anabaptists, on the other hand, the emphasis falls much more heavily upon what the human being is able to do or know after the visitation of divine grace. In the Anabaptist view the experience of grace can mean that the believer through the activity of the Holy Spirit is made a participant in the divine nature. Or it can mean the partial restoration of fallen human nature. In either case, grace meant an ontological or metaphysical change within the person's own nature. To be sure, it must be conceded that the Anabaptist "homo spiritualis" was vastly different from his Lutheran cousin. The difference was due to this soteriological resource within human nature which had to be humanly activated in preparation for Christ. The Lutheran "homo spiritualis" had to depend upon *nititur fide* as a gift that was bestowed solely from without.

Yet the Anabaptist "homo spiritualis" was not simply a carbon copy of his mystical counterpart. Nothing in Anabaptist theology even remotely resembles the elaborate anatomies of the soul which Ozment has described in the anthropologies of Johannes Tauler and Jean Gerson. Compared with these elaborate designs to preserve a region or faculty in human nature that has retained soteriological capacities despite the fall, the Anabaptist effort to do the same thing becomes little more than an *anknüpfungspunkt*.

Even in the mystical theology of Hans Denck, whose mysticism is in many respects closer in spirit and "feeling tone" to that of Johannes Tauler than to any other representative of the Radical Reformation whose thought has been examined in this study, nothing is quite so crassly commercial as Tauler's "*gleich Kauff*" or "fair bargain policy." The abandonment of the love of the creaturely in Denck's theology is somewhat similar to Tauler's demand that the soul in order to achieve the ultimate goal of union with God, give nature its "walking papers." The difference is, however, that in Denck this possibility is seen as resident within the Word that dwells within us but is not of us, while Tauler sees it as resident within unaided human nature.

As for the remainder of the representatives of the Radical Reformation whose thought has provided the basis for this study, their emphasis falls even more strongly upon what human nature can do *after* the reception of divine grace through regeneration, rather than upon what unaided human nature must previously accomplish in preparation for grace. Balthasar Hubmaier's tripartite person, with the unfallen will of the unfallen spirit, was after all only half free until the fallen will of the fallen soul had been restored through regeneration and its lost capacity to distinguish between good and evil recovered. *Then*, but not *before*, the will of the spirit and the will of the soul together could make the flesh go, contrary to its nature, even into the fire.

Similarly, Pilgram Marbeck saw the person endowed with first or original grace

---

24 Ozment, *Homo Spiritualis*, p. 32.

as unable to accomplish anything through this anthropological resource other than to learn that in its depths human nature is sick and ill and in need of Christ, the Great Physician. He it is who can make persons whole through the grace of regeneration and genuine forgiveness of sins. According to Melchior Hoffmann, human nature has in the work of Christ as Second Adam once more been endowed with a will that has been given the freedom to make a real decision. Yet that freedom is not complete until the believer exercises it in the covenant of baptism, which is at the same time a betrothal to Christ, the Heavenly Bridegroom.[25]

Dirk Philips and Menno Simons made the Celestial Flesh Christology, which was carried to the Netherlands by Melchior Hoffmann, the very center of their theology of redemption. They did so by seeing salvation as a dynamic process of the divinization of human nature, and hence as a reversal of the process of the incarnation of God in Jesus Christ. The main emphasis in their theology of redemption is likewise on what the regenerate person can do *after* the reception of the new creature in Christ, rather than on what the natural or unregenerate person *must* do to prepare for this experience. Both Dirk and Menno were very firm in their conviction that if the new birth, mediated through the grace of regeneration in Christ as the Second Adam, did not take place, the result of the first birth out of the first Adam could be only sin, misery, and death. They were thus pessimistic about the capacities of unregenerate human nature to rise above the level of its fallenness, but optimistic about the regenerate person's ability to live in harmony with the nature of the new creature in Christ.

Furthermore, although their Celestial Flesh Christology and the way they related this to the New Testament image of the Church as the Bride of Christ[26] made both Dirk and Menno vulnerable to the pantheism which is so much a part of mysticism whether Christian or non-Christian, both took very conscious and deliberate steps to avoid this danger. Their theological formula with the precise use of prepositions, as William Keeney defines it, was developed with the express purpose of showing the difference between the source of the "humanity of Jesus" and "the source of the divine in regenerate man and the Church."[27] Just as Christ's humanity comes from God according to this formula, so also does his divinity. He is, therefore, divine by nature, but the divinity of the regenerate person is received or conferred through the new birth and, therefore, comes from beyond human nature. And even though both Dirk and Menno saw salvation as a process of divinization which would not be completed until the earthly pilgrim had arrived in the Heavenly City, Dirk especially was very careful to note that this process will not result in the elimination of the distinction between Creator and creature throughout all eternity.[28]

---

25 See Hoffmann's "The Ordinance of God," *SAW*, p. 187, and Armour, *op. cit.*, p. 99.
26 See Chap. IV, Pp. 92–93, above
27 William E. Keeney, *The Development of Dutch Anabaptist Thought and Practice from 1539–1564* (Nieuwkoop: B. De Graaf, 1968), Appendix II, p. 207, and "The Incarnation, A Central Theological Concept" by the same author in *A Legacy of Faith*, ed. Cornelius J. Dyck (Newton, KS: Faith and Life Press, 1962), pp. 55–68.
28 See Chap. III, p. 73, above.

The claim made above is not that the similarity between the Anabaptists and the mystics implies the *conscious* dependence of the former upon the latter at every point. It may very well be, as William Keeney has suggested, "that for the most part [the Anabaptists] arrive at their position independently of Protestants, Roman Catholic scholastics, or mystics through their attempt to put their religious questions to the Scriptures directly."[29]

However, the Scriptures are never approached by any individual or group in a cultural vacuum. What we find in the Scriptures is always colored, at least to some extent, by the cultural presuppositions which we bring to them. Mysticism was abroad in the culture in which the Anabaptists lived. Klaassen and Krahn have both noted that some of the Anabaptists in the Netherlands were directly influenced by the mystical tradition of the Brethren of the Common Life.[30] Klaassen has noted that one of the peculiar features of mysticism was that

> it developed a broad view of God's activity and of the human knowledge about God which went beyond the borders of the church. It allowed that God spoke to man in a variety of ways and that the Bible and the church were only two ways among others. It insisted that pagans, Jews and Moslems had knowledge of God by the direct presence of God in their souls.[31]

Williams has pointed out that such a view was widespread among the Anabaptists, who, despite their more restricted view of the membership of the true Church, manifested surprising ecumenical concerns. He discusses these concerns under the titles of "The Eternal Sacrifice of Christ," "The Gospel of All Creatures," "The Universal Company of the Elect Friends of God," and "The Redemptive Descent of Christ into Hell."[32]

In all of these examples the Anabaptists expressed their concern for the salvation of pious persons who were not only outside the membership of their disciplined congregations but outside the entire Christian tradition as well. The Anabaptists also expressed their conviction that such persons could be saved through these extra-biblical and extra-ecclesiastical means.

J. A. Oosterbaan has noted a similar emphasis in the thought of Menno Simons without attributing it, however, in any way to the influence of mysticism. In Oosterbaan's view Menno arrived at this position through his emphasis upon the sovereign freedom of God's grace.[33] Oosterbaan has thus shown that it is possible to interpret the ecumenical concerns of the Anabaptists without any reference to the influence of mysticism upon them. The article by Williams, however, makes it appear highly unlikely that where these ecumenical concerns are present among the Anabaptists, the influence of mysticism is totally absent.

---

29 William Keeney, in a personal letter to the author, dated Nov. 22, 1975.
30 Walter Klaassen, *op. cit.*, p. 67, and Cornelius Krahn, *Dutch Anabaptism: Origin, Spread, Life and Thought (1450–1600)* (The Hague: Martinus Nijhoff, 1968), pp. 21–25.
31 Walter Klaassen, *op. cit.*, p. 67.
32 Williams, *Review and Expositor*, LXIV (Spring, 1967), 154–58.
33 J. A. Oosterbaan, "Grace in Dutch Mennonite Theology," *A Legacy of Faith*, pp. 55–68.

III. THE CHURCH ON EARTH AS THE PARTIAL
REALIZATION OF PARADISE REGAINED

Armour came to the conclusion in his *Anabaptist Baptism* that the doctrine of regeneration was a key to Anabaptism.[34] Since his study is devoted to the discernment of the theological basis for believer's baptism in Anabaptist thought, the following quotation may serve as a summary of his conclusion:

> However, they were at one in saying that the only legitimate basis for receiving baptism and entering the baptismal covenant was the experience of regeneration within, a regeneration which gave the believer power to make a valid confession of faith and to keep the commands of Christ under the watchful eve of a disciplining church.[35]

It would be equally legitimate to see regeneration as the key to the Anabaptist view of the Church. And the Church on earth is, therefore, already in some measure the beginning of Paradise Regained. In the Hutterite community the abolishment of the ownership of private property is at least a partial return to the original Eden, where no private property existed. Hubmaier's disciplined congregation had the "power of the keys," because in the regenerate members the capacity to distinguish between good and evil had been restored. This was the very faculty, which according to Hubmaier had been lost through the fall. Though Pilgram Marbeck postponed complete regeneration to the time of the future life, it is only those in whom regeneration had already begun to take place who were qualified to be enrolled in the Church as members of Christ's suffering body on earth. For the Dutch Anabaptists the Church was that fellowship of "holy beings," who because of the new birth and the new creature in Christ, which this birth engendered within the believer,

> was a spiritual fellowship of believers who were united with one another and Christ was the meeting point of the divine and human, the eternal and temporal. This was the Kingdom of Heaven to the degree that it was possible of fulfillment on earth, and by men who were still assailed by the weakness of the Adamic nature, even though already granted the divine nature.[36]

The doctrine of regeneration carried within itself the implication that the Church was already in some degree Paradise Regained though still on earth. This explains why the Anabaptists had such a strong sense of transition from the Old to the New as they enrolled in their "Believer's Only" congregations. Ruether has caught something of the excitement the Anabaptists themselves must have felt as they risked their lives by submitting to the capital offense of believer's baptism.

> To join the church is to separate out from the world and to stand as the avant-garde of a new world that is being founded by God in the midst of the old world that is dying. Believer's baptism is the sign that the Christian has forsaken this dying world and the

---

34 See Armour, *op. cit.*, p. 135.
35 *Ibid.* The "however" in the above quotation refers to the different ways in time and manner in which the four representatives of the Anabaptist movement considered in Armour's study understood regeneration as taking place.
36 Keeney, ... *Dutch Anabaptist Thought and Practice* ..., p. 155.

whole principle of existence on which it is founded, and has entered the new creation and principle of existence that is being built up as the old order dies. This new order subsists within the present era as a hostile and antagonistic beachhead of a new and coming world, which will soon take over completely as the messianic community of the New Heaven and Earth which is to be openly manifest with the return of the victorious Christ.[37]

IV. ANABAPTIST PACIFISM: STRATEGY FOR SURVIVAL OR PRINCIPLE OF CHRISTIAN EXISTENCE?

According to James M. Stayer in his recent book, *Anabaptists and the Sword*, Anabaptist pacifism emerged in the process of what could well be called the development of a strategy for survival in a hostile environment rather than as a principle of Christian existence. Stayer argues that the Anabaptists "seemed to oscillate between the polar antitheses of pacifism and revolution in their early history," but that at the same time they "were only tangentially concerned with revolution and pacifism as theoretical issues. They were wrestling rather with the ethics of coercion and they called the theme about which they were thinking the teaching on the Sword."[38]

Stayer holds further that the Anabaptists shared with the non-radical Reformers the rejection of the medieval papalist doctrine of the Two Swords, based upon Luke 22:38, in which two powers, the civil *regnum* and the ecclesiastical *sacerdotium*, each had its own realm of coercive jurisdiction. In sixteenth-century Germany, says Stayer, the Lukan text was rejected in favor of Romans 13:4, which was interpreted to mean that only the civil or temporal *regnum* or *Obrigkeit* had the legitimate right of coercive jurisdiction.[39]

Although the language of both radical and non-radical Reformers with respect to the sword may sound strange in the ears of twentieth-century persons to whom the distinction between the public and the private spheres is common, Stayer argues that "the Anabaptists and the Reformers of the sixteenth century struggled with a problem that has perennial human significance, even for persons who do not share their Christianity. The issue is the relation of force and ethical values."[40]

Stayer then identified what he calls "four points on the compass of this issue."[41] These may be summarized as follows:

---

37 Ruether, *op. cit.*, p. 24.
38 James M. Stayer, *Anabaptists and the Sword* (Lawrence, KS: Coronado Press, 1972), p. 1. Dr. Stayer has been kind enough to grant me permission to quote from his book even though he maintains that my phrase "strategy for survival" would make the Anabaptists guilty of a calculation and theological insincerity which he would never attribute to them. I wish to make it clear that I do not charge Stayer of accusing the Anabaptists of either calculation or theological insincerity. I simply maintain that my term "strategy for survival" is from my perspective a not unfair description of his interpretation of the manner in which the Anabaptists arrived at their pacifist position.
39 *Ibid.*
40 *Ibid.*, p. 2.
41 *Ibid.*

1. The "crusading" standpoint, which may become revolutionary when the persons holding it are out of power.

2. The "realpolitical" approach, which sees that no value remains unperverted when imposed by force, but maintains it is better to use whatever force necessary than to live in a society that is value free.

3. The "apolitical moderate," which sees no possibility of force ever achieving any ethical goals and yet sees an "ordered" society as the necessary precondition for the achievement of any ethical values. This position, therefore, accepts the necessity of using whatever coercion may be necessary to cement politics, but is without the illusion that such coercion can ever be anything more than ethically neutral.

4. A "radical apoliticism," which denies that there can be any ethically neutral coercion among human beings. It asserts that to exercise force is to corrupt oneself and make impossible any achievement of true worth."[42]

Stayer maintains that the Anabaptist teaching on the *Sword* touched virtually all four points on this compass before finally coming to terms with the "radical apolitical" stance. He thus, in my opinion, makes of Anabaptist pacifism a strategy for survival rather than a principle of Christian existence. According to Stayer, the Swiss Brethren were at first "crusading and realpolitical" people who were called to "radical apoliticism" only by the Schleitheim Confession. The Dutch Anabaptists, he maintains, had to be recalled from the revolutionary crusading position of the Münsterites to "radical apoliticism" by Menno Simons. Balthasar Hubmaier, who was not a pacifist but did renounce the use of coercion in matters of faith, is the model which Stayer finds least typical of the Anabaptist teaching on the *Sword*.[43]

Stayer designates himself as "a profane historian with a liberal perspective." He believes that from this vantage point he will be better able to discern what the Anabaptist teaching on the *Sword* really was, because he will approach it from the angle of intellectual history rather than that of theology.[44]

Stayer is justly critical of contemporary American Mennonite scholars who have approached Anabaptist studies with a bias which led them to eliminate from the Anabaptist movement any person or doctrine not in doctrinal uniformity with the contemporary Mennonite Church. The criticism is more than justified when because of this bias men like Balthasar Hubmaier and Melchior Hoffmann are excluded from the Anabaptist movement, the former because he was not a pacifist, and the latter because his chiliastic ideas contributed to the tragedy of Münster – indirectly, however.[45] Yet a "profane historian with a liberal

---

42 *Ibid.*, p. 3. The "four points on the compass" summarize Stayer with the material in quotation marks taken directly from his writings. He does not examine a fifth, that of the anarchist, because he says it did not occur within the sixteenth-century situation.
43 See *Ibid.*, pp. 22, 93–131, and 211–38.
44 *Ibid.*, p. 6.
45 *Ibid.*, pp. 9–14. The criticism, which is rather severe, is directed against John Horsch and Harold S. Bender. Though Stayer sees younger American Mennonite Anabaptist scholars with "more refined professional training" on the horizon, he laments that they work still under the influence of Bender's premise that a so-called Evangelical Anabaptism with Biblical non-resis-

perspective" is not without his own bias. He may, indeed, be able to discern some motifs from his bias or perspective which would be obscured for the Christian theologian because of his theological bias. But by the same logic the secular historian will also be unable to see some of the motifs which are open to the Christian theologian precisely because of his particular bias.

This is why Stayer does not understand that Anabaptist pacifism, or as he would prefer to call it "radical apoliticism," emerged among the Swiss Brethren, in the South German Anabaptist circles, and among the Dutch Anabaptists as a principle of Christian existence rather than as a strategy for survival which was tried only as a last resort after other methods had failed.

Stayer's view that the Swiss Brethren came to the "radical apoliticism" represented in the *Programmatic Letters of 1524* in a gradual way no doubt has a great deal of validity. However, the view that the pacifism found among the Brethren at an earlier date was entirely dependent on Erasmus is open to question. John Howard Yoder has shown that a central Anabaptist hermeneutical principle, by means of which the Old Testament was subordinated to the New, was already present among the Zurich radicals prior to 1524, although its precise origin has yet to be traced.[46]

It may be, therefore, that it was in the Bible study circles, meeting in private homes, that the Brethren tapped the spiritual resources which enabled them to respond to the Zurich Council's rejection of their proposals for more radical reform in a nonviolent rather than a violent manner. The Council's response to the independent radical reformation of the dissenters was the edict of November 19, 1526. The fact that the edict made drowning the means of exacting the death penalty was a cruel and deliberate irony. The waters of rebaptism were now to become the waters of execution.

The Brethren had reason to hope, on the basis of Zwingli's earlier leadership, that the Council's final response to their appeals for a more radical reformation in Zurich would be more positive than the one which they received. The edict of November 19, 1526, however, seems not to have caught them by surprise. That they would eventually have to suffer for their faith Grebel had predicted as early as 1524 when he wrote to Thomas Müntzer:

---

tance at its center began with the Swiss Brethren in Zurich. European Anabaptist scholars, he thinks, have more fully freed themselves of Bender's premise that Evangelical Anabaptism began with the Swiss Brethren and early became normative for the whole sweep of the Anabaptist movement.

46 John Howard Yoder, "The Hermeneutics of the Anabaptists," *MQR*, XLI, No. 4 (October, 1967), 306–308. The above conclusion may have to be revised if, as Kenneth R. Davis maintains, Erasmus is the real progenitor of Anabaptist theology and piety, and Anabaptism is better understood as a radicalization of Erasmus than a radicalization of Luther. In that case Erasmus does become the possible source of the Anabaptist insistence that a way or ways must be found to subordinate the Old Testament to the New. See Kenneth R. Davis, "Erasmus as Progenitor of Anabaptist Theology and Piety," *MQR*, XLVII, No. 3 (July, 1973), 163–78.

> Our shepherds are so furious and enraged against us that they rail at us from the pulpit, calling us boys and Satans [disguised as] angels of light. We will also, in the course of time, see persecution come upon us through them.[47]

Despite this anticipated suffering, the *Letters* advocate neither violence to ward off their own suffering nor a reduction of their demands for reform in order to avoid it. Rather they clearly enunciated what was to become another central principle of Anabaptism, namely, that in this world the true Church will always be a suffering Church.

> True believing Christians are sheep among wolves, sheep for the slaughter. They must be baptized in anxiety, distress, affliction, persecution, suffering, and death. They must pass through the probation of fire, and reach the Fatherland of eternal rest, not by slaying their bodily [enemies] but by mortifying their spiritual enemies.[48]

That Grebel and Mantz should have been at such pains to communicate these views to Thomas Müntzer, and yet had made no effort to communicate them to their colleagues in Zurich, as Stayer implies, does not seem plausible.

The fact that Balthasar Hubmaier continued to hold the "realpolitical" position of the Reformers, in general, does not so much indicate the failure of Grebel and Mantz to make their "radical apoliticism" known to him as it does Hubmaier's rejection of their basic position.

Hubmaier's involvement with the Zurich radicals prior to their open break with Zwingli and the city council was at best marginal. Even so, the Brethren made an effort to inform Hubmaier, who was then in Waldshut, of the latest developments in Zurich.

Yoder has noted that on five separate occasions Hubmaier was either directly or indirectly involved in events within the city of Zurich before he arrived there as a refugee from Waldshut in early December of 1525. The first of these was late October of 1523, when Hubmaier at Grebel's request took part in the Second Disputation in Zurich and

> spoke against certain abuses in the observance of the Mass (Latin Language, withholding the cup), but he showed no interest in the problem raised by Grebel and Simon Stumpf, that of the proper procedure and authority for carrying out the reformation.[49]

The second occasion was the publication of Hubmaier's *Theses Against John Eck* in late October of 1523, in which he designated himself as "a brother of Ulrich Zwingli."[50] The third concerned a letter which bears no date, but Yoder estimated that it was written late in 1524. In this letter Hubmaier "repeated an earlier request that Zwingli respond 'for God's sake' to his questions on baptism."[51] The fourth occasion involved Hubmaier's letter to Johannes

---

47 *Conrad Grebel's Programmatic Letters of 1524*, p. 41.
48 *Ibid.*, p. 29.
49 John Howard Yoder, "Balthasar Hubmaier and the Beginnings of Swiss Anabaptism," *MQR*, XXXIII, No. 1 (January, 1959), 5–6.
50 *Ibid.*, p. 6.
51 *Ibid.*

Oecolampadius in January of 1525. In this letter Hubmaier informed the Basel reformer that he had come to doubt the rightness of infant baptism, though he "was still willing to baptize infants if their parents were so weak in the faith as to request it."[52] What involved Hubmaier with Zurich in this letter addressed to the Basel reformer is that Hubmaier's arguments against infant baptism were so convincing that Oecolampadius wrote to Zwingli for assistance in refuting them.

The fifth occasion, and for our purposes in this study the most important one, was Hubmaier's publication of his *Public Challenge to All Christian Believers* on February 2, 1525. As Yoder states, the pamphlet or tract was an invitation to a disputation on baptism, which Hubmaier assumed would be held in Waldshut. Yoder's analysis of Hubmaier's opportunity to become aware of the "radical apoliticism" of the Zurich radicals is an effective refutation of Stayer's view that no attempt had been made to communicate their position to Hubmaier. He writes:

> Though convinced "that infant baptism is a work without any foundation in the Divine Word," Hubmaier had not yet come to the corollary of believers' baptism, even though the first baptisms in Zurich had taken place two weeks earlier. Hubmaier was not ignorant of the events in Zurich; he had been visited late in January by some of the Zurich leaders, presumably Reublin, Grebel, and Brötli. This indicates that in full awareness of the issues involved, Hubmaier had refused to join the Brethren. He had not made with them the long pilgrimage in which they had been engaged since 1523. The rejection of state authority in matters of faith (October-December, 1523), the understanding that the true Church must be a persecuted minority (spring and summer of 1524), the rejection of Thomas Müntzer's gospel of revolution (September, 1524), and the repeated unsuccessful attempts to carry on a conversation with Zwingli (ending in mid-December, 1524) had all gone on outside the realm of his interest and knowledge. This difference of orientation remained significant even after he finally had accepted believer's baptism. Precisely because he came to the problem of baptism as a trained thinker dealing with a theological problem as such, he was ever to remain distinct in his emphasis from the Swiss Brethren, for whom believers' baptism was only one expression of a whole new way of understanding faith and the church."[53]

This difference in orientation, not the failure of the Brethren to make an attempt to share their "radical apolitical" views with Hubmaier, accounts for the fact that he took the "real-political" position. Although Hubmaier referred to the Zurich radicals as his "fellows in persecution" and as "righteous people"[54] after his arrival in Nicolsburg, he never really joined their company.

> Until his death he continued to follow the Reformers rather than the Brethren in letting the state be master in its own home even if it demanded of Christians that they disobey biblical injunctions (oath, armed defense, interest, defense of the property structure), as well as when it chose to reform the church. That the state which affirms its gracious willingness to reform the church thereby also lays claim to a right to direct, brake, or even halt and reverse the Reformation, is a truth which had become part of the basic spiritual orientation of the Zurich Brethren by 1523, even before baptism became any issue, but which Hubmaier never learned.[55]

52 *Ibid.*
53 *Ibid.*, pp. 6–7.
54 *Ibid.*, p. 17.
55 *Ibid.*

The "radical apoliticism" of the Schleitheim Confession was thus present among the Swiss Brethren well before the Confession itself was written. Schleitheim no doubt helped to solidify a position that had growing acceptance from 1523 onward. But to see Schleitheim itself as breaking completely new ground among the Brethren, except for Grebel and Mantz, is to ignore both the *preparation* for Schleitheim, which these leaders had made among the Brethren prior to their deaths, and the ready acceptance of "radical apoliticism" by the Swiss Brethren after Schleitheim. That a few Swiss Brethren pastors should have defected under the threat of persecution is not surprising. The defections of the few, however, cannot be regarded as the norm for the many. Stayer himself admits that it is not clear "that the peasant protectors of the Brethren ministers were themselves Swiss Brethren."[56]

Moreover, the Schleitheim Confession does not imply hatred of the world, as Stayer maintains, but simply the Anabaptist concept of the Two Kingdoms. Within the framework of this concept Anabaptists did not consider the state to be demonic even when it persecuted them but rather provisional. Their ultimate allegiance belonged not to the present temporal order but to the coming universal Kingdom of Christ.[57] Perhaps it is Stayer's bias as a "profane historian" that prevents him either seeing the Anabaptist idea of the Two Kingdoms or of having any sympathy for it.

Nor, in my opinion, is Stayer correct in his view that Pilgram Marbeck and the South German Anabaptists, in general, had a more positive attitude toward the state than the one implied in the Schleitheim Confession. Michael Sattler at his trial did not dispute either the right or the authority of the judges to rule in civil matters. They were simply not competent to judge the affairs of the Kingdom of Christ.[58] This does not imply hatred of the world but rather the persistent Anabaptist idea of Two Kingdoms — the one provisional, the other ultimate — which Stayer because of his secular orientation does not consider decisive.

Pilgram Marbeck was speaking in support of this same concept when he recognized not only the right of the civil authorities of Strasbourg to expel him from the city but also his own right and duty to return to the city in the event that the Holy Spirit should lead him to do so, even though his banishment had not been revoked.[59] The same principle is applicable when Marbeck concedes, on the one hand, the necessity and even the divinely ordained right and duty of the *Obrigkeit* to wield the sword but, on the other hand, questions the possibility of the Christian as a *gelassener mensch* serving in the *Obrigkeit*.[60]

As for the influence of Melchior Hoffmann and the Melchiorites at Münster or afterward, we have conceded that too many American Anabaptist scholars have been reluctant to admit any connection between Hoffmann, the Melchiorites,

---

56 Stayer, *op. cit.*, p. 111.
57 Williams, *Review and Expositor*, LXIV (Spring, 1967), 146.
58 See George H. Williams, *The Radical Reformation* (Philadelphia: The Westminster Press, 1962), p. 186.
59   See Chap. VI, p. 163, above. See also my article, "A Case Study in Civil Disobedience," *Mennonite Life,* XXV, No. 1, (January, 1970), 12–14.
60 See Chap. VI, p. 160, above, and Stayer, *Op. Cit.*, p. 183.

Münster, and the Dutch Anabaptists. But that deficiency has now been overcome by Cornelius Krahn in his *Dutch Anabaptism*.[61]

However, Stayer's claim that Münster and the events that followed amounted to a complete repudiation of the "radical apoliticism" of Melchior Hoffmann, to which the Dutch Anabaptists had to be recalled by Menno Simons, overlooks two important facts. The first is the transformation of Münster from a Catholic to a Protestant city under the theological leadership of Bernhard Rothmann and his sympathetic political support by the guildsmen well before the arrival of the Melchiorite emissaries in the city. The ensuing ferment in the struggle between Catholics and Protestants for control of the city, and the economic unrest among the peasants beyond it, made Münster a fertile field for the chiliastic ideas of Hoffmann as they were transmitted and distorted to the populace by John of Leiden and other Melchiorites. In fact, it was this ferment in Münster that drew these men to this city rather than to Strasbourg as the probable site of the New Jerusalem.[62]

While Hoffmann may be faulted for not sending messages from his prison cell in Strasbourg in an attempt to curb the abuses at Münster, if, as Stayer maintains, he had opportunity to do so, it remains doubtful that this advice would have been heeded had it arrived. He who withstood Hoffmann to his face on the issue of the *Stillstand* would scarcely have been likely to submit to Hoffmann's advice in his absence.[63] There is thus no firm evidence beyond Hoffmann's silence in the face of the unsavory event at Münster that he himself ever departed from his peaceful chiliasm or "radical apoliticism."

The second fact which Stayer overlooks is that the internal history of Dutch Anabaptism itself does not support his view that all the Dutch Anabaptists had gone whoring, as it were, after the violent revolutionary ways of Münster and hence had to be recalled to "radical apoliticism" by Menno Simons. Whence came that small group of peaceful disciples who abhorred not only the abomination of Münster but also the abomination of established Christendom and implored Menno to become their shepherd, if, as Stayer maintains, the whole of Dutch Anabaptism turned to violence after Münster?[64] The testimony of Obbe Philips that he alone resisted the extremists, to which Stayer appeals in support of his view, is reminiscent of the complaint of Elijah that he was the only person left in Israel who had not bowed the knee to Baal, but Elijah like Obbe was mistaken,[65] as the story of Jacob van Campen, Anabaptist bishop of Amsterdam, reveals. Although Van Campen entered the Anabaptist movement as one of the apostles of Jan Mathis sent out from Haarlem, efforts to win him to the revolutionary violence of Münster proved fruitless. Not only did Van Campen refuse to participate in violence himself but sent out twelve letters to the Amsterdam Anabaptists urging them to do likewise.

---

61 See Krahn, *op. cit.*, pp. 80–164.
62 See Williams, *The Radical Reformation*, pp. 362–81.
63 *Ibid.*, p. 357.
64 Menno Simons, *Reply to Gellius Faber*, 1554, *CWMS*, p. 671.
65 See I Kings 19:9–18 and Stayer, *op. cit.*, pp. 211–328.

Jacob van Campen arrived in Amsterdam in May of 1534 and devoted his energies to preaching and baptizing rather than to the promoting of violent revolution. He was opposed to the use of weapons, save in the cause of self-defense. When the Amsterdam Anabaptists vigorously debated the hermeneutical question whether Scripture should be interpreted according to the principle of the single or the cloven hoof, Van Campen argued for the latter position. His intention, like that of Dirk Philips, was to find a consistent method of subordinating the Old Testament to the New. The failure to develop such a method was one of the factors contributing to the tragedy of Münster.

Jacob van Campen's reward for his refusal to resort to violence and his exhortation to others to do likewise was his own violent death. He was burned at the stake on July 10, 1535.[66] Yet it is highly probable that the peaceful remnant imploring Menno a year later to lead them had earlier been led by Van Campen.

Finally, Stayer does not take into account the fact that after Münster and well before Schleitheim all major Anabaptist groups self-consciously and deliberately developed a clearly Christo-centric hermeneutic. Both in the Netherlands and in South Germany within the Marbeck circle this hermeneutic involved a method of subordinating the Old Testament to the New without the Marcionite heresy of discarding the Old Testament as Christian Scripture. In the Netherlands this hermeneutical method was developed by Dirk Philips in his *Spiritual Restitution*. This was one Dutch Anabaptist response to the Münsterite episode. In South Germany a similar hermeneutic was developed by Pilgram Marbeck in his controversy with Caspar Schwenckfeld. But whether it is Dirk Philips writing his *Spiritual Restitution* or Pilgram Marbeck writing his *Testamentserläuterung*, the Epistle to the Hebrews serves as a model in both cases to stress the fact that from the Anabaptist point of view the New Testament was newer and better than the Old and the commands and example of Christ more binding upon the Christian disciple than those of Moses and Joshua. It was this Christocentric hermeneutic which led to separatist nonresistance in an obedience, if need be, that led "even unto death." Anabaptist pacifism thus becomes a principle of Christian existence rather than a strategy for survival.[67]

---

66 *Verhooren en Vonnissen der Wederdoopers, Betrokken bij de de Aanslagen op Amsterdam in 1534 en 1535*, medegedeeld door Mej. G. Grosheide. This book, which is in the Mennonite Historical Library of Eastern Mennonite College and Seminary, has no name of publisher or date of publication.
67 For a fuller discussion of the above issues see Chaps. V and VI, above, as well as the following authors: William Klassen, *op. cit.*, especially Chap. III, "Marpeck's Use of the Old Testament," giving particular attention to Sec. 4, "The Decisiveness of the 'Life of Christ' "; Keeney, ... *Dutch Mennonite Thought and Practice* ..., Chap. II, "The Word of God and Servants of the Word," Sec. A (1), "The Old Testament and the New Testament"; and Henry Poettcker, "Menno Simons' View of the Bible as Authority" in *A Legacy of Faith*. All three authors point out the importance of a Christo-centric hermeneutic as a foundation for separatist nonresistance or to use Stayer's term, "radical apoliticism."

V. CONCLUSION

The concept of grace which prevailed within the continental Magisterial Reformation was inseparably linked with double predestination and the bondage of the will. Double predestination was, in fact, the solution to the problem posed by the bondage of the will. Within this frame of reference grace from God's side was regarded as God's act of forensic justification wherein the righteousness of the Christian becomes the imputed righteousness of Christ. Where grace is understood in this manner, spiritual health or wholeness is not something that becomes possible within this world. The Christian is throughout life both justified and sinner. He stumbles through this life as one who is half ill, though also as one who has the promise that eventually he will be well. Yet the promise of health is not health itself.

Luther and Calvin were in essential agreement on this forensic view of grace as expressed in the formula, *simul iustus et peccator*. The Magisterial Reformers arrived at their concept of grace by reading Paul through the eyes of Augustine. So understood, justification by grace through faith means a change in status before God, who for Christ's sake regards the sinner as righteous. It does not mean that within this life there is an ontological or metaphysical change within the believer himself.

Among the Radical Reformers, on the other hand, there is found an outright and resolute rejection of the doctrine of double predestination and its corollary, the bondage of the will. The Radical Reformers rejected the doctrine of double predestination and the anthropology of the bondage of the will, not only because they saw that the first, pushed to its ultimate logical conclusion, would make God the mediate or the immediate source of sin, and the second would serve as a screen behind which human beings could evade responsibility for their own moral behavior. At a deeper level the Radicals rejected both these positions because of the influence of the Christian mystics of the two previous centuries upon their anthropology. Like these mystics, they saw human nature as retaining some region or faculty even after the fall that was not vitiated by original sin. Because of this faculty the possibility of preparing the ground of the soul for the coming of God's grace exists within human nature. The exercise of this anthropologically-based soteriological resource was, with the mystics, made a prior condition for the reception of divine grace.

Luther at first followed the lead of the mystics in this respect but later transferred the work of the anthropological resource known as the *gemuete* or *synteresis* to the work of the Holy Spirit. Because the Anabaptists retained the mystical heritage which Luther discarded, the question must be raised whether Anabaptism was more the revival of mysticism than the radicalization of classical Protestantism with the emphasis on discipleship being merely the logical extension of the Protestant emphasis on justification by grace through faith.

Compared with the elaborate anatomies of the soul found within the theologies of the Christian mystics, however, the anthropologically-based soteriological resource within Anabaptism was little more than an *anknüpfungspunkt*. The Anabaptists emphasized far more what the Christian believer can do *after* being made a participant in the divine nature through the activity of the Holy Spirit in the experience of regeneration than they emphasized what *must* be done as a prior condition for the coming of divine grace.

Where the Magisterial Reformers read Paul through the eyes of Augustine, the Radical Reformers reached back beyond Paul to the Gospels. Among the Gospels they had a preference for the Gospel of John, and this was often read through the eyes of the Christian mystics of the preceding century. Five of the seven representatives of the Radical Reformation included in this study state specifically that their concept of salvation is that of the divinization of man, which is also true of the fourth Gospel and of the Johannine epistles. The concept of grace which prevailed within the Radical Reformation was consequently colored by this concept of salvation. Thus, grace is for the Radical Reformers not so much a forensic change in status before God as it is an ontological change within the believer himself. Grace is God's act of regeneration whereby he renews the divine image in man and through the Holy Spirit makes the believer an actual participant in the divine nature itself.

The Radical Reformers did not think that this grace could be earned through any meritorious work. It came as a sheer gift from God. Yet once received, the gift of grace so understood did enable one to rise higher in the scale of Christian perfection than was generally thought possible where the forensic concept of grace prevailed. Even Balthasar Hubmaier and Pilgram Marbeck, the two men included in this study who did not make the Johannine concept of salvation explicitly their own, still stressed grace as that act of God which brings about an ontological change within the believer more than they stressed the act of forensic justification which brings about a change in status before God.

There was present also throughout the Radical Reformation <u>a rudimentary doctrine of natural law</u>, which was sometimes referred to as a first grace. <u>The break between nature and grace was thus not as abrupt for them as it was for either Luther or Calvin</u>. The emphasis upon good works as the fruit of grace in the Radical Reformation led to the accusation of "work's righteousness" from the Magisterial Reformers. On the other hand, the emphasis upon forensic justification by the Magisterial side often led the Radicals to denounce them as peddlers of "cheap grace." That the two sides of the Reformation were in effect working with two different concepts of grace evidently was not clear to the participants in the struggle of the sixteenth century.

Viewed synoptically and according to the chronological age of the person from the cradle to the grave, grace in Radical Reformation thought is, indeed, a complex and many-sided concept. With regard to infants or young children and their freedom from the stain and guilt of original sin, grace was largely soteriologically based upon what might well be called a forensic view of the atonement which was believed to be universally efficacious, so that no child of believer or unbeliever was damned because of Adam's sin. What remained of original sin in the infant or the child was, for Christ's sake, not imputed as sin until the child reached the age of responsibility. Texts which were frequently quoted in support of this forensic and universal view of grace by the Anabaptists, in both South

Germany and in the Netherlands, included such widely divergent passages as Genesis 22:18 and John 1:29b.

While the base of this universal grace was largely soteriological, it was also to a limited extent anthropological. Both in South Germany and in the Netherlands Anabaptist leaders maintained that Christ would not have set little children before men as an example which they should follow, if he had not seen something innately good in them. In the thought of Pilgram Marbeck the anthropological and the soteriological graces are both available to children until they reach the age of responsibility. Through the universal grace which Christ has won for children through his forensic atonement they are again in the state of innocence, which Adam and Eve enjoyed before the fall. At the same time, because they were potentially in Adam when he sinned and when he received the promise of redemption, children have inherited not only original sin but also the *lux naturalis* as the opposite and positive side of original sin. As the child grows to maturity, the innocence won by Christ through the atonement dies off, and he must come to Christ through his own faith, while the *lux naturalis* remains throughout life and is the necessary precondition to lead men to faith in Christ. The Scriptural support for grace, as viewed from its anthropological side, was found by Marbeck in Romans 1 and 2 and in Ecclesiastes 13. The significance of this dual aspect of the concept of grace is that it includes a doctrine of creation as well as a doctrine of redemption.

The theological significance of Christ as the Second Adam was taken with utmost seriousness by such men as Melchior Hoffmann, Dirk Philips, and Menno Simons. This again led, particularly in the case of Hoffmann, to a doctrine of universal grace, which was soteriologically oriented and not limited to infants and children only. Hoffmann argued that as the transgression of the first Adam had plunged mankind into universal bondage to Satan, so the obedience and death of Christ as the Second Adam had brought a partial universal liberation. Man's will, which was through the transgression of the first Adam placed into universal bondage, is now liberated through the atonement of Christ as the Second Adam. Because of the atonement, and only because of it, the power of making a real decision is again placed within the capacity of otherwise still fallen man. Thus, the universal grace purchased through the atonement brings about a partial restoration of man's original humanity. This was actually a radical shift in the doctrine of the atonement which since the days of Anselm had been based upon the solidarity of the race in Adam. Whether the Anabaptists were fully aware of all the implications of this shift is open to question. They also linked grace inseparably with the concept of salvation as the divinization of man. Through grace as God's act of regeneration man is actually made a participant in the divine nature itself. On this level grace is the active agent in a gradual process of divinization which begins when the divine image is recreated in the believer through the work of the Holy Spirit. The recreated divine image is "the new creature in Christ," and this is nourished through an inner and spiritual eating of the Lord's Supper, which is in a restricted sense a means of grace. Because the believer must also carry throughout this life the burden of the sinful nature, which he has received from the first Adam, participation in the divine nature does not mean the possibility of a sinless life in the present world. Yet the presence of grace in the believer's life, as it actualizes his participation in the divine nature, means that the believer now has the possibility of striving against sin and, in a measure, of overcoming it. The process of divinization is not completed until the believer reaches his eternal destiny as a theanthropic individual.

It is not surprising that this view of grace led to a sharp dualism between the Church and the world. The disciple who endeavored to live by the *imitatio Christi* ethic always had to resist the world. Sometimes he could make his protest against the worldiness of the world only by the patient endurance of persecution, while he in turn might persecute no one. In the area of Christian ethics this sometimes led to a sharp limitation of the acceptance of social responsibility, but it also helped to keep alive the necessary tension between the believing Church and the nonbelieving world.

BIBLIOGRAPHY

Armour, Rollin Stely. *Anabaptist Baptism: A Representative Study*. Scottdale, PA: Herald Press, 1966.

Beachy, Alvin J. "A Case Study in Civil Disobedience," *Mennonite Life*, XXV, No. 1 (1970), 12–15.

Conrad Grebel's Programmatic Letters of 1524. Transcribed and translated by J. C. Wenger. Scottdale, PA: Herald Press, 1970.

Davis, Kenneth R. "Erasmus as Progenitor of Anabaptist Theology and Piety," *Mennonite Quarterly Review*, XLVII, No. 3 (1973), 163–178.

Friedmann, Robert. *The Theology of Anabaptism*. Scottdale, PA: Herald Press, 1973.

Hillerbrand, Hans J. "Anabaptism and the Reformation: Another Look," *Church History*, XXIX, No. 4 (December, 1960), 404–23.

Hoffmann, Melchior. "Ordinance of God," *Spiritual and Anabaptist Writers*. Vol. XXV of *The Library of Christian Classics*. Edited by George Huntston Williams and Angel M. Mergal. Philadelphia: The Westminster Press, 1957.

Keeney, William Echard. *The Development of Dutch Anabaptist Thought and Practice from 1539–1564*. Nieuwkoop: B. de Graaf, 1968.

— "The Incarnation, A Central Theological Concept," *A Legacy of Faith*. Edited by C. J. Dyck. Newton, KS: Faith and Life Press, 1962.

Klaassen, Walter. *Anabaptism: Neither Catholic Nor Protestant*. Waterloo, Ontario: Conrad Press, 1973.

Klassen, William. *Covenant and Community: The Life, Writings and Hermeneutics of Pilgram Marpeck*. Grand Rapids, MI: William B. Eerdmans Publishing Company, 1968.

Krahn, Cornelius. *Dutch Anabaptism: Origin, Spread, Life and Thought (1450–1600)*. The Hague: Martinus Nijhoff, 1968.

Oosterbaan, J. A. "Grace in Dutch Anabaptist Theology," *A Legacy of Faith*. Edited by C. J. Dyck. Newton, KS: Faith and Life Press, 1962.

Ozment, Steven E. *Homo Spiritualis: A Comparative Study of the Anthropology of Johannes Tauler, Jean Gerson and Martin Luther (1509–16) in the Context of Their Theological Thought*. Leiden: E. J. Brill, 1969.

— *Mysticism and Dissent: Religious Ideology and Social Protest in the Sixteenth Century*. New Haven: Yale University Press, 1973.

Poettcker, Henry. "Menno Simons' View of the Bible As Authority," *A Legacy of Faith*. Edited by C. J. Dyck. Newton: KS: Faith and Life Press, 1962.

Ruether, Rosemary Radford. *The Radical Kingdom: The Western Experience of Messianic Hope*. New York: Harper & Row, 1970.

Simons, Menno. "Reply to Gellius Faber, 1554," *The Complete Writings of Menno Simons, c. 1496–1561*. Translated from the Dutch by Leonhard Verduin and edited by John C. Wenger, with a biography by Harold S. Bender. Scottdale, PA: Mennonite Publishing House, 1956.

Stayer, James M. *Anabaptists and the Sword*. Lawrence, KS: Coronado Press, 1972.

Steinmetz, David C. "Scholasticism and Radical Reform: Nominalist Motifs in the Theology of Balthasar Hubmaier," *Mennonite Quarterly Review*, XLV, No. 2 (April, 1971), 123–44.

Williams, George Huntston. *The Radical Reformation*. Philadelphia: The Westminster Press, 1962.

— "German Mysticism in the Polarization of Ethical Behavior in Luther and the Anabaptists," *Mennonite Quarterly Review*, XLVIII, No. 3 (July, 1974), 274–304.

— "Sectarian Ecumenicity: Reflections on a Little Noticed Aspect of the Radical Reformation," *Review and Expositor*, LXIV, No.,2 (Spring, 1967), 141–60.

Yoder, John Howard. "The Hermeneutics of the Anabaptists," *Mennonite Quarterly Review*, XLI, No. 4 (October, 1967), 291–308.

— "Balthasar Hubmaier and the Beginnings of Swiss Anabaptism," *Mennonite Quarterly Review*, XXXIII, No. 1 (January, 1959), 5–17.

Verhooren en Vonnissen der Wederdoopers, Betrokken bij de Aanslagen op Amsterdam in 1534 en 1535. Medegedeeld door Mej. G. Grosheide. (No name of publisher nor date of publication.)

INDEX

Abraham, 211, 213 n
Adam, 211; first, 208, 216; Second, 202, 204 f, 208–214, 229
Adamic manhood, 193, 201; nature, 218
Agape, 13, 17, 19 f, 25
Anabaptist, 1, 32, 90 n, 92 n, 100, 124, 169, 173, 188, 203; anthropology, 202–207, 214–217, 227; hermeneutical principle, 221; justification, 202–207; pacifism, 219–221, 226; sword, 219 f; theology of redemption, 209; Two Kingdoms, 224
Anabaptists, 7–10, 13–16, 29, 33, 42 f, 79, 87, 103, 109, 114, 120 n, 123, 125 f, 144, 149, 151, 161 n, 163 n, 164 f, 171 n, 173, 179, 188, 195, 197 f, 203, 207–210, 212–214, 217; Contemplative, 1, 89, 125; Dutch, 3, 8, 18, 20, 25 f, 29, 38 n, 42 n, 58, 60, 62, 65, 77, 83, 92 n, 102, 117 n, 120, 122 n, 125, 127, 140, 146, 162, 166, 169 f, 178 f, 220 f, 225; Evangelical, 2, 87 f, 100, 117, 125–127, 130, 155–157, 178; Revolutionary, 2, 168; South German, 2, 10 n, 14 n, 20, 25, 29 n, 62, 89, 125, 179, 221, 224; Swiss, 123 n
Anselm of Canterbury, 210
Anthropology, 189, 206, 214; mystical, 202, 204, 206, 214, 227
Aquinas, Thomas, 212
Armour, Rollin S., 207, 214, 218
Athanasius, 4, 79
Atonement, 6, 20, 37, 40, 42, 54 n, 56, 60–65, 69, 75, 81, 83 f, 96, 98, 101, 103, 143, 150, 174, 178, 203, 210; forensic, 173; theories of, 213
Augsburg, Germany, 2, 103, 121 n, 131, 133, 136 n, 212
Augsburg Confession, 20, 115 n, 211
Augsburg Evangelicals, 211
Augustine, 4, 13 n, 41, 88 n, 113, 117 n, 227
Augustinian, 10, 13 n, 37 f, 113, 134 n
Augustinianism, 207
Ausbund, 10 n
Austria, 2, 67

Bainton, Roland, 1
Ban, 88–90, 93, 117–122, 125, 163, 178
Baptism, 13, 22, 36, 39 f, 42 n, 67, 88 n, 89 f, 93, 99, 126, 147, 153, 155 n, 222; believer's, 88, 103–110, 128, 209, 218, 223; infant, 26, 39 n, 47 n, 96, 99–103, 203, 208 f, 223
Barth, Karl, 36
Basel, Switzerland, 54 n
Bender, Harold S., 1, 188, 195, 205, 220 n
Bergsten, Torsten, 68, 73, 121 n
Bethel College, 3
Bibliolatry, 140, 152, 177 n
Birth, New (see New Birth)
Bitsch, Rauf, 9
Bondage of the Will (see Will)
Brethren of the Common Life, 30 n, 217
Brethren, Swiss (see Swiss Brethren)
Brown, Harold O.J., 57
Brunner, Emil, 36
Bucer, Martin, 6–8, 10–12, 15–17, 48 n, 124, 149
Bullinger, Heinrich, 8, 10–12, 151 n, 210

Calvin, John, 4 f, 8, 10 f, 14–16, 18 f, 111, 120, 130 n, 131 n, 151 n, 161 n, 164, 166 n, 171, 227
Calvinism, 33
Campanus, John, 117 n
Capital punishment, 64 n, 119, 164, 169 n, 170 n
Capito, Wolfgang, 6 f, 10, 149, 157 f
Catholic, Roman, 1, 110, 112; Church, 26 f, 84, 146 n, 211 f; merit system, 197
Catholicism, Roman, 17, 25–27, 31, 197, 203, 206
Catholics, 114, 165, 208, 211
Celestial Flesh (see Christology)
Chiliasm, 57 n, 157 f
Christ, as Great Physician, 216; as Heavenly Bridegroom, 216; as Redeemer, 213 n; as Second Adam, 213 f, 216
Christology, 3, 42 n, 98 n, 111, 159 n; Celestial Flesh, 2, 14 n, 35 n, 79–86, 88, 96, 103, 117 n, 120, 122 n, 178 f, 216
Church, 1, 15 f, 18, 47 n, 59, 68, 87–128, 129, 136, 139, 146, 150 f, 155 f, 163–165, 170 f, 174–179; authority, 129; Church-kingdom, 89 n; Church-kingdom-state, 89 n; Church-state, 176, 179; Paradise regained, 218 f; suffering, 124, 126–128, 222

233

Cloven hoofs, 141
Coccijus, Johannes, 151 n
Commentary on Romans, 12 n, 195
Community of goods, 169, 218
Community, Holy (see Holy Community)
Conversion, 44, 67–70
Corpus Christi, 87, 171
Corpus Christianum, 87, 171
Covenant, 104, 108, 131, 146–152; natural, 190, 192 f, 214; new, 58, 65, 87–99, 156, 169, 171, 177
Creation, 35 f, 71 f, 173 n

Dathenus, Peter, 9, 10 n
Davis, Kenneth R., 221 n
Day of Grace (see Grace)
Denbeaux, Fred, 173 n
Denck, Hans, 6, 10, 14 n, 15, 32, 37, 188, 198 f, 215; antinomianism, 29 f; baptism, 101; Church, 89, 125; discipline, 119; divinization of man, 29; eschatology, 61; fall, 35; freedom of the will, 47–50; hermeneutics, 130; inner Word, 132, 134, 139, 176; law, 66; legalism, 20 f; Lord's Supper, 104 f; mystical anthropology, 199 f; mystical theology, 215; mysticism, 131, 137, 188, 199; oath, 165; original sin, 37; regeneration, 71 f; sacraments, 99, 103; Scripture, 132–136, 140; sin, 153; soldier, 167; state, 156, 162 f; universalism, 16; work's righteousness, 27 f
De Ries, Hans, 20
Diet of Speyer, 92 n
Discipleship, 9, 153, 155 f, 158, 188 f, 195, 205 f
Discipline, 90, 117–122, 163, 178
Divinization of man, 28 f, 70 f, 77, 174, 216, 229 f
Dorpat, USSR, 31

Eck, John, 25, 212
Eckhart, Meister, 134
Elect, 17, 69
Election, 11, 33, 41, 69, 102
Emden, Germany, 9 n, 106 f
Erasmus, 33, 221
Eschatology, 56–58, 61
Eternal life, 14 n, 35, 64, 66
Ethics, 153–172
Eutychian heresy, 80
Evangelicals, 20, 168, 211
Excommunication, 120, 123, 163

Faber, Gellius, 8, 125, 225
Faith, 9 f, 14, 18–20, 25, 27, 43, 56, 62, 70, 75, 77, 92, 100, 105 f, 109, 116, 119 n, 127, 132, 139, 151 f, 154, 162, 164, 168, 175, 177
Fall, 11, 35–37, 39, 41 n, 50 f, 66, 70, 83, 136, 188
Fellman, Walter, 21
Flensburg, Disputation at, 107 n
Footwashing, 93
Franck, Sebastian, 79, 117 n, 125 f, 134
Frankenthal Disputation, 3, 8–10
Free will (see Will)
Friedmann, Robert, 14 n, 123, 201
Fundhenk, Johannes, 22 n

Gansfort, Wessel, 30 n
Garrett, James Leo, 89, 92 f
Gelassenheit, 27, 49, 190, 196 f, 199 f
Geneva, Switzerland, 8
Germany, 171 n; North, 89 n; South, 32, 42 n, 62, 67 f, 70, 103, 106, 155, 173, 214, 226, 228 f
Gerson, Jean, 187–189, 191–195, 201, 214; mystical anthropology, 191–193
Glaid, Oswald, 157 f, 163
Gospel, 18–20, 30, 59 f, 69, 75, 91, 109, 115 n, 142, 164
Government, 124, 156, 159
Grace, 4–13, 17–21, 23–34, 39–43, 45 f, 53 f, 56, 59, 61, 62–79 *passim*, 214 f; cheap, 5, 32, 122; day of, 58 f; first, 23–25, 44, 52, 68; forensic, 5, 29; means of, 105, 112, 114; new, 52; of today, 95, 150; of tomorrow, 64 n; of yesterday, 65, 95, 150; original, 37, 41, 68, 73; second, 25, 44, 72 f; time of, 56, 58–67, 141–143; universal, 40 f, 42 n, 69, 101, 103, 173 f, 228 f
Grebel, Conrad, 208, 211 n, 222, 224

Haetzer, Ludwig, 198
Harding, Vincent G., 109 n
Harvard Divinity School, 3
"Heaven stormers," 6, 33
Heidelberg Confession, 20
Hermeneutics, 57, 129–152, 166, 171, 177, 226
Hilary of Poitiers, 79
Hillerbrand, Hans J., 88 n, 187 f, 202 f, 206
Hoekstra, Syste, 20, 29
Hoffmann, Melchior. 2 f, 7 n, 8, 39, 42 n, 124 n, 213 n, 220, 224 f; atonement, 42 n, 54 n, 69, 84, 176; ban, 120 f; baptism, 107, 153 f; Celestial Flesh Christology, 2, 79–83, 96, 178 f, 216; Church, 90 f, 94, 121, 178; divinization of man, 29; eschatology, 56–58, 60; fall, 35–37; freedom of the will, 34, 47, 53–56;

government, 159; hermeneutics, 130, 140 f; Incarnation, 74, 81 f, 84; infant baptism, 101; inner Word, 140 f; Law, 70; Lord's Supper, 107 f; martyrdom, 108 n; oath, 165; predestination, 53–55; revolutionary, 158; salvation, 29, 31; soldier, 167; sword, 159; time of grace, 58, 62; universal grace, 42 n, 69, 174; universal salvation, 17
Holland, 2, 17, 26, 30 n, 32, 42 n, 103, 107, 155, 214
Holy Community, 15, 88, 118, 123
Holy Spirit, 58, 105, 142, 152–155, 188, 190, 194, 200, 205, 215, 227–229
Horb, Germany, 6
Horsch, John, 220 n
Hubmaier, Balthasar, 2, 103, 124 n, 157 f, 179, 208, 212, 218, 220; anthropology, 66–68, 200–202, 206 f, 215; ban, 118 f; baptism, believer's, 105 f, 153; infant, 100, 103 n; children, 39; Church, 89 f, 126, 155; eschatology, 61; fall, 34, 36 f, 50–52, 66; freedom of the will, 46 f, 50–53, 72; government, 156–158, 162 f; hermeneutics, 151 n; Holy Spirit, 153; Law, 22; legalism, 17, 20; Lord's Supper, 106; mystical anthropology, 200–202; new birth, 73; sacraments, 99, 103; salvation, 4 f, 25, 29–31, 72, 105; soldier, 167; soul, 51 f, 72; suffering, 126; sword, 125, 156 f; vocation, 122 f
Huss, John, 56, 129 n
Hut, Hans, 14 n, 157, 207 n
Hutterian Brethren, 89 n
Hutterite, 218

Illyricus, Matthias Flacius, 136 n
Imitatio Christi, 155, 162
Immaculate conception, 84
Incarnation, 60, 64 f, 72–85 *passim*, 94, 98, 112, 143, 150, 177
Infant baptism (see Baptism)
Irenaeus, 4, 208

Jelsum, Holland, 8 n
Joachim of Floris, 57 f, 141
John of Leiden, 146 n, 148, 225
Johnston, O.R., 11
Justification, 6, 9, 10 n, 21, 25, 29, 74 n, 195, 197, 203–206; forensic, 4 f, 28, 70–73, 79, 228

Kawerau, Peter, 3, 56, 140 n
Keeney, William, 16, 26 n, 42 n, 85 n, 117, 147 f, 176, 216 f, 226 n
Key of David, 141

Kingdom of Christ, 209
Kingdom of Heaven, 218
Kiwiet, Jan J., 89 n, 101 n, 104 n, 134 n, 136, 161 n
Klaassen, Walter, 189 n, 207, 217
Klassen, William, 150 n, 226 n
Knowledge of God, 191, 201 f
Koehler, Walther, 12, 29, 72
Krahn, Cornelius, 70, 217, 225

Law, 18–23, 25, 30, 59, 62, 64, 66, 69 f, 142 f, 148, 166; natural, 5, 23, 25, 34, 37, 67, 72, 176; time of, 62–66
Leendertz, W.I., 3, 54 n, 81, 140
Leeuwarden, Holland, 8 n, 159 n
Legalism, 17–25
Linden, Friedrich Otto zur, 3, 56
Littell, Franklin, 1, 58 n, 87 n
Locke, John, 176
Logos, 37, 72
Lord's Supper, 89–91, 93, 99, 103–117, 120, 122 n, 126, 155 n, 174
Loserth, Johann, 42 n, 157 n
Löwith, Karl, 58 n
Luther, Martin, 4 f, 7, 11–13, 18–27, 33, 47, 53 f, 72, 74 n, 106 n, 107 n, 120, 122 f, 129, 130 n, 131 n, 136 f, 139, 159, 161, 164, 171, 175, 187–189, 202–207, 213; anthropology, 193–197; forensic justification, 227
Lutheranism, 16, 33
Lutherans, 24, 79 n, 114, 117, 136, 147, 211 f
Lux naturalis, 68, 73, 173, 174 n

McNeill, John, 1
Magisterial Reformation (see Reformation)
Magisterial Reformers (see Reformers)
Magistracy, 162, 164 n, 166
Magistrate, 156 n, 157–163, 166
Mantz, Felix, 208, 222, 224
Marbeck, Pilgram, 2, 25, 89 n, 124 n, 204 f, 224; anthropology, 35, 67 f, 202, 215 f, 229; ban, 121 f; baptism, 99, 101 f, 113–115; children, 39–41, 42 n; Christology, 97 n, 178; Church, 26, 95 f, 98 f, 121–128, 178; conscience, 68, 163; conversion, 44; discipleship, 155; fall, 36 f; freedom of the will, 34, 47 n; government, 124, 159–163, 168; grace of today, 60, 64 f, 95; hermeneutics, 131, 136, 142, 149–152, 226; Holy Spirit, 154 f; infant baptism, 26, 100–102, 165 n; Law, 22 f; legalism, 20; Lord's Supper, 103, 113–117; *lux naturalis*, 68, 73, 173, 174 n; mysticism, 199; natural law, 23,

34, 37, 70, 72, 176; new covenant, 98 f, 121; oath, 165; original grace, 215; original sin, 36–39, 42 n, 43, 68; regeneration, 73, 215 f; sacramentalism, 26; sacraments, 99, 113–117; salvation, 5, 29, 72; sin, 44, 122; soldier, 167; sword, 99, 160, 168; toleration, 126 f; universal grace, 40 f; war, 167
Marcionite heresy, 226
Martyrdom, 108 n, 128
Martyrs' Synod, Augsburg, 212
Melanchthon, Philip, 100, 103, 164, 211 f
Menius, Justus, 7
Mennonites, 14 n, 89 n
Micron, Martin, 166
Miller, William, 158
Ministers, 93, 145
Ministry, 124
Monasticism, 123
Moravia, 2, 42 n, 103, 121 n
Müller, Lydia, 67
Münster, Germany, 57 n, 89 n, 120, 144 n, 146 n, 158, 162, 168, 224–226
Münsterites, 2, 59 n, 158, 220
Müntzer, Thomas, 134, 207 n, 211 n, 222 f
Mutual aid, 171
Mysticism, medieval, 188 f, 195, 207 f

Natural law (see Law)
Natural man, 44
Neff, Christian, 107 n
Netherlands, 2, 62, 67 f, 70, 89 n, 159 n, 165, 173, 216, 226, 229
New birth, 18, 44 f, 58, 70, 72–78, 124, 218
New creature in Christ, 75, 77, 111 f, 174 f, 216, 218
Nicolsburg (Nikolsburg), Czechoslovakia, 2, 50, 67, 105, 153, 157, 223
Nominalism, 206 n
Nomos, 13, 17, 20, 25, 70
Nonviolence, 163, 167, 171
Norden, Germany, 9 n
Nürnberg (Nuremberg), Germany, 3, 16, 20 f, 67, 132
Nürnberg Council, 27, 103
Nygren, Anders, 13 n, 19

Oaths, 147, 165 f
Obedience, 20
Oecolampadius, Johannes, 99 n, 115 n, 165, 223
Oosterbaan, J.A., 217
Origen, 98 n
Osiander, Andreas, 16
Oyer, John, 7 n

Ozment, Steven E., 187–191, 193–201, 207 n, 214 f

Packer, J.I., 11
Pantheism, 74, 216
Papists, 13 f, 168
Paradise Regained, 218
Passau, Germany, 10 n
Paul, the Apostle, 23, 29 f, 46, 51, 115, 124, 127, 153
Pauline, 10, 13, 14 f, 96, 127
Peachey, Paul, 123 n
Peasants' War, 159
Pelagian, 16, 46, 68 n
Pelagianism, 15–17, 38
Perfection, 15, 27 f, 35, 77
Persecution, 126, 147, 164, 171
Philips, Dirk, 2 f, 31, 59 f, 65, 69, 124 n, 151, 174, 216, 226, 229; atonement, 83 f, 101–103; ban, 119 f; baptism, 108–110, 117 n; Celestial Flesh Christology, 14 n, 80–86, 93, 96, 117 n, 178, 216; cheap grace, 32; Church, 18, 26, 87 f, 93–97, 111 f, 125 f; conscience, 163 f; discipline, 119 f; divinization of man, 29, 216; fall, 36 f; freedom of the will, 47 n, 69; hermeneutics, 131, 142–146, 226; Holy Spirit, 58, 154; Incarnation, 74, 81–86, 94; infant baptism, 26, 101–103; Law, 18, 20, 22, 25; Lord's Supper, 110–113, 116, 117 n; magistrate, 161 f; ministers, 33; new birth, 74–76; new covenant, 90 f; new creature in Christ, 75 f, 78, 112; nonviolence, 164, 171; oath, 165; original sin, 39–42, 44 f, 101; regeneration, 109; repentance, 18, 70; salvation, 29, 216; Scripture, 26 f; sin, 38, 46; soldier, 167; state, 161 f, 171; sword, 164, 168; theology of redemption, 216; time of grace, 142–146; time of law, 62 f, 65, 142–146; universal grace, 39 f, 69, 102 f; warfare, 171; work's righteousness, 26
Philips, Obbe, 9 n, 225
Piper, Otto, 134 n
Poettcker, Henry, 226 n
Polygamy, 144 n
Predestination, 11, 16 f, 27, 33 f, 46, 53, 55, 89 n, 176, 214
Prussia, 89 n

Quiring, Horst, 73

Radical Reformation (see Reformation)
Radical Reformers (see Reformers)
Radicals, 7–10, 13, 15, 25, 27 f, 35, 41, 46, 70, 87, 123, 164, 174–177, 179; Dutch, 74; South German, 17

Rationalists, Evangelical, 1
Reformation, 1, 6, 36, 56, 129; left wing, 1, 35; Magisterial, 1, 3-6, 8, 10, 17, 29 f, 32, 37 f, 41, 50, 55 n, 70 f, 77, 99, 110, 120, 123 f, 145 n, 147, 164, 176, 209, 227; Radical, 1-6, 10, 28, 32, 37-39, 56, 58 n, 62, 70 f, 79, 87-90, 103, 123 f, 130, 132, 151, 153, 155 f, 161-165, 173, 175-178, 228
Reformed, 1, 6, 9 f, 16, 26 f, 69, 122, 165 f
Reformers, 26, 209, 219, 222; Magisterial, 25, 28, 31, 33, 35 f, 46, 87 n, 125, 129, 147, 156, 166 n, 175, 179, 188; Radical, 29, 34-36, 41, 46, 56, 58 n, 66-68, 103, 129, 188, 227
Regeneration, 46, 58, 67, 69 f, 72 f, 76, 78, 86, 92, 108 f, 122, 136, 153, 174, 216
Rembert, Karl, 131
Repentance, 18 f, 21, 32, 45, 59, 70, 73 n, 114, 119
Restitution, 59, 87 n, 144, 146, 175
Revolutionary, 157 f, 162
Rhegius, Urbanus, 211 f
Riedemann, Peter, 203
Righteousness, 11; actual, 29; imputed, 29
Righteousness, works (see Work's righteousness)
Roman Catholic (see Catholic)
Rome, Italy, 195
Rörich, T.W., 80
Rothmann, Bernard (Bernhard Rotmann), 59 n, 142-144, 146, 225
Rottenburg, (Rottenberg), Germany, 6, 24
Ruether, Rosemary Radford, 206 f, 218 f

Sachsse, Carl, 22
Sacramentarians, 42 n
Sacramentist, 42 n
Sacraments, 99-117, 120, 129, 136, 175
Salvation, 4-6, 9, 11 f, 17, 26, 28 f, 31, 42 n, 47, 49, 53, 55 n, 56, 65, 70, 72, 76-78, 86, 88, 102, 105, 115 n, 174; order of, 192; universal, 48 n
Sanctification, 197, 202, 204
Sattler, Michael, 6, 224
Scharnschlager, Leopold, 42 n, 202
Schiemer, Leonhard, 14 n, 24 f, 67 f, 72 f, 174 n, 202
Schlaffer, Hans, 14 n
Schleitheim Confession, 8 n, 14, 220, 224
Schoeffer, Peter, 198
Schrenk, Gottlob, 151 n
Schwenckfeld, Caspar, 2 f, 124 n, 158, 175, 178 f, 199, 205, 226; actual sin, 42 f; atonement, 84; ban, 121; baptism, 103, 113 f, 117 n; bondage of the will, 47 n;
Celestial Flesh Christology, 35 n, 79-81, 84-86, 96 n, 97 n, 126 n, 178; Church, 88, 89 n, 97 f, 122 n, 125 f, 178; covenant, 97 f; divinization of man, 29, 77; eschatology, 61; fall, 35 f, 41 n, 66, 136; freedom of the will, 47; government, 156-158, 160; hermeneutics, 130-132, 136-140, 149-152; Holy Spirit, 155; inner Word, 136-140; justification, forensic, 79; Lord's Supper, 99, 103, 113, 115-117; magistrate, 162 f, 167 f; new birth, 78; oath, 165; original sin, 36, 38, 41 n, 43, 68 n, 136; sacrament, 113 f, 136; salvation, 77-79, 85 f; sin, 43 f; sword, 163
Scotus, Duns, 73 n, 74 n
Scriptures, 10, 17, 55, 58, 93 f, 132-141, 145 n, 146, 177; authority of, 129
Separation, 119, 125
Servetus, Michael, 14 n, 164
Shunning, 121 n, 122 n
Silesia, 158
Simons, Menno, 2 f, 8 n, 20, 69, 124 n, 174, 220, 225, 229; actual sin, 42, 44-46; atonement, 84; ban, 119 f; baptism, 99 n, 108-110, 117 n; capital punishment, 64 n; Celestial Flesh Christology, 14 n, 42 n, 80-86, 93, 96, 111, 178, 216; children, 40-42, 69; Church, 26, 90-97; community of goods, 169 f; discipline, 119 f; divinization of man, 29, 216; eschatology, 59; ethics, 155; excommunication, 123; fall, 36-38; freedom of the will, 46 f, 69; gospel, 19; hermeneutics, 131, 146-149, 151; Holy Spirit, 154; Incarnation, 74, 80-86, 112; infant baptism, 101 f; Law, 18-22, 25; Lord's Supper, 110-113, 116, 117 n; magistrates, 161-164, 169; ministers, 32 f, 124; new birth, 31 f, 74-77; new creature in Christ, 74 f, 77 f, 111; nonviolence, 163 f; oath, 165 f; original sin, 37-39, 42, 44-46, 76; salvation, 18, 29, 216; Scriptures, 129; state, 161-164; sword, 161, 164 n, 168-170; theology of redemption, 216; time of grace, 59 f, 62-64; toleration, 126 f, 163 f; universal grace, 69; vocation, 123; war, 168 f, 171
Sin, 12 f, 17 f, 20, 43 f, 46, 48 f, 56, 68, 73, 76, 78, 118, 122, 150, 153, 178 f; actual sin, 42-46, 69; original sin, 11, 15, 36-45, 68, 71, 76, 83, 100 f, 136, 173, 179, 192, 203, 208, 210-214, 228 f
Sixtus IV, Pope, 84
Socinus, 14 n
Soldier, 156 n, 167-172

237

Soteriology, 3, 85 n, 111, 173 f, 203
Soul, 51 f, 66, 72 f, 84, 122, 192 f; powers of, 192 f; sleep of, 14; anatomy of, 191 f; immortality of, 14 n
Spirit, Age of, 56–58
Spiritualists, 1 f, 29, 130, 138 n; Evangelical, 1 f, 88, 124 n, 155 f; Rationalist, 2; Revolutionary, 1 f
State, 155–165, 179
Stayer, James M., 187, 219–226; apolitical moderate, 220; crusading standpoint, 220; radical apoliticism, 220–226; realpolitical approach, 220, 222 f
Steinmetz, David C., 206 n
Strasbourg (Strassburg), Germany, 2, 6, 10, 17, 53, 54 n, 56, 58, 62, 80, 100 n, 106, 122, 124, 126, 133, 157, 159, 163, 224 f; Council, 47 n; Reformers, 22; Synod of, 8, 17, 69
Suffering (see Church)
Supper, Lord's (see Lord's Supper)
Swiss Brethren, 2, 10 n, 17 n, 89 n, 122 n, 187, 210, 221 f; pacifism, 220
Sword, 99, 125, 144 n, 147, 151 n, 156–164, 168–170, 220

Tauler, Johannes, 131, 137, 187–195; mystical anthropology, 189–191
Tavard, George H., 129 n
Tetzel, 195
Theologia Deutsch, 188, 195 f, 198 f, 202, 204, 208, 210
Theology, Lutheran, 203; mystical, 188 n, 189–193 *passim*, 196, 200, 203 f, 214
Thomistic, 190
Time of Grace (see Grace)
Time of Law (see Law)
Toleration, 163
Transubstantiation, 110
Trinity, 35, 57, 134 n
Troeltsch, Ernst, 1
Two Swords, doctrine of, 219

Ulm, Germany, 2
Universalism, 16 f

Valentinian heresy, 80
Valentinus, 80
Van Campen, Jacob, 225 f
Vedder, Henry C., 51
Verduin, Leonhard, 3
Vienna, Austria, 157
Violence, 119, 126, 160, 162, 167 f, 175
Vocation, 122–124
Voluntarism, 176 f, 179
Von Leichtenstein, Baron Leonhard, 157 f

Waldshut, Germany, 122, 157 n, 223
Warfare, 147, 160, 167–169, 171, 175
Wenger, John C., 85 n, 92 n, 151, 211 n
Westphalian, 99
Will, bondage of, 10 f, 15 f, 20, 33 f, 38, 46–56, 71 f, 176, 206, 214; free, 6, 15, 25, 52 f; freedom of, 10, 20, 33 f, 46–56, 69, 72, 176
Williams, George H., 1–3, 16, 51, 53, 79, 89, 108 n, 187 f, 197 f, 201–214, 217
Wittenberg, Germany, 196; University of, 7
Witzel, George, 58 n
Word, 76, 94, 114, 137 n, 152; eternal, 24, 130; of God, 18, 105, 108, 127, 131, 136, 149, 151, 161; of the Lord, 108, 147; inner Word, 24 f, 130–140 *passim*, 176; living Word, 137; outer Word, 130–136, 138, 140
Works, good, 7–10, 28; of merit, 25
Work's righteousness, 6–10, 25–28, 179
Wray, Frank J., 87 n
Wycliffe, John, 129 n

Yoder, John Howard, 222 f

Zurich, 79, 103, 122, 151 n, 210, 221–223; radicals, 221–223; Second Disputation, 222
Zwickau prophets, 7 n
Zwingli, Ulrich, 10, 18 n, 47, 53, 79, 99, 106 n, 108, 115 n, 151, 210 f, 213, 222 f
Zwinglian, errors, 99, 115; views of Supper, 114